Computation, Information, Cognition

Computation, Information, Cognition
The Nexus and the Liminal

Edited by

Gordana Dodig Crnkovic and Susan A. J. Stuart

Cambridge Scholars Publishing

Computation, Information, Cognition: The Nexus and the Liminal,
Edited by Gordana Dodig Crnkovic and Susan A. J. Stuart

This book first published 2007. The present binding first published 2008.

Cambridge Scholars Publishing

12 Back Chapman Street, Newcastle upon Tyne, NE6 2XX, UK

British Library Cataloguing in Publication Data
A catalogue record for this book is available from the British Library

Copyright © 2008 by Gordana Dodig Crnkovic and Susan A. J. Stuart and contributors

All rights for this book reserved. No part of this book may be reproduced, stored in a retrieval system, or transmitted, in any form or by any means, electronic, mechanical, photocopying, recording or otherwise, without the prior permission of the copyright owner.

ISBN (10): 1-4438-0040-6, ISBN (13): 978-1-4438-0040-2

Table of Contents

Preface ix

Introduction xi

Part I: Information 1

Chapter One 2
Epistemology as Information Theory: From Leibniz to Ω
Gregory Chaitin

Chapter Two 18
Information Logic
Luciano Floridi

Chapter Three 41
Formalising Semantic Information: Lessons From Logical Pluralism
Patrick Allo

Chapter Four 53
Getting Closer to Iconic Logic
Ahti-Veikko Pietarinen

Chapter Five 75
Causation: A Synthesis of Three Approaches
Lars-Göran Johansson

Chapter Six 87
An Oriental Approach to the Philosophy of Information
Gang Liu

Part II: Ontology **103**

Chapter Seven 104
Ontology as the Core Discipline of Biomedical Informatics - Legacies
of the Past and Recommendations for the Future Direction of Research
Werner Ceusters and Barry Smith

Chapter Eight 123
Functions and Prototypes
Katherine Munn

Chapter Nine 134
Knowledge in Action
Ruth Hagengruber and Uwe V. Riss

Chapter Ten 147
Towards a Programming Language Ontology
Raymond Turner and Amnon H. Eden

Part III: Bioinformation and Biosemantics **161**

Chapter Eleven 162
The Informational Architectures of Biological Complexity
Pedro C. Marijuán and Raquel del Moral

Chapter Twelve 178
The Cybersemiotic Framework as a Means to Conceptualize
the Difference between Computing and Semiosis
Søren Brier

Chapter Thirteen 195
Meaning and Self-Organisation in Cognitive Science
Arturo Carsetti

Part IV: Cognitive Science and Philosophy **205**

Chapter Fourteen 206
A Neurophysiological Approach to Consciousness: Integrating Molecular,
Cellular and System Level Information
Peter Århem

Chapter Fifteen 218
Does dynamical modelling explain time consciousness?
Paavo Pylkkänen

Chapter Sixteen 228
Complexity, Cognition, and Logical Depth
Pauli Brattico

Chapter Seventeen 236
Is Computationalism Trivial?
Marcin Miłkowski

Chapter Eighteen 248
On Facing Up to the Semantic Challenge
Otto Lappi

Part V: Computational Linguistics 259

Chapter Nineteen 260
Computational Linguistics as an Applied Science
Pius ten Hacken

Chapter Twenty 270
Views of Text Meaning in Computational Linguistics:
Past, Present, and Future
Graeme Hirst

Chapter Twenty One 280
Language Technological Models as Epistemic Artefacts: The Case
of Constraint Grammar Parser
Tarja Knuuttila

Part VI: Ethics and Education 291

Chapter Twenty Two 292
The Paradox of Autonomy: The Interaction Between Humans
and Autonomous Cognitive Artifacts
Alexander Riegler

Chapter Twenty Three 302
A Copernican Revolution in Ethics?
Terrell Bynum

Chapter Twenty Four 330
Building Epistemological Infrastructures- Interventions At A Technical University
Lena Trojer

Chapter Twenty Five.. 341
Computer Ethics in (Higher) Education
Philip Brey

Contributors 364

PREFACE

In this book we have tried to draw together a number of important strands in contemporary approaches to the philosophical and scientific questions that emerge when dealing with the issues of computing, information, cognition and their overlap. It is a work that has come about as a result of establishing a European forum for, what were initially, a series of North American Computing and Philosophy (NA-CAP) conferences whose broad concern was with all aspects of the computational turn that was occurring within the discipline of philosophy. Initially the emphasis was on computer-assisted instruction, but quickly it grew to encompass the possibility of creating minimally self-conscious artificial agents, the ethics of artificial intelligence and machine consciousness, intellectual property rights, issues surrounding perceptual software and questions of representation *versus* non-representation, adaptation and autonomy in robotics, and philosophical issues in the domains of analogue and digital librarianship and archiving. These meetings also saw the development and flourishing of a new perspective, the Philosophy of Information, concerned with the conceptual issues that arise at the intersection of computer science, information technology and philosophy. As Luciano Floridi explains, the Philosophy of Information is concerned with

– the critical investigation of the conceptual nature and basic principles of information, including its dynamics, utilisation and sciences
– the elaboration and application of information-theoretic and computational methodologies to philosophical problems.

["What is the Philosophy of Information", *Metaphilosophy*, 2002, (33), 1/2.]

The first conference of the European Computing and Philosophy (E-CAP) took place in 2003 at the University of Glasgow, Scotland. This was followed in 2004 with a conference at the University of Pavia, Italy, and in 2005 at the Mälardalen University, Västerås, Sweden. It is from the 2005 conference that the papers in this volume are derived.

The presentations in the European, North American, and now Asian-Pacific (AP-CAP) conferences continue to be shaped by the computational turn but, as the fields of enquiry advance and expand, new elements appear and, once again, new perspectives emerge. It is with considerable pleasure that we present this volume not only with a rich opening section dealing with the Philosophy of Information, but also with a section on the Philosophy of Ontology and the ontological considerations involved in the creation of controlled vocabularies and the semantic relations between their terms in software environments. From their work on the development of a programming language ontology (this volume) Eden & Turner have gone on to establish, with an internationally-based group of colleagues, the Philosophy of Computer Science as a fresh and potentially rich perspective from which to address all aspects, physical and metaphysical, of computer science and its objects. The Philosophy of Computer Science was also one of the main themes at E-CAP 2006 at the Norwegian University for Science and Technology, Trondheim, Norway.

So, the background to this volume is exciting being informed by, at least, three new philosophical perspectives, and it is dynamic for the conferences and dialogue have now spread to become truly international.

With so much activity there are a great many people to thank for their vision, influence, good-judgement, and kindness. The first of these must be Robert Cavalier, for without his enthusiasm to see CAP conferences spread to Europe, E-CAP would not have become what it is today. Then there's a clutch of really great people who are a delight to know and work with in the International Association for Philosophy and Computing (IA-CAP), and who can always be relied upon for sound advice, they include but are not limited to, Ron Barnette, Charles Ess, Marvin Croy, and Luciano Floridi.

And, finally, it is essential that we thank the authors for the excellent collaboration and everyone who reviewed submissions for the E-CAP05 conference and to those who helped with the subsequent tough selection process for papers most appropriate for the book. In the latter category we must include Peter Århem, Gustaf Arrhenius, Birgitta Bergsten, Rikard Bonner, Søren Brier, Göran Collste, Chris Dobbyn, Kaj Börje Hansen, Lars-Göran Johansson, Torbjörn Lager, Staffan Larsson, Pedro C. Marijuán, Christina Mörtberg, Joakim Nivre, Jan Österberg, Bertil Rolf, May Thorseth, and Tom Ziemke.

All that is left to say is that we hope you enjoy reading this book and are as stimulated by the papers as we have been.

Susan A. J. Stuart and Gordana Dodig-Crnkovic

March 2007

INTRODUCTION

SUSAN STUART
AND GORDANA DODIG-CRNKOVIC

Every epoch and culture has a different conception of the Universe. For Ptolemy, Descartes, and Newton the Universe was best conceived in a mechanistic way as some vast machine. For others it is, in its entirety, a living organism. [*Viz.* Thales of Miletus, Spinoza, and Kafatos & Nadeau 1999.] Our current understanding in terms of information and computing has led to a conception of the Universe as, more or less explicitly, a computer. On such a pancomputational and paninformational view (Zuse 1967; Lloyd 2006; Chaitin this volume), if all physics is expressible as computation – so the whole universe can be represented as a network of computing processes at different levels of granularity – then we can consider information as a result of (natural) computation, and the Universe as a network of computing processes that are defined by the information they manipulate and produce. Under this conception information is that which constitutes the computing structure, the Universe, at any given moment; the structure changes continuously and that change can be understood as computation. Thus, computation is what happens dynamically to information from one moment to the next.

Under this conception information and computation are elements of a dual-aspect theory, providing a dichotomy with which we can begin to grasp the more fundamental classical energy / matter dichotomy that, embedded within space / time, is generally taken to constitute reality. The elements in such pairings are not only complementary, they are also interdependent, like discreteness and continuum, like time and space, like wave and particle, like form and content; computation and information presuppose one another and can only be understood fully in their conjunction. (Dodig-Crnkovic 2006) On the semantic level, that there might be a wealth of computational processes underlying our communication is insufficient if there is nothing to communicate; that there might be information to be communicated is insufficient without the computational process. One is reminded very clearly of

Kant's dictum: "Thought without content is empty, intuitions without concepts are blind" [A52/B76].

In expanding its domain to the whole Universe computation goes well beyond the limits set by the Church-Turing computability hypothesis. Being process-oriented, pancomputationalism is not so much interested in the structure of the Universe, that is, whether it is ultimately digital, analogue, some hybrid of the two, or none of these, for it takes structure as a given and develops its dynamical behaviour over time. In this way, pancomputationalism in its most general form, natural computation, works equally well for both digital and analogue computing processes.

But, if we are interested in structures and adopt an information realism where entities are informational (including semiotic) structures – the first view we can see expressed in the biological work of Marijuán & Moral and the second in Brier in this volume – then we can opt instead for information structuralism. (Floridi this volume). With regard to this position, Floridi (2004) identifies information semantics as one of the Open Problems in the Philosophy of Information. Among the advantages the informational view brings with it is its finer granularity when put into context of wisdom, knowledge, information, and data. In the adoption of this view we must concern ourselves with the dynamics of information and, more specifically, with whether there is an *information logic* (IL) that is distinct from *epistemic logic* (EL) and *doxastic logic* (DL). It is with this particular issue that Floridi is concerned in his article in this volume; his fundamental claim is that being informed is a transitive state, but that knowing and believing are not.

The pursuit and acquisition of knowledge, and thus also information, has frequently been thought to be a double-edged sword. We seek knowledge so that we can progress in our culture, our science and our technology, but there are times when our discoveries can have a Pyrrhic feel to them In the Abrahamic traditions gaining knowledge is associated with expulsion from paradise, with the loss of safety and certainty. However, in being expelled from one Paradise, we search for or create new ones; in our abandonment of the Ptolemaic astronomy of ideal spheres embrace the Newtonian-Laplacean perfection of heavenly clockwork.

In an echo of the Genesis story and its sentiment Hilbert (1926) said "No one will drive us from the paradise which Cantor created for us". But, one by one our once firmly held convictions are having to be abandoned. We have been removed from our position as the absolute centre of the Universe with its unique and privileged system of co-ordinates, and now find ourselves in the outskirts of our galaxy, a galaxy which is in no way special amongst galaxies. We have left behind absolute space and absolute time. It is time to leave the absolute truth of there being one, and only one, true system of logic (logical monism). Logical pluralism (Beall & Restall, 2000) is motivated by an analysis of disagreement within the classical first-order logic, relevant logic and intuitionistic logic in the account of logical consequence (and hence of logical truth). Allo (this volume) argues that logical pluralism could also entail semantic informational pluralism as information content depends upon the underlying logic one assumes. One of the consequences of this view is that, when a formal account of semantic information is elaborated, the absolute validity of logic cannot be relied upon and some further domain-specific motivations will be required if we are to be assured of the appropriateness of the logic we choose to use.

It is to the external world that we now look for motivations and specifically to the interdisciplinary work being done in the overlapping fields of information, biology and biosemantics, cognitive science, computational linguistics, technology, ontology, ethics, and ultimately – closing the circle – education. We are attempting to draw together some of the most significant work that exists at, what are often conceived to be, the borders of traditional disciplines. In other words we are attempting to establish a nexus in the liminal.

We begin with a speculative metaphysics provided by Greg Chaitin's article 'Epistemology as Information Theory: From Leibniz to the Omega Number'. Chaitin's mix of digital philosophy and digital physics presents a "neo-Pythagorean vision of the world" in which "everything is made out of 0/1 bits, everything is digital software, and God is a computer programmer, not a mathematician!". The challenge is to find how much will fit this new theory, how much will fail to fit, and what it will help us to understand. Chaitin makes the eminently computationalist claim that "we only understand something if we can program it" and, since what we can program depends on the laws of physics that hold in this universe, the things that don't fit the theory will be those things we can't program and, thus, cannot understand. Then he confronts the possibility of uncomputable real numbers by arguing that real numbers don't exist. In support of his position Chaitin presents an algorithmic information theory based on Leibniz's dictum (1686) that the universe has been created simplest in hypotheses and richest in phenomena, thus any explanation has to be simpler than that which it attempts to explain. In terms of digital philosophy and the pancomputational universe this becomes the claim that an elegant program has the property that no program written in the same programming language, that produces the same output, is smaller than it, that is to say: "an elegant program is the most concise, the simplest, the best theory for its output." But what happens if it is not possible to deduce the truth of something from any principle simpler than itself; well, Chaitin concludes, "proofs become useless, because **anything** can be proven from principles that are equally complicated", and this is what happens with any static formal and axiomatic theory for all mathematics. [*Viz.* Hilbert's programme 1920's] There is no one single, simple and basic proof or axiom upon which all else depends; mathematics is more like biology, a world of infinite complexity which cannot be explained in a finite bit theory. However, Chaitin's ambitious programme is not simply to suggest a pluralism of axioms, but rather that, in our attempt to understand mathematics, biology, the universe, we must be willing to add new axioms that need not be self-evident but which can be justified pragmatically. He is a thinker with great energy and panache, and the courage of his ideas is conveyed to the reader very well through his text.

Pancomputationalism, paninformationalism, complexity, axiomatic and logical pluralism, ontology, and Leibniz are some of the leitmotivs that emerge from Chaitin's article and which arise in many of the other contributions in this volume. Pietarinen's article connects with the dichotomy of the continuous and the discrete in the context of an attempt to bridge the current division between analogue and digital accounts of the mind. His emphasis is on visual and non-symbolic representational systems in logic, computing and cognitive sciences, and he examines Peirce's iconic logic – a logic Peirce, himself, thought to be superior to his symbolic system – that employs the diagrammatic logic of Existential Graphs. Graphs may be discrete objects in one sense, but they are also a summation of non-verbalised reasoning processes, in effect, a different, direct form of visual reasoning. Again we are confronted with claims for complexity and a need for an expanded logical system, though this time it is one that is necessary if we are to eventually comprehend the logic of icons and the nature of the non-discrete, analogue mind.

Of perennial concern to philosophy, physics, and now the cognitive sciences, are the notions of causation and causal relations; their importance is no less considerable in the domains of information and computation. "Intuitively there is conceptual connection between causation and transfer of information, because we can't get any information from a system without interacting causally with it ... Thus transfer of information is a causal process.". [Johansson, this volume] Johansson addresses this concern by first establishing four, quite different, proposals: causation is (i) the transfer of a conserved quantity; (ii) analysed in terms of counterfactuals; (iii) explicable in terms of INUS-conditions, that is, a cause can be an insufficient [I] but necessary [N] part of a condition which is itself unnecessary [U] but exclusively sufficient [S]; and (iv) something we humans – agents – can manipulate in, for example, the transfer of information which can be a cause of something else. Johansson's suggestion is that, in an attempt to understand this rather complicated notion of causality, we must drop the counterfactual approach – it leads us up a blind alley when we try to determine its truth-value – and unify the other three approaches to provide a robust concept of cause as it is used in ordinary language, and in the natural and social sciences.

In Gang Liu's essay we return to Leibniz as a key figure in the convergence of computing and philosophy, but this time as a proto-Sinologist who interprets the *I-Ching* hexagrams and attempts to integrate elements of oriental organic philosophy into his metaphysics and especially into the semantics of possible worlds. Taking this as his starting point Liu presents a new synthesis with modal information theory (MIT) or modal informationalism in an effort to deal with the indecisive ontological status of information and its shift within the idealism / materialism dichotomy. He closes his essay by urging us to re-examine Leibniz's work in the context of the philosophy of information and pancomputationalism: "A re-discovery of Leibniz's philosophy is essential; his ideas might have been too radical to be accepted in his own age, let them not be too radical to be accepted by ours, especially with the advent of a new field, the philosophy of information."

From questions about the ontological status of information *per se* we move to the ontology of controlled vocabularies with Smith & Ceusters; we find, even here, Leibniz's influence, though this time it is his vision of a universal language, a *mathesis universalis*.

Now that all states, transactions, and relations – in business, medicine, administration, astronomy, and so on – are to be formalised to enable automatic communication and sharing, we must solve the problems of ambiguity and indeterminacy common to all concepts embedded in natural language. The creation of appropriate ontologies confronts this problem head on. "Ontology, as conceived from the realist perspective, is not a software implementation or a controlled vocabulary. Rather, it is a theory of reality, a *'science of what is, of the kinds and structures of objects, properties, events, processes and relations in every area of reality*' (Smith 2003)." In their essay 'Ontology as the Core Discipline of Biomedical Informatics. Legacies of the Past and Recommendations for the Future Direction of Research' Smith & Ceusters provide an eloquent account of the misapplication of controlled vocabularies which provide an inflexible uniform framework within which it is supposed that items and their relations can be adequately described. The prominent example of a controlled vocabulary is the Gene Ontology which, in its use of the very limited 'is-a' and 'part-of' relations, runs counter to the rules of logic. They identify one very telling failure, when 'is-a' is used tacitly to mean 'within'; for example, when wanting to express the fact that the embryo is in the uterus the gene ontologist writes completely falsely that the embryo 'is-a' uterus. Their paper, whilst wryly amusing, is a very stark warning about the urgent need for a coherent ontology, and not just for biomedical informatics.

In a very similar vein Munn addresses the ontologies, the taxonomical hierarchies, of biomedical information systems, but her focus is on the use of the term 'function'. In her analysis of the National Library of Medicine's clinical resource, Medical Subject Headings (MeSH), she discovers that 'function' is used to mean 'role' and that 'role' has two characteristics: it is something carried out in relation to a biological system, and it is associated with repeated patterns of action. These characteristics presuppose that function is normative and, thus, something which provides a standard from which we can judge *with respect to what* conditions X functions well. It is these normative standards that bioinformatics must specify if it is to be successful.

Chaitin's computationalist dictum, that you can only really understand something if you can program it, is clearly evident in each of the ontology papers in this volume.

In Eden & Turner's essay we have an analysis of the ontology of programming languages and subsequent possibility of a philosophical analysis of software design. They begin by considering the different possible ontological perspectives and settle on a *denotational semantics* (DS) as "the most ontologically self-conscious", it being the one that makes explicit what set theoretic constructions are required to interpret the language in set theory. Doing this, they argue, will lead back to a Quinean distinction between the ontological commitments of a scientific theory and the actual choice of a theory. They examine the assumptions of compositionality, extensionality and completeness that are the underpinning of DS, and question the set-theoretic account of programming languages which accepts sets as a basic ontological structure. Like constructive logicians and mathematicians who appeal to notions such as *operation* and *constructive proof*, computer scientists, they argue, have their own basic ontology in *data types*.

Again in the context of the relation of information to knowledge Hagengruber & Riss address the issue of knowledge management, the problem of transforming human knowledge into machine representations, and knowledge domain extensionality and integration. In particular, their focus is on the dynamic nature of the switch from implicit to explicit knowledge and, since their view of knowledge is related to action, they adopt a dynamic approach. Critically, they ask why is it possible for us to put together our knowledge of different domains reasonably successfully when in reality they are each described in innumerable individually coherent ways but which, when brought together, do not amount to a unified and coherent world theory.

To understand and resolve this issue we might examine the very interesting distinction that arises between communication and computation when the computer is conceived as an open system in communication with the environment; so, in the case of biological computing where, crucially, the boundary is dynamic. For many of the authors in this volume biology is at the centre of an 'information revolution'. The new fields of, for example, genomics, proteomics, and bioinformatics are capturing both enormous investment and a great deal of the lime-light; and at the same time, they are producing copious realms of specialized biomolecular data. Paradoxically, not much theoretical effort is being devoted to the elaboration of an integrated 'informational perspective' of the living cell, or to make sense of the whole 'informational architectures' withstanding the multicelullar complexity evolved by eukaryots – the nascent integrative field of systems biology is mostly concerned with empirically-oriented problems.

In this regard, the Marijuán & Moral essay provides an interesting theoretical starting-point. It is based on a taxonomy of the molecular recognition events occurring in the cell, progressively advancing towards a unitary contemplation of the informational organization of life. Along the way, one can make sense of the overall convergence of informational architectures and signaling systems upon an organismic cycle decomposable in multiple cell-cycles. Of particular interest in their approach are the taxonomy of molecular recognition events, the stochastic nature of enzyme function, the combination of 'functional addresses' and 'secondary address' in a type of von Neumann computing scheme in the eukaryotic DNA, the functioning of the Cellular Signaling System, and their discussion of how the cell builds 'meaning' for the different combinations of received signals. Ultimately they argue that the organization of life, that which distinguishes animate from inanimate matter, would not evolve only on the existence of a genetic 'code', or on a series of nested 'codes', but on a series of evolutionary inventions of an 'informational' nature, that is, related to combinatoric arrangements of molecular recognition events.

Brier's contribution to this volume is written from the perspective of biosemiotics – the study of signs, communication and information in living systems. It is semiosis which raises living systems above the purely physical, chemical and, even, informational explanations, and, with Sebeok's work (*Viz.* Sebeok 1976, 1989) biosemiotics has extended to a description of semiosis between body cells and within the cells (*endosemiotics*) (Uexküll et al. 1993). Peirce's semiotics deals with non-intentional bodily and natural signs, but un-interpreted 'natural' and technological objects are merely protosemiotic, displaying only 'Secondness' in Peircean terminology. For Brier the big question is whether a biosemiotic Peircian framework can encompass these protosemiotic objects. Following on from this he asks whether any of the human signs that computers manipulate can be said to be signs for the computer *per se*; in other words, why is it that we focus only on humans in language, culture and society as producers of meaning? In response he offers a cybersemiotics which embraces the evolutionary view of system science, cybernetics, and information science arguing that semiosis is "immanent in the universe, manifesting itself clearly in living systems and becoming emancipated and self-organized in social systems".

Carsetti's essay is also concerned with information patterns and meaning, but specifically with the emergence of meaning at the level of system-organisation. This meaning is necessarily connected to specific linguistic and logical operations, and to specific observational procedures. His emphasis is on a synergetic methodology – the formation and self-organiation of patterns and structures in 'open' systems. He examines Kanizsa's work in Gestalt theory and the problem of amodal completion – where we know perceptually that an object is occluded but we do not actually see it, arguing that a synergetic order-formation theory, like that used in non-linear dynamical systems, is the only one to offer a robust explanatory model of what we take the emerging pattern to mean. However, even this is not sufficient for the understanding we have of the temporally enduring conscious mind; for that we need a continuous interplay with the environment.

In the section on Cognitive Science and Philosophy we focus on consciousness, in juxtaposition with our other themes. Århem's paper addresses the question of consciousness at two different levels: on evolutionary level in neuroanatomical features critical for sustaining consciousness and at cellular level by studying the neural impulse patterns characteristic of a conscious state. He examines Crick and Koch's phylogenetic approach to consciousness extending it into and beyond Edelman's, Cotterill's and Eccles' work respectively. The thrust of this part of his essay is that to understand the evolution of consciousness we should focus on the reptilian brain; the reptile-bird brain evolution transition reveals a greater continuity than was initially expected, and this makes the consciousness cut-off point at birds particularly problematic. In the second part of his paper he emphasises the importance of understanding anaesthesiology because, although there is still very little known about what happens at either the system or the molecular level when anaesthetics are administered, we do know that they switch a network of neurons from high-frequency firing to low-frequency firing. Århem concludes that if further analysis reveals what it is that is being inhibited, we might have some better indication of what is important as the underpinning for consciousness.

In his essay on consciousness Pylkkanen focuses on the temporal structure of conscious experience when, for example, we hear music. He weaves together Husserl's tri-partite analysis of time consciousness – the primal impression of now, the retention of just past, and the protention of what is to come – with

Bohm's implicate order framework to present a critique of van Gelder's dynamical model of auditory pattern recognition and to present a richer account of the perception of previously experienced elements in our awareness of temporally enduring objects. Crucial to his account is the notion of the 'enfoldment' of these retained or previously experienced elements; a conclusion that presents a resolution for Husserl's seeming paradox of experiencing the past and future in the present.

Contemporary philosophy of mind is for the most part inspired by the naturalist intuition that the mind is part of the natural universe. A majority of contemporary philosophers assume a physicalist concept of mind according to which mental phenomena derive from neurophysiological phenomena, if they are not neurophysiological *per se*. In their attempt to naturalise the concept of mind many cognitive scientists rely on computational and / or informational metaphors and tools. This is the direction taken by the remaining three papers in this section of the book; each deals with the notion of computationalism and, more or less, explicitly the computational theory of mind (CTM). Brattico's interest is in Fodor's continuing objection to the CTM as providing an account of global cognition, that is, the kind of logically deep, complex thinking that goes in to deciding, for example, whether you let your children have the puppy they keep asking for or, in Brattico's much neater, but still computationally complex, example, whether or not you should carry an umbrella. This kind of everyday thinking involves pragmatic reasoning, problem solving, abductive reasoning and imagination, and in coming to a decision there must be a trade-off between efficiency and reason. In Artificial Intelligence modelling this becomes the 'frame problem' – distinguishing between computationally relevant and computationally irrelevant facts or, as Fodor puts it: "Hamlet's problem: when to stop thinking" (1987, p.140) – and a trade-off between rationality and computational complexity must be reached. In his attempt to resolve the problem of the poor trade-off between rationality and efficiency in cognitive modelling Brattico adopts Bennett's complexity theoretical notion of *logical depth* (Bennett 1988), and concludes that the logical depth of the knowledge underpinning our everyday decision-making is the result of an evolutionary process, a process which has been enriched by the learning of lessons communicated to us from previous generations.

Milkowski's focus is on the triviality threat to computationalism, that is, the fact that simultaneously some deny that cognition involves computation, yet others claim that all physical processes are computational (pancomputationalism), possibly even algorithmic, and he argues that even if these claims are true, computationalism need not be rendered trivial. He begins by distinguishing two main forms of computationalism: (i) that cognitive processes could be described algorithmically, and (ii) that cognitive processes are algorithmic or computational; and by distinguishing three varieties of computationalism: (i) that cognitive processes can be simulated computationally, (ii) that cognitive processes can be realised computationally, and (iii) that cognitive processes are generated by overall computational processes. In doing this he establishes a multi-level model of cognition where a base level, on which higher levels are supervenient, might be conceived of algorithmically but the emergent computational levels might not or, at least, not in the same algorithms. The result is a taxonomy of possible computationalisms, some of which are weak and trivial, and some of which are robust and non-trivial.

Finally, in this section, Lappi takes up the challenge to computational neuroscience presented by Grush (2001): How do you distinguish between computation – understood as computational processing of semantic information – and any other complex causal process that is governed by a computationally tractable rule? Grush's analysis of the problem is given in terms of a-semantics (isomorphism between the causal neural processes and some abstract algorithm) and e-semantics (isomorphism between the causal neural process and the physical causal processes within the environment), and he claims that recent computational neuroscience treats computation and representation a-semantically and, thus, inadequately; what is needed is a more genuinely semantic notion of computation and representation in terms of e-semantics. Lappi agrees with Grush about the limitations of a-semantics but suggests, instead, a c-semantic construal of computation and representation, that is, one which makes essential reference to the cognitive mechanisms of the organism that represent a systematic and genuine contribution of the organism to semantic content and which provides not merely a reflection of structure in the environment.

From a concern with CTM, we move to applications in the domain of computational linguistics (CL) and, in the first instance, to ten Hacken's claim that CL should be conceived as an applied science. He begins by using the example of parsing to show that CL can be pursued as an empirical science, as an applied science or as mere technology. However, since applied sciences are problem-oriented, they have both a practical orientation and an explanatory focus; it is this explanatory focus, he argues, that facilitates the expression of well-formed problems in terms of their *identification*, *evaluation*, *decomposition*, and appropriate *knowledge selection*.

Knuuttila also makes, as she herself says, a "short philosophical visit into the world of parsing" but to her the interesting question is an ontological one about the manner in which we tend to treat language technological models, like the Constraint Grammar Parser, as abstract, theoretical representations of the world rather than as epistemic artefacts. In arguing that models should be treated more robustly and not simply as substitutes for the 'real' thing, Knuuttila emphasises the artificiality, workability and experimentability of scientific models, and suggests that in treating them less like Platonic ideals we might begin to rethink our approach to science more generally.

According to Hirst much of the success of recent computational linguistics (CL), natural language processing (NLP), and human language technologies (HLT) has been achieved by adapting the problem we are trying to solve. He presents three computational views of text-meaning: (i) objective text-meaning, (ii) authorial intent, and (iii) subjective text-meaning, and argues that if CL is to progress it must incorporate all three approaches and not just the first. Moreover, it must develop ways of dealing with the reader's purposiveness and the possibility of what the author might have said but didn't, not just with the familiar notions of pragmatics and implicature.

Dynamics, process, change, and agency are central concepts in the computationalist view. As a result of giving (human) agency and thus intentionality such a prominent role, computationalists must address the ethical aspects and consequences of that agency. Ethics must be an explicit constitutive element in the whole computationalist / informationalist epistemic enterprise.

The issues surrounding pancomputationalism, paninformationalism, biosemantics, cognition, ontology, logical pluralism, and technology are of paramount importance to us, yet they are academically liminal, awkwardly interdisciplinary with no clearly-defined disciplinary responsibility. Thus, no text that deals with these topics as they are currently perceived and conceived can fail to consider the relevant ethical and educational issues that accompany them.

To this end the final section of the book begins with an examination by Bynum of an ethics for the new millennium. Bynum's *Flourishing Ethics*, that draws its inspiration from biological systems, argues for ethical pluralism. In a context of globalization it is likely that this pluralism will become a commonplace reality for everybody and, for this reason alone, it deserves scholarly attention.

Since, it is argued, information ethics is presenting us with a revolution in ethical discourse we need a Copernican Revolution in ethical theory. This is exactly what Bynum's essay does; it introduces us to a nascent ethical theory in the field of Computer Ethics: *Flourishing Ethics*. It is a theory that will provide new tools for dealing with the 'policy vacuums' (Moor 1985) that are presented, almost daily, by the advent of new technologies and our current scientific understanding of life, human nature and the universe. It will also make it possible for us to revisit the shortcomings of already long-established ethical theories. Taking a lead from Aristotle, Bynum argues that excellence in information processing will produce excellence in action and, thus, human flourishing.

It is an invigorating ethics that stresses the role of human beings as caretakers rather than exploiters of others and our planet's resources. It encourages moral agents to see themselves not as independent from each other and the universe but as part of a continuum, the information, and possibly computation, continuum. "The shift in perspective advocated by Flourishing Ethics, then, brings human beings back into the fold with the rest of the universe. It views humans, like all other beings, as fellow participants in the creative unfolding of the cosmos – fellow travelers in the cosmic river of flowing information." (Bynum, this volume)

Riegler analyses the paradox of autonomy in which he argues quite forcefully that when an artificial, self-organising system has reached a state of proper autonomy, that is, where their goals are independent from our own, it will be impossible for us to interact with them. The consequences of this are, it is needless to say, serious and never more so than in the context of personal service robots – systems that are being developed to aid in the care of the elderly and those a suffering chronic illness. The development of increasingly *e*-autonomous agents and the autonomy paradox that this might present is something we must consider carefully, especially if we want their interaction with us to continue in our favour.

Trojer depicts the challenges a technical university, with an explicit profile of applied Information and Communication Technology (ICT), encounters in a region with strong development and when the cooperation with public and private partners outside the university becomes a necessary and predominant reality. It is a situation that calls for knowledge and information transformation processes, and an epistemological openness among people active at the university is a prerequisite for successful functional cooperation. The main questions concern resources for staying confident, future-oriented and innovative as an ICT researcher and a member of the academic teaching staff. Trojer makes reference to her five year development experience, involving student recruitment, research and campus building, and the securing of resources for the epistemological framework within which she has developed a feminist techno-science programme within a technical faculty. Her paper contributes to the epistemological pluralism and multiculturalism of the book, alongside Baynum's ethical pluralism and Allo's logical pluralism.

The final essay in this volume, and another which addresses the issue of computer ethics, has been contributed by Brey. In his paper Brey states that "Computer ethics is a major new field of study that addresses ethical issues in the use, development and management of information technology, as well as in the formulation of general societal policies regarding the regulation of information technology in society". Universities are beginning to develop the teaching of computer ethics as a subject and, he maintains, they must concentrate on two central areas: (i) *computer ethics policies*, and (ii) *computer ethics education*. Brey presents an outline for a field of study which he refers to as social and humanistic studies of computing (SHC) and contrasts it with the applied study of societal aspects of computing (ASC). Both must have a place in the university curriculum if they are to generate awareness of the complex issues we now confront.

We have brought this collection of essays together in an attempt to establish the interconnecting themes within a pancomputational and paninformational, process-oriented conception of the universe. The interdisciplinary nature of the essays can occasionally mean that they exist in the liminal regions of two or more fields of inquiry, the result of which can be that they are overlooked in a discipline-orientated academy. What we have established, in bringing them together, is a perspective and a series of perspectives from, on, and within a burgeoning domain where no single discipline is pre-eminent.

That these particular essays have been brought together does not imply that they provide a set of answers, or even necessarily that there are answers, but in your interaction with them we anticipate that a further series of dialogues will be established. Thus, we offer them both individually and in their compilation as "new metaphors, new starting points". [Winograd 1997]

References

Beall JC & Restall G, 2000. Logical Pluralism, Australasian Journal of Philosophy, 78, pp 475–493

Bennett, C. H. 1988. 'Logical depth and physical complexity', in The Universal Turing Machine; A Half-Century Survey, 227—257. Edited by R. Herken. Oxford: Oxford University Press

Dodig-Crnkovic G. 2006. Investigations into Information Semantics and Ethics of Computing, Mälardalen University Press, forthcoming

Floridi, L. 2004. 'Open Problems in the Philosophy of Information', Metaphilosophy, 35.4

Fodor, J.A. 1987. 'Modules, frames, fridgeons, sleeping dogs and the music of the spheres'. In The robot's dilemma: The frame problem in artificial intelligence, ed. Z. Pylyshyn. Norwood, NJ: Ablex.

Grush, R. 2001. 'The Semantic Challenge to Computational Neuroscience', in Machamer, P. Grush, R. & McLaughlin, P. (Eds.), Theory and Method in the Neurosciences, Pittsburgh, PA: University of Pittsburgh Press.

Hilbert, D, 1926. 'Über das Unendliche'. Mathematische Annalen, 95: 161—90. Translated as "On the infinite" in van Heijenoort, From Frege to Gödel: A source book in mathematical logic, 1879-1931, Harvard University Press

Kafatos, M. & Nadeau, R. 1999. The Conscious Universe: Parts and Wholes in Physical Reality, Springer, 2nd Edition

Kant, I. 1929. The Critique of Pure Reason, trans. Norman Kemp Smith, Macmillan Press (A edition 1781 + B edition 1787)

Lloyd, S. 2006. Programming the Universe: A Quantum Computer Scientist Takes on the Cosmos, Jonathan Cape

Moor, J. H. 1985. "What Is Computer Ethics?", in Terrell Ward Bynum, ed., Computers and Ethics, Blackwell, pp. 266-75 (first published in Metaphilosophy October 1985)

Sebeok, T. 1976. Contributions to the Doctrine of Signs. Bloomington: Indiana University Press

—. 1989 The Sign & Its Masters. Sources in Semiotics VIII. New York: University Press of America.

Uexküll, Thure von, Geigges, W., Herrmann J. M. 1993. 'Endosemiosis', Semiotica 96 (1/2), pp 5-51

Winograd, T. 1997. The design of interaction. Beyond Calculation: The next 50 years of computing. Copernicus, pp 149-161

Zuse, K. 1967. Rechnender Raum, Elektronische Datenverarbeitung, vol. 8, pp 336-344

PART I:
INFORMATION

Chapter One

Epistemology as Information Theory: From Leibniz to Ω

Gregory Chaitin

Abstract

In 1686 in his *Discours de métaphysique*, Leibniz points out that if an arbitrarily complex theory is permitted then the notion of "theory" becomes vacuous because there is always a theory. This idea is developed in the modern theory of algorithmic information, which deals with the size of computer programs and provides a new view of Gödel's work on incompleteness and Turing's work on uncomputability. Of particular interest is the halting probability Ω, whose bits are irreducible, i.e., maximally unknowable mathematical facts. More generally, these ideas constitute a kind of "digital philosophy" related to recent attempts of Edward Fredkin, Stephen Wolfram and others to view the world as a giant computer. There are also connections with recent "digital physics" speculations that the universe might actually be discrete, not continuous. This *système du monde* is presented as a coherent whole in my book *Meta Math!*, which will be published this fall.

Introduction

I am happy to be here with you enjoying the delicate Scandinavian summer; if we were a little farther north there wouldn't be any darkness at all. And I am especially delighted to be here delivering the Alan Turing Lecture. Turing's famous 1936 paper is an intellectual milestone that seems larger and more important with every passing year.

[For Turing's original paper, with commentary, see Copeland's The Essential Turing.]

People are not merely content to enjoy the beautiful summers in the far north, they also want and need **to understand**, and so they create myths. In this part of the world those myths involve Thor and Odin and the other Norse gods.

In this talk, I'm going to present another myth, what the French call a *système du monde*, a system of the world, a speculative metaphysics based on information and the computer.

[One reader's reaction (GDC): "Grand unified theories may be like myths, but surely there is a difference between scientific theory and any other narrative?" I would argue that a scientific narrative is more successful than the Norse myths because it explains what it explains more precisely and without having to postulate new gods all the time, i.e., it's a better "compression" (which will be my main point in this lecture; that's how you measure how successful a theory is).]

The previous century had logical positivism and all that emphasis on the philosophy of language, and completely shunned speculative metaphysics, but a number of us think that it is time to start again. There is an emerging digital philosophy and digital physics, a new metaphysics associated with names like Edward Fredkin and Stephen Wolfram and a handful of like-minded individuals, among whom I include myself. As far as I know the terms "digital philosophy" and "digital physics" were actually invented by Fredkin, and he has a large website with his papers and a draft of a book about this. Stephen Wolfram attracted a great deal of attention to the movement and stirred up quite a bit of controversy with his very large and idiosyncratic book on *A New Kind of Science*.

And I have my own book on the subject, in which I've attempted to wrap everything I know and care about into a single package. It's a small book, and amazingly enough it's going to be published by a major New York publisher a few months from now. This talk will be an overview of my book, which presents my own personal version of "digital philosophy," since each of us who works in this area has a different vision of this tentative, emerging world view. My book is called *Meta Math!*, which may not seem like a serious title, but it's actually a book intended for my professional colleagues as well as for the general public, the high-level, intellectual, thinking public.

"Digital philosophy" is actually a neo-Pythagorean vision of the world, it's just a new version of that. According to Pythagoras, all is number — and by number he means the positive integers, 1, 2, 3, ... — and God is a mathematician. "Digital philosophy" updates this as follows: Now everything is made out of 0/1 bits, everything is digital software, and God is a computer programmer, not a mathematician! It will be interesting to see how well this vision of the world succeeds, and just how much of our experience and theorizing can be included or shoe-horned within this new viewpoint.

[Of course, a system of the world can only work by omitting everything that doesn't fit within its vision. The question is how much will fail to fit, and conversely, how many things will this vision be able to help us to understand. Remember, if one is wearing rose colored glasses, everything seems pink. And as Picasso said, theories are lies that help us to see the truth. No theory is perfect, and it will be interesting to see how far this digital vision of the world will be able to go.]

Let me return now to Turing's famous 1936 paper. This paper is usually remembered for inventing the programmable digital computer via a mathematical model, the Turing machine, and for discovering the extremely fundamental halting problem. Actually Turing's paper is called "On computable numbers, with an application to the *Entscheidungsproblem*," and by computable numbers Turing means "real" numbers, numbers like e or $\pi = 3.1415926...$ that are measured with infinite precision, and that can be computed with arbitrarily high precision, digit by digit without ever stopping, on a computer.

Why do I think that Turing's paper "On computable numbers" is so important? Well, in my opinion it's a paper on epistemology, because we only understand something if we can program it, as I will explain in more detail later. And it's a paper on physics, because what we can actually compute depends on the laws of physics in our particular universe and distinguishes it from other possible universes. And it's a paper on ontology, because it shows that some real numbers are **uncomputable**, which I shall argue calls into question their very existence, their mathematical and physical existence.

[You might exclaim (GDC), "You can't be saying that before Turing and the computer no one understood anything; that can't be right!" My response to this is that before Turing (and my theory) people could understand things, but **they couldn't measure how well** they understood them. Now you can measure that, in terms of the degree of compression that is achieved. I will explain this later at the beginning of the section on computer epistemology. Furthermore, programming something forces you to understand it better, it forces you to really understand it, since you are explaining it **to a machine**. That's sort of what happens when a student or a small child asks you what at first you take to be a stupid question, and then you realize that this question has in fact done you the favor of forcing you to formulate your ideas more clearly and perhaps even question some of your tacit assumptions.]

To show how strange uncomputable real numbers can be, let me give a particularly illuminating example of one, which actually preceded Turing's 1936 paper. It's a very strange number that was invented in a 1927 paper by the French mathematician Emile Borel. Borel's number is sort of an anticipation, a partial anticipation, of Turing's 1936 paper, but that's only something that one can realize in retrospect. Borel presages Turing, which does not in any way lessen Turing's important contribution that so dramatically and sharply clarified all these vague ideas.

[I learnt of Borel's number by reading Tasic's *Mathematics and the Roots of Postmodern Thought,* which also deals with many of the issues discussed here.]

Borel was interested in "constructive" mathematics, in what you can actually compute we would say nowadays. And he came up with an extremely strange non-constructive real number. You list all possible yes/no questions in French in an immense, an infinite list of all possibilities. This will be what mathematicians call a denumerable or a countable infinity of questions, because it can be put into a one-to-one correspondence with the list of positive integers 1, 2, 3, ... In other words, there will be a first question, a second question, a third question, and in general an Nth question.

You can imagine all the possible questions to be ordered by size, and within questions of the same size, in alphabetical order. More precisely, you consider all possible strings, all possible finite sequences of symbols in the French alphabet, including the blank so that you get words, and the period so that you have sentences. And you imagine filtering out all the garbage and being left only with grammatical yes/no questions in French. Later I will tell you in more detail how to actually do this. Anyway, for now **imagine** doing this, and so there will be a first question, a second question, an Nth question.

And the Nth digit or the Nth bit after the decimal point of Borel's number answers the Nth question: It will be a 0 if the answer is no, and it'll be a 1 if the answer is yes. So the binary expansion of Borel's number contains the answer to every possible yes/no question! It's like having an oracle, a Delphic oracle that will answer every yes/no question!

How is this possible?! Well, according to Borel, it isn't really possible, this can't be, it's totally unbelievable. This number is only a mathematical fantasy, it's not for real, it cannot claim a legitimate place in our ontology. Later I'll show you a modern version of Borel's number, my halting probability Ω. And I'll tell you why some contemporary physicists, real physicists, not mavericks, are moving in the direction of digital physics.

[Actually, to make Borel's number as real as possible, you have to avoid the problem of filtering out all the yes/no questions. And you have to use decimal digits, you can't use binary digits. You number all the possible finite strings of French symbols including blanks and periods, which is quite easy to do using a computer. Then the Nth digit of Borel's number is 0 if the Nth string of characters in French is ungrammatical and not proper French, it's 1 if it's grammatical, but not a yes/no question, it's 2 if it's a yes/no question that cannot be answered (e.g., "Is the answer to this question "no"?"), it's 3 if the answer is no, and it's 4 if the answer is yes.]

Geometrically a real number is the most straightforward thing in the world, it's just a point on a line. That's quite natural and intuitive. But *arithmetically*, that's another matter. The situation is quite different. From an arithmetical point of view reals are extremely problematical, they are fraught with difficulties!

Before discussing my Ω number, I want to return to the fundamental question of what does it mean to understand. How do we explain or comprehend something? What is a theory? How can we tell whether or not it's a successful theory? How can we measure how successful it is? Well, using the ideas of information and computation, that's not difficult to do, and the central idea can even be traced back to Leibniz's 1686 *Discours de métaphysique*.

Computer Epistemology: What is a mathematical or scientific theory? How can we judge whether it works or not?

In Sections V and VI of his *Discourse on Metaphysics,* Leibniz asserts that God simultaneously maximizes the variety, diversity and richness of the world, and minimizes the conceptual complexity of the set of ideas that determine the world. And he points out that for any finite set of points there is always a mathematical equation that goes through them, in other words, a law that determines their positions. But if the points are chosen at random, that equation will be extremely complex.

This theme is taken up again in 1932 by Hermann Weyl in his book *The Open World* consisting of three lectures he gave at Yale University on the metaphysics of modern science. Weyl formulates Leibniz's crucial idea in the following extremely dramatic fashion: If one permits arbitrarily complex laws, then the concept of law becomes vacuous, because there is always a law! Then Weyl asks, how can we make more precise the distinction between mathematical simplicity and mathematical complexity? It seems to be very hard to do that. How can we measure this important parameter, without which it is impossible to distinguish between a successful theory and one that is completely unsuccessful?

This problem is taken up and I think satisfactorily resolved in the new mathematical theory I call *algorithmic information theory.* The epistemological model that is central to this theory is that a scientific or mathematical theory is a computer program for calculating the facts, and the smaller the program, the better. The complexity of your theory, of your law, is measured in bits of software:

program (bit string) —> **Computer** —> output (bit string)

theory —> **Computer** —> mathematical or scientific facts

Understanding is compression!

Now Leibniz's crucial observation can be formulated much more precisely. For any finite set of scientific or mathematical facts, there is always a theory that is exactly as complicated, exactly the same size in bits, as the facts themselves. (It just directly outputs them "as is," without doing any computation.) But that doesn't count, that doesn't enable us to distinguish between what can be comprehended and what cannot, because there is always a theory that is as complicated as what it explains. A theory, an explanation, is only successful to the extent to which it compresses the number of bits in the facts into a much smaller number of bits of theory. Understanding is compression, comprehension is compression! That's how we can tell the difference between real theories and *ad hoc* theories.

[By the way, Leibniz also mentions complexity in Section 7 of his *Principles of Nature and Grace,* where he asks the amazing question, "Why is there something rather than nothing? For nothing is simpler and easier than something."]

What can we do with this idea that an explanation has to be simpler than what it explains? Well, the most important application of these ideas that I have been able to find is in metamathematics, it's in discussing what mathematics can or cannot achieve. You simultaneously get an information-theoretic, computational perspective on Gödel's famous 1931 incompleteness theorem, and on Turing's famous 1936 halting problem. How?

[For an insightful treatment of Gödel as a philosopher, see Rebecca Goldstein's *Incompleteness.*]

Here's how! These are my two favorite information-theoretic incompleteness results:

- You need an N-bit theory in order to be able to prove that a specific N-bit program is "elegant."
- You need an N-bit theory in order to be able to determine N bits of the numerical value, of the base-two binary expansion, of the halting probability Ω.

Let me explain.

What is an elegant program? It's a program with the property that no program written in the same programming language that produces the same output is smaller than it is. In other words, an elegant program is the most concise, the simplest, the best theory for its output. And there are infinitely many such programs, they can be arbitrarily big, because for any computational task there has to be at least one elegant program. (There may be several if there are ties, if there are several programs for the same output that have exactly the minimum possible number of bits.)

And what is the halting probability Ω? Well, it's defined to be the probability that a computer program generated at random, by choosing each of its bits using an independent toss of a fair coin, will eventually halt. Turing is interested in whether or not individual programs halt. I am interested in trying to prove what are the bits, what is the numerical value, of the halting probability Ω. By the way, the value of Ω depends on your particular choice of programming language, which I don't have time to discuss now. Ω is also equal to the result of summing 1/2 raised to powers which are the size in bits of every program that halts. In other words, each K-bit program that halts contributes $1/2^K$ to Ω.

And what precisely do I mean by an N-bit mathematical theory? Well, I'm thinking of formal axiomatic theories, which are formulated using symbolic logic, not in any natural, human language. In such theories there are always a finite number of axioms and there are explicit rules for mechanically deducing consequences of the axioms, which are called theorems. An N-bit theory is one for which there is an N-bit program for systematically running through the tree of all possible proofs deducing all the consequences of the axioms, which are all the theorems in your formal theory. This is slow work, but in principle it can be done mechanically, that's what counts. David Hilbert believed that there had to be a single formal axiomatic theory for all of mathematics; that's just another way of stating that math is static and perfect and provides absolute truth.

Not only is this impossible, not only is Hilbert's dream impossible to achieve, but there are in fact an infinity of irreducible mathematical truths, mathematical truths for which essentially the only way to prove them is to add them as new axioms. My first example of such truths was determining elegant programs, and an even better example is provided by the bits of Ω. The bits of Ω are mathematical facts that are true for no reason (no reason simpler than themselves), and thus violate Leibniz's principle of sufficient reason, which states that if anything is true it has to be true for a reason.

In math the reason that something is true is called its proof. Why are the bits of Ω true for no reason, why can't you prove what their values are? Because, as Leibniz himself points out in Sections 33 to 35 of *The Monadology,* the essence of the notion of proof is that you prove a complicated assertion by analyzing it, by breaking it down until you reduce its truth to the truth of assertions that are so simple that they no longer require any proof (self-evident axioms). But if you cannot deduce the truth of something from any principle simpler than itself, then proofs become useless, because **anything** can be proven from principles that are equally complicated, e.g., by directly adding it as a new axiom without any proof. And this is exactly what happens with the bits of Ω.

In other words, the normal, Hilbertian view of math is that all of mathematical truth, an infinite number of truths, can be compressed into a finite number of axioms. But there are an infinity of mathematical truths that cannot be compressed at all, not one bit!

This is an amazing result, and I think that it has to have profound philosophical and practical implications. Let me try to tell you why.

On the one hand, it suggests that pure math is more like biology than it is like physics. In biology we deal with very complicated organisms and mechanisms, but in physics it is normally assumed that there has to be a theory of everything, a simple set of equations that would fit on a T-shirt and in principle explains the world, at least the physical world. But we have seen that the world of mathematical ideas has infinite complexity, it cannot be explained with any theory having a finite number of bits, which from a sufficiently abstract point of view seems much more like biology, the domain of the complex, than like physics, where simple equations reign supreme.

On the other hand, this amazing result suggests that even though math and physics are different, they may not be as different as most people think! I mean this in the following sense: In math you organize your computational experience, your lab is the computer, and in physics you organize physical experience and have real labs. But in both cases an explanation has to be simpler than what it explains, and in both cases there are sets of facts that cannot be explained, that are irreducible. Why? Well, in quantum physics it is assumed that there are phenomena that when measured are equally likely to give either of two answers (e.g., spin up, spin down) and that are inherently unpredictable and irreducible. And in pure math we have a similar example, which is provided by the individual bits in the binary expansion of the numerical value of the halting probability Ω.

This suggests to me a quasi-empirical view of math, in which one is more willing to add new axioms that are not at all self-evident but that are justified pragmatically, i.e., by their fruitful consequences, just like a physicist would. I have taken the term quasi-empirical from Lakatos. The collection of essays *New Directions in the Philosophy of Mathematics* edited by Tymoczko in my opinion pushes strongly in the direction of a quasi-empirical view of math, and it contains an essay by Lakatos proposing the term "quasi-empirical," as well as essays of my own and by a number of other people. Many of them may disagree with me, and I'm sure do, but I repeat, in my opinion all of these essays justify a quasi-empirical view of math, what I mean by quasi-empirical, which is somewhat different from what Lakatos originally meant, but is in quite the same spirit, I think.

In a two-volume work full of important mathematical examples, Borwein, Bailey and Girgensohn have argued that experimental mathematics is an extremely valuable research paradigm that should be openly acknowledged and indeed vigorously embraced. They do not go so far as to suggest that one should add new axioms whenever they are helpful, without bothering with proofs, but they are certainly going in that direction and nod approvingly at my attempts to provide some theoretical justification for their entire enterprise by arguing that math and physics are not that different.

In fact, since I began to espouse these heretical views in the early 1970's, largely to deaf ears, there have actually been several examples of such new pragmatically justified, non-self-evident axioms:

- the P not equal to NP hypothesis regarding the time complexity of computations,
- the axiom of projective determinacy in set theory, and
- increasing reliance on diverse unproved versions of the Riemann hypothesis regarding the distribution of the primes.

So people don't need to have theoretical justification; they just do whatever is needed to get the job done.

The only problem with this computational and information-theoretic epistemology that I've just outlined to you is that it's based on the computer, and there are uncomputable reals. So what do we do with contemporary physics which is full of partial differential equations and field theories, all of which are formulated in terms of real numbers, **most of which are in fact uncomputable,** as I'll now show. Well, it would be good to get rid of all that and convert to a *digital physics.* Might this in fact be possible?! I'll discuss that too.

Computer Ontology: How real are real numbers?
What is the world made of?

How did Turing prove that there are uncomputable reals in 1936? He did it like this. Recall that the possible texts in French are a countable or denumerable infinity and can be placed in an infinite list in which there is a first one, a second one, etc. Now let's do the same thing with all the possible computer programs (first you have to choose your programming language). So there is a first program, a second program, etc. Every computable real can be calculated digit by digit by some program in this list of all possible programs. Write the numerical value of that real next to the programs that calculate it, and cross off the list all the programs that do not calculate an individual computable real. We have converted a list of programs into a list of computable reals, and no computable real is missing.

Next discard the integer parts of all these computable reals, and just keep the decimal expansions. Then put together a new real number by changing every digit on the diagonal of this list (this is called Cantor's diagonal method; it comes from set theory). So your new number's first digit differs from the first digit of the first computable real, its second digit differs from the second digit of the second computable real, its third digit differs from the third digit of the third computable real, and so forth and so on. So it can't be in the list of all computable reals and it has to be uncomputable. And that's Turing's uncomputable real number!

[*Technical Note:* Because of **synonyms** like .345999... = .346000... you should avoid having any 0 or 9 digits in Turing's number.]

Actually, there is a much easier way to see that there are uncomputable reals by using ideas that go back to Emile Borel (again!). Technically, the argument that I'll now present uses what mathematicians call *measure theory*, which deals with probabilities. So let's just look at all the real numbers between 0 and 1. These correspond to points on a line, a line exactly one unit in length, whose leftmost point is the number 0 and whose rightmost point is the number 1. The total length of this line segment is of course exactly one unit. But I will now show you that all the computable reals in this line segment can be covered using intervals whose total length can be made as small as desired. In technical terms, the computable reals in the interval from 0 to 1 are a set of measure zero, they have zero probability.

How do you cover all the computable reals? Well, remember that list of all the computable reals that we just diagonalized over to get Turing's uncomputable real? This time let's cover the first computable real with an interval of size $\varepsilon/2$, let's cover the second computable real with an interval of size $\varepsilon/4$, and in general we'll cover the Nth computable real with an interval of size $\varepsilon/2^N$. The total length of all these intervals (which can conceivably overlap or fall partially outside the unit interval from 0 to 1), is exactly equal to ε, which can be made as small as we wish! In other words, there are arbitrarily small coverings, and the computable reals are therefore a set of measure zero, they have zero probability, they constitute an infinitesimal fraction of all the reals between 0 and 1. So if you pick a real at random between 0 and 1, with a uniform distribution of probability, it is infinitely unlikely, though possible, that you will get a computable real!

What disturbing news! Uncomputable reals are not the exception, they are the majority! How strange!

In fact, the situation is even worse than that. As Emile Borel points out on page 21 of his final book, *Les nombres inaccessibles* (1952), without making any reference to Turing, most individual reals are not even uniquely specifiable, they cannot even be named or pointed out, no matter how non-constructively, because of the limitations of human languages, which permit only a countable infinity of possible texts. The individually accessible or nameable reals are also a set of measure zero. Most reals are un-nameable, with probability one! I rediscovered this result of Borel's on my own in a slightly different context, in which things can be done a little more rigorously, which is when one is dealing with a formal axiomatic theory or an **artificial** formal language instead of a natural human language. That's how I present this idea in *Meta Math!*.

So if most individual reals will forever escape us, why should we believe in them?! Well, you will say, because they have a pretty structure and are a nice theory, a nice game to play, with which I certainly agree, and also because they have important practical applications, they are needed in physics. Well, perhaps not! Perhaps physics can give up infinite precision reals! How? Why should physicists want to do that?

Because it turns out that there are actually many reasons for being skeptical about the reals, in classical physics, in quantum physics, and particularly in more speculative contemporary efforts to cobble together a theory of black holes and quantum gravity.

First of all, as my late colleague the physicist Rolf Landauer used to remind me, no physical measurement has ever achieved more than a small number of digits of precision, not more than, say, 15 or 20 digits at most, and such high-precision experiments are rare masterpieces of the experimenter's art and not at all easy to achieve.

This is only a practical limitation in classical physics. But in quantum physics it is a consequence of the Heisenberg uncertainty principle and wave-particle duality (de Broglie). According to quantum theory, the more accurately you try to measure something, the smaller the length scales you are trying to explore, the higher the energy you need (the formula describing this involves Planck's constant). That's why it is getting more and more expensive to build particle accelerators like the one at CERN and at Fermilab, and governments are running out of money to fund high-energy physics, leading to a paucity of new experimental data to inspire theoreticians.

Hopefully new physics will eventually emerge from astronomical observations of bizarre new astrophysical phenomena, since we have run out of money here on earth! In fact, currently some of the most interesting physical speculations involve the thermodynamics of black holes, massive concentrations of matter that seem to be lurking at the hearts of most galaxies. Work by

Stephen Hawking and Jacob Bekenstein on the thermodynamics of black holes suggests that any physical system can contain only a finite amount of information, a finite number of bits whose possible maximum is determined by what is called the Bekenstein bound. Strangely enough, this bound on the number of bits grows as the surface area of the physical system, not as its volume, leading to the so-called "holographic" principle asserting that in some sense space is actually two-dimensional even though it appears to have three dimensions!

So perhaps continuity is an illusion, perhaps everything is really discrete. There is another argument against the continuum if you go down to what is called the Planck scale. At distances that extremely short our current physics breaks down because spontaneous fluctuations in the quantum vacuum should produce mini-black holes that completely tear spacetime apart. And that is not at all what we see happening around us. So perhaps distances that small **do not exist**.

Inspired by ideas like this, in addition to *a priori* metaphysical biases in favor of discreteness, a number of contemporary physicists have proposed building the world out of discrete information, out of bits. Some names that come to mind in this connection are John Wheeler, Anton Zeilinger, Gerard 't Hooft, Lee Smolin, Seth Lloyd, Paola Zizzi, Jarmo Mäkelä and Ted Jacobson, who are real physicists. There is also more speculative work by a small cadre of cellular automata and computer enthusiasts including Edward Fredkin and Stephen Wolfram, whom I already mentioned, as well as Tommaso Toffoli, Norman Margolus, and others.

And there is also an increasing body of highly successful work on quantum computation and quantum information that is not at all speculative, it is just a fundamental reworking of standard 1920's quantum mechanics. Whether or not quantum computers ever become practical, the workers in this highly popular field have clearly established that it is illuminating to study sub-atomic quantum systems in terms of how they process qubits of quantum information and how they perform computation with these qubits. These notions have shed completely new light on the behavior of quantum mechanical systems.

Furthermore, when dealing with complex systems such as those that occur in biology, thinking about information processing is also crucial. As I believe Seth Lloyd said, the most important thing in understanding a complex system is to determine how it represents information and how it processes that information, i.e., what kinds of computations are performed.

And how about the entire universe, can it be considered to be a computer? Yes, it certainly can, it is constantly computing its future state from its current state, it's constantly computing its own time-evolution! And as I believe Tom

Toffoli pointed out, actual computers like your PC just hitch a ride on this universal computation!

So perhaps we are not doing violence to Nature by attempting to force her into a digital, computational framework. Perhaps she has been flirting with us, giving us hints all along, that she is really discrete, not continuous, hints that we choose not to hear, because we are so much in love and don't want her to change!

For more on this kind of new physics, see the books by Smolin and von Baeyer in the bibliography. Several more technical papers on this subject are also included there.

Conclusion

Let me now wrap this up and try to give you a present to take home, more precisely, a piece of homework. In extremely abstract terms, I would say that the problem is, as was emphasized by Ernst Mayr in his book *This is Biology*, that the current philosophy of science deals more with physics and mathematics than it does with biology. But let me try to put this in more concrete terms and connect it with the spine, with the central thread, of the ideas in this talk.

To put it bluntly, a closed, static, eternal fixed view of math can no longer be sustained. As I try to illustrate with examples in my *Meta Math!* book, math actually advances by inventing new concepts, by completely changing the viewpoint. Here I emphasized new axioms, increased complexity, more information, but what really counts are new ideas, new concepts, new viewpoints. And that leads me to the crucial question, crucial for a proper open, dynamic, time-dependent view of mathematics,

"Where do new mathematical ideas come from?"

I repeat, math does not advance by mindlessly and mechanically grinding away deducing all the consequences of a fixed set of concepts and axioms, not at all! It advances with new concepts, new definitions, new perspectives, through revolutionary change, paradigm shifts, not just by hard work.

In fact, I believe that this is actually the central question in biology as well as in mathematics, it's the mystery of creation, of creativity:

"Where do new mathematical and biological ideas come from?"
"How do they emerge?"

Normally one equates a new biological idea with a new species, but in fact every time a child is born, that's actually a new idea incarnating; it's reinventing the notion of "human being," which changes constantly.

I have no idea how to answer this extremely important question; I wish I could. Maybe **you** will be able to do it. Just try! You might have to keep it cooking on a back burner while concentrating on other things, but don't give up! All it takes is a new idea! Somebody has to come up with it. Why not you?

[I'm not denying the importance of Darwin's theory of evolution. But I want much more than that, I want a profound, extremely general mathematical theory that captures the essence of what life is and why it evolves. I want a theory that gets to the heart of the matter. And I suspect that any such theory will necessarily have to shed new light on mathematical creativity as well. Conversely, a deep theory of mathematical creation might also cover biological creativity.

A reaction from Gordana Dodig-Crnkovic: "Regarding Darwin and Neo-Darwinism I agree with you — it is a very good idea to go beyond. In my view there is nothing more beautiful and convincing than a good mathematical theory. And I do believe that it must be possible to express those thoughts in a much more general way... I believe that it is a very crucial thing to try to formulate life in terms of computation. Not to say life is nothing more than a computation. But just to explore how far one can go with that idea. Computation seems to me a very powerful tool to illuminate many things about the material world and the material ground for mental phenomena (including creativity)... Or would you suggest that creativity is given by God's will? That it is the very basic axiom? Isn't it possible to relate to pure chance? Chance and selection? Wouldn't it be a good idea to assume two principles: law and chance, where both are needed to reconstruct the universe in computational terms? (like chaos and cosmos?)"]

Appendix: Leibniz and the Law

I am indebted to Professor Ugo Pagallo for explaining to me that Leibniz, whose ideas and their elaboration were the subject of my talk, is regarded as just as important in the field of law as he is in the fields of mathematics and philosophy.

The theme of my lecture was that if a law is arbitrarily complicated, then it is not a law; this idea was traced via Hermann Weyl back to Leibniz. In mathematics it leads to my Ω number and the surprising discovery of completely lawless regions of mathematics, areas in which there is absolutely no structure or pattern or way to understand what is happening.

The principle that an arbitrarily complicated law is not a law can also be interpreted with reference to the legal system. It is not a coincidence that the words "law" and "proof" and "evidence" are used in jurisprudence as well as in science and mathematics. In other words, the rule of law is equivalent to the rule of reason, but if a law is sufficiently complicated, then it can in fact be completely arbitrary and incomprehensible.

Acknowledgements

I wish to thank Gordana Dodig-Crnkovic for organizing E-CAP'05 and for inviting me to present the Turing lecture at E-CAP'05; also for stimulating discussions reflected in those footnotes that are marked with GDC. The remarks on biology are the product of a week spent in residence at Rockefeller University in Manhattan, June 2005; I thank Albert Libchaber for inviting me to give a series of lectures there to physicists and biologists. The appendix is the result of lectures to philosophy of law students April 2005 at the Universities of Padua, Bologna and Turin; I thank Ugo Pagallo for arranging this. Thanks too to Paola Zizzi for help with the physics references.

References

Borel, Emile. 1952. *Les nombres inaccessibles.* Gauthier-Villars.
Borwein, Jonathan, Bailey David, Girgensohn Roland. 2003, 2004. *Mathematics by Experiment, Experimentation in Mathematics.* A. K. Peters.
Chaitin, Gregory. 2005. *Meta Math!* Pantheon.
Copeland B, Jack. 2004. *The Essential Turing.* Oxford University Press.
Fredkin, Edward. http://www.digitalphilosophy.org/.
Goldstein, Rebecca. 2005. *Incompleteness.* Norton.
Jacobson, Ted. "Thermodynamics of spacetime." http://arxiv.org/gr-qc/9504004.
Leibniz, G. W. 1686, 1714, 1714. *Discourse on Metaphysics, Principles of Nature and Grace, The Monadology.*
Lloyd, Seth. "The computational universe." http://arxiv.org/quant-ph/0501135.
Mayr, Ernst. 1998. *This is Biology.* Harvard University Press.
Mäkelä, Jarmo. "Accelerating observers, area and entropy." http://arxiv.org/gr-qc/0506087.
Smolin, Lee. 2001. *Three Roads to Quantum Gravity.* Basic Books.
't Hooft, Gerardus. "The holographic principle." http://arxiv.org/hep-th/0003004.
Tasic, Vladimir. 2001. *Mathematics and the Roots of Postmodern Thought.* Oxford University Press.

Tymoczko, Thomas. 1998. *New Directions in the Philosophy of Mathematics.* Princeton University Press.
von Baeyer, Hans Christian. 2004. *Information.* Harvard University Press.
Weyl, Hermann. 1932. *The Open World.* Yale University Press.
Wheeler, John. 1992. "The 'It from bit' proposal." Sakharov Memorial Lectures on Physic., vol. 2, Nova Science.
Wolfram, Stephen. 2002. *A New Kind of Science,* Wolfram Media.
Zeilinger, Anton. 1999. "The principle of quantization of information." *Found Phys.* 29:631-643.
Zizzi, Paola. "A minimal model for quantum gravity." http://arxiv.org/gr-qc/0409069.

CHAPTER TWO

INFORMATION LOGIC

LUCIANO FLORIDI

Abstract

One of the open problems in the philosophy of information is whether there is an *information logic* (*IL*), different from *epistemic* (*EL*) and *doxastic logic* (*DL*), which formalises the relation "*a* is informed that *p*" ($I_a p$) satisfactorily. In this paper, the problem is solved by arguing that the axiom schemata of the normal modal logic (*NML*) **KTB** (also known as **B** or **Br** or Brouwer's system) are well suited to model the relation of "being informed".

Keywords

Brouwer's system; Doxastic logic; Entailment property; Epistemic logic; Gettier problem; Information logic; Normal modal logic **KTB**; Veridicality of information.

Introduction

As anyone acquainted with modal logic (*ML*) knows, *epistemic logic* (*EL*) formalises the relation "*a* knows that *p*" ($K_a p$), whereas *doxastic logic* (*DL*) formalises the relation "*a* believes that *p*" ($B_a p$). One of the open problems in the philosophy of information (Floridi [2004b]) is whether there is also an *information logic* (*IL*), different from *EL* and from *DL*, that formalises the relation "*a* is informed that *p*" ($I_a p$) equally well.

The keyword here is "equally" not "well". One may contend that *EL* and *DL* do not capture the relevant relations very well or even not well at all. Hocutt [1972], for example, provides an early criticism. Yet this is not the point here, since all I wish to argue in this paper is that *IL* can do for "being informed" what *EL* does for "knowing" and *DL* does for "believing". If one objects to the last two, one may object to the first as well, yet one should not object to it more.

The proposal developed in the following pages is that the normal modal logic (*NML*) **KTB** (also known as **B**, **Br** or Brouwer's system[1]) is well suited to model the relation of "being informed", and hence that *IL* can be constructed as an informational reading of **KTB**. The proposal is in three sections.

In section one, several meanings of "information" are recalled, in order to focus only on the "cognitive" sense. Three main ways in which one may speak of a "logic of (cognitive) information" are then distinguished. Only one of them is immediately relevant here, namely, "*a* is informed that *p*" as meaning "*a* holds the information that *p*". These clarifications are finally used to make precise the specific question addressed in the rest of the paper.

In section two, the analysis of the informational relation of "being informed" provides the specifications to be satisfied by its accurate formalization. It is then shown that **KTB** successfully captures the relation of "being informed".

In section three, the conclusion, I sketch some of the work that lies ahead, especially as far as the application of information logic is concerned to deal with some key issues in epistemology.

Throughout the paper the ordinary language of classical, propositional calculus (*PC*) and of normal, propositional modal logic (see for example Girle [2000]) will be presupposed. Implication ($\rightarrow$) is used in its "material" sense; the semantics is Kripkean; Greek letters are metalinguistic, propositional variables ranging over well-formed formulae of the object language of the corresponding *NML*; and until section 2.6 attention is focused only on the axiom schemata of the *NMLs* in question.

1. Three logics of information

"Information" may be understood in many ways, e.g. as signals, natural patterns or nomic regularities, as instructions, as content, as news, as synonymous with data, as power or as an economic resource and so forth. It is notoriously controversial whether even most of these senses of "information" might be reduced to a fundamental concept.[2] However, the sort of "information" that interests us here is arguably the most important. It is "information" as

---

[1] The name was assigned by Becker [1930]. As Goldblatt [2003] remarks: "The connection with Brouwer is remote: if 'not' is translated to 'impossible' ($\neg \Diamond$), and 'implies' to its strict version, then the intuitionistically acceptable principle p $\rightarrow$ $\neg\neg$p becomes the Brouwersche axiom". For a description of **KTB** see Hughes and Cresswell [1996].

[2] For an overview see Floridi [2004a] and Floridi [2005b]. Personally, I am very sceptical about attempts to find a unified theory of information and hence a unique logic that would capture all its interesting features.

semantic content that, on one side, concerns some state of a system, and that, on the other side, allows the elaboration of an agent's propositional knowledge of that state of the system. It is the sense in which Matthew is informed that *p*, e.g. that "the train to London leaves at 10.30 am", or about the state of affairs *f* expressed by *p*, e.g. the railway timetable. In the rest of the paper, "information" will be discussed only in this intuitive sense of *declarative*, *objective* and *semantic content* that *p* or about *f* (Floridi [2005a]). This sense may loosely be qualified as "cognitive", a neutral label useful to refer here to a whole family of relations expressing propositional attitudes, including "knowing", "believing", "remembering", "perceiving" and "experiencing". Any "non-cognitive" sense of "semantic information" will be disregarded.[3]

The scope of our inquiry can now be narrowed by considering the logical analysis of the *cognitive* relation "*a* is informed that *p*". Three related yet separate features of interest need to be further distinguished, namely

a) how *p* may be informative for *a*.

For example, the information that $\neg p$ may or may not be informative depending on whether *a* is already informed that $(p \vee q)$. This aspect of information – the *informativeness* of a message – raises issues of e.g. novelty, reliability of the source and background information. It is a crucial aspect related to the quantitative theory of semantic information (Bar-Hillel and Carnap [1953], see Bar-Hillel [1964]; Floridi [2004c]), to the logic of transition states in dynamic system, that is, how change in a system may be informative for an observer (Barwise and Seligman [1997]) and to the theory of levels of abstraction at which a system is being considered (Floridi and Sanders [2004]; Floridi and Sanders [forthcoming]);

b) the process through which *a* becomes informed that *p*.

The informativeness of *p* makes possible the process that leads from *a*'s uninformed (or less informed) state *A* to *a*'s (more) informed state *B*. Upgrading *a*'s state *A* to a state *B* usually involves receiving the information that *p* from

---

[3] There are many plausible contexts in which a stipulation ("let the value of x = 3" or "suppose we discover the bones of a unicorn"), an invitation ("you are cordially invited to the college party"), an order ("close the window!"), an instruction ("to open the box turn the key"), a game move ("1.e2-e4 c7-c5" at the beginning of a chess game) may be correctly qualified as kinds of information understood as semantic content. These and other similar, non-cognitive meanings of "information" (e.g. to refer to a music file or to a digital painting) are not discussed in this paper, where semantic information is taken to have a declarative or factual value i.e. it is suppose to be correctly qualifiable alethically.

some external source *S* and processing it. It implies that *a* cannot be informed that *p* unless *a* was previously uninformed that *p*. And the logical relation that underlies this state transition raises important issues of timeliness and cost of acquisition, for example, and of adequate procedures of information processing, including introspection and metainformation, as we shall see. It is related to communication theory (Shannon and Weaver [1949 rep. 1998]), temporal logic, updating procedures (Gärdenfors [1988]), and recent trends in dynamic epistemic logic (Baltag and Moss [2004]);

c) the state of the epistemic agent *a*, insofar as *a holds* the information that *p*.

This is the *statal* condition into which *a* enters, once *a* has acquired the information (actional state of being informed) that *p*. It is the sense in which a witness, for example, is informed (holds the information) that the suspect was with her at the time when the crime was committed. The distinction is standard among grammarians, who speak of passive verbal forms or states as "statal" (e.g. "the door *was shut* (state) when I last checked it") or "actional" (e.g. "but I don't know when the door *was shut* (act)").[4] Here, we are interested only in the *statal* sense of "is informed". This sense (c) is related to cognitive issues and to the logical analysis of an agent's "possession" of a belief or a piece of knowledge.

Point (a) requires the development of a logic of "being informative"; (b) requires the development of a logic of "becoming informed"; and (c) requires the development of a logic of "being informed (i.e. holding the information)". Work on (a) and (b) is already in progress. Allo [2005] and Sanders [forthcoming], respectively, develop two lines of research complementary to this paper. In this paper, I shall be concerned with (c) and seek to show that there is a logic of information comparable, for adequacy, flexibility and usefulness, to *EL* and *DL*.

Our problem can now be formulated more precisely. Let us concentrate our attention on the most popular and traditional *NML*, obtainable through the analysis of some of the well-known characteristics of the relation of accessibility (reflexivity, transitivity etc.). These fifteen[5] *NMLs* range from the weakest **K** to the strongest **S5** (see below Figure 1). They are also obtainable

---

[4] I owe to Christopher Kirwan this very useful clarification; in a previous version of this paper I had tried to reinvent it, but the wheel was already there.
[5] The number of *NMLs* available is infinite. I am grateful to Timothy Williamson and John Halleck who kindly warned me against a misleading wording in a previous version of this paper.

through the combination of the usual axiom schemata of *PC* with the fundamental modal axiom schemata (see below Figure 2). Both *EL* and *DL* comprise a number of cognitively interpretable *NML*, depending on the sets of axioms that qualify the corresponding *NML* used to capture the relevant "cognitive" notions. If we restrict our attention to the six most popular *EL* and *DL* – those based on systems **KT**, **S4**, **S5** and on systems **KD**, **KD4**, **KD45** respectively – the question about the availability of an information logic can be rephrased thus: among the popular *NMLs* taken into consideration, is there one, not belonging to {**KT**, **S4**, **S5**, **KD**, **KD4**, **KD45**}, which, if cognitively interpreted, can successfully capture and formalise our intuitions regarding "*a* is informed that *p*" in the (c) sense specified above?

A potential confusion may be immediately dispelled. Of course, the logical analysis of the cognitive relation of "being informed" can sometimes be provided in terms of "knowing" or "believing", and hence of *EL* or *DL*. This is not in question, for it is trivially achievable, insofar as "being informed" can sometimes be correctly treated as synonymous with "knowing" or "believing". *IL* may sometime overlap with *EL*. The interesting problem is whether "being informed" may show properties that typically (i.e., whenever the overlapping would be unjustified) require a logic different from *EL* and *DL*, in order to be modelled accurately. The hypothesis defended in the following pages is that it does and, moreover, that this has some interesting consequences for our understanding of the nature of the relation between "knowing" and "believing".

Computation, Information, Cognition - The Nexus and the Liminal

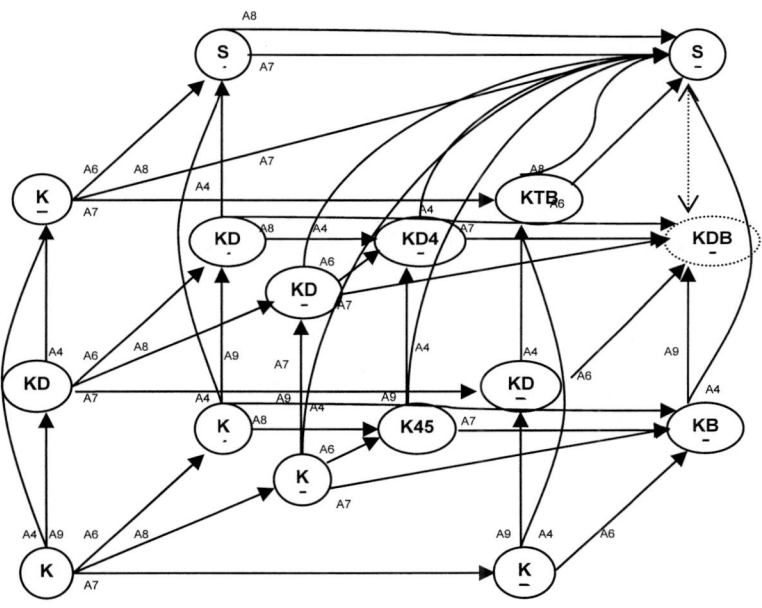

Figure 1 Fifteen Normal Modal Logics

Note that **KDB5** is a "dummy" system: it is equivalent to **S5** and it is added to the diagram just for the sake of elegance.

Synonymous
T = M = KT
B = Br = KTB
D = KD

Equivalent axiomatic systems
B = TB
KB5 = KB4, KB45
S5 = T5, T45, TB4, TB5, TB45, DB4, DB5, DB45

Cartesian axis
Transitive R
Aristotelian axis   A6   Socratic axis
Reflexive R   Euclidean R
A9-A4   A8-A6-A7
                     Platonic axis
                     Symmetric R
                     A7

2. Modelling "being informed"

Let us interpret the modal operator $\Box$ as "is informed that". We may then replace the symbol $\Box$ with I for "being informed", include an explicit reference to the informed agent a, and write

$\Box p = I_a p$ to mean a is informed (holds the information) that p.[6]

As customary, the subscript will be omitted whenever we shall be dealing with a single, stand-alone agent a. It will be reintroduced in § 2.4, when dealing with multiagent *IL*. Next, we can then define $\Diamond$ in the standard way, thus

$U_a p =_{\text{def}} \neg I_a \neg p$ to mean a is uninformed   (is not informed, does not hold the information) that $\neg p$; or
for all a's information (given a's information base), it is possible that p.

Simplifying, a's information base can be modelled by representing it as a *dynamic* set D_a of sentences of a language L.[7] The intended interpretation is that D_a consists of all the sentences, i.e. all the information, that a holds at time t. We then have that $I_a p$ means that $p \in D_a$, and $U_a p$ means that p can be uploaded in D_a while maintaining the consistency of D_a, that is, $U_a p$ means $\Diamond \, (p \in D_a)$ "salva cohaerentiae".[8] Note that a need not be committed, either doxastically

---

[6] A *de re* interpretation is obtainable by interpreting $I_a p$ as "there is the information that p".

[7] Dynamic sets are an important class of data structures in which sets of items, indexed by keys, are maintained. It is assumed that the elements of the dynamic set contain a field (called the key) by whose value they can be ordered. The phone directory of a company is a simple example of a dynamic set (it changes over time), whose key might be "last name". Dynamic sets can change over the execution of a process by gaining or losing elements. Of the variety of operations usually supported by a dynamic set, three are fundamental and will be assumed in this paper:
Search(S,k) = given a set S and a key value k, a query operation that returns a pointer x to an element in S such that $key[x] = k$, or nil if no such element belongs to S.
Insert(S,x) = an operation that augments the set S with the element x.
Delete(S,x) = an operation that removes an element pointed to by x from S (if it is there).

[8] As Patrick Allo has noted in a personal communication, this can also be expressed in terms of safety of inclusion of p in D_a.

(e.g. in terms of strengths of belief, Lenzen [1978]) or epistemically (e.g. in terms of degrees of certainty) in favour of any element in D_a.

Given that *IL* might actually overlap and hence be confused with *EL* or *DL*, the most plausible conjecture is that an *IL* that can capture our intuitions, and hence satisfy our requirements regarding the proper formalization of I_p, will probably bear some strong resemblance to *EL* and *DL*. If there is any difference between these three families of cognitive logics it is likely to be identifiable more easily in terms of satisfaction (or lack thereof) of one or more axioms qualifying the corresponding *NML*. The heuristic assumption here is that, by restricting our attention to the fifteen *NMLs* in question, we may be able to identify the one which best captures our requirements. It is a bit like finding where, on a continuous map, the logic of information may be placed: even if we succeed in showing that **KTB** is the right *NML* for our task, there is still an infinite number of neighbouring *NMLs* extending **KTB**.[9]

For ease of reference, the axiom schemata in question are summarised and numbered progressively in Figure 2, where φ, χ and ψ are propositional variables referring to any wff of *PC*.

Following Hintikka's standard approach (Hintikka [1962]), a systematic way to justify the choice of some axiom schemata is by trying to identify a plausible interpretation of a semantics for the corresponding *NML*. We shall now consider the 12 axiom schemata and show that *IL* shares only some of them with *EL* and *DL*.

Label	Definitions of Axiom Schemata	Name of the axiom or the corresponding *NML*	Frame
A_1	$\varphi \to (\chi \to \varphi)$	1st axiom of *PC*	
A_2	$(\varphi \to (\chi \to \psi)) \to ((\varphi \to \chi) \to (\varphi \to \psi))$	2nd axiom of *PC*	
A_3	$(\neg \varphi \to \neg \chi) \to (\chi \to \varphi)$	3rd axiom of *PC*	
A_4	$\Box \varphi \to \varphi$	**KT** or **M**, K2, veridicality	Reflexive
A_5	$\Box(\varphi \to \chi) \to (\Box \varphi \to \Box \chi)$	**K**, distribution, deductive cogency	
A_6	$\Box \varphi \to \Box\Box \varphi$	4, **S4**, K3, KK, reflective thesis or positive introspection	Transitive

---

[9] Many thanks to John Halleck for calling my attention to this point and to Miyazaki [2005].

26 Chapter Two

A_7	$\varphi \to \Box\Diamond\varphi$	**KTB**, **B**, **Br**, Brouwer's axiom or Platonic thesis	Symmetric
A_8	$\Diamond\varphi \to \Box\Diamond\varphi$	**S5**, reflective, Socratic thesis or negative introspection	Euclidean
A_9	$\Box\varphi \to \Diamond\varphi$	**KD**, **D**, consistency	Serial
A_{10}	$\Box(\varphi \to \chi) \to (\Box(\chi \to \psi) \to \Box(\varphi \to \psi))$	Single agent transmission	
A_{11}	$\Box_x\Box_y\varphi \to \Box_x\varphi$	**K4**, multiagent transmission, or Hintikka's axiom	

Figure 2 Axiom schemata of the propositional *NMLs* discussed in the paper

2.1 *IL* satisfies A_1, A_2, A_3, A_5

Trivially, we may assume that *IL* satisfies the axioms A_1-A_3. As for A_5, this specifies that *IL* is distributive, as it should be. If an agent *a* is informed that $p \to q$, then, if *a* is informed that *p*, *a* is also informed that *q*. Note that, although this is entirely uncontroversial, it is less trivial. Not all "cognitive" relations are distributive. "Knowing", "believing" and "being informed" are, as well as "remembering" and "recalling". This is why Plato is able to argue that a "mnemonic logic", which he seems to base on **K4**, may replace *DL* as a foundation for *EL*.[10] However, "seeing" and other experiential relations, for example, are not: if an agent *a* sees (in a non metaphorical sense) or hears or experiences or perceives that $p \to q$, it may still be false that, if *a* sees (hears etc.) *p*, *a* then also sees (hears etc.) *q*.

The inclusion or exclusion of the remaining seven axioms is more contentious. Although logically independent, the reasons leading to their inclusion or exclusion are not, and they suggest the following clustering. In § 2.2, *IL* is shown to satisfy not only A_9 (consistency) but also A_4 (veridicality). In § 2.3, it is argued that *IL* does not have to satisfy the two "reflective" axioms, that is A_6 and A_8. And in § 2.4, it is argued that *IL* should satisfy the "transmissibility" axioms A_{10} and A_{11}. This will leave us with A_7, to be discussed in § 2.5.

---

[10] On Plato's interpretation of knowledge as recollection see especially *Phaedo* 72e-75 and *Meno* 82b-85.

2.2 Consistency and Truth: *IL* satisfies A_9 and A_4

In *DL*, A_9 replaces the stronger A_4, which characterizes *EL*: whereas *p* must be true for the epistemic agent *a* to know that *p*, the doxastic agent *a* only needs to be consistent in her beliefs. There are at least four reasons why *IL* should be characterized as satisfying A_9:

1) A_9 specifies that, in *IL*, the informational agent *a* is consistent, but so can be our ordinary informed agent in everyday life: $Ip \rightarrow Up$. If *a* holds the information that the train leaves at 10.30 am then, for all *a*'s information, it is possible that the train leaves at 10.30 am, in other words, *p* can be uploaded in *a*'s information base D_a while maintaining the consistency of D_a;

2) even if (1) were unconvincing, *IL* should qualify *a* as consistent at least normatively, if not factually, in the same way as *DL* does. If *a* holds the information that the train leaves at 10.30 am, then *a* should not hold the information that the train does not leave at 10.30 am. The point is not that doxastic or informational agents cannot be inconsistent,[11] but that A_9 provides an information integrity constraint: inconsistent agents should be disregarded. Again, to appreciate the non-trivial nature of a normative approach to A_9, consider the case of a "mnemonic logic": it might be factually implausible and only normatively desirable to formalise "*a* remembers that *p*" as implying that, if this is the case, then *a* does not remember that $\neg p$. Matthew may remember something that actually never happened, or he might remember both *p* (that he left the keys in the car) and $\neg p$ (that he left the keys on his desk) and be undecided about which memory is reliable. Likewise, if a database contains the information that *p* it might, unfortunately, still contain also the information that $\neg p$, even if, in principle, it should not, because this would seriously undermine the informative nature of the database itself (see next point 3), and although it is arguable (because of A_4, see below) that in such case either *p* or $\neg p$ fail to count as information;

3) objections against *IL* satisfying A_9 appear to be motivated by a confusion between "becoming informed" and "being informed", a distinction emphasised in § 2.1. In the former case, it is unquestionable that *a* may receive and hence hold two contradictory messages (e.g., *a* may read in a printed timetable that the train leaves at 10.30 am, as it does, but *a* may also be told by *b* that the train does not leave at 10.30 am). However, from this it only follows that *a* has the information that the train leaves at 10.30 am, but since *p* and $\neg p$ erase each other's value as pieces of information *for a*, *a* may be unable, subjectively, to

---

[11] It might be possible to develop a modal approach to QC (quasi-classical) logic in order to weaken the integrity constraint, see Grant and Hunter [forthcoming].

identify which information a holds. It does not follow that a is actually informed both that the train leaves at 10.30 am and that it does not;

4) if *IL* satisfies the stronger A_4 then, *a fortiori*, *IL* satisfies A_9. Accepting that *IL* satisfies A_9 on the basis of (1)-(3) is obviously not an argument in favour of the inclusion of A_4. At most, it only defuses any argument against it based on the reasoning that, if *IL* did not satisfy A_9, it would fail to satisfy A_4 as well. The inclusion of A_4 requires some positive support of its own, to which we now turn.

According to A_4, if a is informed that p then p is true. Can this be right? Couldn't it be the case that one might be qualified as being informed that p even if p is false? The answer is in the negative, for the following reason. Including A_4 as one of *IL* axioms depends on whether p counts as information only if p is true. Now, some critics (Colburn [2000], Fox [1983], Dodig-Crnkovic [2005] and, among situation theorists, Devlin [1991]) may still be unconvinced about the necessarily veridical nature of information, witness the debate between Floridi [2004c] and Fetzer [2004]. However, more recently, it has been shown in Floridi [2005a] that the Dretske-Grice approach to the so-called standard definition of information as meaningful data[12] remains by far the most plausible. In short, p counts as information only if p is true because:

"[...] *false* information and *mis*-information are not kinds of information – any more than decoy ducks and rubber ducks are kinds of ducks" (Dretske [1981], 45).

"False information is not an inferior kind of information; it just is not information" (Grice [1989], 371).

As in the case of knowledge, truth is a necessary condition for p to qualify as information. In Floridi [2005a] this is established by proving that none of the reasons usually offered in support of the alethic neutrality of information is convincing, and then that there are several good reasons to treat information as encapsulating truth and hence to disqualify misinformation (that is, "false information") as pseudo-information, that is, as not (a type of) information at all. The arguments presented there will not be rehearsed here, since it is sufficient to accept the conclusion that either one agrees that information encapsulates truth or (at least) the burden of proof is on her side.

Once the veridical approach to the analysis of semantic information is endorsed as the most plausible, it follows that, strictly speaking, to hold (exchange, receive, sell, buy, etc.) some "false information", e.g. that the train leaves at 11.30 am when in fact it leaves at 10.30 am, is to hold (exchange,

---

[12] Other philosophers who accept a truth-based definition of information are Barwise and Seligman [1997] and Graham [1999].

receive, sell, buy, etc.) no information at all, only some semantic content (meaningful data). But then, a cannot hold the information (be informed) that p unless p is true, which is precisely what A_4 states. Mathew is not informed but misinformed that Brazil lost the world cup in 2002 because Brazil won it. And most English readers will gladly acknowledge that Matthew is informed about who won the world cup in 1966 only if he holds that England did.

The mistake – arguing that a may be informed that p even if p is false, and hence that *IL* should not satisfy A_4 – might arise if one confuses "holding the information that p", which we have seen must satisfy A_4, with "holding p as information", which of course need not, since an agent is free to believe that p qualifies as information even when p is actually false, and hence counts as mere misinformation.

As far as A_4 is concerned, "knowing that p" and "being informed that p" work in the same way. This conclusion may still be resisted in view of a final objection, which may be phrased as dilemma: either the veridical approach to information is incorrect, and therefore *IL* should not satisfy A_4, or it is correct, and therefore *IL* should satisfy A_4, yet only because there is no substantial difference between *IL* and *EL* (information logic becomes only another name for epistemic logic). In short, the inclusion of A_4 among the axiom schemata qualifying *IL* is either wrong or trivial.

The objection is interesting but mistaken. So far, *IL* shares all its axiom schemata with *EL*, but information logic allows truth-encapsulation without epistemic collapse because there are two other axiom schemata that are epistemic but not informational. This is what we are going to see in the next section.

2.3 No reflectivity: *IL* does not satisfy A_6, A_8

Let us begin from the most "infamous" of *EL* axiom schemata, namely A_6. One way of putting the argument in favour of A_4 and against A_6, is by specifying that the relation of "informational accessibility"[13] H in the system that best formalises "being informed/holding the information that p" is *reflexive* without being *reflective*, reflectivity being here the outcome of a transitive relation in a single agent context, that is, "introspection", a rather more common label that should be used with some caution given its psychologistic overtones.

If H were reflective (if the informational agent were introspective), *IL* should support the equivalent of the *KK* or *BB* thesis, i.e., $Ip \rightarrow IIp$. However,

---

[13] The choice of the letter H is arbitrary, but it may graphically remind one of the H in Shannon's famous equation and in the expression "holding the information that p".

the *II* thesis is not merely problematic, it is unjustified, for it is perfectly acceptable for *a* to be informed that *p* while being (even in principle) incapable of being informed that *a* is informed that *p*, without adopting a second, meta-informational approach to *Ip*. The distinction requires some unpacking.

On the one hand, "believing" and "knowing" (the latter here understood as reducible to some doxastic relation) are mental states that, arguably, in the most favourable circumstances, could implement a "privileged access" relation, and hence be fully transparent to the agents enjoying them, at least in principle and even if, perhaps, only for a Cartesian agents. Yet *KK* or *BB* remain controversial (see Williamson [1999], Williamson [2000] for arguments against them). The point here is that defenders of the inevitability of the *BB* or *KK* thesis may maintain that, in principle, whatever makes it possible for *a* to believe (or to know) that *p*, is also what makes it possible for *a* to believe (or to know) that *a* believes (or knows) that *p*. *B* and *BB* (or *K* and *KK*) are two sides of the same coin. More precisely, if *a* believes (or knows) that *p*, this is an internal mental fact that could also be mentally accessible, at least in principle, to a Cartesian *a*, who can be presumed to be also capable of acquiring the relevant, reflective mental state of believing (knowing) that *a* believes (or knows) that *p*. Translating this into information theory, we are saying that either there is no communication channel that allows *a* to have a doxastic (or epistemic) access to *p*, or, if there is, this is also the same channel that, in principle, allows *a* to have a doxastic (or epistemic) access to *a*'s belief (or knowledge) that *p*. So a defender of the *BB* or *KK* thesis may argue that the mental nature of doxastic and epistemic states may allow *BB* and *KK* to piggyback on *B* and *K* without requiring a second, meta-channel of communication. Call this the single-channel nature of doxastic and epistemic relations.

On the other hand, all this does not hold true for "being informed/holding the information", because the latter is a relation that does not necessarily require a mental or conscious state. Beliefs and knowledge (again, analysed doxastically) are in the head, information can be in the pocket. Less metaphorically, artificial and biological agents may hold the information that *p*, even if they lack a mind or anything resembling mental states concerning *p*. As a result, "being informed" should be analysed as providing an unprivileged access to some *p*. A dog is informed (holds the information) that a stranger is approaching the house only if a stranger is actually approaching the house, yet this does not imply that the dog is (or can even ever be) informed that he is informed that a stranger is approaching the house. Indeed, the opposite is true: animals do not satisfy any of the *KK*, *BB* or *II* thesis. There are no Cartesian dogs. Likewise, a computer may hold the information that "the train to London leaves at 10.30 am", but this, by itself, does not guarantee, even in principle, that the computer also holds the information that it holds the information about the train timetable, or we might be much closer to true AI than anybody ever seriously claimed. Finally, Matthew might have the information that "the train to London leaves at 10.30 am" written in a note in his pocket, and yet not be informed that he holds the information that p. Actually, Matthew might even have it stored in his brain, like Johnny Mnemonic, who in William Gibson's homonymous novel is a mnemonic data courier hired to carry in his brain 320 gigabytes of crucial information to safety from the Pharmacom corporation. Note the difference: Johnny holds the information that he holds some precious information, yet this is like a black box, for he does not hold the information that he holds the information that p.

The distinction may be further clarified if, once again, it is translated into information theory. We are saying that either there is no communication channel that allows a to have an informational access to p, or, if there is, it is such that, even with a Cartesian agent placed in favourable circumstances (no malicious demon etc.), it may still fail to allow a to have an informational access to a's information that p. The possibly non-mental nature of informational states impedes II from piggybacking on I through the same channel of communication. An II relation requires in fact a second, meta-channel that allows an I relation between a and Ip, but then this channel too is not, by itself, reflective, since any III relation requires a third channel between I and IIp, and so forth. As far as reflectivity is concerned, "being informed that p" is not like "believing that p" or "knowing that p" but more like "having recorded that p" or "seeing that p". The former two require mental states, whose nature is such as to allow the possibility in principle of the *BB*-thesis or *KK*-thesis. The latter two do not require mental states and hence do not include the possibility of a reflective state: information, records and perceptual sensations do not come with metainformation or metarecords or metasensations by default, even in principle, although there may be a second layer of memory, or another channel of communication or of experience, that refers to the first layer of memory or the first channel of information or the more basic experience. Call this the double-channel nature of the information relation.

The distinction between the single and double channel of information may be compared to the distinction between a reflective sentence that speaks of itself (single-channel, e.g. "this sentence is written in English") and a meta-sentence that speaks of another sentence (double-channel, e.g. "the following sentence is written in English" "the cat is on the mat"). Natural languages normally allow both. Consider Matthew again. He may have in his pocket a note about the first note about the train timetable, yet this would be irrelevant, since it would just be another case of double-channel condition or meta-information. As Wittgenstein succinctly put it: "nothing in the visual field allows you to infer that it is seen by an eye" (*Tractatus*, 5.633). Likewise, nothing in a piece of information p allows you to infer that an information system that holds p also holds the information that it holds p (compare this to the fact that nothing in Matthew's ignorance allows you to infer that he is aware of his ignorance), whereas nothing in a belief or in a piece of knowledge allows you to infer that a doxastic or epistemic agent holding that belief or enjoying that piece of knowledge does not also believe that she believes that p, or does not also know that she knows that p. Knowledge and beliefs are primed to become reflective, information is not.

Consider now the following two objections against the distinction between the single-channel (or reflective or conscious or introspective, depending on the technical vocabulary) nature of epistemic and doxastic states and the double-channel (or opaque, or unreflective, or unconscious) nature of informational states.

First, one may point out that the *II* thesis seems to be implemented by some artificial systems. Actually, there are so-called "reflective" artificial agents capable of proving the classic knowledge theorem (Brazier and Treur [1999]), variously known as the "muddy children" or the "three wise men" problem, the drosophila of epistemic logic and distributed AI.[14] The description, however, is only evocative. Artificial agents may appear to be "reflective" only because of some smart tricks played at the level of interfaces and human-computer interactions, or because of a multi-layer structure. In particular, architectures or programs for computational systems (of AI) and systems for machine learning are technically called "reflective" when they contain an accessible representation of themselves that can be used (by themselves) e.g. to monitor and improve their performance. But what is known as *reflective computing* is only a case of metaprogramming or a communication channel about another communication channel, precisely as expected.[15] It is what has been labelled above the double-channel nature of the *II* states. One may compare it to a dog being informed that (or barking because) another dog is informed that (or is barking because) a stranger is approaching. At a higher level of abstraction the two dogs may form a single security system, but the possibility of multiagent

---

[14] The classic version of the theorem is related to the Conway-Paterson-Moscow theorem and the Conway paradox (see Groenendijk et al. [1984], pp. 159-182 and Conway and Guy [1996]) and was studied, among others, by Barwise and Seligman [1997]. For some indications on its history see Fagin and Halpern [1988], p. 13.

[15] Barklund [1995] and Costantini [2002] are two valuable surveys with further references to the "three wise men" problem. Note that, for those who object to *EL*, the axiomatization of the reasoning involved in the classic knowledge game may be done in standard (i.e. non-modal) FOL (Mccarthy [1971-1987] and Mccarthy [1990]); at the same time, it is amenable to a treatment in terms of BDI (Belief, Desire, Intention) architecture (Rao and Georgeff [1991]).

(e.g. n dogs or n computational) informational systems does not contradict the deflationist view that "being informed" is not a reflective relation.

Second, the *II* thesis seems to be implemented at least by some human agents. In this case, the reply is that this is so only because information relations can be implemented by human agents by means of mental states, which can then lend their reflective nature to *H*. It is not *H* to be reflective; rather, if an agent *a* can manage *Ip* through some epistemic or conscious state, for example, then, if the corresponding relation of accessibility is reflective the *II* thesis may become acceptable.

To summarise with a slogan: information entails no iteration. The point concerning the rejection of A_6 is not that "being informed" cannot appear to be a reflective relation: this is possible because *Ip* may be the object of a second relation *I* (double-channel nature of *II*), when *a* is a multiagent system, or because *Ip* may be implemented mentally, when *a* is a human agent, and hence be subject to reflection, consciousness or introspection. The point concerning the rejection of A_6 is that doxastic and epistemic accessibility relations, interpreted as mental states, may require in principle only a single-channel communication to become reflective, so the *BB* and *KK* theses may be justifiable as limit cases; whereas *H*, by itself, is not necessarily mental, and requires a double-channel communication to become reflective. But then (a) the second channel may be absent even in the most idealised, animal or artificial agents, even in principle, and (b) in any case, we are developing a logic of the communication channel represented by the information relation between *a* and *p*, and this channel is not reflective. The conclusion is that adopting A_6 to formalise *Ip* would be a misrepresentation.

There is a further objection to the latter conclusion, but we shall see it in the next section, since it is connected to A_{10}. Before, we may briefly look at a consequence of the exclusion of A_5 by considering A_8. This axiom too is reflective, and therefore equally inappropriate to qualify *IL*. From the fact that an artificial agent does not hold the information that $\neg p$ it does not follow that it holds the information that it is missing the information that $\neg p$. We shall return to this point in § 2.5. In this case too, the previous considerations regarding the possibility of meta-information (two-channel) or mental implementation of the information relation apply, but do not modify the conclusion.

2.4 Transmissibility: *IL* satisfies A_{10} and A_{11}

The exclusion of A_6 from the group of axiom schemata characterizing *IL* might still be opposed on the basis of the following reasoning: if the relation of informational accessibility is not interpreted as transitive, then it becomes impossible to transfer information, but this is obviously absurd, so A_6 must be included.

The objection is flawed for three reasons. First, transmission does not necessarily depend on transitivity: in the **KD**-based *DL*, a belief may be transferred from *a* to *b* despite the fact that the axiom schema $(B_a\varphi \rightarrow B_aB_a\varphi)$ and the corresponding relation of accessibility do not characterize ***KD***. Second, the exclusion of A_6 does not concern the exclusion of the transitivity of modal inferences formulated in A_{10}, which can easily be shown to be satisfied by *IL*. A_{10} is a theorem in all *NML* and, being a weaker version of the K-principle, it formulates a very weak property, unlike the *KK*-principle.[16] Third, the exclusion of A_6 concerns the transitive nature of *H* when a single, standalone agent is in question. It does not preclude the inclusion of A_{11} (Hintikka's axiom of transmission) in a multiagent context. On the contrary, in this case, A_{11} correctly characterizes *IL*, as it is perfectly reasonable to assume that $(I_aI_b\varphi \rightarrow I_a\varphi)$: if Matthew is informed that Jenny is informed that the train to London leaves at 10.30 am, then he is also informed that it does. Note that this is made possible also thanks to A_4, i.e. the assumption that to be informed that *p* the latter must the true.

2.5 Constructing the information base: *IL* satisfies A_7

A_7 is the defining axiom schema of the system **KTB**. *IL* satisfies A_7 in the sense that, for any true *p*, the informational agent *a* not only cannot be informed that $\neg p$ (because of A_4), but now is also informed that *a* does not hold the information that $\neg p$.

The inclusion of A_7 in *IL* does not contradict the anti-reflective (i.e., zero introspection) constraint supported in § 2.3. True, the conclusion *IUp* can be inferred both from *Up* and from *p*. However, in the former case (A_8), one would have to assume some form of negative reflection (introspection), in order to allow the agent *a* to draw the inference from an informational state *Up* to the relevant, meta-informational state *IUp*. Whereas in the latter case (A_7) the inference is drawn externally, by an observer, who concludes that, for any piece of information *p*, one can attribute to the agent *a* the information that *a* does not have the information that $\neg p$, irrespective of whether *a* lacks any kind of reflection on *a*'s informational states. This holds true for theorems such as *II*(*p* ∨ ~*p*), which are demonstrable in *KTB-IL*: as we saw in 2.3, the point here is not denying the possibility of meta-information – it is trivially true that computers

---

[16] I am very grateful to Patrick Allo for having called my attention to this point.

can have information about their information that p, for example – but objecting against the reflective (introspective, single-channel) nature of it.

The distinction may be better appreciated if we look at a second objection against the inclusion of A_7, which actually turns in its favour. It concerns the provability of $\Diamond\Box\varphi \to \varphi$ in **KTB**. Ontologically, this is known to be a rather controversial result. Yet, informationally, $UI\varphi \to \varphi$ has a very intuitive reading. We already know from A_9 that a is an informationally consistent agent and, from A_4, that a is informed that p only if p, so we only need now an axiom of *constructability of a's information base*: if, for all a's information it is possible that a holds the information that p (if, according to a's information base D_a, D_a can be consistently extended to include the information that p) then p must be the case. In other words, the negation of $UI\varphi \to \varphi$ would make no sense: if φ is false, then no coherent incrementation of the information database is possible by uploading the information that φ. This shows, quite interestingly, that the connection between the intuitionistically-inspired **KTB** and *IL* is not accidental. What lies behind both is a concern for direct methods to expand the information base.

It might seem that, by satisfying A_7, *IL* embeds a closed-world assumption.[17] The similarity is indeed there, but there is also a fundamental difference. In any interesting formalization of "being informed", it is plausible to assume that the agent has only incomplete information about the world. This precludes, as inappropriate, the assumption that, if a is not informed that φ then φ is false.[18] What A_7 guarantees is that any possible extension of a's information base corresponds to a genuine state of the world. Since the dual (A_{7d}) $\Diamond\Box\varphi \to \varphi$ can replace A_7 as the characterizing axiom schema of any **KTB**-based system, in the next section we shall adopt it as a more intuitive alternative.

2.6 KTB-*IL*

We have now completed the analysis of all the axiom schemata. The result is a **KTB**-based information logic (*KTB-IL*). Compared to *EL* and *DL*, **KTB-*IL*** satisfies the following minimal set of axiom schemata and inference rules (modus ponens and necessitation):

A_1 $(\varphi \to (\chi \to \varphi))$
A_2 $((\varphi \to (\chi \to \psi)) \to ((\varphi \to \chi) \to (\varphi \to \psi)))$

---

[17] I am grateful to Daniel Lemire for having called my attention to this point. I agree with Patrick Allo that an elegant way of reading Lemire's suggestion is by explaining the weakening of the closed-world assumption by saying that being informed is 'prospectively or purposefully consistent / true', and hence 'closed for the limiting case'.
[18] For a qualified assumption, in terms of local closed-world, see Golden et al. [1994].

A_3 $\quad ((\neg \varphi \to \neg \chi) \to (\chi \to \varphi))$
A_4 $\quad (I\varphi \to \varphi)$
A_5 $\quad (I(\varphi \to \chi) \to (I\varphi \to I\chi))$
A_{7d} $\quad (UI\varphi \to \varphi)$
MP $\quad \vdash \varphi, \vdash (\varphi \to \chi) \Rightarrow \vdash \chi$
Nec $\quad \vdash \varphi \Rightarrow \vdash I\varphi$

Two birds with the same stone, as the saying goes: we have a NML-based logic for "being informed" and a cognitive reading of **KTB**.

3. Conclusion

The results just seen pave the way to a better understanding of the relations between "knowing", believing" and "being informed". More specifically, four consequences of a **KTB**-based *IL* have not been explored here, namely: the debate on information overload; the veridical nature of information ($Ip \to p$); the unsatisfactory state of the $Kp \to Bp$ principle, according to which knowledge implies belief; and hence the relation between *IL* and *EL*, and more generally the "Gettierisable" nature of the tripartite definition of knowledge as justified true belief. These are issues discussed in another article (Floridi [forthcoming]), but they are the motivations behind the development of *IL*. In the long run, the project is to provide a solid justification for a non-doxastic foundation of knowledge, and for a non-psychologistic, non-mentalistic and non-anthropomorphic approach to epistemology, which could then easily be applied to artificial or synthetic agents such as computers, robots, webbots, companies, and organizations. There is, admittedly, quite a lot of work to be done, but, as far as the tasks of this article are concerned, we have come to an end of our toil.

Acknowledgements

I discussed several drafts of this paper at many meetings: at the 10th Workshop of Topika, Mesta, Chios (September, 2002); at the Department of Philosophy, University of Hertfordshire (January, 2005); at the Department of Computer Science, UCL (February 2005); at the Dipartimento di Scienze della Formazione, Università degli Studi di Salerno (March, 2005); at the Unité d'enseignement et de recherché, Sciences humaines, Lettres et Communication, Télé-Université (Teluq) Université du Québec (May 2005); at the Departamento de Filosofia and the Faculdade de Letras, Universidade do Porto (June 2005); at ECAP 2005, the Fourth European Computing and Philosophy Conference,

Mälardalen University (June 2005); and at Regensburg Universität (November 2005). I wish to thank Gerassimos Kouzelis; Brendan Larvor; Mel Slater; Roberto Cordeschi; Armando Malheiro da Silva and Fernanda Ribeiro; Jean Robillard; Gordana Dodig-Crnkovic; and Rainer Hammwöhner for their kind invitations, which gave me the opportunity to discuss and clarify several ideas contained in this paper. I am also grateful to the participants in these meetings for their helpful discussions. In particular, I would like to acknowledge the help, useful comments and criticisms by Patrick Allo, Fred Dretske, Rod Girle, John Halleck, Daniel Lemire, Paul Oldfield, Gianluca Paronitti, Claudio Pizzi, Hans Rott, Jeff Sanders, Sebastian Sequoiah-Grayson, Timothy Williamson. As usual, they are responsible only for the improvements and not for any remaining mistakes.

References

Allo, P. 2005. "Being Informative" in WSPI '05 - Proceedings of the Second International Workshop on Philosophy and Informatics, Third Conference Professional Knowledge Management edited by Gregor Büchel, Bertin Klein, and Thomas Roth-Berghofer (Kaiserslautern (Germany), April 11-13, 2005):http://sunsite.informatik.rwth-aachen.de/Publications/CEUR-WS//Vol-130/.

Baltag, A., and Moss, L. S. 2004. "Logics for Epistemic Programs" *Synthese*. 139(2), 165-224.

Bar-Hillel, Y. 1964. *Language and Information: Selected Essays on Their Theory and Application.* (Reading, Mass ; London: Addison-Wesley).

Bar-Hillel, Y. and Carnap, R. 1953. "An Outline of a Theory of Semantic Information." repr. in Bar-Hillel [1964], pp. 221-74.

Barklund, J. 1995. "Metaprogramming in Logic." in *Encyclopedia of Computer Science and Technology.* edited by A. Kent and J. G. Williams (New York: Marcel Dekker), vol. 33, 205-227.

Barwise, J., and Seligman, J. 1997. *Information Flow: The Logic of Distributed Systems.* (Cambridge: Cambridge University Press).

Becker, O. 1930. "Zur Logik Der Modalitaten." *Jahrbuch für Philosophie und phänomenologische Forschung.* 11, 497-548.

Brazier, F. M. T., and Treur, J. 1999. "Compositional Modelling of Reflective Agents." *International Journal of Human-Computer Studies.* 50, 407-431.

Colburn, T. R. 2000. *Philosophy and Computer Science.* (Armonk, N.Y.: M.E. Sharpe).

Conway, J. H., and Guy, R. K. 1996. *The Book of Numbers.* (New York: Copernicus).

Costantini, S. 2002. "Meta-Reasoning: A Survey." in *Computational Logic: Logic Programming and Beyond - Essays in Honour of Robert A. Kowalski*. edited by A. C. Kakas and F. Sadri (Springer-Verlag),

Devlin, K. J. 1991. *Logic and Information*. (Cambridge: Cambridge University Press).

Dodig-Crnkovic, G. 2005. "System Modeling and Information Semantics." in Proceedings of the Fifth Promote IT Conference. Borlänge, Sweden, edited by Janis Bubenko, Owen Eriksson, Hans Fernlund, and Mikael Lind (Studentlitteratur: Lund),

Dretske, F. I. 1981. *Knowledge and the Flow of Information*. (Oxford: Blackwell). Reprinted in 1999 (Stanford, CA: CSLI Publications).

Fagin, R., and Halpern, J. Y. 1988. "Belief, Awareness and Limited Reasoning." Artificial Intelligence, 34 39-76.

Fetzer, J. H. 2004. "Information, Misinformation, and Disinformation." Minds and Machines. 14(2), 223-229.

Floridi, L. 2004a. "Information." in *The Blackwell Guide to the Philosophy of Computing and Information*. edited by L. Floridi (Oxford - New York: Blackwell), 40-61.

—. 2004b. "Open Problems in the Philosophy of Information." *Metaphilosophy*. 35(4), 554-582.

—. 2004c. "Outline of a Theory of Strongly Semantic Information." 14(2), 197-222.

—. 2005a. "Is Information Meaningful Data?" Philosophy and Phenomenological Research. 70(2).

—. 2005b. "Semantic Conceptions of Information." *Stanford Encyclopedia of Philosophy*. Edward N. Zalta (ed.), URL = <http://plato.stanford.edu/entries/information-semantic/>.

—. forthcoming, "The Logic of Being Informed." *Logique et Analyse*.

Floridi, L. and Sanders, J. W. 2004. "The Method of Abstraction." in Yearbook of the Artificial. Nature, Culture and Technology. Models in Contemporary Sciences, edited by M. Negrotti (Bern: Peter Lang), 177-220.

Floridi, L. and Sanders, J. W. forthcoming, "Levellism and the Method of Abstraction." The final draft of this paper is available as IEG – Research Report 22.11.04, see www.wolfson.ox.ac.uk/~floridi/pdf/latmoa.pdf

Fox, C. J. 1983. *Information and Misinformation: An Investigation of the Notions of Information, Misinformation, Informing, and Misinforming*. (Westport, Conn: Greenwood Press).

Gärdenfors, P. 1988. *Knowledge in Flux: Modeling the Dynamics of Epistemic States*. (Cambridge, Mass ; London: MIT).

Girle, R. 2000. *Modal Logics and Philosophy*. (Teddington: Acumen).

Goldblatt, R. 2003. "Mathematical Modal Logic: A View of Its Evolution." *Journal of Applied Logic.* 1(5-6), 309-392.

Golden, K., Etzioni, O., and Weld, D. 1994. "Omnipotence without Omniscience: Efficient Sensor Management for Software Agents." in Proceedings of the twelfth national conference on Artificial intelligence. Seattle, Washington, United States, edited by O. Etzioni (AAAI Press), 1048-1054.

Graham, G. 1999. *The Internet: A Philosophical Inquiry.* (London: Routledge).

Grant, J., and Hunter, A. forthcoming, "Measuring Inconsistency in Knowledgebases." *Journal of Intelligent Information Systems.*

Grice, H. P. 1989. *Studies in the Way of Words.* (Cambridge, Mass.: Harvard University Press).

Groenendijk, J. A. G., Janssen, T. M. V., and Stokhof, M. J. B. (ed.) 1984. *Truth, Interpretation, and Information: Selected Papers from the Third Amsterdam Colloquium.* (Dordrecht, Holland ; Cinnaminson, U.S.A: Foris Publications).

Hintikka, J. 1962. *Knowledge and Belief: An Introduction to the Logic of the Two Notions.* (Ithaca: Cornell University Press).

Hocutt, M. 1972. "Is Epistemic Logic Possible?" Notre Dame Journal of Formal Logic. 13 (4), 433-453.

Hughes, G. E., and Cresswell, M. J. 1996. *A New Introduction to Modal Logic.* (London: Routledge).

Lenzen, W. 1978. *Recent Work in Epistemic Logic.* (Amsterdam: North-Holland).

McCarthy, J. 1971-1987. "Formalization of Two Puzzles Involving Knowledge."

McCarthy, J. 1990. *Formalizing Common Sense: Papers by John Mccarthy.* (Norwood, NJ: Ablex).

Miyazaki, Y. 2005. "Normal Modal Logics Containing Ktb with Some Finiteness Conditions." Advances in Modal logic. 6, 171-190. http://www.aiml.net/volumes/volume5/

Rao, A., and Georgeff, M. 1991. "Modeling Rational Agents within a Bdi-Architecture." in Proceedings of the Second International Conference on Principles of Knowledge Representation and Reasoning. edited by J. Allen, R. Fikes, and E. Sandewall (San Mateo, CA: Morgan Kaufmann), 473-484.

Sanders, J. W. forthcoming, "On Information."

Shannon, C. E., and Weaver, W. 1949 rep. 1998. *The Mathematical Theory of Communication.* (Urbana: University of Illinois Press). Foreword by Richard E. Blahut and Bruce Hajek.

Williamson, T. 1999. "Rational Failures of the Kk Principle." in *The Logic of Strategy*, edited by C. Bicchieri, R. Jeffrey, and B. Skyrms (Oxford: Oxford University Press), 101-118.
—. 2000. *Knowledge and Its Limits.* (Oxford: Oxford University Press).

CHAPTER THREE

FORMALISING SEMANTIC INFORMATION: LESSONS FROM LOGICAL PLURALISM

PATRICK ALLO

Abstract

Up to now theories of semantic information have implicitly relied on logical monism, or the view that there is one true logic. The latter position has been explicitly challenged by logical pluralists. Adopting an unbiased attitude in the philosophy of information, we ask whether logical pluralism could also entail informational pluralism. The basic insights from logical pluralism and their implications for a theory of semantic information are therefore explored.
The present paper provides a non-technical and informal motivation for a pluralist conception of informational content.

1. Introduction and motivation

Despite several authors' attention for the multi-faceted character of the concept of information (see Floridi (2003) and Bremer & Cohnitz (2004)), actual attempts to formalise the concept of information all too often tend towards an implicit logical monism (the view that there is *one true logic*). The core aim of this paper is to provide an alternative for the assumption that there is a single logic of (semantic) information. The plan, however, is not to deny the possibility of a logic of information being better than others, but to provide a conceptual framework in accordance with both the polyvalence of information and an unbiased approach in the philosophy of information.

Our starting point is two-fold. On the one hand different theories of semantic information are available, all relying to a certain extent on formal logic. On the other there is the pluralist claim from Beall & Restall (2000) that there is more than one true logic. Basically, a logical pluralist claims that there are several ways to give a precise account of the pre-theoretical notion of logical consequence (and hence of logical truth). Above all (s)he holds that none of these is a priori better than the others. A logical pluralist, however, does not claim that every *true logic* is suited for all contexts of application. Taking logical pluralism seriously, we ask what kind of theory of semantic information logical pluralists should adopt.

An elementary consequence of this point of view is that, when a formal account of semantic information is elaborated, the absolute validity of a logic cannot be taken for granted. Some further — external — evidence for its applicability is needed. Taking the implications of logical pluralism further, one might make the stronger claim that the pre-theoretical notion of semantic information does not in itself warrant a unique logic, but also needs pluralistic formalisation. In other words, a pluralist position about logic may be equally reflected in a formal theory of semantic information. Both the elementary (henceforth weak), and the strong implication of logical pluralism for formalising the concept of information need further investigation.

The aim of this paper is essentially to take the idea of logical pluralism seriously, and use it as an underlying philosophy of logic when formalising semantic information. It is thought that logical pluralism and the informational pluralism it entails contributes to a more general pluralist attitude which is fundamental to the philosophy of information. To show the specific benefits of our approach, it is argued that (i) logical pluralism and semantic information are mutually compatible, and that (ii) a pluralist approach provides a versatile and more discriminating account of semantic information.

2. Pluralism about logical consequence

A precise characterisation of logical pluralism requires an answer to the preliminary question of what a logic is. Following Beall and Restall's account,[1] logic's aim is to give a formal account of logical consequence.[2] Therefore, a logical pluralist should be considered as a pluralist with respect to logical consequence. This comes down to the idea that there is no unique formalisation of the pre-theoretical notion of consequence when conceived as truth-preservation over all cases. Or, more precisely:

Definition 1 (V) *A conclusion A follows from premises* Σ *iff any* case *in which each premise in* Σ *is true is also a* case *in which A is true.*

---

[1] The following outline is essentially based upon Beall & Restall (2000) (2001).
[2] A logic can either be characterised by a consequence relation or as a set of tautologies. Since Tarski the former has taken a dominant position in the philosophy of logic.

Allowing for a variety of cases, the following picture arises: (i) if cases are taken to be Tarskian Models (complete and consistent), then we get plain classical logic, (ii) if cases are constructions (consistent but possibly incomplete), the corresponding logic is intuitionistic, and (iii) if cases turn out to be situations (both possibly inconsistent and incomplete) we obtain relevant logic.

To get a glimpse of how these logics stand apart, consider the following schema rehearsing some basic theorems:[3]

Theorem	*CL*	*IL*	*RL*
$p \vee \sim p$ (excluded middle)	√		(√)
$q \rightarrow (p \vee \sim p)$ (irrelevance)	√		
$(p \;\&\sim p) \rightarrow q$ (explosion)	√	√	
$\sim\sim p \rightarrow p$ (double negation elimination)	√		√

A logical pluralist who wishes to hold more than the trivial claim that there are distinct logical systems[4], should endorse the claim that none of the preceding characterisations captures all there is to say about logical consequence. As explained by Beall and Restall, all three logics — classical, intuitionistic and relevant — can be mutually related. One might, for instance, say that classical logic includes both other logics, for every Tarskian Model is both a situation and a construction.[5] On the other hand, it could be claimed that relevant logic is the most general approach, for it puts less constraints on what counts as a case.

The crux of Beall and Restall's argument lies in the rejection of any view putting forward the most general approach to logical consequence as the ultimate and unique one. There is a sense in which, for instance, disjunctive syllogism (henceforth DS), i.e. $A, \sim A \vee B \Rightarrow B$, is correct (viz. classically), but

---

[3] The case of relevant logics is quite complex as it is a family of logics, e.g. excluded middle is a theorem for mainstream relevant logics, while it is not for depth- or contraction-free relevant logics.
[4] A logical monist, for example, will endorse the claim that there are different logical systems while maintaining that there is only one *true* logic.
[5] Traditionally one might say that every intuitionistic / relevant tautology is also a classical tautology, but in this case it is better to focus on the fact that a complete and consistent situation is a model, and that a completed construction is also a model.

also a sense in which it is incorrect (viz. relevantly, for a situation can make both A and $\sim A$ true while keeping B false).[6] Choosing either logic as being the One True Logic, this distinction (which the pluralist takes to be useful) is dismissed. Put differently, if one wants to take DS as being valid in one sense, but invalid in another, a pluralist account of logical consequence should follow.[7]

A final point which might prove useful when arguing for informational pluralism, is that there is a sense in which — from a pluralist standpoint — the relevant road is superior to the classical one. Viz., a relevant logic does not exclude classical logic, for situations might indeed be complete and consistent. Thus, at first sight, a pluralist interpretation of relevant logic remains possible, whereas a classically based pluralism is not.

3. Semantic Information

By semantic information, one usually refers to information as content. This means that, contrary to Shannon's original explication of the notion, meaning *does* matter for semantic information. When investigating the consequences of logical pluralism for the concept of semantic information, we essentially rely on three views on information as content. As a starting point, the general definition of information (GDI) remains very general (Floridi, 2003).

Definition 2 (GDI) *An infon σ classifies as semantic information iff:*

1. *σ consists of a* non-empty *set (D) of data (d),*
2. *the data in D are* well-formed *(wfd)), and*
3. *the wfd in D are* meaningful *(mwfd = δ).*

Seeking a criterion to check whether a pluralist view on information can count as information, (GDI) provides too weak constraints to be of any real interest. More is to be obtained from Floridi (2005)'s analysis which stresses the fact that semantic information ought to be *declarative, objective and semantic information* (henceforth, DOS-information). Based on that insight, he proposes a revised definition which incorporates the truth of information.

---

[6] An analogous argument can be given for the case of excluded middle, $A \vee \sim A$, in classical and intuitionistic logic, for a construction might satisfy neither A nor $\sim A$.

[7] Another approach, due to Read (2004), rephrases the distinction as follows: $A, \sim A \vee B \Rightarrow B$, but $A, \sim A + B \Rightarrow B$, for + is an intentional disjunction. This approach will not be further pursued. Of a totally different order is the logical monist's approach to the problem of DS. Whereas a classical logical monist can simply assert that DS will never lead one from truth to falsity, the paraconsistent monist has to explain the usefulness of DS despite its invalidity. One way to meet this problem is the instrumental acceptance of DS, while maintaining that it is not part of Logic.

From (GDI) and its revision, we obtain two important constraints on the notion of information, viz. (i) information is factual and hence true, (ii) information has a fixed and informee-independent meaning.[8]

Of a different kind is Carnap & Bar-Hillel (1952)'s explication of the pre-theoretical notion of semantic information, as it does not provide a strong criterion for *being information*,[9] but gives a measure for informational content. The basic idea underlying the latter, is the so-called *Inverse Relationship Principle*, and its formal version by Carnap & Bar-Hillel.

> Whenever there is an increase in available information there is a decrease in possibilities, and vice versa. (Barwise, 1997, 491)

Definition 3 $CONT(\sigma)$ = *the set of state descriptions inconsistent with* σ

Property 3.1 $CONT(T)$ = *MIN, for* T *is a tautology*

Property 3.2 $CONT(\bot)$ = *MAX, for* $\bot$ *is a contradiction*

Leaving technical matters aside, a few comments are still in place. A first one concerning two major properties of the resulting calculus. Viz. (i) tautologies or logical truths have no informational content because they are true of any state description, and (ii) contradictions have maximal informational content because they exclude all state descriptions. Especially the latter has been challenged, as assigning maximal content to a necessary falsehood is rather counterintuitive.

A second comment, aims at the way in which definition 3 is presented as the one formalisation of the *Inverse Relationship Principle*. Reformulating the latter as to match definition 1 (V), a more general view is obtained:

Definition 4 (CONT) *The informational content of a piece of information is given by the set of cases it excludes.*

Reconsidering definition 3, it is obvious that by taking the relevant cases to be state descriptions, a choice is made which is not fully warranted by the idea of informational content alone. State descriptions being no more than the syntactical counterpart of Tarskian models, the analogy with classical logic arising as a natural elucidation of definition 1 (V) is striking. Thus, if logical pluralism questions the truth of classical logic (or any other logic) as the one specification of the concept of logical consequence, then it is not such a strange

---

[8] It is nevertheless important to distinguish the user-independence posited by Floridi (2005) — also referred to as the genetic neutrality of semantic information — from Dretske's more radical (language independent) realism according to which a user-independent meaning is to be situated at the level of the data (Floridi, 2003, 45).

[9] The latter fact motivated Floridi (2004)'s revision of their theory such as to account for strongly semantic information — which is closer to the constraints fixed by DOS-information.

move to question along the same lines the correctness of definition 3 as the unique formalisation of the *Inverse Relationship Principle*. This view will be called *informational pluralism* and is defended in the subsequent sections through some examples.

4. Pluralism and Semantic Information

For working purposes, the idea of informational pluralism is best described as the view that informational content is not uniquely determined by its basic principle, but is instead fully determined by adding what one takes to be the relevant cases. Or, in other words, informational content depends upon the underlying logic one assumes.[10] This view will be illustrated with three examples, two of them involving the weaker notion of *being informative for someone* (focus on underlying logic of an agent), and a last one using the more objective notion of *being informative* (focus on context and perspective of any receiver); see also Allo (2005).

Pluralism in Communication

Consider the following communication-context involving (i) a first agent called Bertie — a classical reasoner, and (ii) a second agent called Bertus — an intuitionistic reasoner. Let now, for the first case (left illustration), Bertie send the message that $p \vee \sim p$ to Bertus, and for the second case (right illustration) Bertus sending the same message to Bertie.

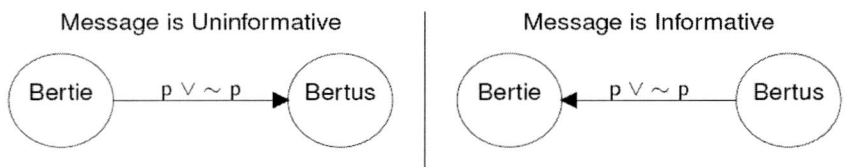

Trying to determine the informational content of this message, one stumbles upon the limits of the measure CONT, as previously defined. Obviously, $p \vee \sim p$ being a classical tautology, it should be assigned minimal content, but: (i) while Bertie did utter a tautology (according to his logic), Bertus did not, hence (ii) Bertus gets a message he does not consider a tautology, but which has minimal informational content, and (iii) Bertie gets a message which is tautological to

---

[10] This is, not only the language's expressive power, but essentially its deductive strength.

him, but which has more than minimal informational content.

Remains the question what information is conveyed by the message $p \vee \neg p$. In the first case it is a message which does not rule out any (complete) case, but in the second case it rules out all (possibly incomplete) cases which do not decide whether p. Or, in other words: Bertie is informed that Bertus knows whether p. If, however, any of these agents had taken its own logic as the one and true logic for determining the content of the message, they would have misjudged its value. This fact validates at least an instrumental motivation of informational pluralism, but only insofar as we make the additional assumption that agents do know of their opponents logic.

Pluralism in Multi-Agent Systems

A similar, but more radical, example can be formulated using rule-based agents. These are agents which do not necessarily dispose of the complete set of rules which usually constitute a logic. In an informal context they can simply be considered as reasoners disposing of a non-empty set of conditional rules which they apply to incoming formulae. Consider now the following setting in which each agent can fire only two rules of a system of natural deduction according to the schema given below.[11]

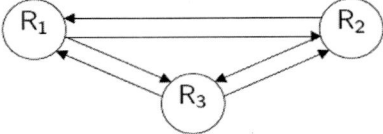

R_1 : $[E \wedge][I \wedge]$
R_2 : $[E \vee][I \vee]$
R_3 : $[E \sim][I \sim]$

From the set of rules it follows that, as a whole, the system disposes of all of classical logic ($\Rightarrow$), while for each individual agent ($\Rightarrow_i$), this does not hold.

Determining the informational content of a message in such a system, again, forces one to go beyond the standard approach. Let us, for instance, begin with each agent getting the same non-tautological formula ϕ as an input. Informational content and conditional informational content, then should satisfy the following properties:

---

[11] One might think of it as a graphical representation of a proof (like a proof-net, but much more loosely) in which the nodes are agents/programs and the edges are communication channels.

Property 4.1 (Generally)

1. The initial formula ϕ is informative for all agents.

More important is the informational value of $CONT(\psi_i | \phi)$ for all ψ_i which agents communicate. The latter is a measure for the informational content added by the system to the initial input.

Property 4.2 (System's Perspective)

1. For all communicated ψ_i it holds that $\varphi \Rightarrow \psi_i$
2. $CONT(\psi_i | \varphi) = MIN$
3. The system cannot produce content beyond that of φ.
4. Logic does not add informational content.

Property 4.3 (Individual Agent's Perspective)

1. $CONT(\psi_i | \varphi) = MIN$ iff $\varphi \Rightarrow_a \psi_i$
2. Agents get messages with more than minimal content.
3. Logic does add informational content.

If the original input φ had been the classical tautology $p \lor \sim p$, then any message would be a tautology too. Nevertheless, even in that case it would not be sound to infer that from $CONT(\psi_i | \varphi) = CONT(\psi_i | T) = CONT(\psi_i) = CONT(T) = MIN$ it follows that $CONT_a(\psi_i | \varphi) = MIN$, for even if ψ_i is necessarily a tautology itself, it might come as a surprise to some agent in the system.

This example, being a purely instrumental one (agents can hardly be said to be *logical* in any strong sense), merely motivates a user-dependent defence of informational pluralism. Of special interests is, however, the introduction of the distinction between internal and external perspectives on informational content. The latter feature is crucial to the following example in which pluralism is shown to be relatively independent from pragmatical or instrumental considerations.

Pluralism and Situated Information

In a last example, we rely on the informational interpretation of relevant logic, which essentially boils down to the following two facts: (i) the semantics for relevant logics are best understood in terms of information (situations satisfying infons, and relevant entailments as information flow between situations), (ii) relevant logics provide a proof-theory and a syntax for situation semantics (see: Restall, 1995; Mares, 1997). Suffice it to say that thinking of information states in terms of situations is a very natural approach for it values the partiality and locality of what it means to be informed. The overall picture arising from these results might tempt one to start thinking about relevant logics as the ultimate information logic. A pluralist interpretation is, as shown below, an even more natural option. Such an interpretation of situated information rephrases the idea of a pluralist reading of relevant logics into informational terms.

For both the left and the right example given below, a pluralist interpretation of information arises from the distinction between local and global perspectives, which is not unlike the case discussed in the previous section, but essentially stems from relevant logic's frame semantics.

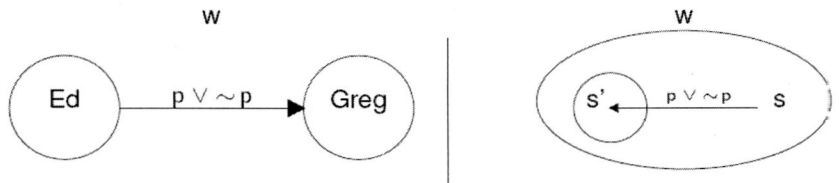

Let, for instance, Ed be sending a message to Greg, saying that $p \vee \sim p$. In such a case, that message has non-zero informational content for it allows Greg to exclude all cases in which Ed is in a situation which fails to satisfy $p \vee \sim p$. In other words: Greg is informed that Ed's local situation decides whether p, and the message $p \vee \sim p$ can be said to have more than minimal informational content.[12]

To an external observer the evaluation of informational content is quite different as his perspective is that of completed situations or worlds w. Thus, even if from an internal perspective (e.g. Greg's) the message has a non-zero content, to our external observer it hardly comes as a surprise to hear that either p or $\sim p$ for Ed's situation cannot be completed without satisfying one or the other. Contrary to the previous examples, pluralism arising from this communication context does not follow from a difference in logic between two agents, nor does it need pragmatical considerations to motivate it. The second example — a special case of the first one — makes this even more obvious.

---

[12] Using Devlin (1991)'s infon-based notation, it can be said that for Ed's situation (s) it holds that either $s \models \ll P, a_1, ..., a_n, l, t, 1 \gg$ or $s \models \ll P, a_1, ..., a_n, l, t, 0 \gg$.

Consider situations s and s' for which it holds that s properly extends situation s' such that all information which is true of s' is also true of s, but such as to make $p \vee \sim p$ only true in s.[13] From this reformulation one has to conclude that for any receiver in situation s' the message $p \vee \sim p$ has non-zero informational content (it contains some factual information about situation s), while at the same time for any receiver in world w the same message has minimal content.

5. Concluding Remarks

Basic motivation for writing this paper was to show that the idea of logical pluralism could be applied to the notion of semantic information, and more specifically to that of informational content as it arises from the *Inverse Relationship Principle*.

Thus far the following has been argued for: (i) logical pluralism arises in fairly simple communication contexts, and (ii) the formulation of a pluralistically inspired measure for informational content is necessary to get a firm grip on what is informative in such contexts. More generally it could be claimed that, on the one hand, logical pluralism provides an elucidation (if not a way out) of the problem of assigning informational content to logical truths, while on the other hand the informational perspective on logic makes the idea of logical pluralism more plausible (for it represents a useful application).

Notwithstanding the fact that a comprehensive theory of informational pluralism is not a part of the present paper, its basic features have been outlined. Most importantly, it is shown to be not only a viable alternative to a monist understanding of information, but also a fundamentally superior one. The key argument in favour of informational pluralism could be summarised by appealing to the notion of a logic's discriminatory power. The idea of the latter being that deductive strength varies with discriminatory strength: the more a logic proves, the fewer distinctions (or discriminations) it registers (Humberstone, 2005, 207), it appears that a weaker logic leads to a more discriminatory measure of informational content. Informational pluralism then, is precisely the idea that from a certain perspective (called global or external) these discriminations should partly be disregarded.

As to the blindspots in this exposition, a few need to be highlighted. First and foremost, very little attention was paid to the requirement for semantic information to have an informee-independent meaning. Despite the non-pragmatic character of the last example's informational pluralism, the meaning

---

[13] Contrary to what the illustration suggests, this should not be interpreted as standard set inclusion, but as $s' \leq s$ for $\leq$ is a partial information ordering on the set of situations.

invariance of a message was not as such established. In other words, no argument was provided to show that a difference in informational content between internal and external perspective should not entail a change in meaning. This being a serious threat to a purported pluralist theory of semantic information, it should be treated in detail when designing such a theory. For the moment, such a defence could be restricted to pointing out that, when adopting a minimalist understanding of meaning, the meaning-invariance requirement can be fulfilled within the bounds of a pluralist understanding of information.

Next, the problem of assigning informational content to contradictions — the so-called Bar-Hillel/Carnap-paradox from property 3.2 (see Floridi, 2004) — was not treated either. The semantics of relevant logic allowing for inconsistent situations, one might be tempted to think that a solution would arise in a very similar way to its dual problem (the content of logical truths). Inconsistent situations being very different from their incomplete siblings, it is doubtful whether they could count as genuine (that is, possibly factual) cases in the sense of definition 4 and the concept of information as being true in virtue of what is factual (Israel & Perry, 1990). Assigning less than maximal content to a contradiction, would require one to either adopt a (non-semantic) dialetheist position (the world is possibly inconsistent), or to reject the factuality requirement on semantic information. Both options need an extensive discussion which lies beyond present paper's aim.

Apart from mentioned omissions, further research on the topic of informational pluralism might include the formulation of an independent motivation of pluralism which relies on methodological considerations emerging from the philosophy of information. Reconsidering the notion of *logical discrimination*, one might easily start to think of a logic as an *interface* in the sense of Floridi & Sanders (2004), thus leading to a reformulation of informational pluralism in terms of *levels of abstraction*. This being only one possible suggestion for further research, the broad topic of informational pluralism as a part of the philosophy of information shows itself as a promising line of enquiry into the nature of semantic information.

References

Allo, P., 2005. "Being Informative - Information as Information Handling", in: *WM2005: Professional Knowledge Management Experiences and Visions*, Althoff, Dengel, Bergmann, Nick and Roth-Berghofer, eds., DFKI Gmbh, Kaiserslautern: 579–586.

Barwise, J., 1997. "Information and Impossibilities", *Notre Dame Journal of Formal Logic*, 38(4): 488–515.

Beall, J.C. & Restall, G., 2000. "Logical Pluralism", *Australasian Journal of*

Philosophy, 78: 475–493.
Beall, J.C. & Restall, G., 2001. "Defending Logical Pluralism", in: *Logical Consequence: Rival Approaches*, Brown, B., Woods, J., eds., Hermes, Stanmore: 1–22.
Bremer, M. E. & Cohnitz, D., 2004, *Information and Information Flow: An introduction*. Ontos Verlag, Frankfurt.
Carnap, R. & Bar-Hillel, Y., 1952. "An Outline of a Theory of Semantic Information", MIT, Cambridge, Massachusetts, *Technical Report 247*. Reprinted in: Bar-Hillel, Y., 1964, *Language and Information. Selected Essays on Their Theory and Application*, Addison-Wesley, London.
Devlin, K., 1991. *Logic and Information*. Cambridge University Press, Cambridge.
Floridi, L., 2003. "Information", in: *The Blackwell Guide to the Philosophy of Computing and Information*, Floridi, L., ed., Blackwell Publishing, Oxford: 40–61.
—. 2004. "Outline of a Theory of Strongly Semantic Information", *Minds & Machines*, 14(2): 197–222.
—. 2005. "Is Information Meaningful Data?", *Philosophy and Phenomenological Research*, 70(2): 351–370.
Floridi, L. and Sanders, J.W., 2004. "Levellism and the Method of Abstraction", *Information Ethics Group* - Oxford University,
Hintikka, J., 1970. On *Semantic Information, in: Information and Inference*, Hintikka, J. and Suppes, P., eds., Reidel, Dordrecht: 3–27.
Humberstone, I.L., 2005. *Logical Discrimination, in: Logica Universalis*, Béziau, J.-Y., ed., Birkhäuser Verlag, Basel: 207-228.
Israel, D. & J. Perry, 1990. *What is Information, in: Information, Language and Cognition*, P. Hanson, ed., University of British Columbia Press, Vancouver: 1–19.
Mares, E., 1997. "Relevant Logic and The Theory of Information", *Synthese*, 109(3): 345–360.
Read, S., 2004. "In Defence of the Dog: Response to Restall", in: *Logic, Epistemology, and the Unity of Science*. Rahman, Symons, Gabbay & Van Bendegem, eds., Dordrecht/Boston/London, Kluwer Academic Publishers: 175–180.
Restall, G., 1995. "Information Flow and Relevant Logic", in: *Logic, Language and Computation: The 1994 Moraga Proceedings*, Seligman, J. and D. Westerståhl, eds., CSLI Press, 463–477.
Tanaka, K., 2003. "Three Schools of Paraconsistency", *Australasian Journal of Logic*, 1.

CHAPTER FOUR

GETTING CLOSER TO ICONIC LOGIC

AHTI-VEIKKO PIETARINEN

Abstract

Visual and non-symbolic representational systems are increasingly important in logic, computing and cognitive sciences. Peirce proposed a logic for representing and reasoning about "actions of the mind in thought" using iconic signs, in other words to represent the connections and similarities exhibited in the relationships that exist, on the one hand, in the representational system, and, on the other, in the objects being so represented. The proposed means towards that end was the system of icons that employs the diagrammatic logic of Existential Graphs. Some of the key notions of his systems are explored and placed into the context of our cognitive and computational realm. It is argued that a diagrammatic logic needs to be expanded in multiple ways in order to attain a comprehensive logic of icons.

Key words

Peirce, logic, icons, diagrams, existential graphs.

1. Introduction

Visual and non-symbolic representations are becoming increasingly important in the intersections of logic, cognitive and computing sciences. What are the best systems to be used for such multi-lateral yet logically rigorous purposes? If the goal is to strive for as iconic representations as possible while not sacrificing any expressive power or logical and inferential accuracy, then the best method in town is, I will contend, what Charles S. Peirce proposed with his diagrammatic logic of Existential Graphs (EGs). His purpose was to attain a comprehensive representational system for the "action of the mind in thought" and its "moving picture" (MS 298: 1, 1906, *Phaneroscopy*; see Pietarinen

2006a).[1] Such graphs provide, according to him, a "system for diagrammatizing intellectual cognition" (MS 292: 41, 1905, *Pragmatism*). He stated never to "*reflect* in words", but to "employ visual diagrams", because that was his "natural language of self-communion" and because he was "convinced that it is the best system for the purpose" (MS 619: 8, 1909, *Studies in Meaning*).

Peirce's purpose was to derive a comprehensive logical analysis of thought through such iconic means, and to analyse reasoning that is rigorous and valid also when symbolic expressions fall short of fulfilling the expressive and inferential purposes and practices of such cognitively grounded representations. And short must they fall, Peirce avers, since "there are countless Objects of consciousness that words cannot express; such as the feelings a symphony inspires or that which is in the soul of a furiously angry man in [the] presence of his enemy" (MS 499, 1906, *On the System of Existential Graphs Considered as an Instrument for the Investigation of Logic*). One has yet to invent logical diagrams for such purposes, but in the very least, their plausibility is strongly suggested by our occasional emotional inexpressivity.

Using pictures, pictographs, pictograms, ideographs and other iconic and heterogeneous system of representation for analytic purposes fell into limbo during the 20th-century philosophy, marked by the wide-spread belief in the supremacy of symbol crunching.[2] Witness Tim Crane's assertion:

> Much thought is not pictorial or imagistic in any case ... pictures too cannot explain the logical structure of thoughts or sentences: how could a purely pictorial representation represent the thought that 'If it isn't raining next Saturday, we'll go to the sea'? (Crane, 1995, p. 770).

Earlier, Eco (1982) and Goodman (1968) had made related attacks, arguing that perceived similarities and representations belong to logically distinct categories and that iconic signs, just as the symbolic ones, hinge on conventions. Peirce, in contrast, did not conceive our realm of thought as narrowly. On the contrary, he wanted to "extend logic to embrace all the necessary principles of

---

[1] Reference is to Peirce (1967) by manuscript and page number, followed by year and title.

[2] See e.g. the *Diagrams* Conference Series; the special issue on Pictograms in *Information Design Journal* 10, 2001; or Midtgarden (2002), Hookway (1994), Jappy (2005), Barwise & Etchemendy (1996), Kazmierczak (2001), Hoffman (2004), Nyíri (2003) among others for the resurgence of the idea. Recall that, before early hominids were able to talk, they used gestures. Now we have mastered how to communicate by speech and text, and are rapidly moving towards a visual age of communication. What, then, is the next major transition in our evolution of communication?

semeiotic", and to duly "recognize a logic of icons, and a logic of indices, as well as a logic of symbols" (4.9, 1906, *The Simplest Mathematics*).[3]

Beginning with the diagrammatic logic of existential graphs, the remainder of this paper explores a logic of icons, challenging the aforementioned critical views.

2. Iconicity and Logic

2.1 What is an Iconic Representation?

Iconic signs come in many forms and guises. To begin with, Peirce took much of our mathematical cerebration to be at bottom iconic:

> Logic may be defined as the science of the laws of the stable establishment of beliefs. Then, *exact* logic will be that doctrine of the conditions of establishment of stable belief which rests upon perfectly undoubted observations and upon mathematical, that is, upon *diagrammatical*, or, *iconic*, thought. (3.429, 1896, *The Regenerated Logic*).

What is, then, essential in iconic thought? According to Peirce, "we form in the imagination some sort of diagrammatic, that is, *iconic*, representation of the facts, as skeletonized as possible" (2.778, 1901, *Notes on Ampliative Reasoning*). He then distinguished visual and other forms of iconic representations. "With ordinary persons", he explained, iconic representation "is always a visual image, or mixed visual and muscular". Visual images may further be either "*geometrical*, that is, such that familiar spatial relations stand for the relations asserted in the premisses", or "*algebraical*, where the relations are expressed by objects which are imagined to be subject to certain rules, whether conventional or experiential" (*ibid.*).

2.2 Diagrammatic Logic

To believe in an iconic logic of thought is to believe that the essential representational and inferential aspects of the processes of the mind can be articulated by certain diagrams. According to Peirce, logical diagrams are precise snapshots of the thought that the mind produces. On the contents of the mind diagrams give "rough and generalized" pictures (4.582), which

---

[3] Reference is to Peirce (1931-58) by volume and paragraph number, followed by year and title.

nevertheless are logically as precise as any conceptual or abstract framework can possibly reveal. The reason is, Peirce explains, that diagrams are icons that reflect continuous relationships between "rationally related objects" (MS 293: 11, *untitled*). Our knowledge about rational connections is not ultimately based on experience or mathematical certainty, but is something "which anybody who reasons at all must have an inward acquaintance with" (*ibid.*: 11).

To recall the famous trichotomy, observe that Peirce thought three kinds of signs to be necessary in all comprehensive logical conceptions:

> The first is the diagrammatic sign or *icon*, which exhibits a similarity or analogy to the subject of discourse; the second is the *index*, which like a pronoun demonstrative or relative, forces the attention to the particular object intended without describing it; the third [or *symbol*] is the general name or description which signifies its object by means of an association of ideas or habitual connection between the name and the character signified. (1.369, c.1885, *A Guess at a Riddle*).

Conventions and indices may affect some properties of such rational relationships, but diagrams should nevertheless be "as iconic as possible" in order to represent "visible relations" (MS 492: 22, c.1903, *Logical Tracts*). In Peirce's words, "a *Diagram* is a [sign] which is predominantly an icon of relations and is aided to be so by conventions. Indices are also more or less used" (MS 492: 22).

Recall that there are the 'heterogeneous' logics that are not, in fact, iconic in the full sense, since they not only combine diagrammatic with symbolic signs, but replace some of the constituents (such as predicates) that Peirce argued to be at bottom iconic images with symbolic expressions.[4] Conversely, one may hold symbolic logic also to be 'heterogeneous', since for Peirce, for instance algebraic, model-theoretic and inferential thinking all involve considerations that are iconic in nature.

What is essential in logical diagrams? Being iconic, they denote objects by some likeness, semblance or analogy.

> Every picture (however conventional its method) is essentially a representation of that [iconic] kind. So is every diagram, even although there be no sensuous resemblance between it and its object, but only an analogy between the relations of the parts of each. (2.279, c.1895, *Speculative Grammar*).

---

[4] On heterogeneous logics, see e.g. Barwise & Etchemendy (1995). Peirce on images see Pietarinen (2006d).

Model-theoretic entities and logical formulas being 'true-in-a-model', structure-preserving maps, etc., are examples of such iconicity, exhibiting some abstract, structural and intellectual rather than perceptual and visual likeness.

2.3 Image, Diagram, Metaphor

Not all iconicity is in diagrams, however. Pure iconic signs, which Peirce termed *hypoicons*, fall into three classes:

> Those which partake of simple qualities, or First Firstnesses, are *images*; those which represent the relations, mainly dyadic, or so regarded, of the parts of one thing by analogous relations in their own parts, are *diagrams*; those which represent the representative character of a representamen by representing a parallelism in something else, are *metaphors*. (EP 2:274, 1903, *Sundry Logical Conceptions*).[5]

Some images, such as photographs, resemble their objects because the connection is physically forced. Diagram, on the other hand, is like "a mental formula always more or less general" (1.592, 1903, *Ideals of Conduct*). A diagram need not be like its object according to some visual appearance, but according to the extent to which the relationships in different parts of the diagram resemble the relationships between the different parts of the object. In metaphors, representations are translocated from one medium into another, effecting, for example, a change in meaning from linguistic or literal to non-linguistic or non-literal meaning. The upshot is that any fully iconic logic should really encompass also the logic of images and the logic of metaphors.

2.4 Schematic Recap

To summarise the discussion above, let us draw the following chart:

---

[5] Reference is to Peirce (1998) by page number, followed by year and title.

58   Chapter Four

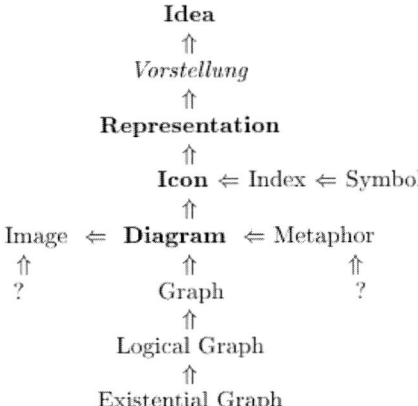

The topmost and the most general level concerns ideas.[6] They are articulated by the kinds of representations listed underneath in the decreasing chains of generality. *Vorstellung* is a 'cluster of ideas', an image-schema or a percept, while representation is a more active notion of it. Of the remaining trichotomies expounded above, the logic of images as well as the logic of metaphors have hardly been tackled in the literature at all.

3. Peirce's Existential Graphs

As witnessed by the above schema, Peirce's articulation of diagrams is in terms of an expressive system of Existential Graphs (EGs).

3.1 Initial Concepts

3.1.1 Remark on the History of Diagrams in Logic

Precursors of the use of diagrams in logic include Juan Luis Vives (1492-1540), Leonhard Euler (1707-1783), F.A. Lange (1828-1875) and John Venn (1834-1923). Nevertheless, the emergence of the 'moving-pictures' idea coincides with Peirce's living in New York 1895-97, where first commercial films were premiered, under Thomas Alva Edison's name, using the newly-established technology of the *Vitascope*. Year 1895 was the annus mirabilis of

---

[6] These are preceded still by *feelings*, which for Peirce were fundamental in giving rise to ideas.

film industry, and also the year Peirce announced his EGs. (Peirce and Edison were personal acquaintances competing on affordable domestic lighting for houses.) Peirce also catalogued the *Vitascope* for the attempted classification of the 'Practical Sciences' in around 1903, keeping a close eye on these developments (MS 1135; see Pietarinen 2006c).

3.1.2 Graph, Logical Graph, Existential Graph

Peirce believed that the logical nature of a diagram is revealed in a graph composed of four main components: "The *sheet* [Sheet of Assertion] upon which it is written or drawn, of *spots* or their equivalents, of *lines of connection*, and (if need be) of *enclosures*" (4.419). Enclosures are also called *cuts*, and spots *rhemas*. A *graph* is a *type*, resembling structural formulas of the chemist. A *logical graph* "is a graph representing logical relations iconically, so as to be an aid to logical analysis" (4.420).

We then also need a theory, the *existential graphs*, which comprise instances of logical graphs and which are "governed by a system of representation founded upon the idea that the sheet upon which [a logical graph] is written, as well as every portion of that sheet, represents one recognized universe, real or fictive, and that every graph drawn on that sheet, and not cut off from the main body of it by an enclosure, represents some fact existing in that universe" (4.421, c.1903, *On Existential Graphs, Euler's Diagrams, and Logical Algebra*).

3.2 Alpha, Beta, Gamma

3.2.1. Preamble

EGs amount to expressive logics going beyond classical propositional and first-order languages. In general, Peirce's classification was threefold:

1. Alpha Graphs (propositional logic) express propositional concepts (*Cat and dog are on a mat*).
2. Beta Graphs (predicate logic) express first-order concepts (*Every man is mortal*).
3. Gamma Graphs express, among others:
    a. Modalities (*It is possible that it rains*);
    b. Higher-order reasoning (*Aristotle has all the virtues of a philosopher*);

c. Meta-logical graphs: (*Every point on a line of identity is a dot*);
d. Non-declarative assertions (interrogatives, imperatives, emotions, interpretation of music, etc.).

Let us briefly address the three main parts in turn.[7]

3.2.2. System Alpha

3.2.2.1. Language

1. EGs are scribed on a surface, the *Sheet of Assertion* (SA), which provides the Universe of Discourse. An empty SA is a tautology.

2. Graphs are *juxtaposed* on SA, which is the diagrammatic counterpart to a (commutative) conjunction. For example:

A pear is ripe

A dog stumbles over a quick fox

That is, *A pear is ripe and a dog stumbles over a quick fox*.

3. Graphs may be enclosed or *cut* by continuous closed circles. This provides the diagrammatic counterpart to negation:

(*You are a good goalkeeper*)

That is, *It is not the case that you are a good goalkeeper*. A recursive application of juxtaposition and cuts amounts to the set G_α of well-formed diagrams of alpha graphs.

---

[7] Reference is to Peirce (1931-58) by volume and paragraph number, followed by year and Expositions of EGs include Pietarinen (2005a), Roberts (1973), Shin (2002) and Zeman (1964).

3.2.2.2. Proofs in Alpha

Nests are produced by sequences of areas of cuts as we read graphs 'from outside in' (Peirce compared this to osmosis in cells). *Negative* (resp. *positive*) areas are those enclosed within an odd (resp. *even*) number of cuts.

Now, alpha graphs have the following four sound rules of transformation, which also comprise a complete set:

1. **Add/remove double cuts**:

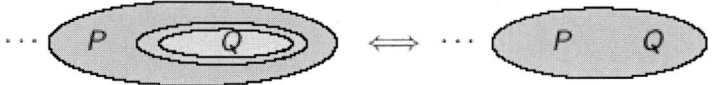

2. **Insertion**: Any $P \in G_\alpha$ may be *added on negative* area:

3. **Erasure**: Any $P \in G_\alpha$ may be *erased from positive* area:

4. **Iteration/Deiteration**: Any copy of $P \in G_\alpha$ may be *scribed on* (resp. *removed from*) the same area or *on* (resp. *from*) the area in its nest (which is not part of $P \in G_\alpha$):

3.2.3. System Beta

3.2.3.1. Spots and Lines of Identities

Beta graphs add two more signs to the alpha part.

4. *Spots* are bounded regions on SA that differ from other regions in terms of quality. They are the diagrammatic and iconic counterparts to predicate terms.

5. *Lines of identities* (LI), attached to the *hooks* on the boundaries of spots, are continuous connections between spots and between areas of cuts. They provide diagrammatic counterparts to quantification, identity and predication.

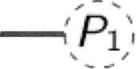

Two readings of LIs are distinguished in beta graphs:

- *Existential assertion*: The outermost portion of an LI rests on a positive area.
- *Universal assertion*: The outermost portion of an LI rests on a negative area.

By recursively applying the idea, the set G_β of well-formed beta diagrams is constructed.

3.2.3.2. Example

The following two sentences have their respective beta graphs:

Computation, Information, Cognition - The Nexus and the Liminal   53

There is a woman (possibly the same) who loves (and is loved by) every man:

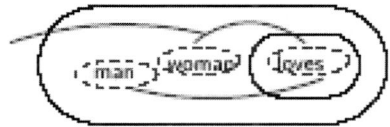

Every man loves (and is loved by) a woman:

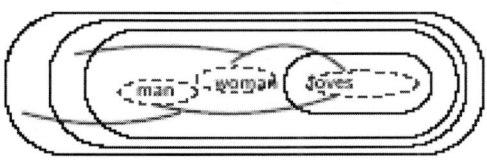

For simplicity, it is assumed that all relations, expressed by the attachments of LIs to the *hooks* of spots, are symmetric. (This is not without loss, as it amounts to a diagrammatic logic that correlates with a subsystem of a full predicate logic with identity.)

No new transformation rules are needed for the beta part beyond the previous four ones, but care must be taken in manipulating the LIs. Moreover, an axiom of well-definedness is needed, which states that an unattached dot or an LI not crossing a cut may be added on the sheet or assertion or on any area.

3.2.4. Systems Gamma

3.2.4.1. Broken Cut (1903)

Scribing a broken cut around a graph G *denies the necessity of* G.[8]

---

[8] Do not confound broken cuts with bounded regions of spots. The latter are typically not explicitly drawn.

The following transformation rules go with the broken cut, while several others can be devised to build new modal systems, depending on the properties of the modalities.

5. Opening/Closing Cuts:

5.1 Any evenly enclosed continuous cut may be *opened* to a broken cut:

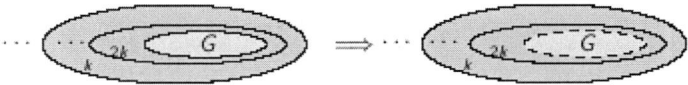

5.2 Any oddly enclosed broken cut may be *closed* to a continuous cut:

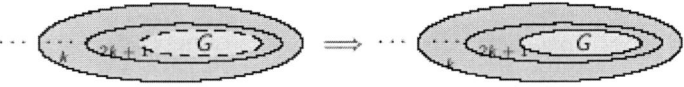

Imposing various restrictions on iteration/deiteration across modal, i.e. broken cuts and across continuous cuts yields different modal systems. A few of them have been studied in Zeman (1964).

3.2.4.2. Tinctured Existential Graphs (1906)

The *verso* of the SA on the area of the broken cut represents possibility, while the reversal of the SA's *verso*, that is, the *recto*, represents actuality. Beginning with this idea, Peirce employed different colours/tinctures to express different kinds of modalities the *verso* may expose, including the following:

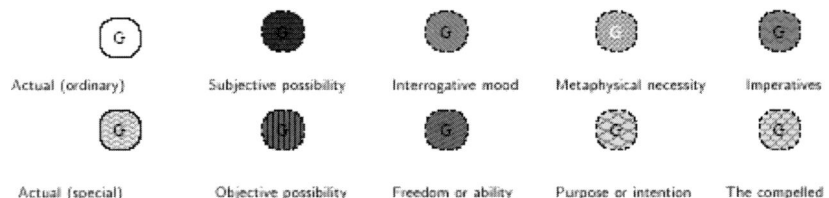

3.2.4.3. Tinctures with Identity Lines

Combining LIs with modalities gives rise to a diagrammatic counterpart to a modal predicate logic. Now the *de dicto*/*de re* distinctions can be diagrammatised. How the 'cross-world' identity functions in such diagrams when quantification and modality are interspersed has not been discussed in the literature so far.

3.2.4.4. Example ("Peirce's Puzzle")

Consider the sentence

There is a person who will commit suicide if she fails.

The diagram for this is

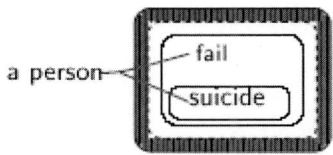

The sentence above is clearly different in meaning from

There is a person who will commit suicide if everyone fails.

However, representing the two sentences in first-order logic amounts to having two logically equivalent formulas!

But a logical diagram for the latter sentence is rather the following:

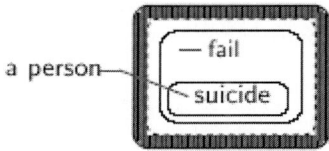

The crucial difference is that, unlike in the first diagram, the outermost end of the LI connected to the spot *fail* lies inside the objective possibility of *will* marked by the tinctured area, not outside of that area. This renders the two diagrams not logically equivalent.

3.2.4.5. Collections

Yet another (but certainly not the final) idea that Peirce suggested in order to extend the expressivity of diagrams was to accommodate plurals and collections. Examples are the following:

Something is one of Z's collections:

Something is a collection of all Z :

3.2.4.6. Example

A collection of philosophers is a collection of human beings:

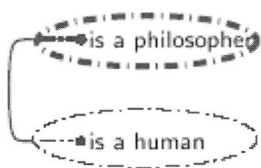

As to further extensions such as higher-order graphs and the meta-graphs ('graphs of graphs'), see, for example, Pietarinen (2005a) and Roberts (1973).

4. Iconicity and Diagrams

4.1 Further Beyond

Iconic diagrams are not meant to substitute symbolic languages of logic. On the contrary, in spreading along more than one dimension, Peirce believed that they provide an *exhaustive* method to logically represent and reason about assertions:

> Three dimensions are necessary and sufficient for the expression of all assertions; so that, if man's reason was originally limited to the line of speech (which I do not affirm), it has now outgrown the limitation. (MS 654: 6, 1910, *Preface to Essays on Meaning*).

Logical analysis of human thought in higher-dimensional spaces needs also preserve the dynamics of representations, Peirce avers:

> At great pains, I learned to think in diagrams, which is a much superior method [to algebraic symbols]. I am convinced that there is a far better one, capable of wonders; but the great cost of the apparatus forbids my learning it. It consists in *thinking in stereoscopic moving pictures*. (MS L 231, 1911, *Letter to Kehler*).

It is not known what the logic of "stereoscopic moving pictures" could have been, but see Pietarinen (2004b, 2005a) for some suggestions.

The insight concerning logic as a spatial form of expression was reinstated much later by many logicians:

> We speak in real time, and real time progresses linearly ... But formal languages are not spoken (at least not easily). So there is no reason to be influenced by the linearity of time into being narrow-minded about formulas. And linearity is the ultimate in narrowness. (Enderton, 1970, p. 393).

Indeed, the rational parts exhibited in diagrammatic syntax, Peirce maintains, "are really related to one another in forms of relations analogous to those of the assertions they represent". And if so, "in studying this syntax we may be assured that we are studying the real relation of the parts of the assertions and reasoning", which is not, according to him, the case "with the syntax of speech" (MS L 231: 10).

4.2 Shin's Account

In *Iconic Logic of C. S. Peirce*, Sun-Joo Shin (2002) embraces the iconicity of Peirce's EGs. But several features are missing or distorted in that account.

1. Shin's interpretation is not as iconic as possible (e.g., it uses predicate terms, not spots, and so is heterogeneous).
2. The interpretation is preoccupied by compositionality, which runs counter to the original semantics of EGs as 'endoporeutic', i.e., spelling out the 'outside-in' interpretation of graphs.[9]
3. It lacks discussion on non-diagrammatic icons, and does not go beyond the beta part.
4. The treatment is idiosyncratic on what "visually clear" and "intuitive" ways of "reading off" EGs are (Shin, 2002, p. 63). As noted, iconicity need not be visual and in that sense actually readable.
5. Even when iconicity is readable, there are multiple ways of reading graphs. This is not an issue under Peirce's conception. To wit, consider the following alpha graph and all the logically equivalent ways of translating it into propositional logic:

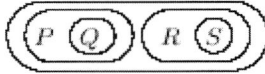

Conjunctions:

$$\neg((\neg(P \land \neg Q) \land \neg(R \land \neg S))), \neg((\neg(R \land \neg S) \land \neg(P \land \neg Q))),$$
$$\neg((\neg(\neg Q \land P) \land \neg(\neg S \land R))), \neg((\neg(R \land \neg S) \land \neg(\neg Q \land P))),$$
$$\neg((\neg(P \land \neg Q) \land \neg(\neg S \land R))), \neg((\neg(\neg S \land R) \land \neg(P \land \neg Q))),$$
$$\neg((\neg(\neg Q \land P) \land \neg(R \land \neg S))), \neg((\neg(\neg S \land R) \land \neg(\neg Q \land P))),$$
$$\neg((P \to Q) \land (R \to S)), \neg((R \to S) \land (P \to Q)).$$

---

[9] On compositionality and endoporeutics of EGs, see Pietarinen (2005b,c).

Disjunctions:

$$(P \wedge \neg Q) \vee (R \wedge \neg S), (P \wedge \neg Q) \vee (\neg S \wedge R),$$
$$(\neg Q \wedge P) \vee (R \wedge \neg S), (\neg Q \wedge P) \vee (\neg S \wedge R),$$
$$(R \wedge \neg S) \vee (P \wedge \neg Q), (\neg S \wedge R) \vee (P \wedge \neg Q),$$
$$(R \wedge \neg S) \vee (\neg Q \wedge P), (\neg S \wedge R) \vee (\neg Q \wedge P).$$

Implications:

$$(P \rightarrow Q) \rightarrow (R \wedge \neg S), \neg(R \wedge \neg S) \rightarrow (P \wedge \neg Q),$$
$$(P \rightarrow Q) \rightarrow (\neg S \wedge R), \neg(R \wedge \neg S) \rightarrow (\neg Q \wedge P),$$
$$(R \rightarrow S) \rightarrow (P \wedge \neg Q), \neg(\neg S \wedge R) \rightarrow (P \wedge \neg Q),$$
$$(R \rightarrow S) \rightarrow (\neg Q \wedge P), \neg(\neg S \wedge R) \rightarrow (\neg Q \wedge P),$$
$$\neg(P \wedge \neg Q) \rightarrow (R \wedge \neg S), \neg(P \wedge \neg Q) \rightarrow (\neg S \wedge R),$$
$$\neg(\neg Q \wedge P) \rightarrow (R \wedge \neg S), \neg(\neg Q \wedge P) \rightarrow (\neg S \wedge R).$$

All these 30 readings are readily available in the given alpha graph.

5. Conclusions

5.1 Summary

EGs have a lot of potential for development. In particular, the gamma part and the various extensions have been little studied. Yet according to Peirce, "*The Gamma Part* supposes the reasoner to invent for himself such additional kinds of signs as he may find desirable" (MS 693: 282, n.d.). He also suggested a delta part in 1911, which he might have wanted to have in order to improve upon the treatment of modalities and quantification. At all events, with EGs, Peirce believed that one is capable of representing "All that is in any way or in any sense present to the mind" (1.284, 1905, *Phenomenology*). In that sense, the theory strongly suggests where our true logic of cognition might reside in.

5.2 Towards a Logic of Icons

Recall that diagrams and the logic of graphs both pertain to the secondness of iconic signs. They profess literal, truth-conditional meaning by *continuity in*

70 Chapter Four

relations with our universes of discourse. Diagrams exhibit context-dependence and spatiality, and are multi-modal and perceptible by one of our sensory modes.

What to expect next? A theory development matching the accuracy of diagrams is needed for images and metaphors. In contrast to diagrams, metaphors exhibit non-literal meaning by various forms of *similarity*—including analogy, comparison and parallelism—*in qualities* with the universe of discourse.[10] They are more context-independent and abstract, but less spatial and visual than diagrams. Images, on the other hand, have meaning by *causal connection in kind* with the universe of discourse. Like diagrams, they are context-dependent and spatial, while markedly concrete and visual.[11] Beginning with this broader view to iconic representations, logicians, philosophers and cognitive scientists are in an excellent position to develop comprehensible logics of cognition.

5.3 Crane's Err

Crane's allusion concerning non-visual character of language is now seen to be dubious. Let us take his example and draw an existential graph for it (the components used here are explained under Section 3):

If it isn't raining next Saturday, we'll go to the sea.

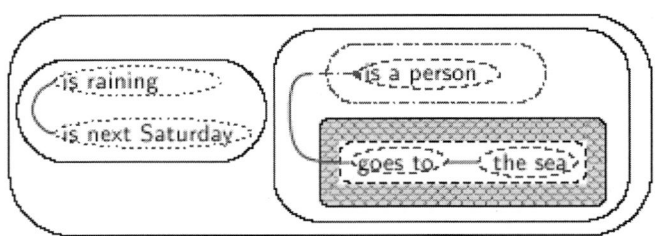

---

[10] See Steinhart (2001) for a take on the logic of metaphors in the framework of possible-worlds semantics.

[11] See e.g. Otto Neurath's (1936) 'International System Of Typographic Picture Education' (ISOTYPE) for an attempt at a generic system of communication using pictograms.

So, EGs can capture such scenarios after all. This is a telling argument in favour of the representations of thoughts constantly formed and presented to the mind as analytic 'snapshots' whose logical properties can be studied by logical diagrams.

While such diagrams are often markedly visual, other diagrammatic modes of representation ranging from geometric and algebraic to haptic, tactile, olfactory and proprioceptive ones are conceivable, too, as long as they are rooted in the iconicity of form.

Moreover, there is much less conventionality in icons than what Goodman and Eco would have us believe. It is the *modes* of representation that are conventional, not the *form*. It usually does not matter which particular tincture, colour or contour we use for the expression of some specific modality, as long as the expression is iconic, in other words employs a broken cut of some suitable kind that exposes new possible worlds within which the meaning of modal expressions may then be evaluated.[12]

5.4 Future Uses of Iconic Logic

Unlike symbolic logic, diagrammatic methods involve multi-modal reasoning, in other words information obtained through several media. Several prospects arise:

1. *The Philosophy of Mind and Cognitive Science*: How do humans actually represent information and reason about non-linguistic, multi-modal mental representations?

2. *Formal Logic*: Study the properties of diagrammatic and iconic systems (expressive power, soundness/completeness of transformation rules, length of transformations, restrictions on transformations for different modal systems, substructural logics, etc.)?

3. *Linguistics and Computer Science*: How to diagrammatically represent information coded in assertions? How to best reason about such knowledge or information? Would a comprehensive logic software

---

[12] See Pietarinen (2006b) for a discussion of Peirce's graphs and modalities in view of the later development of possible-worlds semantics. On game semantics for graphs, see Pietarinen (2004a, 2003, 2006a).

based on EGs have pedagogical and educational value superseding that of the kinds of heterogeneous logics employed, say, in *Hyperproof*?[13]

Endeavours in logic and in cognitive and computing sciences are still a far cry from meeting Peirce's criteria for iconicity. At any rate, icons exhibit "the only really fertile reasoning" (4.571, 1905, *Prolegomena*), which is key not only to abduction and Peirce's philosophy of pragmaticism (Pietarinen & Snellman 2006) but also to a comprehensive theory likely to emerge as a powerful candidate for a new synthesis of the human mind and the computer.

Acknowledgments

Supported by the Academy of Finland (*Logic and Game Theory*) and the Jenny and Antti Wihuri Foundation (*Pragmatic Theories of Meaning*).

References

Barwise, J. and Etchemendy, J. 1995. "Heterogeneous logic." in J. Glasgow, N. Hari Narayanan and B. Chandrasekaran eds, *Diagrammatic Reasoning: Cognitive and Computational Perspectives*. Cambridge, Mass.: MIT Press, 211-234.
Barwise, J. and Etchemendy, J. 1996. "Visual information and valid reasoning." in G. Allwein and J. Barwise eds, *Logical Reasoning with Diagrams*. Oxford: Oxford University Press, 160-182.
Crane, T. 1995. "Representation." *Oxford Companion to Philosophy*. Oxford & New York: Oxford University Press, 769-770.
Eco, U. 1982. "Critique of the image." in Burgin, V. ed, *Thinking Photography*. London: Macmillan, 32-38.
Enderton, H.B. 1970. "Finite partially ordered quantifiers." *Zeitschrift für Mathematische Logic und Grundlagen der Mathematik*. 16, 393-397.
Goodman, N. 1968. *Languages of Art: An Approach to a Theory of Symbols*. Indianapolis: Bobbs-Merrill Company.
Hoffman, M.H.G. 2004. "How to get it: Diagrammatic reasoning as a tool of knowledge development and its pragmatic dimension." *Foundations of Science*. 9, 282-305.
Hookway, C. 1994. "Iconicity and logical form." *Histoire Épistémologie Language*. 16, 53-64.
Jappy, T. 2005. "In defense of iconicity." *Visio*. 10.

---

[13] Barwise, J. and Etchemendy, J. (1994). "Hyperproof", New York: Cambridge University Press.

Kazmierczak, E. 2001. "On diagrammatic nature of representation: Art, design, and information as modeling forms of thinking." *in 6th World Congress of the International Association for Visual Semiotics: The Visual in the Age of Post-Visual.* Quebec: Laval University.

Midtgarden, T. 2002. "Iconic aspects of language and language use: Peirce's work on iconicity revisited." *Semiotica.* 139, 227-244.

Neurath, O. 1936. *International Picture Language: The First Rules of Isotype.* London: Kegan Paul. (Reprint Edition 1980: University of Reading: Department of Typography & Graphic Communication.)

Nyíri, K. ed, 2003. Mobile Learning: Essays on Philosophy, Psychology and Education. Vienna: Passagen Verlag.

Peirce, C. S. 1931-58. *Collected Papers of Charles Sanders Peirce.* 8 vols, P. Weiss, C. Hartshorne and A.W. Burks eds, Cambridge, Mass.: Harvard University Press.

—. 1967. Manuscripts in the Houghton Library of Harvard University, identified by R. Robin, Annotated Catalogue of the Papers of Charles S. *Peirce,* Amherst: University of Massachusetts Press.

—. 1998. *The Essential Peirce, 2,* Peirce Edition Project. Bloomington: Indiana University Press.

Pietarinen, A.V. 2003. "Peirce's game-theoretic ideas in logic." *Semiotica* 144, 33-47.

—. 2004a. "Diagrammatic logic and game-playing." in G. Malcolm ed, *Multidisciplinary Approaches to Visual Representations and Interpretations.* Amsterdam: Elsevier, 115-133.

—. 2004b. "Peirce's diagrammatic logic in IF perspective." in A. Blackwell, K. Marriott and A. Shimojima eds, *Diagrammatic Representation and Inference: Third International Conference.* Lecture Notes in Artificial Intelligence 2980, Berlin: Springer-Verlag, 97-111.

—. 2005a. *Signs of Logic: Peircean Themes on the Philosophy of Language, Games, and Communication.* (Synthese Library 329), Dordrecht: Springer.

—. 2005b. "Compositionality, relevance and Peirce's logic of existential graphs." *Axiomathes.* 15, 513-540.

—. 2005c. "The composition of concepts and Peirce's pragmatic logic." in E. Machery, M. Werning and G. Schurtz eds, *The Compositionality of Concepts and Meanings: Foundational Issues.* Frankfurt: Ontos-Verlag, 247-270.

—. 2006a. "Peirce's magic lantern: moving pictures of thought." *Transactions of the Charles S. Peirce Society.* to appear.

—. 2006b. "Peirce's contributions to possible-worlds semantics." *Studia Logica.* 82, 345-369.

—. 2006c. "Interdisciplinarity and Peirce's classification of the sciences: A centennial reassessment." *Perspectives on Science* 14, 127-152.

—. 2006d. "Peirce and the logic of image." *Semiotica*. to appear.
Pietarinen, A.V. and Snellman, L. 2006. "On Peirce's proof of pragmaticism." in T. Aho and A.-V. Pietarinen eds, *Truth and Games. Acta Philosophica Fennica* 78, Helsinki: Societas Philosophica Fennica, 275-288.
Roberts, D.D. 1973. *The Existential Graphs of Charles S. Peirce*. The Hague: Mouton.
Shin, S.-J. 2002. *The Iconic Logic of Peirce's Graphs*. Cambridge, Mass.: MIT Press.
Steinhart, E. 2001. *The Logic of Metaphor*. Dordrecht: Kluwer.
Zeman, J.J. 1964. *The Graphical Logic of C. S. Peirce*. dissertation, University of Chicago. web.clas.ufl.edu/users/jzeman/ (2002 Online Edition).

Chapter Five

Causation: A Synthesis of Three Approaches[1]

Lars-Göran Johansson

Introduction

The word 'cause' and its cognates, such as 'bring about', 'produce', 'make', etc., are all common in our vernacular. In many cases we have no problems to determine whether we should use the word 'cause' or not; our intuitions are clear. But when we try to spell out our criteria it has proven all too easy to invent counterexamples. This is a philosophical challenge and an incentive for debate. Another reason for discussing causation is that in many sciences we are interested in causal relations and we urgently need a well-defined concept.

Disagreements about the nature of causation have been a perennial trait in philosophy. In recent years at least four quite different views are proposed. One is the conserved quantity theory according to which causation is transfer of a conserved quantity. Another is the agency theory according to which a cause is something we humans can manipulate; a third popular approach is to analyse causes in terms of counterfactuals and a fourth account is to define causes in terms of INUS-conditions. Each approach can muster strong intuitions and paradigmatic examples in favour of its view, but all have difficulties which become visible when generalising beyond paradigmatic examples.

In response to this, some have suggested an ecumenical approach, saying that causation should be analysed as a disjunction of all these accounts. One could then in each different case apply the analysis that fits best. But this sounds a bit ad hoc; what is the unifying principle? Why do we call all these apparently different things for cases of causation? Something stronger than mere disjunction is needed.

---

[1] I thank Bertil Rolf for much appreciated and valuable comments on an earlier draft of this paper.

In this paper I will propose a more unified approach involving three of the abovementioned approaches, viz., Mackie's analysis in terms of INUS-conditions, the agency theory and the conserved quantity theory. But why leave out counterfactual analysis?

My reason is that it appears to me to be a blind alley. It is of course correct that we often explain a causal statement such as, '*a* caused *b*', by saying 'if *a* had not occurred, *b* would not have happened'. But suppose we ask about the meaning of this counterfactual? How do we decide whether such a statement is true or false? Counterfactuals cannot be viewed as mere material conditionals (if so, all counterfactuals would be true) and in order to decide the truth conditions for counterfactuals we need something stronger than first order predicate logic, as was shown already by Goodman (1955).

Adherents to counterfactual analysis of causation reply that such an analysis we have had since Lewis [1973] used possible world semantics to formulate truth-conditions for counterfactuals. His idea was that a counterfactual is true if the antecedent and consequent are true in a possible but non-actual world, which is sufficiently *similar* to ours. How, then, do we measure similarity? Obviously, this measure must respect our intuitions about causation and Lewis elaborated on the idea, but was the result illuminating? Judea Pearl comments:

"Lewis (1979) subsequently set up an intricate system of weights and priorities among various aspects of similarity- size of 'miracles' (violation of laws), matching of facts, temporal precedence and so forth, - in attempting to bring similarity closer to causal intuition. But these priorities are rather post hoc and still yield counterintuitive inferences (J. Woodward, personal communication)." (Pearl 2000, 239)

Thus, counterfactuals are not of much help as an illuminating analysis of causation. We should rather reverse the order of explanation and explain counterfactuals in terms of causes. In his [2000] Pearl does this by giving an account of counterfactuals in terms of causal mechanisms, i.e., laws. This is the right way to go; laws and mechanisms are fundamental for understanding both causation and counterfactual statements. In my view, the conserved quantity theory, which is a theory about mechanisms, i.e., laws, goes directly to the hart of the problem.

Many writers, Cartwright and Pearl for example, have used directed acyclic graphs to construct models of causal relations in such areas as econometrics or epidemiology. The aim is to display how variables causally depend on each other. For example, if a variable x affects another variable z only by affecting an intermediate variable y, this is displayed in a directed acyclic graph as that there is no path from x to z, which does not pass through y. I think these models are of great heuristic and pedagogical value, but they do not provide any philosophical analysis of causation. The reason is that the axioms of these models are motivated by causal intuitions. The point of graph models is not to analyse causation but to sort out possible causal structures behind statistical data; hence in this paper I will leave this approach out.

In the sequel I will give an outline of a reductive analysis of causation based on Mackie's analysis of causation in terms of INUS-conditions, the conserved quantity theory and the agency (or manipulability) theory. It seems to me that von Wright (1971) was on the right track when saying that the concept of cause identifies what we can manipulate and that it is at least partly related to our interests. But it also contains an aspect having to do with objective mechanisms in the world, because these restrict what and how we can manipulate. Furthermore, we sometimes talk about causes where manipulability is out of the question, which shows that agency cannot be the sole aspect of causation; more is needed in a complete account.

Hume on causation

As so many others I think Hume's account of causation is a good starting point. He claimed that the idea of cause was based on three observable traits:
- The cause precedes its effect,
- Cause and effect are contiguous,
- The same type of effects regularly follows events of the same type of cause.

(He also hinted at a counterfactual analysis, but I'll leave that aside for reasons given above.) This account fits our use of the concept of cause in a number of paradigmatic cases, but there are also several problematic ones. There are for example obvious examples of cause and effect not being in direct contact and cause-effect correlations are often less than strict. Hume discussed some of these objections and he added caveats. For example, in cases where the correlation is not strict he suggested that there is more than one cause for a particular effect.

The most controversial part of Hume's account was his denial that causes *necessitate* their effects in a stronger sense than 'are always followed by'. He frankly claimed that causation is nothing but correlation. When we have described all particular facts about events we have basically said everything there is to say; causal laws supervene on these particular facts. This view is not consonant with the fact that we require explanations of correlations and sometimes our curiosity is satisfied by a causal explanation; if causation were no more than regularity, the explanation would beg the question. Hence, we take for granted that causation is something more than regular connection, something which explains the regularity. Hume claimed this to be a mistake, but in that I think Hume made a mistake. Do I then accept metaphysical necessity? No. I fundamentally agree with Hume in grounding our knowledge on sensory experience, but he made a mistake in taking for granted that experience of single objects or events is basic. Seeing an object is seeing it as an object of a certain kind; the observation is a categorisation and the categories we use are not inborn and fixed once and for all. They are affected by our experiences and to some extent malleable. Hence, a more holistic view on observation is needed and in such a perspective it is not correct to say that causal laws supervene on particular facts. In a sense, formulating laws and construing categories for sorting our observations are two sides of the same coin. Correlations are not brute facts. I have elaborated on this idea in my [2005], [2006a] and [2006b].

Thus, although Hume was wrong in saying that regularities are brute facts, his three criteria for causation were the correct starting point and we need some elaboration and modification of them. I will take up three such elaborations and modifications: i) relaxing the strict regularity condition, ii) bringing in the human perspective in the analysis of causation, and iii) elaboration of the contiguity condition. The first task was taken care of by Mackie.

Mackie's theory; Regularity and INUS-conditions

As already mentioned, there are cases in which we say that a particular cause has a particular effect, while the generalisation to a strict generality is not valid. The natural move is to relax Hume's demand, thus saying that cause and effect must be positively correlated, but the correlation need not be strict. Mackie's account of cause in terms of INUS-conditions has precisely this consequence. According to Mackie, a cause is an *Insufficient, but Necessary part of a complex of factors, the complex being Unnecessary but Sufficient for the occurrence of the effect*; in short an *INUS-condition*. It follows immediately that the old rule 'same cause, same effect' is not generally valid.

The cause of influenza provides an illuminating example of the first part of the definition. We know that a virus of certain kind is a necessary but not sufficient condition for flu, since not all individuals exposed to the virus become diseased. Other factors must be present, such as a weakened immune system in the body. If we collect statistical information about the occurrence of the virus, the flu and the state of immune system among people we will get less than strict correlations.

The correlation between cause and effect need not be high. Consider smoking and lung cancer. The incidence of lung cancer among those who have been smokers for 30 years or more is only around 7%. Nevertheless, we consider smoking the cause, or the most important cause, of lung cancer. It is obvious that there must be other factors than smoking, known or unknown, which are positively correlated with lung cancer. Why not call any of these the cause? Or in the case of the influenza virus and the flu, why not saying that the low efficiency of the immune system is the cause of the flu? What are the selection principles among the INUS-factors when calling one of the as the cause? For, clearly, that is what we do.

Selection among INUS-conditions

Germund Hesslow has [1984] given some simple and illuminating examples, which display the operative selection principle in identifying the cause among the INUS-conditions. One such example is a genetic experiment with two populations of fruit flies, one with normal genetic set up, one with a mutation. The mutation results in very short wings provided the temperature is around 22 centigrade. We say that the mutation is the cause of the shortened wings. However, if we raise the temperature to 32 centigrade, the wings become normal also in the mutated population. Now, Hesslow asks us instead to compare two mutated populations, one raised in lower temperature, the other in higher temperature. Since the population raised in lower temperature has shortened wings it seems obvious that it is the low temperature, which caused short wings.

Hesslow's conclusion is that low temperature and mutation both are INUS-conditions for short wings and which to call the cause depends on which comparison we make. This observation suggests that the selection of one of the INUS-conditions as *the cause* is determined by the observer's perspective.

Let us, as a second example, consider the following, not implausible little story. An early winter morning Mr Smith drives his car on his way to his job. Being late he drives rather fast. In a curve there is ice on the road, the car slips and goes of the road into the ditch. What was the cause of this accident? Smith would, I guess, claim that the cause was the ice on the road. The police might say that Smith's driving too fast was the cause; one could expect of every driver that morning to be prepared of ice on the road since the temperature was below zero. Since Smith had not been properly careful he himself, or his action, was the cause.

A physicist describing the physics of the event might claim that the cause was insufficient friction due to blank tyres. A meteorologist might say that it was the fall of temperature to below zero together with the humid air that morning which caused the accident, since he observe a peak in accidents this very morning in this area. A road construction engineer might say that the cause of the accident was a wrongly built road; he has measured the side-inclination of the road at the bend and found it insufficient, which results in many accidents of this kind at this place.

It seems to me that all can give plausible arguments for their causal statements. Moreover, they are not contradicting each other, and hence there are several causes for this event. But very often we ask about *The Cause*, thus supposing there is only one cause, or one most important cause, and in such cases people with different perspectives or different interests focus attention on different causes. It seems to me that the purported causes all are INUS-conditions, and the selection among them depends on perspective.

Numerous examples of this kind could be imagined. The general conclusion to be drawn is that the analysis of causation in terms of INUS-conditions has two steps. First we identify the INUS-factors, which are a matter of science, and then one such factor is selected as *the cause*. This selection is guided by pragmatic considerations; it depends on perspective, interest, legal or moral norms, etc.

Now, it is time to bring the agency theory of causation into the picture. Perspective, interests, norms and manipulability could be subsumed under the label 'agent-perspective'. Selecting one INUS-condition as *the cause* is made from our perspective as agents in the world. The road construction engineer wants to rebuild roads and make better roads in the future. The policeman's duty is to decide whether the driving was a criminal act or not. The driver doesn't want to be accused of criminal driving, etc.

This conception of causation has been argued for by von Wright [1971] and Price & Menzies [1993] under the name of *agency theory* or the *manipulability theory* of causation.

Agency

Knowledge about causes helps us bringing about desirable states of affairs and avoiding unpleasant ones. Therefore, agency theorists claim, the concept of cause should be analysed from the perspective of ourselves as agents in the world. Causation is seen as primarily belonging to the intentional idiom of actions, beliefs and desires. We are interested in causes just because they tell us what to do to satisfy our desires and to avoid unpleasant events. This is the basic intuition in the agency theory of causation. Here is how Price & Menzies argue:

> The basic premise is that from an early age, we all have direct experience of acting as agents. That is, we have direct experience not merely of the Humean succession of events in the external world, but of a very special class of such successions: those in which the earlier event is an action of our own, performed

in circumstances in which we both desire the later event, and believe that it is more probable given the act in question than it would be otherwise. To put it more simply, we all have direct personal experience of doing one thing and thence achieving another. ... It is this common and commonplace experience that licenses what amounts to an ostensive definition of the notion of 'bringing about'. In other words, these cases provide direct non-linguistic acquaintance with the concept of bringing about an event. Acquaintance, in turn, does not depend on prior acquisition of any causal notion. An agency theory thus escapes the threat of circularity. (1993, p. 194-5)

I find this convincing as long as it concerns human actions. But when adherents to this theory try to generalise to situations, which are not manipulable, they run into trouble. Their general idea is that we think analogously; we apply causal notions in situations, which are sufficiently similar to situations in everyday life that we in fact can manipulate. This idea can be formulated in counterfactual terms, something like "A causes B if and only if B would change if an appropriate manipulation on A were to be carried out."

There are difficulties with this generalisation, the most serious being that it cannot distinguish between genuine and spurious causes. Furthermore, in order to really be illuminating we need an analysis of counterfactuals, i.e., a theory telling us under what conditions a counterfactual is true and when not. As already indicated, I think this is a detour since the counterfactuals are best analysed in terms of laws and we need laws anyway in the analysis of causation

But the notion of *causing* or *bringing about* is connected to our deliberations and actions. Judea Pearl [2000] claims that this was the original content of the notion:

"The agents of causal forces in the ancient world were either deities, who cause thing to happen for a purpose, or human beings and animals, who possess free will, for which they are punished or rewarded. This notion of causation was naïve, but clear and unproblematic. The problem began, as usual, with engineering; when machines had to be constructed to do useful jobs. ... And, once people started building multistage systems, an interesting thing happened to causality - physical objects began acquiring causal character. " (2000, 333)

I think he is right in this historical analysis of the evolution of the concept of cause. And he is also right in insisting that the concept of cause still has this two-sided character, it is both related to our *first-person perspective* as agents and to a *third-person perspective* on interactions between physical objects.

These two perspectives can be brought together using Mackie's analysis in terms of INUS-conditions. The third-person-perspective is adopted when determining the INUS-conditions and the first-person perspective is operative when we select one of these as *the cause*.

But sometimes we ask about the cause of an event without having the slightest idea of how to manipulate states of affairs. (What is the cause of the sun's shining? Answer: the fusion of hydrogen in its nucleus. How do we manipulate that?). Here nature itself is seen as the causal agent and the first-person perspective is inadequate. But then, what do we rely on when we decide the cause of such things? My guess is that a contact criterion is used for determining causes. But what is more precisely meant by contact?

Contact

To begin, we must say something about cases of causation in which cause and effect are not directly in contact. In such cases we assume something is transmitting the causing, as Hume himself suggested. This intuition has been developed by Reichenbach (1956), Salmon (1984, 1994, 1998) and Dowe (1992, 1999, 2000). The first step is to introduce two causal concepts, *causal interaction* and *causal process*. The first refers to direct contact between two objects; the later refers to propagation of causing over spatial distances. Electromagnetic signals are typical examples of causal processes; they propagate from place to place in space and transmit energy between distant objects. When such an electromagnetic signal arrives at a piece of matter, an interaction might occur and energy is transferred. Thus both interaction and propagation are involved in this and many other cases of causation.

Reichenbach's original idea was to take the cause-effect asymmetry as basis for defining the direction of time. Since causes are propagated in space and this takes time, effects must necessarily occur later than causes. This idea is no longer popular, but Reichenbach's idea that causes are propagated physically remains; transmitting a causal effect is done by using one of four kinds of interaction in nature; gravitation, electromagnetism, the weak or the strong nuclear force. Wesley Salmon took up this idea in his [1984]. However, not only causes form continuous chains in space. For example, the motion of a shadow along a wall is continuous, albeit not a causal chain. Hence Salmon introduced the distinction between *causal process*es and *pseudo processes*. The distinction was made in terms of the possibility of marking; if it is possible to mark the process and this mark continues to exist later in the process, it is a causal process, otherwise not. The disadvantage with this approach, from an empiricist point of view, was the modal formulation, which proved unavoidable. Hence, he later dropped the mark approach and adopted the *conserved quantity approach* (1994), first inaugurated by Phil Dowe (1992). The core idea is to say that a causal process is one in which a conserved quantity is propagated, whereas in a pseudo process no quantity is conserved and the distinction is made without using modal expressions. For example, transfer of light from a light source to a target is a causal process since energy is conserved, whereas the motion of a shadow on a wall is a pseudo-process because no such quantity can be attributed to the shadow. The quantities thought of could be any recognized as such by physics, such as mass-energy, momentum or charge.

Processes take time, hence the conserved quantity theory need to give a criterion for identity over time of such processes. Dowe proposes something, which he calls *strict identity*: an object is wholly existent at each and every instant in its history (1999, 250). I must say that I don't find this criterion very helpful; what does it mean to say that something is wholly existent? This point needs improvement but I will not pursue that point here.

Furthermore, we need to replace the notion of contact with something more precise, since objects can, in a sense, be in contact without changing their states. An example is provided by neutrinos passing through our bodies all the time without doing anything at all with us; they are in a sense in contact with us (they are inside us!) but they do no cause anything since they don't change our bodily state the slightest. Hence the correct criterion for causal interaction is exchange of a conserved quantity between the interacting systems.

This account also provides reasons for Reichenbach's principle. This principle says that a correlation between two stochastic variables X and Y is, if the correlation obtains in an entire population and not only in a sample, due to the fact that either i) X causes Y, or ii) Y causes X, or iii) there is a common cause to X and Y. The principle is intuitively acceptable and it is explained by the thought that causation requires contact. Thus real correlations, i.e., correlations obtaining not only in samples but also in populations, have causal explanations, but we need physical information to tell which of the alternatives is correct.

Causation in the social sciences

One could reasonably ask if transfer of conserved physical quantities has any relevance at all when discussing causes of social, political or historical events. My answer is *yes*. Consider for example the beginning of World War I. The common view is that the cause of this event was the assassination of archduke Franz Ferdinand in Sarajevo. I will take for granted that this event was at least one of the causes of the World War I. It is clear that knowledge about this event is a necessary condition for the Austrian government to declare war against Serbia. This knowledge is transmitted by personal communication, telegrams or telephone calls. Knowledge transmission needs transfer of information and transfer of information requires physical contact, see the next section. So, even if we usually don't focus attention on physical connections when discussing causation in social sciences, it is nevertheless a necessary prerequisite. We see once more the agency perspective in operation; physical contact is an INUS-condition also for historical, social events, but in those areas we are not particularly interested in physical aspects of causation. We focus on people's actions or lack of actions, their beliefs and motives.

Causation and Information

Intuitively there is conceptual connection between causation and transfer of information, because we can't get any information from a system without interacting causally with it; for example, when looking at something, the object causes (by reflecting light) stimuli on the observer's retina. Thus transfer of information is a causal process. This deserves a closer look.

Information in the sense of Shannon-Weaver (defined as $H = -\int p(x) \ln p(x)\, dx$, where $p(x)$ is the probability density over the set of possible states) is a measure of structure, or order. The information contained in a state description gives us a measure of how many microstates are possible given the description. If information, in this sense, is transmitted from one system to another, an abstract structure of the first system is copied in the second, and this cannot be anything but a causal process. We can represent it theoretically as a mapping and this mapping is a theoretical representation of a physical process, viz., a process in which a conserved quantity is transmitted from one system to another. Thus it fulfils our demands on a causal process.

But it is not entirely in accord with ordinary language to say that the stored information on for example a CD causes the music heard when playing it. Rather we would say that *playing the* CD causes us to hear music. The point is that the word 'cause' usually takes events as relata, and *playing CD and hearing music* are events, but not 'stored information'.

In the discussion about the logic of the concept of cause there is another proposal, viz. to construe it as relating states of affairs, not events. There are reasons for this approach (see for example Needham (2003)) and if this construal is adopted, it is possible to say that information stored in one system ca be the cause of stored information in another system. Hence in either view it is possible to construe transfer of information as a causal process.

Summary

Causation is a notion used for singling out those connections in nature, in society and in history, which we find worth caring about as agents. Both the third-person and the first-person perspective must be used in a complete account. By adding the agency perspective and the conserved quantity theory to Mackie's theory of causes as INUS-conditions, we can integrate these aspects into a unified account of our concept of cause as it is used in ordinary talk, in natural and social sciences.

References

Dowe, P. 1992. "Wesley Salmon's Process Theory of Causality and the Conserved Quantity Theory." *Philosophy of Science* 59: 195-216.
—. 1999. "Good Connections: Causation and Causal Processes." In H. Sankey ed, *Causation and Laws of Nature*. Dordrecht: Kluwer, pp. 247-63.
—. 2000. *Physical Causation*. New York: Cambridge University Press.
Hesslow, G. 1984, "What is a Genetic Disease? On the Relative Importance of Causes." in Lindahl & Nordenfeldt eds, *Health, Disease and Causal Explanation in Medicine*. Reidel, Dordrecht, pp. 183-93.
Johansson, L-G. 2005. "The Nature of Natural Laws." pp.171-187 *in* Faye, Needham, Scheffler and Urchs eds, *Nature's Principles*. Berlin, Springer.
—. 2006a. "Induction, Causation and Laws." in Koskinen, Pihlström and Vilkko eds, *Science- a Challenge to Philosophy?* Frankfurt: Peter Lang.
—. 2006b. "Natural Necessity." In Lagerlund, Lindström and Sliwinski eds, Modality *Matters. Twenty-Five Essays in honour of Krister Segerberg*, Uppsala Philosophical Studies 53, pp. 231-245.
Mackie, John. 1974. *The Cement of the Universe*. Oxford: Clarendon Press.
Menzies, P. and Price, H. 1993. "Causation as a Secondary Quality." *British .Journal of the.Philosophy of .Science*. 44, pp. 187-203.
Lewis, D. 1973. *Counterfactuals*. Oxford: Blackwell.
Needham, P. 2003. "On Davidson's Conception of Events." In *A Philosophical Smorgasbord. Essays on action, truth and other things in honour of Frederick Stoutland*. Uppsala Philosophical Studies 52, 2003, pp. 119-142.
Pearl, J. 2000. *Causality*. New York: Cambridge University Press, New York.
Price, H. 1991. "Agency and Probabilistic Causality." *British .Journal of the.Philosophy of .Science*. 42, pp. 157 -76.
Putnam, H. 1962. "It Ain't Necessarily So." *Journal of Philosophy*. LIX, 22.
Quine, W.V.O 1953. "Two Dogmas of Empiricism." in *From a Logical Point of View*. Cambridge, Ma: Harvard University Press.
—. 1981. "Things and Their Place in Theories." In *Theories and Things*. Cambridge, Ma: Harvard University Press, 1981.
Reichenbach, Hans. 1956. *The Direction of Time*. Berkeley and Los Angeles: University of California Press.
Salmon, W. 1984. Scientific *Explanation and the Causal Structure of the World*. Princeton: Princeton University Press.

—. 1994. "Causality Without Counterfactuals." *Phil. of Science*. 61: 297-312.
—. 1998. *Causality and Explanation.* New York: Oxford University Press.
Von Wright, G.H. 1971. *Explanation and Understanding.* Ithaca, N.Y.: Cornell University Press.

CHAPTER SIX

AN ORIENTAL APPROACH TO THE PHILOSOPHY OF INFORMATION

GANG LIU

Abstract

The opening sentence in the brief history of the International Association of Computing and Philosophy (IACAP) history reads as follows: 'the convergence of computing and philosophy has a lineage going back to Leibniz, his "calculus" and his "adding machine."' It is obvious Leibniz is regarded as a key figure in forming the new philosophy. In 1992 and 2002 both the 'computational turn' and the 'information turn' were proposed respectively. Both 'turns' mean that the Philosophy of Computing and Information (PCI) or simply Philosophy of Information (PI) is being taken as an orientative rather than a cognitive philosophy. Cognitive philosophy concerns much more with 'what', taking philosophy as an activity pursuing the establishment of knowledge and the corresponding systems. Orientative philosophy, on the other hand, inquires about 'how', that is, it points out the orientation of our interests to a specific field or direction and more importantly it puts emphasis on the methodological aspect of this philosophy.

The shift based on the PI can be seen as a mirror of the shift from the industrial to the information society. And from the perspective of the history of philosophy, such a shift is regarded as a shift of a large tradition. (Liu 2003b) Any school should be rooted in its own context of thought derived from its particular philosophical traditions. In this essay I will argue that Leibnizian philosophy brings about a new tradition in philosophy, that is, the formal tradition in addition to the classic (Platonic) and modern (Kantian) traditions. The line of argument I will take follows four major milestones in Gottfried Wilhelm Leibniz, Bertrand Russell, Clarence I. Lewis and Saul A. Kripke. The essential notions are logical calculus, the material implication, the strict implication and the semantics of possible worlds, which brings Leibnizian metaphysics into the modern philosophical discourse.

The formal tradition or more narrowly the Russell-Couturat line of interpretation on Leibniz is regarded as rejecting his metaphysics as well as his connection with China. However, in this essay I reveal the symbiosis of Leibniz's logic and metaphysics with his lifelong relationship with China as a proto-Sinologist. Leibniz not only interpreted the formal system of the *Yijing* or *I-Ching* hexagrams, one of the oldest classics in China, with binary arithmetic he also integrated elements of oriental organic philosophy into his metaphysics to try to synthesize the split he was facing.

The ontological position of information in current PI studies is far from clear, meandering between the materialistic and idealistic dichotomy. The question here is whether information itself could occupy an independent ontological category. In the inquiry of the nature of the central doctrine of Leibniz's possible worlds, we have modal Platonism, a radical interpretation claiming that possible worlds are the same ones as our planet (telescopic theory), and *ex post facto* modal realism, claiming that possible worlds are only possible states of affairs. Both of these interpretations have been made entirely within the framework of western philosophy. It is just this point that I will argue should be considered from an oriental perspective. Following Leibniz, I will provide a new synthesis with modal information theory (MIT) or modal informationalism in an effort to address the dilemma concerning the ontological position of information.

In 1992 and 2002 the 'computational turn' (Burkholder 1992) and the 'information turn' (Floridi 2002) were proposed respectively. These resulted in cyberphilosophy, a term designating 'the intersection of philosophy and computing', (Moor and Bynum 2003, Liu 2004) a new philosophical field which refers either to the PCI (Floridi 2004a) or simply to the PI. (Floridi 1999, 2002; Liu 2002, 2003a, 2003b; Benthem and Adriaans 2004) The scientific concept of 'information' has been formally accepted into the realm of philosophical inquiry.

1. Computational/Information Turns as a Shift of Philosophical Tradition

The opening sentence in IACAP's history states that 'the convergence of computing and philosophy has a lineage going back to Leibniz, his "calculus" and his "adding machine."' (IACAP 2005) Clearly Leibniz is regarded as a key figure in forming the new philosophy now under discussion, and it can be argued that Leibniz opened up a formal tradition in philosophy some three hundred years ago with his work on traditional logic.

Generally, there are two approaches to the history of philosophy; one, the usual approach, runs according to the textbooks, and the other, according to the philosophical traditions. G. MacDonald Ross presents the textbook approach in *Leibniz*. (Macdonald Ross 1984) In the Introduction he presents this familiar picture in the following way:

> Traditionally, university courses on the history of modern philosophy have been structured round a pantheon of seven great philosophers: three 'continental rationalists ': Descartes, Spinoza and Leibniz; three 'British empiricists ': Locke, Berkeley and Hume; and Kant. The empiricists were supposed to have believed that all our knowledge was built up out of the data of sense, whereas the rationalists were supposed to have restricted genuine knowledge to what could be deduced from indubitable truths of reason. Kant, on the other hand, created a new synthesis out of what was right in both empiricism and rationalism. Needless to say, this way of viewing the history of philosophy was invented by Kant himself. It has, however, had a remarkably long run for its money. (Ross 1984)

Kant had his own reasons and intentions when he developed the 'new synthesis' in his times. However, whenever the philosophy of Leibniz is concerned there are always particular difficulties when forcing him into the Procrustean bed invented by Kant. I will explore this issue in the next section, but first we must examine how we might bring Leibniz into our present discourse of information. To this end I will explore another scheme following the philosophical tradition. Western philosophy can be categorized as classic, modern, and formal traditions (Liu 2003), or Platonic, Kantian and Leibniz-Russellian traditions. (Mu 1997) Here the formal tradition, or the Russell-Couturat line, (Mungello 2004) is concerned with what is known to the philosophers of the Anglo-American tradition due to the works of Bertrand Russell (Russell 1900, rep. 1975) and Louis Couturat. (Couturat 1901)

Norbert Wiener, the founder of cybernetics, viewed Leibniz as the patron saint for cybernetics, because his work is closely related with two concepts: universal language and logical calculus. (Wiener 1948) It is clear why a scientist would view Leibniz's two great contributions as 'universal language' and 'logic calculus'. In effect, Leibniz presented only an idea with some initial steps; he did not fully realise his ideas. It was Russell who did the technical job. So we have sufficient reason to hook up Leibniz with Russell, that is, from Leibniz's logical algebra to Russell's *Principia Mathematica*.[1] Actually, Russell also takes Leibniz to be a pioneer of mathematical logic. (Russell 1955) And it has been generally acknowledged that he became the father of symbolic logic because of the heuristic of the intelligible features of the Chinese characters. (Lewis 1918)

From the evaluations by Wiener and Russell, Leibniz is important only when he is considered technically and his philosophical theory has been overlooked. Russell even thought his metaphysics was nothing but a vain hope. Russell is clear that almost all of Leibniz's useful philosophy comes from his logic (Russell 1900, rep. 1975), and his logic is simply considered to have been a 'subject-predicate' logic, that is, P existing in S. As a realist, Russell is a philosopher of single-world assumption or real world model, that is, any symbols and formulas in the formal system should be understood as objective, that is to say, all of these abstracts represents their real beings in the real world. After analysis, they are finally inhabitants in our real world. This view of reality is clearly expressed in his *Introduction to Mathematical Philosophy*, where he calls for a sound sense of reality for logicians. (Russell 1930, p.159) To sum up, Leibniz was seen and interpreted by Russell via a single-world perspective, which is partial, possibly misleading, even though Russell is considered to be an expert on Leibniz. It is ridiculous to see that Leibniz's philosophy was divided into good and bad elements in Russell's works. In Russell's opinion, his logic is good but secret and his metaphysics, derived from the logic, is bad and vulgar. Perhaps his logic should not be interpreted only in this narrow, superficial and technical manner, just as Martin Heidegger has pointed out. (Heidegger 1978, Eng. tr. 1984) Logic must have a metaphysical foundation.

Russell turned Leibniz's symbolic logic into the 'classic logic'. However, C. I. Lewis was dissatisfied with the key notion of 'material implication' in Russell's system. He thought it too far away from intuition and too weak for commonsense understanding. According to Lewis, it should be strengthened. He proposes the 'strict implication system', in which two modal words -- 'necessary' and 'possible' -- were used, and on which the 'strict implication' calculus systems were constructed. Thus he initiated the 'modern modal logic'. Lewis not only improved Russell's system with his construction of the strict implication system he also revived Leibniz's theory of possible worlds. Saul Kripke proposes a 'theory of possible worlds' in modal logic semantics, and the phrase 'Kripke à la Leibniz' is not uncommon, but it was Leibniz, writing in the seventeenth century, who employed the concept of 'possible worlds' for the first time when he was constructing his philosophical cosmology. Leibniz said

> Now as in the Ideas of God there is an infinite number of possible universes, and as only one of them can be actual, there must be a sufficient reason for the choice of God, which leads Him to decide upon one rather than another. (Leibniz 1898, § 53)

Alfred Whitehead was the co-author; therefore, Whitehead was as important as Russell (Michael Heim, email correspondence), Whitehead's Process and Reality could be seen as a modern version of Leibniz's Monadology. As

Leibniz's philosophy was divided into good and bad by Russell, it seems to me he took the good one, that is, the mathematical logic and Whitehead took the bad one, that is, the metaphysics!

That is to say, the possible worlds are much richer than the chosen one. However, we have to accept the present actual no matter what it is for it is chosen by God and He has his reason.

The fundamental idea of Kripke's semantics of possible worlds is to prescribe the various conditions of modal propositions with respect to the models constructed according to accessible relations of sets of possible worlds. Hence, his semantics based on the work of Alfred Tarski is also called 'relational semantics'. The semantics of possible worlds have already been widely accepted in the international community of logic, becoming a standard against which to check other kinds of semantics, that is, other newly constructed semantics should be compatible with Kripke's relational semantics. The semantics of possible worlds realizes the idea of a semantics of formal language originally proposed by Leibniz. With the ideas of semantics shifting from the model of the real world to that of possible worlds, the focus in logical inquiry also shifts from syntax to semantics. In a recent essay, Floridi pointed out that there are five concepts of information that are semantically relevant. (Floridi 2004b)

The rise of PI means a series of transformations, for example, from modern to formal tradition; from real world to possible worlds; from syntax to semantics (Floridi 2004b); from the theory of proofs to the theory of models; from geometry to algebra; from classic logic to modern logic; from pursuing diachronic identity to pursuing synchronic similarity; from the philosophy of science to the philosophy of information (Dodig-Crnkovic 2003); and so on and so forth. In terms of *western* philosophy, this change can be viewed as from the 'primacy of forms' to the 'primacy of materials'. However, philosophical empiricists have long doubted the efficacy of any philosophical analysis of contents for they don't believe in such a thing as the primacy of materials. However, the issues discussed by those in favour of the primacy of materials are often related to the fields of metaphysics, ontology or ethics. (Stegmüller 1986, p.151)

2. Leibniz's China Connection

The formal tradition is one part of the splendour of western achievement, it is the brilliance of western culture. From Leibniz to Russell there are active results, which are positive and constructive rather than negative and destructive. However, it should also be pointed out that the fatal deviation along the Russell-

Couturat line is that it is too narrow to encompass Leibniz's profoundness, and especially his lifelong link with China. It is interesting to see that Leibniz's philosophy was divided into good and bad by Russell; with his Anglo-Saxon perspective he said that Leibniz 'had a good philosophy which (after Arnauld's criticisms) he kept to himself, and a bad philosophy which he published with a view to fame and money.' (Russell 1975) Russell failed to see the fact that in Leibniz's philosophy there is 'a concurrence where logic and metaphysics come together in fruitful symbiosis'. (Rescher 1981, p.56) In the next section I will discuss this symbiosis and demonstrate the profound problem of the ontological position of information as well as suggest a possible solution.

The fantastic aspect of Leibniz's philosophy is that it combines with reason rather than with experience. Logic is only a rational tool with which to approach his metaphysics of nature. Before we follow this further let's briefly survey China's impact on Leibniz's philosophy.

Leibniz is considered to be an avid Sinophile. In his inquiry of a *characteristica universalis* on which to order all human knowledge, he was drawn to the Chinese *I-Ching*. (Swetz 2003). Mungello's study of Leibniz shows Chinese thought not as original inspiration but rather as corroboration for his previously and independently developed notions. (Mungello 1977) Nonetheless, the corroboration itself can be seen as an influence. (Mungello 2000) Joseph Needham's special section of *Zhu Xi, Leibniz and the Organic Philosophy* (Needham 1956, 496ff.) points out the Chinese thoughts generalized in *lixue* (lit. studies of reasons and principles, or just Neo-Confucianism (Derk Bodde *viz.* Youlan 1948) contributes to European thought in a much more significant way than has been previously acknowledged. Given that Leibniz's writings have still not been fully edited and published it must be true to say that the whole significance of his philosophy has not yet been apprehended. Ernest R. Hughes, the Oxford Sinologist, claims in the preface of his translations of *Daxue* (Great Learning) and *ZhongyYong* (The Doctrine of Mean) that Leibniz was influenced by the Neo-Confucianism. (Hughes 1942)

Leibniz's connection with China can be explored at least in the following three aspects.

Extensive Reading. The style of scholarship in the seventeenth century is rather different from today's to emphasis on narrow specialization. Scholars had to write extensively and read extensively in different fields of inquiry. When he was 20 years of age Leibniz read *De Re Litteraria Sinensium Commentarius* (Commentary on Chinese Literature) by Gottlieb Spizel (1639-1691), where it introduced Chinese natural philosophy alongside a detailed account of the doctrine of the *I-Ching*. He had also read Athanasius Kircher (1601-1680), a proliferate Jesuit scholar who published around 40 works, most notably in the fields of oriental studies, and so on. Kircher's *China Monumentis Illustrata* (Illustrated Mementos of China) (1667) was an encyclopedia of China, which combined accurate cartography with mythical elements such as dragons. The Belgian Jesuit Philippe Couplet (1623-1693) published a book entitled *Confucius Sinarum philosophus* (Confucius as a Chinese Philosopher 1687). It can be identified from a letter dated on December 19, 1687 that Leibniz read this book in the very year when it was published. (Leibniz an Landgraf Ernst von Hessen-Rheinfels 1687) In this letter Leibniz briefly reviewed Couplet's book.

Novissima Sinica and Correspondence with J. Bouvet. In a letter dated on December 14,1697, Leibniz wrote : 'Je farai donc mettre une affiche à ma porte avec ces mots: bureau d'addresse pour la Chine, afin que chacun sache, qu'on n'a s'addresser à moy pour en apprendre des nouvelles.' (Leibniz 1697, p.869) He was preparing a board on his office door as 'The General Office on Chinese Affairs' and anything concerning China should be handled by this office and would be transferred to the missionaries. Later he met Claudio Filippo Grimaldi (1638-1712) in Rome, an Italian Jesuit who stayed in China for some 17 years. By April 1697, Leibniz had accumulated enough information on China from Grimaldi and others to publish *Novissima Sinica* (Latest News from China 1697). Leibniz was an avid letter writer seeking the news on current events associated with China, especially with Jesuit missionaries to China, among whom were Joachim Bouvet (1656-1730), one of the first French Jesuit missionary members to China. Correspondence proved as important as books in transmitting Chinese philosophy to Europeans. Indeed, in the seventeenth century, letters served to communicate knowledge in the way that scholarly journals do today. (Mungello 2003) As a result, letters among scholars were often lengthy and were reproduced by secretaries for further circulation. The correspondence allowed writers to exchange ideas that were too controversial to obtain the official approval needed for publication. Leibniz's correspondence from 1697 to 1704 is one of the most striking transmissions of philosophic knowledge of that period.

These letters have been cited widely and often by scholars, and in the beginning of 1920s the Japanese scholar Gorai Kinzo went to Hanover to copy all of the letters and saw the diagram Bouvet had sent to Leibniz, that is, the *Xiantiantu* (lit. prior to heaven system) worked out by Shao Yong (1011-1077), a famous Chinese philosopher of Neo-Confucianism. In his doctoral thesis on the impact of Confucianism on German political thoughts Kinzo used some of these letters.

Leibniz studied the diagram of Fuxi's characters , and annotated his copy in red ink. Leibniz must have observed this diagram previously but did not notice its possible connection to binary numbers. (Swetz 2003) He sent his binary arithmetical interpretation to Bouvet and it was Bouvet who pointed out the association. Bouvet was driven by the possibility of revealing an 'Ancient Theology'. In their collaboration, they complemented and reinforced each other's beliefs. Unfortunately, their faulty Sinology also deceived them. In effect, there is also another system called *Houtiantu* (lit. later heaven system) initiated as early as the 11th century BCE. Shao Yong created a revolution in the system by inventing the *Xiantiantu*, initiating a new school of inquiry of the *I-Ching*, thus the mathematical school, in addition to the numerical and rational schools, happened to be present already in China for a thousand years, and Leibniz's inquiry is taken as purely mathematical. (Dong 1987)

Pioneer of Sinology. Enlightenment Europeans admired Chinese cultures, and cultural borrowings and assimilation were apparent in both directions, at least up to the end of the 1700s. There were three groups of people throughout Europe. First, the Jesuits who studied and publicized China at the most serious and deepest level. Second, 'proto-Sinologists' who were serious scholars but took a less focussed approach in their study of the many different aspects of Chinese cultures. Andreas Müller of *Clavis Sinica* (Key to the Chinese Language) fame was a proto-Sinologist, and Leibniz is another good example of a proto-Sinologist. Thirdly, the popularizers, who took a shallower approach to the study of China and sought to find in China support for European political and intellectual movements. (Mungello 1999)

Leibniz's last and most substantive work on Chinese philosophy was the *Discours sur la théologie naturelle des Chinois* (Discourse on the natural theology of the Chinese), which was stimulated by a distorted interpretation of Chinese philosophy given by another influential seventeenth-century philosopher Nicolas Malebranche (1638-1715). Malebranche wrote a small book on the existence and nature of God (Malebranche 1708) based on inadequate sources. Malebranche wrote this dialogue mainly because he perceived the influence of Spinozism in Chinese philosophy. Writing the dialogue gave him the chance to combat these irreligious traces, and to distance his own philosophy from Spinozistic monism, and to rebut critics like theologian Antoine Arnauld (1612-1694). Malebranche attacked the Chinese for recognizing only one substance, which consisted of matter that differed in degree ranging from gross to rarefied. Malebranche's interpretation dealt with a particular school of Confucian philosophy developed by Zhu Xi (1130-1200), known as Neo-Confucianism. Leibniz's *Discours* rebutted Malebranche's interpretation of Neo-Confucianism and showed them to be the distortions of a philosophic Eurocentrism. In addition, Leibniz justified Neo-Confucianism in a manner that made his *Discours* the most knowledgeable explanation of Chinese philosophy by a seventeenth-century European philosopher. (Mungello 2003)

A century later after the publication of *Novissima Sinica*, Johann Gottlieb

Buhle (1763-1821) depicted a different picture of China in his *Course of the History of Philosophy* (1796). He said that it is obvious that the Chinese have commercial exchanges with European countries...but in the aspects of culture and the employment of reason it seems that the Chinese have not made the kinds of progress that might be expected. On the contrary, they remain at a common or vulgar level. He did not mention the failure in the Rites Controversy of the Jesuits. And yet he pointed out that there was a government monopoly, secret police elsewhere, and bound the qualified and talented personnel into this tradition as well. The indifference and suppression hurt the capability and encouragement of these people. Leibniz hope was corrupted. This may be one reason to go back to Leibniz and reconsider his writings. (Poser 2000, 12)

As we have seen, from a narrow line of interpretation Leibniz's lifelong connection with China is regarded as peripheral to his main philosophical concerns. (Mungello 2004) It seems that the Anglo-American philosophers often overlook this historical link. Actually, it seems impossible to have an appropriate understanding of Leibniz's philosophy without his connection with China. He is an 'alternative' in the history of western philosophy for he introduced an oriental organic and naturalistic worldview especially in his doctrine of possible worlds. (Liu 2004)

3. Modal Information Theory: A New Synthesis

Modern modal logic opens up a tremendous promise for its application to both Information and Computing Science (ICS) and Information and Computing Technology (ICT). It can be imagined that this theory will still have more important roles to play with the development of quantum information sciences and a substantial step towards the realization of the idea of building quantum computers. Einstein once said that it was difficult to understand the meaning of a concept when it became more and more universal and came into the horizon of the people more frequently. Hence, it is necessary to carry out inquiry from different perspectives, which would result in more achievements. It seems that information is a 'magic' concept of this sort. However, its ontological position is not determined as yet from the present state of inquiry. Just as Jon Barwise said: 'the place of information in the natural world of biological and physical systems is far from clear.' (Barwise and Seligman 1997, xi) It is not hard to see that on the very planet where we are living, that is, 'the natural world of biological and physical systems', the position of information is still a problem to be settled. On the other hand, Floridi also employed the materialistic and idealistic dichotomy we are familiar with, saying:

> Most people agree that there is no information without (data)

representation....this principle is often interpreted materialistically, as advocating the impossibility of physically disembodied information, through the equation "representation = physical implementation". The view that there is no information without physical implementation is an inevitable assumption when working on the physics of computation, since computer science must necessarily take into account the physical properties and limits of the carriers of information. It is also the ontological assumption behind the Physical Symbol System Hypothesis in AI and cognitive science. (Floridi 2004b, Liu 2004b)

This is obviously the materialistic view of information; however, it is also arguable that the representation of information does not necessarily require a physical implementation. Floridi then presents the idealistic scenario:

...environments in which there are only noetic entities, properties and processes (e.g. Berkeley, Spinoza), or in which the material or extended universe has a noetic or non-extended matrix as its ontological foundation (e.g. Pythagoras, Plato, Leibniz, Hegel), seem perfectly capable of upholding the representationalist principle without also embracing a materialist interpretation. The relata giving rise to information could be monads, for example. (Floridi 2004b)

Essentially, Floridi is arguing that if one drops the Cartesian dichotomy, that information is different from the physical/material and from the mental, then there appears the possibility of a novel independent ontological category for information. It seems that without a better way out, he has to come back to Wiener's complaint that information is information. No materialism which does not admit this can survive at the present day. (Wiener 1948, p.132). It can be concluded that there is still no satisfactory solution to the ontological status of information. Under the framework of western philosophy with its long history of mind-body dualism, it is unlikely to find an acceptable solution for the concept of information.

It seems that our problems encountered today are quite similar to those Leibniz encountered some three hundred years ago. Therefore, when the position of the information is under discussion, we have to go back to Leibniz to make another new synthesis from an oriental perspective. Just as Heidegger pointed out that in Leibniz

'not only does the ancient and medieval tradition of logic converge in him in an independent new form; he becomes at the same time the stimulus for posing new questions, providing suggestions for tasks which are in part taken up only in recent times. From Leibniz we can create for ourselves perspectives reaching back to the ancients and forward to the present, perspectives important for the foundational problems of logic.' (Heidegger 1978, 1984, p.22).

No doubt Heidegger's evaluation of Leibniz is worth praising. But I would like to move a step further to suggest that in Leibniz there not only converged ancient and medieval western tradition, but also the oriental tradition, especially the tradition of Neo-Confucianism. In effect, Leibniz employed Neo-Confucianist thought to make a new synthesis of the split in western philosophy. Such a split cannot be integrated simply dependent on pure western philosophical elements or resources. Neo-Confucianism is an organic knowledge of nature, a theory of synthesis, or an organic naturalism. The system of thoughts of Neo-Confucianism represented by Zhu Xi stands for the highest level of Chinese philosophical ideas (Needham 1969, 1987, p.61). However, it is just this point that has been ignored by the western philosophers. Now, it is still necessary for us to try to make a new synthesis of the concept of information from the Chinese perspective.

This situation is rather similar to the one met by Leibniz three hundred years ago. At that time, he also faced two irreconcilable conflicts of theological idealism and atomistic materialism, which never got a successful solution in the history of European thought. (Needham 1980) Leibniz became a bridge maker trying to solve the antimony. Actually, Leibniz had already made a new synthesis prior to Kant. In effect, he introduced the organic worldview from Neo-Confucianism to integrate the split he was facing. (Liu 2004) That's why I cherish Leibniz in the present situation concerning the ontological status of information.

After the establishment of the semantics, the nature of the possible worlds has been widely discussed among logicians and various views have been proposed. Among these there are two famous realist interpretations, namely David K. Lewis' radical realism (Lewis 1987) and Kripke's soft realism (Kripke 1972). The radical realism is also called modal Platonism, a dualist interpretation in terms of Platonism, which was criticized and scorned as the 'telescopic theory'. While Kripke proposed the soft realism in respect of Aristotle's logic, and possible worlds were understood as Aristotle's *potentia*, in Aristotle's logic the predicate is actually assigned as ontological. Therefore, his logic in effect focuses on the predicate. Now that Kripke is in line with the ontological position of the predicate, he is sure to be in favor of Aristotle's 'potential infinity' rather than the 'actual infinity' in the first order logic. Kripke's interpretation eliminates the possible worlds in reality, which is understood as 'possible states' of affairs. (Kripke 1972) It should be pointed out that these two interpretations have been presented in an entirely western philosophical framework, so they approach Leibniz's philosophy too narrowly to encompass his profoundness.

Now we are going to open an organic naturalistic approach to comprehend Leibniz's theory of possible worlds from an oriental perspective. Possible worlds might be viewed as worlds in information. This would provide one interpretation of modal information theory (MIT) or modal informationalism (MI). According to Leibniz's idea, the number of possible worlds is infinite and then we apply the notion of actual infinity to possible worlds, that is, the 'abstraction of actual infinity' employed in single-world assumption is employed in the multiple worlds assumption. The notion of infinity is no longer seen as an infinite extending process, as it were, rather it is seen as a finished totality, or just 'allatonceness'. In this way, 'infinite' would be seen as 'finite'; alternatively we could treat 'infinite problems' with 'finite methods'. As far as human beings do not have a position of God, we don't have God's eye to view all of the details at one time. Therefore, the axiomatic method could only be confined to a certain model. Models are artifacts by which we can investigate those essentially non-constructive objects. Conversely, we would be able to have an infinite possibility in constructive capability. It is necessary to point out that the MIT proposed here is different from first order logic, in which the three principles of the nonemptiness of individual domains, two-valuedness and extensionality are not necessary and sufficient conditions. This is because the possible worlds on our horizon are no longer limited in the physical or 'natural' world, on the contrary they are informational and metaphysical worlds. And this could ensure the plurality of subjects and analyticity of all propositions. This is coincident with Leibniz's subject-predicate logic, from where his metaphysics is derived, that is, the subject is in the possible world and the predicate in the actual world. Just as Leibniz put it '...every predicate, necessary or contingent, past, present, or future, is comprised in the notion of the subject...' (Leibniz 1686).

In effect, in Leibniz's *Monadology*, each monad represents a unique perspective, and in the totality of monads, each monad has to be accepted. This can be explained via the law of sufficient reason. To my understanding, each monad or perspective stands for a unique modality and what's more, not a single perspective or modality can be partitioned by more than one monad. Otherwise, the chances for larger changes would be missed.

MacDonald Ross provides an interesting example to show this constructively infinite possibility:

> A better model of Leibniz's system would be an elaboration of the example of the cube. Computer graphics can be used to create animated film sequences representing the changing shapes and positions of imaginary objects from particular perspectives. We can imagine an infinity of such films, each from infinitesimally different viewpoints, all being run simultaneously. Even though the objects and their interactions are entirely Fictional, it will be *as if* there had been infinitely many cameras filming one and the same scene from different points of view. The simplest way of describing what they portrayed would be by

adopting that fiction, even though its only reality would be as a formula in a computer program. But although this formula would not be *real* in the sense of having a physical embodiment outside the computer, it would be *objective*. It would be the only representation not biased towards one or other perspective, and all the others could be derived from it. (MacDonald Ross 1984, p.98)

A re-discovery of Leibniz's philosophy is essential; his ideas might have been too radical to be accepted in his own age, let them not be too radical to be accepted by ours, especially with the advent of a new field, the philosophy of information.

References

Barwise J. and Seligman J. 1997. *Information Flow-The Logic of Distributed Systems*. Cambridge: Cambridge University Press.

Burkholder, L. ed, 1992. *Philosophy and the Computer*. Boulder- San Francisco-Oxford: Westview.

Couturat L.1901. *La logique de Leibniz d'après des documents inédits*, Paris, F. Alcan (reprint: Hildesheim, Olms, 1969).

Dodig-Crnkovic G. 2003. "Shifting the Paradigm of the Philosophy of Science: the Philosophy of Information and a New Renaissance", *Minds and Machines*. special issue on the Philosophy of Information, **13**: 471-501.

Dong, Guangbi. 1987. *Mathematical Structures of the Hexagrams in I-Ching*. Shanghai: Shanghai People's Press (in Chinese).

Floridi, L. 1999. *Philosophy and Computing: An Introduction*. London-New York: Routledge.

—. 2002. "What is the Philosophy of Information?" *Metaphilosophy*. special issue edited by T. W. Bynum and J. H. Moor with the title *CyberPhilosophy: The Intersection of Philosophy and Computing*. volume 33, issues 1/2, January, pp. 123-145.

—. ed, 2004a. *Blackwell Guide to the Philosophy of Computing and Information*. Oxford - New York: Blackwell.

—. 2004b. "Open Problems in the Philosophy of Information", *Metaphilosophy*. No. 4, Vol. 35, pp. 554-582.

Hughes, E. R. 1942. *The Great Learning and the Mean-in-Action*. Dent, London.

Kripke, S. A. 1963. "Semantical considerations on modal logic", *Acta Philosophica Fennica* 16.

—. 1972. "Naming and necessity", in *Semantics of Natural Language*. Ed, Herman and Davison. Dordrecht-Boston-London: Reidel.

Lewis, C. I. 1918. *A Survey of Symbolic Logic*. Berkeley: University of California Press.
Lewis, D. K. 1987. *On the Plurality of the Worlds*. Oxford-New York: Blackwell.
Moor, J. H. and Bynum B. T. 2003, *Cyberphilosophy: The Intersection of Philosophy and Computing (Metaphilosophy)*, Oxford - New York: Blackwell.
Liu, Gang. 2002. "Context, Content and Programme of the Philosophy of Information, Philosophical Trends". (Beijing, in Chinese), No. 9, pp. 17-21.
—. 2003a. From the *Philosophical Issues of Information to the Philosophy of Information, Studies in Dialectics of Nature*. (Beijing, in Chinese), No. 1, Vol. 19, pp. 45-49.
—. 2003b. "Background Shift of Science and the Philosophy of Information, Philosophical Trends". (Beijing, in Chinese), No. 12, pp.11-14.
—. 2004. "Cyberphilosophy and a Possible Foundation for the Future Oriental Philosophy of Technoscience in a Framework of Metaphilosophical Pluralism", A keynote presented at Section 4 *Modernization and Intercultural Communication in the Cyberage: A Philosophical Inquiry* held at Chinese Academy of Social Sciences on afternoon of November 20th, during the 27th General Assembly of the International Council for Philosophy and Humanistic Studies (CIPSH), International Social Sciences Council (ISSC) and Chinese Academy of Social Sciences (CASS) Meeting on Cultures and the Internet, Beijing November 19-20.
IACAP. 2005. http://www.iacap.org/history.php, accessed on the 17th January, 2005.
Leibniz, W. G. 1687. *Sämtliche Schriften und Brief*, hrsg. von der Preussischen (spatter Deutschen). Akademie der Wissenschaften zu Berlin, 1687-90.Akademie-V·BERLIN, 1970.25.
—. 1697. *Sämtliche Schriften und Brief*, hrsg. von der Preussischen (spatter Deutschen). Akademie der Wissenschaften zu Berlin, XIV, 1923 to present.
—. 1697. *Writings on China*. Daniel J. Cook and Henry Rosement, Trs. and eds, Open court, Chiago, 1994.
—. 1716. *Discours sur la théologie naturelle des Chinois (Lettre sur la philosophie chinoise à M. de Remond)*. Hannover, Niedersachsische Landersbibliothek, MS 37, 1810, no. 1. For a Chinese translation, see Pang Jing-ren (tr.) "A Letter from Leibniz to M. Remond: On the Philosophy of China", *Studies for the History of Philosophy of China*. nos., 3, pp. 20-30 and 4, pp. 89-97, 1981 and no. 1, pp. 101-107, 1982. And English translation, see Writings on China. 1994. pp. 75-138.
—. 1686. *Extracts from Leibniz*, in Appendix A Critical Exposition of the Philosophy of Leibniz. p. 205.

—. 1898. *Monadology*, Monadology. (Robert Latta tr.), in the public domain elsewhere.
Mu, Zongsan. 1997. *Fourteen Lectures on the Converging of the Oriental and Occidental Philosophies*. Shanghai: Shanghai Classics Press (in Chinese).
Malebranche, N. 1708. *Entretien d'un philosophe Chrétien et d'un philsophe chinois sur l'existence et la nature de Dieu*. (Dialogue between a Christian philosopher and a Chinese philosopher on the existence and nature of God), in Mal. OC XV.
Mungello, D. E. 1977. *Leibniz and Confucianism: The Search for Accord*. *Honolulu*: University of Hawaii Press.
—. 1999. *The Great Encounter of China and the West, 1500-1800*. New York: Rowman & Littlefield.
—. 2000. "How important of China in Leibniz's philosophy", in. Wenchao Li and Hans Poser (eds.) Leibniz and China—An International Symposium in Memory of the 300 Anniversary of the Publication of *Novissima Sinica*. Beijing Science Press (Chin. trs. Wenchao Li, et al.) pp. 44-65.
—. 2003. "European responses to non-European philosophy: China", in Daniel Garber and Michael Ayers eds., *The Cambridge History of Seventeenth-Century Philosophy*. Vol. 1.
—. 2004. Book Review on Leibniz and China: a Commerce of Light. (by F. Perkins), Notre Dame Philosophical Reviews 11.04.
Poser, H. 2000. "Leibniz's *Novissima Sinic*a and the European's Interest in China", in (Eds. Wenchao Li and Hans Poser) Leibniz and China—An International Symposium in Memory of the 300 Anniversary of the Publication of *Novissima Sinica*. Beijing Science Press (Chin. trs. Wenchao Li, et al.) pp. 1-18.
Rescher, N. 1981. *Leibniz's Metaphysics of Nature: A Group of Essays*. Dordrecht, Boston, London: Reidel.
Ross, G.M. 1984. *Leibniz*, New York: Oxford University Press.
Russell, B. 1900. *A Critical Exposition of the Philosophy of Leibniz*. London: George Allen & Unwin Ltd (reprint 1975).
—. 1930. *Introduction to Mathematical Philosophy*. Edinburgh: Neil & Co., Ltd.
—. 1955. *A History of Western Philosophy: And its Connection with Political and Social Circumstances From the Earliest Times to the Present Day*. London: George Allen and Unwin Ltd.
Swetz, F. J. 2003. "Leibniz, the Yijing, and the religious conversion of the Chinese", *Mathematics Magazine*. vol. 76, no. 4 (October), pp. 276-291.
Stegmüller W. 1986. *Hauptströmmungen der Gegenwartsphilosophie Eine Kritische Einführung*. Band II, Stuttgart: Alfred Kröner.

Wiener, N. 1948. *Cybernetics or Control and Communication in the Animal and the Machine*. 2nd ed, Cambridge, Massachusetts: MIT Press, 1961.
Youlan, F. 1948. *A Short History of Chinese Philosophy*. (Collier-Macmillan), reprinted 1997: Free Press

PART II:
ONTOLOGY

CHAPTER SEVEN

ONTOLOGY AS THE CORE DISCIPLINE OF BIOMEDICAL INFORMATICS - LEGACIES OF THE PAST AND RECOMMENDATIONS FOR THE FUTURE DIRECTION OF RESEARCH

WERNER CEUSTERS AND BARRY SMITH

1. Introduction

The automatic integration of rapidly expanding information resources in the life sciences is one of the most challenging goals facing biomedical research today. Controlled vocabularies, terminologies, and coding systems play an important role in realizing this goal, by making it possible to draw together information from heterogeneous sources – for example pertaining to genes and proteins, drugs and diseases – secure in the knowledge that the same terms will also represent the same entities on all occasions of use. In the naming of genes, proteins, and other molecular structures, considerable efforts are under way to reduce the effects of the different naming conventions which have been spawned by different groups of researchers. Electronic patient records, too, increasingly involve the use of standardized terminologies, and tremendous efforts are currently being devoted to the creation of terminology resources that can meet the needs of a future era of personalized medicine, in which genomic and clinical data can be aligned in such a way that the corresponding information systems become interoperable.

Unfortunately, however, these efforts are hampered by a constellation of social, psychological legal and other forces, whose countervailing effects are magnified by constant increases in available data and computing power. Patients, hospitals and governments are reluctant to share data; physicians are reluctant to use computerized forms in preparing patient reports; nurses, physicians and medical researchers in different specialities each insist on using their own terminologies, addressing needs which are rarely consistent with the needs of information integration.

Here, however, we are concerned with obstacles of another type, which have to do with certain problematic design choices made thus far in the development of the data and information infrastructure of biomedicine. The standardization of biomedical terminologies has for some years been proceeding apace. Standardized terminologies in biomedicine now exist in many flavours, and they are becoming increasingly important in a variety of domains as a result of the increasing importance of computers and of the need by computers for regimented ways of referring to objects and processes of different kinds. The Unified Medical Language System (UMLS), designed to *"facilitate the development of computer systems that behave as if they 'understand' the meaning of the language of biomedicine and health"* (NLM 2004), contains over 100 such systems in its MetaThesaurus (NLM 2004a), which comprehends some 3 million medical and biological terminological units. Yet very many of these systems are, as we shall see, constructed in such a way as to hamper the progress of biomedical informatics.

2. International Standard Bad Philosophy

Interestingly, and fatefully, many of the core features which serve as obstacles to the information alignment that we seek can be traced back to the influence of a single man, Eugen Wüster (1898-1977), a Viennese saw-manufacturer, professor of woodworking machinery, and devotee of Esperanto, whose singular importance turns on the fact that it was he who, in the middle of the last century, founded the technical committee devoted to terminology standardization of the International Organization for Standardization (ISO). Wüster was almost single-handedly responsible for all of the seminal documents put forth by this committee, and his ideas have served as the basis for almost all work in terminology standardization ever since.

ISO is a quasi-legal institution, in which earlier standards play a normative role in the formulation of standards which come later. The influence of Wüster's ideas has thus been exerted in ever wider circles into the present day, and it continues to make itself felt in many of the standards being promulgated by ISO not only in the realm of terminology but also in fields such as healthcare and computing.

Unfortunately these ideas, which have apparently never been subjected to criticism by those involved in ISO's work, can only be described as a kind of

International Standard Bad Philosophy. Surveying these ideas will thus provide us with some important insights into a hitherto unnoticed practical role played by considerations normally confined to the domain of academic philosophy, and will suggest ways in which a good philosophy of language can help us develop and nurture better scientific terminologies in the future.

We surmise further that Wüster's ideas, or very similar ideas which arose independently, could be embraced by so many in the fields of artificial intelligence, knowledge modelling, and nowadays in Semantic Web computing, because the simplification in our understanding of the nexus of mind, language and reality which they represent answers deep needs on the side of computer and information scientists. In subjecting Wüster's ideas to critical analysis, therefore, we shall also be making a contribution to a much larger project of exploring possibilities for improvement in the ways in which computers are used in our lives.

3. Terminologies and Concept Orientation

The thinking of ISO Technical Committee (TC) 37 is that of the so-called Vienna School of Terminology, of which Wüster (1991) and Felber (1984) are principal movement texts (for a survey see Temmerman (2000, chapter 1)). Terminology, for Wüster and Felber, starts out from what are called *concepts*. The document ISO CD 704.2 N 133 95 EN, which bears the stamp of Wüster's thinking, explains what concepts are in psychological terms. When we experience reality, we confront two kinds of objects: the concrete, such as a tree or a machine, and the abstract, such as society, complex facts, or processes:

As soon as we are confronted with several objects similar to each other (all the planets in the solar system, all the bridges or societies in the world), certain essential properties common to these objects can be identified as characteristics of the general concept. These characteristics are used to delimit concepts. On the communicative level, these concepts are described by definitions and represented by terms, graphic symbols, etc. (ISO CD 704.2 N 133 95 EN)

A concept itself, we read in the same text, is "a unity of thought made up of characteristics that are derived by categorizing objects having a number of identical properties." To understand this and the many similar sentences in 150 documents, we need to understand what is meant by 'characteristic'. On the one hand, again in the same ISO text, we are told that a characteristic is a property that we identify as common to a set of objects. In other texts of ISO, however (for example in ISO 1087-1), we are told that a characteristic is a "mental representation" of such a property. This uneasy straddling of the boundary between world and mind, between property and its mental representation, is a feature of all of ISO's work on terminology, as it was a feature of Wüster's own thinking. Terminology work is seen as providing clear delineations of concepts in terms of characteristics as thus (confusingly) defined. When such delineations have been achieved, then terms can be assigned to the corresponding concepts. Wüster talks in this connection of a 'realm' (*Reich*) of concepts and of a 'realm' of terms (Wüster 1991, p. 1), the goal being that each term in a terminology should be associated with one single concept through "permanent assignment" (Felber 1984, p. 182).

4. Problems with the Concept-Based View of Terminologies

The above should seem alien to those familiar with the domain of medicine, however, because there we often have to deal with classes of entities for which we are unable to identify characteristics which all their members share in common. Terms are often introduced for such classes of entities long before we have any clear delineation of some corresponding concept.

The reason for this miscalibration between the ISO view of terminology and the ways terms in medicine are actually used turns on the fact that the notion of concept which underlies the terminology standards of ISO TC 37 and its successors *has nothing to do with medicine at all*. As Temmerman points out (2000, p. 11), Wüster was 'an engineer and a businessman ... active in the field of standardisation' and was concerned primarily with the standardisation of *products*, entities of the sort which truly are such as to manifest characteristics identifiable in encounters of similars *because they have been manufactured as such*. Vocabulary itself is treated by Wüster and his TC 37 followers 'as if it could be standardised in the same way as types of paint and varnish' (Temmerman, p. 12).

In those areas – like manufacturing or trade – which were uppermost in the mind of Wüster and of TC37 in its early incarnations, the primary purpose of standardization is precisely to bring about a situation in which entities in reality (such as machine parts) are *required* to conform to certain agreed-upon standards. Such a requirement is of course quite alien to the world of medicine, where it is in every case the entities in reality which must serve as our guide and benchmark. However, even in medicine – for reasons which increasingly have to do not only with ISO edicts but also with the expectations of those involved in the development of software applications – terminologists have been encouraged to focus not on entities in reality but rather on the concepts putatively associated therewith. The latter, it is held, enjoy the signal advantage that they can be conveyed as input to computers. At the same time they can be identified as units of knowledge and thus serve as the basis for what is called 'knowledge modelling', a term which itself embodies what we believe is a fateful confusion of *knowledge* with the true and false *beliefs* to which, in a domain like medicine, many of the concepts in common use correspond.

Some critical remarks about certain conceptions in ISO TC 37 documents have been recently advanced (Areblad and Fogelberg 2003), and the proposed alternative certainly represents an advance on Wüster in its treatment of individual objects. As concerns what is general, however, this new work still runs together objects and concepts, identifying specific kinds or types of phenomena in the world with the general concepts created by human beings. In this way, like Wüster, it leaves itself with no benchmark in relation to which given concepts or concept-systems could be established as correct or incorrect. Moreover, it leaves no way of doing justice to the fact that bacteria would still have properties different from those of trees even if there were no humans able to form the corresponding concepts.

The Kantian Confusion

We can get at the roots of the problem of Wüsterian thinking if we examine what ISO CD 704.2 N 133 95 EN has to say about individual particulars and the proper names associated with them:

If we discover or create a singular phenomenon (individual object, e.g., the planet Saturn, The Golden Gate Bridge, the society of a certain country), we form an individual concept in order to think about that object. For communication purposes we assign *names* to individual concepts so that we can talk or write about them.

When parents assign names to their children, according to this view, and when they use such names for purposes of communication with others *they are not talking about their children at all*. Rather, they are talking about certain individual concepts which they have formed in their minds. This confusion of objects and concepts is well known in the history of philosophy. It is called "Kantianism".

Wüster and Felber and (sadly) very many of the proponents of concept-based terminology work who have followed in their wake, as also very many of those working in the field of what is called 'knowledge representation', are subject to this same Kantian confusion. One implication of the fact that one is unsure about whether one is dealing with objects or with concepts is that one writes unclearly. This, for example, is how Felber in his semi-official text on terminology (presenting ideas incorporated in relevant ISO terminology standards) defines what he calls a 'part-whole definition':

The description of the collocation of individual objects revealing their partitive relationships corresponds to the definition of concepts. Such a description may concern the composite. In this case the parts, of the composite are enumerated. It may, however, also concern a part. In this case the relationship to an individual object subordinate to the composite and the adjoining parts are indicated. (Felber, *op. cit.*, cited exactly as printed)

The Realist Alternative

The alternative to Kantianism in the history of philosophy is called realism, and we have argued in a series of papers that the improvement of biomedical terminologies and coding systems must rest on the use of a *realist ontology* as basis (Smith 2004, Fielding *et al* 2004, Simon *et al*. in press). Realist ontology is not merely able to help in detecting errors and in ensuring intuitive principles for the creation and maintenance of coding systems of a sort that can help to prevent errors in the future. More importantly still, it can help to ensure that the coding systems and terminologies developed for different purposes can be provided with a clear documentation (thus helping to avoid many types of errors), and that they can be made compatible with each other (thus supporting information integration). Note that we say '*realist ontology*' (or alternatively, with Rosse and Mejino (2003), '*reference ontology*') in order to distinguish ontology on our understanding from the various related things which go by this name in contexts such as knowledge representation and conceptual modelling.

Ontology, as conceived from the realist perspective, is not a software implementation or a controlled vocabulary. Rather, it is a theory of reality, a '*science of what is, of the kinds and structures of objects, properties, events, processes and relations in every area of reality*' (Smith 2003). It is for our purposes here a theory of those higher-level categories which structure the biomedical domain, the representation of which needs to be both unified and coherent if it is to serve as the basis for terminologies and coding systems that have the requisite degree and type of interoperability.

Ontology in this realist sense is already being used as a means of finding inconsistencies in terminologies and clinical knowledge representations such as SNOMED (Ceusters W, Smith B. 2003; Ceusters *et al.* 2004; Bodenreider et al. 2005), the Gene Ontology (Smith, Köhler and Kumar 2004), or the National Cancer Institute Thesaurus (Ceusters, Smith and Goldberg, in press). The method has also proved useful in drawing attention to certain problematic features of the HL7 RIM, more precisely on its confused running together of acts, statements about acts, and the reports in which such statements are registered (Vizenor 2004). This makes the HL7 RIM inadequate as a model for electronic patient records (so that it is to be regretted that experiments in this direction are already taking place). On the positive side, it has been embraced by the Foundational Model of Anatomy and by the Open Biomedical Ontologies Consortium as a means whereby precise formal definitions can be provided for the top-level categories and relations used in terminologies, in a way that will both support automatic reasoning and be intelligible to those with no expertise in formal methods (Smith *et al.*, 2005).

5. Formal methods for coding systems

Biomedical terminologies or coding systems can be integrated together into larger systems, or used effectively within an EHR system (which means: without loss or corruption of information), only on the basis of a shared common framework of top-level ontological categories. Often one talks in this connection merely of the sort of regimentation that can be ensured through the use of languages such as XML, or through technologies such as RDF(S) (W3C 2004) or OWL (W3C 2004a) – ontology languages that currently enjoy wide support through their association with the Semantic Web project.

On closer inspection, however, one discovers that the 'semantics' that comes with languages like RDF(S) and OWL is restricted to that sort of specification of meaning that can be effected using the formal technique of mathematical model theory. This means that meanings are specified by associating with the terms and sentences of a language certain abstract set-theoretic structures in line with the understanding of semantics that has followed in the wake of Alfred Tarski's 'semantic' definition of truth for artificial languages (Hodges n.d.). Model theory allows us to describe the minimal conditions that a world must satisfy in order for a 'meaning' (or 'interpretation' in the model-theoretic sense) to be assignable to every expression in an artificial language with certain formal properties. Unfortunately, however, entities in reality are hereby substituted by abstract mathematical constructs embodying only the properties shared in common by all such interpretations. A formal semantic theory makes as few assumptions as possible about the actual nature or intrinsic structure of the entities in an interpretation, in order to retain as much generality as possible. In consequence, however, the chief utility of such a theory is not to provide any deep analysis (or indeed any analysis at all) of the nature of the entities – for example of the biomedical kinds and instances – described by the language. Rather, the power of formal semantics resides at the logical level, above all in providing a technical way to determine which inferences are valid (Guha and Hayes 2002).

In our view, in contrast, the job of 'semantics' as this term is used in phrases such as 'semantic interoperability' is identical to that of ontology as traditionally understood. Thus it does not consist in the construction of simplified models for testing the validity of inferences. Rather, its task is to support the alignment of the different perspectives on reality embodied in different types of coding and classification systems; to this end it must provide us with a common reference framework which mirrors the structures of those entities in reality to which these different perspectives relate.

6. Basic Formal Ontology

One such reference framework, which has been developed by the Institute of Formal Ontology and Medical Information Science in Saarbrücken, is Basic Formal Ontology (BFO) (Grenon and Smith 2004, Grenon et al. 2004), one of several closely related ontological theories proposed in the recent literature of realist ontology (for a survey and comparison see Masolo et al. 2004). BFO rests on the idea that it is necessary to develop an ontology that remains as close as possible to widely shared intuitions about objects and processes in reality.

It consists in a number of sub-ontologies, the most important of which are:

• SNAP, ontologies indexed by time instants and analogous to instantaneous snapshots of what exists at a given instant

• SPAN, ontologies indexed by time intervals and analogous to videoscopic representations of the processes unfolding across a given interval

– corresponding to the fundamental division between continuants (entities, such as organisms or blood corpuscles, which endure self-identically through time), and occurrents (processes, such as heart bypass surgeries or increases in temperature, which can be divided along the temporal axis into successive phases). Each SNAP ontology is a partition of the totality of objects and their continuant qualities, roles, functions, etc., existing in a given domain of reality at a given time. Each SPAN ontology is a partition of the totality of processes unfolding themselves in a given domain across a given temporal interval. SNAP and SPAN are complementary in the sense that, while continuants alone are visible in the SNAP view and the occurrents in which they are involved are visible only in the SPAN view, continuants and occurrents themselves exist only in mutual dependence on each other.

SNAP and SPAN serve as the basis for a series of sub-ontologies at different levels of granularity reflecting the fact that the same portion of reality can be apprehended in an ontology at a plurality of different levels of coarser or finer grain from whole organisms to single molecules. What appears as a single object at one level may appear as a complex aggregate of smaller objects at another level. What is a tumour at one level may appear as an aggregate of cells or molecules at another level. What counts as a unitary process at one level may be part of a process-continuum at another level. Since no single ontology can comprehend the whole of reality at all levels of granularity, each of the ontologies here indicated is thus partial only (Kumar et al. 2004).

Dependent entities, both within the SNAP and within the SPAN ontologies, are entities which require some other entity or entities which serve as their bearers. Dependent entities can be divided further into relational (for entities – such as processes of infection – dependent on a plurality of bearers) and non-relational (for entities – such as a rise in temperature – dependent on a single bearer).

Processes are examples of dependent entities on the side of occurrents: they exist always only as processes of or in some one or more independent continuants which are their bearers. Qualities, roles, functions, shapes, dispositions, and powers are examples of dependent entities on the side of continuants: they exist always only as the qualities (etc.) of specific independent continuants as their bearers: a smile smiles only in a human face; the function of your heart exists only when your heart exists.

Universals and particulars: Entities in all categories in the BFO ontology exist both as universals and particulars. You are a particular human being, and you instantiate the universal human being; you have a particular temperature, which instantiates the universal temperature; you are currently engaging in a particular reading act, which instantiates the universal reading act. In each case we have a certain universal and an associated plurality of instances, where the term 'instance' should be understood here in a non-technical way, to refer simply to those objects, events and other entities which we find around us in the realm of space and time (and thus not, for example, to entries, records or values in databases). 'Universal', too, connotes something very simple, namely the general kinds or patterns which such particular entities have in common. Thus to talk of the universal red is just to talk of that which this tomato and that pool of ink share in common; to talk of the universal aspirin is to talk of that which these aspirin pills and those portions of aspirin powder share in common. That universals in this sense exist should be uncontroversial: it is universals which are investigated by science. It is in virtue of the existence of universals that medical diagnoses are able to be formulated by using general terms, and that corresponding standardized therapies can be tested in application to pluralities of different cases (instances) existing at different times and locations (Swoyer 1999).

Again, in part because of the influence of Wüsterian thinking, both universals and particulars have been poorly treated in biomedical terminologies and in electronic health records thus far. While biomedical terminologies ought properly to be constructed as inventories of the universals in the corresponding domains of reality (Smith et al. 2005), they have been conceived instead as representations of the concepts in peoples' heads. While electronic health records ought properly to be constructed as inventories of the instances salient to the health care of each given patient (including particular disorders, lesions, treatments, etc.), they have in fact been put together in such a way that in practice only human beings (patients, physicians, family members) are represented on the level of instances, information about all other particular entities being entered in the form of general codes – in ways which cause the problems outlined in (Ceusters and Smith 2005). Instances have also been inadequately treated in the various logical tools used in the fields of terminology and EHR. (The Tarskian approach referred to above encourages, again, the logical treatment, not of actual particular entities in corporeal reality, but rather of those abstract mathematical surrogates for such entities which are created ad hoc for the logician's technical purposes.)

Ontology and epistemology: The BFO framework distinguishes, further, between ontology and epistemology. The former is concerned with reality itself, the latter with our ways of gaining knowledge of reality. These ways of gaining knowledge can themselves be subjected to ontological treatment: they are processes of a certain sort, with cognitive agents as their continuant bearers. This fact, however, should not lead us to confuse epistemological issues (pertaining to what and how we can know) with ontological issues (pertaining to how the world is). Thus 'finding' is a term which belongs properly not to ontology but rather to epistemology, and so also do UMLS terms such as 'experimental model of disease'. It is the failure to distinguish clearly between ontology and epistemology – a failure that is comparable in its magnitude to the failure to distinguish, say, between physics and its history or between eating and the description of food) – which is at the root of the confusions in Wüster/ISO thinking, and in almost all contemporary work on terminologies and knowledge representation and which leads for example to the identification of blood pressure with result of laboratory measurement or of individual allele with observation of individual alleles.

Already a very superficial analysis of a coding system like the ICD (for: International Classification of Diseases: World Health Organization, n.d.) reveals that this system is not in fact a classification of diseases as entities in reality (Bodenreider et al. 2004). Rather it is a classification of statements on the part of a physician about disease phenomena which the physician might attribute to a patient. As an example, the ICD-10 class B83.9: Helminthiasis, unspecified does not refer (for example) to a disease caused by a worm belonging to the species unspecified (some special and hitherto uninvestigated sub-species of Acanthocephalia or Metastrongylia). Rather, it refers to a statement (perhaps appearing in some patient record) made by a physician who for whatever reason did not specify the actual type of Helminth which caused the disease the patient was suffering from. Neither OWL nor reasoners using models expressed in OWL would complain about making the class B83.9: Helminthiasis, unspecified a subclass of B83: Other helminthiasis; from the point of view of a coherent ontology, however, such a view is nonsense: it rests, again, on the confusion between ontology and epistemology.

A similar confusion can be found in EHR architectures, model specifications, message specifications or data types for EHR systems. References to a patient's gender/sex are a typical example (Milton 2004). Some specifications, such as the Belgian KMEHR system for electronic healthcare records (Kmehr-Bis, n.d.) include a classification of what is called "administrative sex" (we leave it to the reader to determine what this term might actually mean). The possible specifications of administrative sex are then female, male, unknown, or changed. Unknown, here, does not refer to a new and special type of gender (reflecting some novel scientific discovery); rather it refers merely (but of course confusingly) to the fact that the actual gender is not documented in the record.

7. An Ontological Basis for Coding Systems and the Electronic Health Record

Applying BFO to coding systems and EHR architectures means, in the first place, applying it to the salient entities in reality – to actual patients, diseases, therapies – with the goal of making coding systems more coherent, both internally and in their relation to the EHRs which they were designed to support. But it is essential to this endeavour that we establish also the proper place in reality of coding systems and EHRs themselves, and that we understand their nature and their purposes in light of a coherent ontological theory. Coding systems are in fact as real as the words we speak or write and as the patterns in our brains, and we can use the resources of a framework like BFO in order to analyze how both coding systems and EHRs relate a single reality in a way which is compatible with what is known informally by the patients, physicians, nurses, etc. toward whom they are directed.

Referent tracking is a new paradigm for achieving the faithful registration of patient data in electronic health records, focusing on what is happening on the side of the patient (Ceusters W., Smith B. 2005a) rather than on statements made by clinicians (Rector et al. 1991). The goal of referent tracking is to create an ever-growing pool of data relating to concrete entities in reality. In the context of Electronic Healthcare Records (EHRs) the relevant concrete entities, i.e. particulars as described above, are not only particular patients but also their body parts, diseases, therapies, lesions, and so forth, insofar as these are relevant to their diagnosis and treatment. Within a referent tracking system (RTS), all such entities are referred to explicitly, something which cannot be achieved when familiar concept-based systems are used in what is called "clinical coding" (Ceusters W., Smith B. 2005b).

By fostering the accumulation of prodigious amounts of instance-level data along these lines, including also considerable quantities of redundant information (since the same information about given instances will often be entered independently by different physicians), which can be used for cross-checking, the paradigm allows for a better use of coding and classification systems in patient records by minimizing the negative impact that mistakes in these systems have on the interpretation of the data.

The users who enter information in a RTS will be required to use IUIs (Instance Unique Indentifiers) in order to assure explicit reference to the particulars about which the information is provided. Thus the information that is currently captured in the EHR by means of sentences such as: "this patient has a left elbow fracture", would in the future be conveyed by means of descriptions such as "#IUI-5089 is located in #IUI-7120", together with associated information for example to the effect that "IUI-7120" refers to the patient under scrutiny or that "IUI-5089" refers to a particular fracture in patient #IUI-7120 (and not to some similar left elbow fracture from which he suffered earlier). The RTS must correspondingly contain information relating particulars to universals, such as "#IUI-5089 is a fracture" (where 'fracture' might be replaced by a unique identifier pointing to the representation of the universal fracture in an ontology). Of course, EHR systems that endorse the referent tracking paradigm should have mechanisms to capture such information in an easy and intuitive way, including mechanisms to translate generic statements into the intended concrete form, which may itself operate primarily behind the scenes, so that the IUIs themselves remain invisible to the human user. One could indeed imagine that natural language processing software will one day be in a position to replace in a reliable fashion the generic terms in a sentence with corresponding IUIs for the particulars at issue, with the need for manual support flagged only in problematic cases. This is what users already expect from EHR systems in which data are entered by resorting to general codes or terms from coding systems.

If the paradigm of referent tracking is to be brought into existence, at least the following requirements have to be addressed:
- a mechanism for generating IUIs that are guaranteed to be unique strings;
- a procedure for deciding what particulars should receive IUIs;
- protocols for determining whether or not a particular has already been

assigned a IUI (except for some exceptional configurations that are beyond the scope of this paper, each particular should receive maximally one IUI);

• practices governing the use of IUIs in the EHR (issues concerning the syntax and semantics of statements containing IUIs);

• methods for determining the truth values of propositions that are expressed through descriptions in which IUIs are used;

• methods for correcting errors in the assignment of IUIs, and for investigating the results of assigning alternative IUIs to problematic cases;

• methods for taking account of changes in the reality to which IUIs get assigned, for example when particulars merge or split.

An RTS can be set up in isolation, for instance within a single general practitioner's surgery or within the context of a hospital. The referent tracking paradigm will however serve its purpose optimally only when it is used in a distributed, collaborative environment. One and the same patient is often cared for by a variety of healthcare providers, many of them working in different settings, and each of these settings uses its own information system. These systems contain different data, but the majority of these data provide information about the same particulars. It is currently very hard, if not impossible, to query these data in such a way that, for a given particular, all information available can be retrieved. With the right sort of distributed RTS, such retrieval becomes a trivial matter.

This, in turn, will have a positive impact on the future of biomedicine in a number of different ways. Errors will be more easily eliminated or prevented via reminders or alerts issued by software agents responding to changes in the referent tracking database. It will also become possible to coordinate patient care between multiple care organisations in more efficient ways. An RTS will also do a much better job in fulfilling the goals of the ICD and its precursors, namely to enable information integration for public health. It can help specifically in the domain of disease surveillance, an area of vital concern on a global scale that has the potential not only to improve the quality of care but also to provide a means for controling costs, in particular by promoting effective cooperation among healthcare professionals for continuity of care.

8. Toward the Future

European and international efforts towards standardization of biomedical terminology and electronic healthcare records have been focused over the last 15 years primarily on syntax. Semantic standardization has been restricted to issues pertaining to knowledge representation (and resting primarily on the application of set-theoretic model theory, along the lines described in section 5. above). Moves in these directions are indeed required, and the results obtained thus far are of value both for the advance of science and for some concrete uses of healthcare informatics applications. But we can safely say that the syntactical issues are now in essence resolved. The semantic problems relating to biomedical terminology (polysemy, synonymy, cross-mapping of terminologies, and so forth), too, are well understood – at least in the community of specialized researchers. Now, however, it is time to solve these problems by using the theories and tools that have been developed so far, and that have been tested under laboratory conditions (Simon et al. 2004). This means using the right sort of ontology, i.e. an ontology that is able explicitly and unambiguously to relate coding systems, biomedical terminologies and electronic health care records (including their architecture) to the corresponding instances in reality.

To do this properly will require a huge effort, since the relevant standards need to be reviewed and overhauled by experts who are familiar with the appropriate sorts of ontological thinking (which will require some corresponding effort in training and education). Even before that stage is reached, however, there is the problem of making all constituent parties – including patients (or at least the organizations that represent them), healthcare providers, system developers and decision makers – aware of how deep-seated the existing problems are. Having been overwhelmed by the exaggerated claims on behalf of XLM and similar silver bullets of recent years, they must be informed that XML, or Descriptive Logic, or OWL, or even the entire Semantic Web, can take us only so far. And of course we must also be careful to avoid associating similarly exaggerated expectations with realist ontology itself. It, too, can take us only so far.

The message of realist ontology is that, while there are various different views of the world, this world itself is one, and that this one world, because of its immense complexity, is accessible to us only by a corresponding variety of different sorts of views. It is our belief that it is only through reference to this world that the various different views can be compared and made compatible (and not by reference to ethereal entities in some 'realm of concepts'). To allow clinical data registered in electronic patient records by means of coding (and/or classification) systems to be used for further automated processing, it should be crystal clear whether entities in the coding system refer to diseases or to statements made about diseases, to acts on the part of physicians or to documents in which such acts are recorded, to procedures and observations or to statements about procedures or observations. As such, the coding systems used in electronic healthcare records should be associated with a precise and formally rigorous ontology that is coherent with the ontology of the healthcare record as well as with those dimensions of the real world that are described therein. And they should be consistent, also, not with information models concocted by database designers from afar, but rather with the common-sense intuitions about the objects and processes in reality which are shared by patients and healthcare providers.

9. Recommendations

Concrete recommendations for further progress thus include the following:

1. Given that most existing international standards in terminology and related fields were created at a time when the requirements for good ontologies and good controlled vocabularies were not yet clear, efforts should be made to inform people of the urgent need for more up-to-date and more coherent standards.

2. The work of ISO TC 37 (on terminologies) and of the technical committees which have fallen under its sway (CEN/TC251, ISO/TC215, etc.) should be subjected to a radical evaluation from the point of view of coherence of method, intelligibility of documentation, consistency of views expressed, usability of proposed standards, methods for testing, and quality assurance.

3. Through collaboration between users and developers, objective measures should be developed for the quality of ontologies.

4. By applying these quality measures, a publicly available top-level ontology should be developed on the basis of consensus among the major groups involved in biomedical ontology development, almost all of whom are present within the EU; this top-level ontology should be complemented with extensions for biomedicine and bio-informatics.

5. Objective measures should be developed for ascertaining the quality of tools designed for the support of information integration in such a way that, when resources are invested in the development of ontologies and associated software in the future, clear thresholds of success can be formulated and corresponding standards of accountability imposed.

6. Existing terminologies and ontologies should be assessed for their compatibility with the major top-level ontologies, and efforts should be devoted to ensuring such compatibility in the future.

7. Principles should be established setting forth the appropriate use of ontologies in EHR systems, including investigations of the merits of systems which, in addition to general terms from coding systems, also incorporate reference to particulars in a systematic way.

8. The ontological mistakes in the HL7 RIM should be thoroughly

documented and modifications should be proposed to make the HL7 approach consistent with a faithful treatment of the different kinds of entities that exist in the domain of healthcare and are relevant for patient data collection and for the communication of information content between healthcare institutions.

9. A Europe-wide institution should be developed for the coordination of ontology research and knowledge transfer in order to promote high-quality work and to avoid redundancy in investment of ontology-building efforts. Open competitions should be developed which are designed to find the best methodologies for harvesting healthcare data, with real gold standards and real measures of success governing applications of the results to clinical care and public health, integration with genomics-based data to develop personalized care, integration with the data gathered by third parties, e.g. by drug companies.

10. Conclusion

We have argued that what is needed if we are to support the kind of information integration to which we all aspire is not more or better information models but rather a theory of the reality to which both coding systems and electronic health records are directed.

Applying a sound realist ontology to coding systems and to EHR architectures means in the first place ensuring that the latter are calibrated not to the denizens of Wüster's 'realm of concepts' but rather to those entities in reality – such as particular patients, diseases, therapies, surgical acts, and the universals which they instantiate – which form the subject matter of healthcare. In this way we can make coding systems more coherent, both internally and in their relation to the EHRs which they are designed to support, and externally in relation to the patients, physicians, nurses, etc. toward whom they are directed.

Acknowledgments

Work on this paper was carried out under the auspices of the Alexander von Humboldt Foundation, the EU Network of Excellence in Medical Informatics and Semantic Data Mining, and the Project "Forms of Life" sponsored by the Volkswagen Foundation.

References

Areblad, M., Fogelberg, M. 2003. "Comments to ISO TC 37 in the revision of ISO 704 and ISO 1087." CEN/TC251 WGII/N03-17 2003-08-27.
Bodenreider, O., Smith, B., Kumar, A., Burgun, A. 2005. (Forthcoming)

"Investigating subsumption in DL-based terminologies: A case study in SNOMED CT." in *Artificial Intelligence in Medicine*, forthcoming.

Bodenreider, Olivier, Smith, Barry, Burgun, Anita 2004. "The Ontology-Epistemology Divide: A Case Study in Medical Terminology", *Third International Conference on Formal Ontology* (FOIS) 2004, 185-195.

Ceusters W., Smith B., Kumar A., Dhaen C. 2004. "Mistakes in Medical Ontologies: Where Do They Come From and How Can They Be Detected? in Pisanelli DM (ed.) Ontologies in Medicine." *Proceedings of the Workshop on Medical Ontologies*, Rome October 2003. Amsterdam: IOS Press, Studies in Health Technology and Informatics, vol 102, 145–64.

Ceusters W., Smith, B. 2003. "Ontology and Medical Terminology: Why Descriptions Logics are not enough", *Proceedings of the Conference Towards an Electronic Patient Record* (TEPR 2003), San Antonio, 10-14 May 2003 (electronic publication).

Ceusters W., Smith, B. 2005a. "Referent Tracking in Electronic Healthcare Records." Accepted for MIE 2005, Geneva, 28-31 Augustus 2005.

Ceusters W., Smith B. 2005b. Strategies for Referent Tracking in Electronic Health Records. (Download draft). *Proceedings of IMIA WG6 Conference on "Ontology and Biomedical Informatics."* Rome, Italy, 29 April - 2 May 2005. (in press).

Felber, H. 1984. *Terminology Manual*. Unesco: International Information Centre for Terminology (Infoterm), Paris.

Fielding, James M., Simon, Jonathan, Ceusters, Werner and Smith, Barry. 2004. "Ontological Theory for Ontological Engineering: Biomedical Systems Information Integration", *Proceedings of the Ninth International Conference on the Principles of Knowledge Representation and Reasoning* (KR2004), Whistler, BC, 2-5 June 2004, 114-120.

Grenon, Pierre and Smith, Barry. 2004. "SNAP and SPAN: Towards Dynamic Spatial Ontology." *Spatial Cognition and Computation*. 4: 1, 69–103.

Grenon, Pierre, Smith, Barry and Goldberg, Louis. 2004. "Biodynamic Ontology: Applying BFO in the Biomedical Domain." in D. M. Pisanelli ed, *Ontologies in Medicine: Proceedings of the Workshop on Medical Ontologies*, Rome October 2003, Amsterdam: IOS Press, 20–38.

Guha R.V., Hayes P. 2002. "LBase: Semantics for Languages of the Semantic Web. NOT-A-Note." 02 Aug 2002: (http://www.coginst.uwf.edu/~phayes/LBase-from-W3C.html)

Hodges, Wilfrid. n.d. "Model Theory." *Stanford Encyclopedia of Philosophy* (http://plato.stanford.edu/entries/model-theory/).

ISO 2002 ISO 18308: Health Informatics – Requirements for an Electronic Health Record Architecture: (http://www.iso.ch/iso/en/CatalogueDetailPage.CatalogueDetail?CSNUMB

ER=33397).

Jonathan Simon, James Fielding, Mariana Dos Santos, Barry Smith. "Reference Ontologies for Biomedical Ontology Integration and Natural Language Processing." *International Journal of Medical Informatics*, in press.

Kmehr-Bis. n.d. "Kind Messages for Electronic Healthcare Record, Belgian Implementation Standard." (http://www.chu-charleroi.be/kmehr/htm/kmehr.htm).

Kumar, Anand, Smith, Barry and Novotny, Daniel. 2004. "Biomedical Informatics and Granularity." *Comparative and Functional Genomics*, 5, 501–508.

Masolo C., Borgo S., Gangemi A., Guarino N., Oltramari A. 2004. *WonderWeb Deliverable D18: Ontology Library* (http://wonderweb.semanticweb.org/deliverables/documents/D18.pdf).

Milton, Simon K. 2004. "Top-Level Ontology: The Problem with Naturalism." in Achille Varzi and Laure Vieu eds, *Formal Ontology and Information Systems. Proceedings of the Third International Conference* (FOIS 2004), Amsterdam: IOS Press, 2004, 85–94.

NLM (National Library of Medicine.) 2004. UMLS fact sheet, updated 7 May 2004 (http://www.nlm.nih.gov/pubs/factsheets/umls.html).

—. 2004a. UMLS MetaThesaurus fact sheet, updated 7 May 2004. (http://www.nlm.nih.gov/pubs/factsheets/umlsmeta.html).

Rector AL, Nolan WA, and Kay S. "Foundations for an Electronic Medical Record". *Methods of Information in Medicine* 30: 179-86, 1991.

Rosse, C. and Mejino, J. L. V. Jr. 2003. "A Reference Ontology for Bioinformatics: The Foundational Model of Anatomy." *Journal of Biomedical Informatics*, 36:478–500.

Simon, Jonathan, Fielding, James M. and Smith, Barry. 2004. "Using Philosophy to Improve the Coherence and Interoperability of Applications Ontologies: A Field Report on the Collaboration of IFOMIS and L&C", in Gregor Büchel, Bertin Klein and Thomas Roth-Berghofer eds, *Proceedings of the First Workshop on Philosophy and Informatics*. Deutsches Forschungszentrum für künstliche Intelligenz, Cologne, 65–72.

Smith, Barry, Köhler, Jacob, Kumar, Anand. 2004. "On the Application of Formal Principles to Life Science Data: a Case Study in the Gene Ontology," In: Erhard Rahm ed, : *Data Integration in the Life Sciences, First International Workshop*, DILS 2004, Leipzig, Germany, March 25-26, 2004, (Lecture Notes in Computer Science 2994), Springer, 79–94.

Smith, Barry, Werner Ceusters, Bert Klagges, Jacob Köhler, Anand Kumar, Jane Lomax, Chris Mungall, Fabian Neuhaus, Alan Rector, Cornelius Rosse 2005. "Relations in Biomedical Ontologies", *Genome Biology*, 2005, 6 (5), R46.

Smith, Barry. 2003. "Ontology." in Luciano Floridi ed, *Blackwell Guide to the Philosophy of Computing and Information*, Oxford: Blackwell, 155–166.

Swoyer, Chris 1999 "How Ontology Might be Possible: Explanation and Inference in Metaphysics." *Midwest Studies in Philosophy*, 23, 1999; 100–131.

Temmerman R. 2000. "Towards New Ways of Terminology Description." Amsterdam: John Benjamins.

Vizenor, Lowell 2004 "Actions in Health Care Organizations: An Ontological Analysis." *Proceedings of MedInfo* 2004, San Francisco, 1403–10.

W3C 2004 "RDF Semantics." W3C Recommendation 10 February 2004 (http://www.w3.org/TR/rdf-mt/).

—. 2004a. "OWL Web Ontology Language Semantics and Abstract Syntax." W3C Recommendation 10 February 2004 (http://www.w3.org/TR/owl-semantics/).

Werner Ceusters and Barry Smith. 2005. "Tracking Referents in Electronic Health Records." *Medical Informatics Europe* (MIE 2005), Geneva.

Werner Ceusters, Barry Smith, Louis Goldberg. In press. "A Terminological and Ontological Analysis of the NCI Thesaurus." *Methods of Information in Medicine*.

World Health Organisation n.d. ICD-10 - *The International Statistical Classification of Diseases and Related Health Problems*. tenth revision (http://www.who.int/whosis/icd10/).

Wüster, E. 1991. *Einführung in die allgemeine Terminologielehre und terminologische Lexikographie*. Bonn: Romanistischer Verlag, Germany.

CHAPTER EIGHT

FUNCTIONS AND PROTOTYPES

KATHERINE MUNN

1. Function in Biomedical Information Systems

Biomedical information systems have the task of representing the knowledge that is acquired by experts in domains of biology and medicine. This knowledge pertains to types or classes of entities, such as molecules and proteins, and to types or classes of relations, such as parthood and subsumption. Information systems represent this knowledge in the form of lists of terms that refer to these types or classes. These lists are arranged into taxonomical hierarchies called ontologies.

The term function has wide currency in biomedical ontologies, yet its meaning is often unclear (see Smith, et al., 2005). One sense of function which is particularly unclear is the notion of a role within a biological system. This notion is appealed to for example by the National Library of Medicine's clinical resource, Medical Subject Headings (MeSH), which describes function as "used…with biochemical substances, endogenously produced, for their physiologic role". Unfortunately MeSH offers no indication of how "role" is to be understood in the physiological domain. We must garner clues from its usage of this term in the domain of behavioral science. Under the heading behavior and behavior mechanisms it describes role as an "expected and characteristic pattern of behavior". A related characteristic of "function" in its role sense comes to light when MeSH uses function language to describe what a particular part of the organism is for, as in its description of ovary: "In vertebrates, the ovary contains two functional parts: the ovarian follicle for the production of female germ cells…and the endocrine cells…for the production of estrogens and progesterone".

In these examples, MeSH's "role" notion of function incorporates two characteristics. First, it is carried out in relation to a biological system. Second, it is associated with a pattern of actions that may be performed repeatedly, justifying the claim that items which engage in such actions do so because that is what they are for. This notion of function is normative: any statement incorporating it presupposes, implicitly or explicitly, a normative standard. This standard provides the context within which statements such as "X is functioning well", or "X is doing what it is for", are to be understood. It provides justification for the claim that X is for pumping blood and not for causing leukaemia to be spread throughout the body. It tells us, in other words, with respect to what X functions well. Thus bioinformatics, in order to represent the meaning of function statements fully and accurately, must specify the normative standards to which they make appeal.

2. Functions and Normativity

Functions in the role sense admit of normative statements of two sorts: (a) statements based on subjective norms, such as "that was a lovely catalysis"; and (b) statements based on statistical norms, such as "that was a typical catalysis". But they also admit of a third sort: (c) "his heart performs its function particularly well". To what sort of norm do such statements appeal?

Although such statements sometimes do appeal to statistical norms and to subjective standards, they need not. "His heart pumps well" might simply mean that his heart causes his blood to circulate in a way that, all else being equal and barring any unforeseen contingencies, it will contribute to his staying alive for the long-term future. No statistical group need be referred to, and the standard in question is not subjective but physiological.

It is thus possible for standards of measurement to exist in objective reality, even if the norms that we attach to these standards may not. Johansson (2004) points out a similarity between function concepts and metric scales. Metric scales use units as reference points for comparing values such as length or weight. These units exist objectively, even though the precise length of a meter is determined culturally. Similarly, function concepts are often used to compare how effectively an object performs a process with how effectively it could perform it. The ideal performance of that process (e.g. the blood-pumping that would best contribute to long-term survival) is used as a standard to which actual performances may be compared. The contribution to survival made by blood-pumping exists objectively, even if descriptions such as "well" or "poorly" are language-dependent. Johansson calls the ideal a "prototypical standard unit" (111).

One objective standard has been mentioned: contribution to long-term survival. Another example is the persistence of the organism's species. This paper will offer a theory for analyzing such objective normative statements. It will claim that statements such as "X functions well", when made with respect to physiological processes, make an implicit comparison between X and a prototype for Xs, where a prototype is an objectively existing entity.

The goal of this paper is not the analysis of statements about normative functioning, but a metaphysical theory of the entities to which such statements make reference. This distinction is important, for the subject matter of biomedical informatics is not statements, but the entities to which biology and medicine pertain. The closer a bioinformation system comes to representing those entities as they are, the more effective it will be in furthering the ends of the scientists who use it.

3. The Architects' Conception of Prototypes

The notion of prototype is most commonly associated with Eleanor Rosch and cognitive linguistics (see Rosch 1983, Tversky 1982), but its history, sketched by Hennig (2005), dates to classical Greek philosophy, where it is used in a very different way. One of the most important differences is that Rosch's notion of prototype denotes a concept in our minds, whereas the classical notion of prototype denotes an entity in the world.

Proto means first. Typos means (1) the act of impressing something (such as a seal) into a surface (such as wax), (2) the impression or image thereby produced, or (3) exemplar, sketch, or form. Hennig outlines two similar conceptions of prototype originating in classical Greek philosophy; the one which he calls the "architects' conception" is the most relevant here.

On this conception, derived from Plato (1996), a prototype is a three-dimensional scale model of a building, which builders employ as a reference when they construct the actual edifice. This prototype is itself built following a two-dimensional design or blueprint, which is called an archetype. Both the prototype and the archetype are representations of the design conceived in the mind of the architect.

The prototype thus factors into the cause of the building's coming into being. It is not an efficient cause in the Aristotelian sense (see 1984): it does not lay down mortar and brick. Rather, it provides a pattern for those who do lay down mortar and brick. It is a plan, or a representation, existing prior to the building itself, that determines what the building ought to look like when it is finished. The completed edifice may be compared to the prototype, and the builders' work judged according to how well they followed the plan. Building a house is a goal-directed process, and the prototype is a representation of the goal, or end state, toward which the process of building is directed.

But the notion of prototype is not limited to the building of artifacts; it first appears in classical descriptions of how the gods fashioned men and animals. In classical philosophy, and in this paper, a prototype can be compared to a scale model, or design, specifying the qualities that a finished product, or creature, should have. Thus only those entities which come about through goal-directed processes have prototypes. There are two kinds of entities that fit this description, although each in a different way: artifacts, which are generated by processes directed externally to them; and organisms, which develop by means of processes directed from within themselves. Because this paper's main interest is biological functions, it will concentrate on the latter.

4. Goal-directed Processes in Nature

Mechanistic philosophers bristle at any mention of goal-directedness in nature, for they associate it with some variation of the supernaturalist theory of vitalism, the belief that a vital force, whose cause is not governed by physico-chemical laws, pervades all parts of organisms and disappears when they die. Traditional Cartesian mechanism, with its exclusive commitment to physico-chemical causes as well as to explanatory reduction of biological phenomena to causes operating at the lowest systemic levels, has been the dominant assumption especially since the beginning of the 20th century.

However, biologists are increasingly arguing that the traditional mechanistic view does not adequately explain phenomena in the organic world (see Mayr 1988, Gilbert and Sarkar 2000, Webster and Goodwin 1996, Tsikolia 2006). They do not dispute that biological phenomena have material causes. What they call into question is whether biological phenomena at higher levels can be explained only in terms of physico-chemical phenomena occurring at the lowest levels.

They argue that the statement "the heart pumps and blood circulates" does not capture the entire content of the statement "the heart pumps in order to circulate blood". But the reason for this has nothing to do with the linguistic content of statements. It has to do with the facts which such statements assert. On this view, "the heart pumps in order to circulate blood" states a fact about the heart's pumping which is different from that stated by "the heart pumps and blood circulates". In other words, there is a fact of the matter about the goal of the heart's pumping. If this claim sounds dubious, it is because it is difficult to express without reliance upon metaphorical language, such as "goal", or upon language that implies the intentions of thinking agents, such as "in order to". Our language's awkwardness at describing goal-directedness in other ways is unfortunate, and stems from the historical contingencies of its development. But it would be wrong to conclude on the basis of our language alone that no other kind of goal-directedness exists.

The challenge to biologists who observe goal-directedness in nature is to explain it in materialist terms. To this end Mayr suggests the term teleonomy. A teleonomic process, on Mayr's definition, has two characteristics (1988, 46): "[i]t is guided by a 'program,' and it depends on the existence of some endpoint, goal, or terminus which is foreseen in the program that regulates the behavior." The notion of teleonomy is fitting as a naïve description of organic processes, but must acquire flesh through the definition of the terms, such as "program" and "goal", upon which it relies.

Mayr cashes out "program" in terms of an organism's genotype, citing the facts that the latter specifies the qualities that the fully developed phenotype is to have, and that it is causally effective in bringing about the processes by which the organism will develop according to specification. However, Webster and Goodwin (1996) have cautioned against singling out DNA as the sole guiding force behind morphological development. They point out that talk of genes "guiding" or "directing" developmental processes is merely metaphorical, and veils complexities to which an array of embryological and other experiments has called attention. Webster and Goodwin suggest that possession of a genome of a certain type is probably a necessary condition for the occurrence in general of developmental processes, but that talk of this genome "guiding" or "directing" specific goal-directed processes is misleading and simplistic. They believe that goal-directedness in organisms can only be accounted for by an entirely new theory of morphogenesis, which they develop in great detail (1996).

Whatever theoretical structure one accepts to account for goal-directed processes in organisms, there is widespread agreement among biologists that this goal-directedness exists as such and requires explanation. This paper attempts to aid efforts to provide such explanation, by providing a metaphysical theory of prototypes to undergird it.

5. Prototypes

The following is based on the metaphysical view that universals exist in objective reality. A universal, such as blueness or lizard, is an abstract entity that provides the metaphysical correlate to a natural kind. When a particular belongs to a natural kind, it thereby instantiates a universal. When two particulars belong to the same kind, they both instantiate the same universal. A rough corollary in information science is a class into which entities are categorized; but whereas classes reflect our cognitive partitions of the world, universals exist outside and independently of those partitions.

There are property universals, such as softness, and substance universals, such as organism or woman (see e.g. Armstrong 1989). Property universals are instantiated by single traits or qualities which depend for their existence upon other entities which bear them (a lizard's skin bears the color green). Substance universals are instantiated by entities which do not depend upon other entities in this way (the lizard is not dependent upon the color of its skin). Substance universals are complex, incorporating a combination of property universals, but they are not reducible to these property universals.

On the present theory, some substance universals are prototypes: "prototype" is the name for a certain subset of substance universals. This subset consists of substance universals whose instances come into being through goal-directed processes. The only universals that meet this criterion are artifacts, organisms, and other organic entities (such as cells or tissues). The goal of these processes is to instantiate the prototype. Thus a house is built by processes which are directed externally by human beings, who have the goal of making the house look just like its blueprint. In a similar fashion, an organism develops by means of processes which are directed, by mechanisms within the organism itself, toward the goal of making an organism of a certain kind. We have seen that, although there is disagreement as to how these internal goal-directed processes in organisms can be explained, it is nonetheless widely agreed that organisms do develop according to such processes. On the theory to be advanced here, the "goal" toward which such processes are directed is the prototype itself.

Although prototypes (like all universals) exist in the abstract, it is possible to represent them graphically, in writing, or in some other way. Examples of such representations include blueprints, instruction manuals for putting together bicycles, or, in the case of organisms, in DNA (Mayr 1988) or in morphogenetic fields (Webster and Goodwin 1996).

Substance Universals are Underdetermined

Universals of the same kind form taxonomies. Each taxonomy can be represented by a mathematical tree, whose nodes correspond to universals of greater and lesser determinacy. For example, color is a universal at the root of a tree whose nodes include universals for various specific shades, such as blueness, greenness, and so forth. A particular instantiates the most determinate universal on the tree (e.g. blue #1456), and it thereby instantiates as well every node we encounter in moving vertically up the tree (including blue and color). Thus highly general universals, such as color, have many more instantiations than highly specific ones, such as blue #1456.

It is relatively simple to construct trees for property universals, for each such universal is instantiated only by one kind of trait (a color, a texture, a sound). However, the picture quickly becomes complicated in representing substance universals (which include prototypes). For each substance has a vast amount of qualities. Picture an almost infinite number of mathematical trees lined up next to one another, one for each kind of trait that a substance instantiates. This kind of representation is an oversimplification, but it conveys to some extent the complex nature of substance universals.

One reason why this picture is an oversimplification is this: many substance universals leave many traits unspecified. In the same way that the universal color has more instances than the universal blue #1456, the universal organism has many more instances than the universal male ocelot. Organism is extremely unspecified, and can be instantiated by anything from a prokaryote to a giraffe. Even substance universals which are more specific, such as human male, leave many traits unspecified (such as eye color).

Prototypes are More Specified than Most Other Universals

Another reason why the above picture is an oversimplification is that it does not distinguish those traits which belong essentially to the substance in question: those traits which are such that, without them, an entity cannot instantiate the universal in question. It is fairly safe to say that aliveness is a trait which is necessarily instantiated by every organism. But what about traits, such as having eyes, which are shared in common by most cats? We would hardly say that a cat without eyes is no longer an instantiation of the universal cat. Yet precisely because this cat is significantly different from other members of its natural kind, we intuitively regard it somehow as a less complete instantiation of that universal – because there is an important way in which it does not match the blueprint for cat. In other words, although it does instantiate the universal cat, it does not instantiate the prototype cat.

We have seen that there are more instantiations of general universals than there are of specific ones. Thus, although this patch of blue does not instantiate the property universal blue#1456, it does instantiate blue. Similarly, although a cat without eyes instantiates the universal cat, which at its most general level does not specify having eyes as essential, it does not instantiate a more specified level of this universal at which having eyes belongs, in a non-essential way, to the natural kind cat.

Just what constitutes an essential property, and how it differs from a non-essential property, is a deep question which cannot be addressed here (but see Webster and Goodwin 1996). What matters here is that they are different. The instantiation of a substance universal must have the essential properties, whereas the instantiation of a prototype must have many of the non-essential ones as well. A prototype is thus a universal of a certain level of specificity.

To imagine this, recall our representation of a substance universal as a series of mathematical trees lined up next to each other, with the most general universals as roots and the more specific ones branching off into nodes. Each tree represents a different property universal, such as color or sex, and each property belonging to the substance universal is represented by such a tree.

Some trees represent properties that are essential for the substance's instantiating a certain kind (such as aliveness for the universal woman), and some are non-essential (such as brown for lion). Let us stipulate that aliveness comes in different levels which can be represented on a tree, such as physical aliveness and mental aliveness, the latter being a specification of the former. All that is essential for the universal woman is physical aliveness, for a comatose woman is still a woman. The prototype woman, however, is more specified: it is not instantiated by a comatose woman. A similar situation arises with the universal brown, which is a specification on the tree representing color. The prototype lion is instantiated as brown. But instantiating this color is not essential for a lion; an albino lion is still a lion. What is essential to a lion is that it instantiate some color. Thus the universal lion has some color, whereas the prototype lion is specifically brown.

But this is also an oversimplification. Often prototypes specify not a specific trait (such as brown #8476), but a range of traits. For example, I said above that the prototype for lion specifies brownness. But probably closer to the truth is that it specifies any number of brownish shades, ranging from blackish- to reddish-brown. Thus prototypes are, themselves, often underspecified. Nonetheless, they are more specified than most universals.

Let us return to our row of mathematical trees which represents all of the properties a substance universal has. What emerges in this visual representation is this: If we circle the nodes on each tree which correspond to the prototype, and connect them to all of the other circled nodes by a horizontal line crossing through all of the trees, and if we do the same with the nodes corresponding to the other, more general, universals, what results is two jagged lines which may have points in common but which never cross over one another.

Prototypes Instantiated

Because prototypes often specify a range of traits rather than a specific trait, it is conceivable for two particulars to differ from one another and yet instantiate the same prototype. Thus the prototype horse specifies neither maleness nor femaleness; all it specifies is that the instance have some determinate sex. Even though an androgynous horse instantiates the universal horse, it does not instantiate the prototype horse.

We saw that an entity may instantiate a universal without instantiating the prototype of that universal. It is also possible for a prototype to be instantiated to differing degrees. Of two albino lions which are identical except that one has no tail and the other has no tail and a sixth toe, neither instantiates the prototype, but the former instantiates it to a higher degree than the latter. However, of two albino lions which are identical except that one has no tail and the other has no ear, it is difficult to say which comes closer to instantiating the prototype. For neither tails nor ears are essential properties, and it seems that any decision as to whether one is somehow "more essential" would be arbitrary. The current theory of prototypes thus needs to be completed by a theory of essential and non-essential properties.

Recall that prototypes are unique among universals in this: their instances come into being through goal-directed processes, of which the prototype itself is the goal. A house built exactly according to specification is a perfect rendering of its blueprint. Similarly, an entity which exactly instantiates its prototype is a perfect rendering of its natural kind. The questions of just which qualities are specified by the prototype, how narrowly it specifies them, and therefore what constitutes perfection for a certain kind, can only be answered, again, by a theory of essential and non-essential properties. One thing, however, is clear: two entities can be canonical and yet differ. The reason for this is, as we have seen, that for many properties, prototypes do not specify one quality in particular but rather a range of qualities.

6. Conclusion

This paper has sketched a metaphysical theory of prototypes, the entities to which statements about normative functions as "roles" in biomedicine implicitly refer. When an item is said to be functioning "well", this is always with respect to the perfect functioning of a canonical instance of its kind. An instance is canonical when it has all of the traits specified by its prototype.

Prototypes are not concepts existing in our minds, but abstract entities existing in reality. They comprise a subset of substance universals, and are distinguished from other universals in that they are instantiated by particulars which develop according to goal-directed processes. Such particulars include artifacts and organisms. A prototype can be compared to a blueprint which specifies the way in which an artifact or organism should develop.

The theory of prototypes advanced here explains what prototypes are, but it does not explain why they are as they are. It claims that prototypes specify the essential and the non-essential properties which particulars must have in order to belong to natural kinds, but it does not explain what makes a property essential or non-essential. Nor does it explain why particulars have the non-essential traits that they do. The present theory thus needs to be complemented by a theory of essential and non-essential properties.

A theory of prototypes is important for biomedical ontologies. The reason is that such ontologies contain information not about specific instances, but about classes or types (Smith, et al., 2005). Ontologies such as the Foundational Model of Anatomy (Rosse, et al., 1998) deal with canonical instances, which are, in the language of this paper, representations of what a perfect instance of a prototype would be. In order to speak accurately and informatively about what particular items do when they perform a function, it is necessary to appeal to what they are supposed to do, to what they are for. The prototype theory advanced here provides a metaphysical basis for making claims about types and canonical instances.

Acknowledgments

This paper was written under the auspices of the Wolfgang Paul Program of the Alexander von Humboldt Foundation, and the Project Forms of Life sponsored by the Volkswagen Foundation.

References

Aristotle. 1984. *Metaphysics*. In *The complete works of Aristotle*, edited by John Barnes. Princeton: Princeton University Press.
Armstrong, David. 1989. *Universals: an opinionated introduction*. Boulder: Westview Press.
Gilbert, Scott F., and Sahotra Sarkar. 2000. "Embracing complexity: organicism for the 21st century". *Developmental Dynamics* 219:1–9.

Hennig, Boris. 2005. "Prototypesetting". Paper presented at the Institute for Formal Ontology and Medical Information Science, March 21, in Saarbrücken, Germany.

Johansson, Ingvar. 2004. "Functions, function concepts and scales." *The Monist* 87:1:96-114.

Mayr, Ernst. 1988. *Toward a new philosophy of biology*. Cambridge and London: Harvard University Press.

National Library of Medicine, National Institutes of Health. Medical Subject Headings (MeSH), http://www.nlm.nih.gov/mesh/meshhome.html (September 2005).

Plato. 1996. *Timaeus*. In *Plato: collected dialogues*, edited by Edith Hamilton and Huntington Cairns. Princeton: Princeton University Press.

Rosch, E. 1983. "Prototype classification and logical classification: the two systems." In *New Trends in Cognitive Representations: Challenges to Piaget's Theory*. Edited by Ellin Kofsky Scholnick. Hillsdale, NJ: Lawrence Erlbaum Associates.

Rosse, C., L. G. Shapiro, and J. F. Brinkley. 1998. "The digital anatomist foundational model: principles for defining and structuring its concept domain." In *Proceedings, American Medical Informatics Association Fall Symposium*.

Smith, Barry, Werner Ceusters, Jacob Köhler, Anand Kumar, Jane Lomax, Chris Mungall, Fabian Neuhaus, Alan Rector, and Cornelius Rosse. 1995. "Relations in biomedical ontologies." *Genome Biology* 6:5:R46.

Tsikolia, Nikoloz. 2006. "The role and limits of a gradient based explanation of morphogenesis: a theoretical consideration." *International Journal of Developmental Biology* 50:333-340.

Tversky, A., and D. Kahneman. 1982. *Judgments of and by representativeness. In Judgment Under Uncertainty: Heuristics and Biases*. Edited by D. Kahneman D, P. Slovic, and A. Tversky. New York: Cambridge University Press.

Webster, Gerry, and Brian Goodwin. 1996. *Form and transformation*. Cambridge: Cambridge University Press.

CHAPTER NINE

KNOWLEDGE IN ACTION[1]

RUTH HAGENGRUBER AND UWE V. RISS

Abstract

The study starts form the insight that knowledge is essentially related to action. This implies specific requirement concerning the dynamics knowledge which dissents from the widespread view of a static nature of knowledge reflected in the image of explicit knowledge. The gap between universal explications and particular action contexts is bridged by the implicit knowledge of the respective agent. It is argued that explications are described in terms of relational patterns that possess a specific ambit of validity. Transgression of these domains calls for a rearrangement of relations. Rearrangements are described as pointed selection proc-esses based on the agents' experience identifying stable relations in their interaction with the world.

---

[1] We take the term 'implicit knowledge' instead of Polanyi's term 'tacit knowledge'.
As an example he took the finger with which we point at an object and regarded the difference between the awareness of the finger with that of the object. Polanyi describes this as follows: "To integrate a thing B into bearing on some C, amounts to endowing B with a meaning that points at C. An obvious way to do this is to choose as B a finger pointing at C. Suppose a lecturer points his finger at an object, and tells the audience: 'Look at this!' The audience will follow the pointing finger and look at the object....This directive, or vectorial way of attending to the pointing finger, I shall call our subsidiary awareness of the finger...A meaningful relation of the subsidiary to the focal is formed by the action of a person who integrates one to the other, and the relation persists by the fact that the person keeps up this integration. ...[In] general terms, the triad of tacit knowing consists of subsidiary things (B) bearing on a focus (C) by virtue of an integration performed by a person (A). ...we attend from one or more subsidiaries to a focus on which the subsidiaries are to bear." (Polanyi 69: 181/182)

1. Introduction

One of the driving forces behind knowledge management (KM) has been the idea to provide methods that transform human knowledge into machine representations. The core task herein consists in transforming implicit practical into external propositional knowledge and vice versa (Nonaka and Takeuchi 95). However, this concept of KM has not yet been as satisfactory as expected. In our opinion one major reason for this failure is the neglect of the relation between these two concepts in particular concerning processive aspects. In particular representing processive elements requires an explanation of how it is possible to switch from implicit to explicit knowledge. In this paper we show how to deal with this switch. First, we are convinced that both concepts are closely related, i.e., they affect action in a similar way. The representational switch of knowledge is action dependent. Second: Changes in explicit knowledge are related to rearrangements of subsidiaries. We will call them 'patterns'. Third: This rearrangement is a process of approximation to reality. We try to increase the comprehension of the gap between 'implicit' and 'explicit' knowledge in order to deepen the understanding of interdependence of knowing and acting.

The paper is organized as follows. In section 2 we will discuss the question whether knowledge can be understood as a resource that can be arbitrarily exploited. This will lead us to the consideration of dynamic aspects of knowledge in section 3. Here we dissent from this widespread opinion and indicate those aspects of knowledge that suggest a more dynamic view of knowledge. In section 4 we will turn to the distinction of implicit and explicit knowledge and their relevance for this dynamical character. In section 5 we will discuss the influence of this dynamics on explications of knowledge. In particular we will deal with the question how the latter can cope with the dynamic requirements and consider the process of rearrangement of explications. The latter point is deepened in section 6 where we will consider the specific structure of explications. In section 7 we will give a final discussion and emphasize those points of the study which are relevant for an automatic processing of explications of knowledge, e.g., as usual in KM.

2. Knowledge as a Resource?

Philosophical tradition provides famous examples how knowledge is put forth, e.g. in Plato's dialogue Meno. Here Socrates asserts that all knowledge is already within us. Reasoning can be seen as a sort of explication. Thus Socrates asks Meno, an uneducated slave, to draw a square with twice the area of that one he has drawn. Initially Meno fails, but under further questioning by Socrates he starts to develop the answer on the basis of the knowledge that he already possesses. Socratic maieutic technique has enabled the uneducated slave to do mathematics.

KM has to accomplish a similar task. Also here knowledge, which is only indirectly available, must be unfolded. In particular it must be adapted to the specific situation of the person who relies on it. We can relate this task to the following question: How can we formally store knowledge, the relevance of which is not clear at the moment it is stored? In the following we will discuss that the "now knowing" of Meno is nothing else but a rearrangement of the elements (entities), he already knows, where the rearrangement is lead by Socrates. The recombination of the respective elements is based on a certain kind of logic and requires that the pattern is permanently aligned with a goal that we want to achieve. Socrates had this goal and he used it to combine the entities in a way that enabled Meno to succeed.

We can see this as a paragon for the way how we have to deal with knowledge in order to make reasonable use of it. Thus Socrates argues in this example that he has not taught Meno anything that the servant did not already know. This contradicts the wide-spread assumption of knowledge as a resource that is to be transferred from one source to arbitrary recipients and turn the attention to the active process of knowledge transfer leading to the question how we can adaptable knowledge from a static source. In the following we want to cast some light on these questions. We show that application of knowledge requires a continuous adaptation which partly takes place implicitly.

3. Static versus Dynamic Knowledge

Asking for the nature of knowledge many researchers and philosophers have seen it in a close relation to action (Polanyi 62, Tsoukas 01, Wiig 05, Riss 05). However, it is still an open question how knowledge is related to action. In (Riss 05) we have argued that knowledge describes the capability of an agent to control an action leading it to its successful end. Actions cannot be accomplished without knowledge and knowledge without reference to action is not controllable. Here we understand action as realization of knowledge applied to a specific section of reality. Doing so knowledge cannot be regarded as static but varies with the respective action.

The inappropriateness of the separation of knowledge and action results from the fact that there is no knowledge outside action. Of course, we often refer to knowledge in the sense of static explications, e.g., scientific formulae or theories, which seem to be independent of any action. They might be read as action independent laws. However, such laws express expectations of stable relational connections reflected in their successful application (Riss 05). They do not imply the actual success since particular circumstances can frustrate the planned execution. This finally raises the question how static representations can measure up to the process character of knowledge.

We have to assert that knowledge explications are just as little knowledge as hammers are tools without a person who uses them appropriately. In this respect we can revert to the investigations of Michael Polanyi who stated that all explicit knowledge must be rooted in implicit knowledge, which bridges the gap between explication and action. Implicit knowledge determines the production of behaviors and the constitution of mental states but it is not propositionally expressible, or as Polanyi described it: 'we can know more than we can tell' (Polanyi 66: 4). To explain the role of implicit knowledge he took the example of a map which only obtains a knowledgeable character by the person who reads and uses it appropriately (Polanyi 62: 18-20).

Knowledge explications are generally dealing with entities, which are not unfolded further. In sentences these are the words, in formulae the included symbols. It is assumed that the agent who deals with these explications can already cope with these entities and the relations that are evolved between them. For the map this means that entities describe localities that the agent can identify in her actual surroundings and which are related to other entities, i.e., localities, by indicating the distance and direction in which the agent must go to reach them. The knowledge character of a map is based on the fact that the agent relies on her implicit knowledge how to identify the localities in reality and to integrate the provided entities and relations to new implicit knowledge that allows her to physically reach the localities she aims at.

Coming back to the expectation character of knowledge we see that by their very nature expectations are universal in the sense that they must fit to various situations. An instance of knowledge does not only correspond to an individual action but to a variety of actions. If I know how to perform an action successfully and meet a situation that is similar enough to the previous one, I am likely to accomplish this action, too. In contrast to expectations real situations are particular, characterized by an infinite number of clues that might influence any action undertaken in its context. Moreover, no situation is like the other even if we perform the same action many times. The appearing gap between universality of expectation and particularity of situation is bridged by the knowledgeable agent. Therefore knowledge encompasses aspects of universality and particularity. On the one hand, it must be universal to cover the various situations we might face, i.e., it must be repeatedly applicable. On the other hand, it must be adapted to every particular situation. This is what we understand as implicit knowing, in contrast to explicit knowledge that is described in form of laws, rules etc. We will subsume the latter under the generic term stable patterns and express them in terms of entities and relations, therefore also calling them relational patterns. At this point we might ask how these stable patterns are entwined with implicit knowledge and how they lead to successful application in a particular situation.

4. The Entanglement of Implicit and Explicit Knowledge

Explicit knowledge, e.g., formal physical theories, represents stable patterns of interrelated entities referring to certain sections of reality. They refer to these sections but they do not mirror them. They rather serve as instructions how to deal with reality to those who possess the capability to realize them appropriately. Although most people know Einstein famous formula $E = mc2$ most of them do not know how it can be successfully transformed into a physical experiment. Or in other word, they do not know its ambit of validity. However, the latter aspect is a central constituent of knowledge and the ability to recognize the limits of formal representations and their transformation to action is decisive.

Moreover, it is important to recognize the reciprocity between universality and the ambit of validity. The more exactly formal patterns predict reality, the more constrained is their field of applicability since the exactness confines admissible possible contexts. If we take for example the laws of quantum physics we get only unsatisfactory predictions for chemical phenomena since the latter ones are out of reach of the physical patterns. This is not due to the fact that the physical laws are not applicable in these cases but they become so complex that they do not lead to practical predictions concerning complex molecules. In the same way we cannot fully explain most chemical reactions going back to physics although they refer to the same fundament of reality. Chemical and physical patterns allow predictions regarding the same reality but they are only loosely coupled concerning their analytic representation of reality and their ambits of validity are mainly different. Here it is to be emphasized that validity is meant in the practical sense of validation in terms of action. Naturally the physical laws are only valid for molecules but they do not allow us to understand the character of chemical reactions, at least not in the sense of a chemist. While quantum mechanical considerations deal with wave packages chemical investigation work with quantities of chemical substances. Generally we can say that reality can be described in innumerable kinds of patterns that cover distinct domains (Smith 95).

In our reality all possible domains of knowledge are gathering together, in reality, all domains collapse. Whether we regard a chemical reaction from a physical or chemical point of view we must come to the same real phenomena. However, the view might be rather different depending on the ambit of validity.

Every explicit knowledge domain encompasses patterns that allow a consistent description of a section of reality but if we put them together we do not end up with a consistent world theory. Why is it then possible that we can interconnect our knowledge of these different domains successfully? In particular, often successful action (in new areas) is built on integration of knowledge from different domains. This question does not only concern the integration of different do-mains but also their extension.

Relational Patterns can be torn out of domains and integrated in others but this does not imply that the representations of these domains become indistinct. For example, it is possible to describe simple chemical reaction by quantum mechanical means and some of the considered entities can be related to chemical ones. The conclusions concerning experimental findings must even be the same. The result in terms of physical representation, however, is fundamentally different from that of a chemical reaction although both refer to the same phenomenon. On the other hand, such a new representation of the already known gives us new insights in the nature of these reactions. Thus the quantum mechanical investigation allows us to take a look at the particular dynamics of elections in these reactions. That is not possible in a chemical consideration. Within the same section of reality we have different ambits of validity, i.e. we describe sections of our world by means of different relational patterns, even if all of them are part of this reality. Although it is the formalism, that is held by a relational pattern. By means of formalisms, we distinguish different domains. By means of relational patterns we represent implicit knowledge. The world view of a physicist and that of a chemist are quite different as well as the ambits of validity of their views. Nevertheless they focus on the same reality and must explain the same experiments based on implicit knowing that enables the interpretation of formal representations in terms of real phenomena.

So what does it mean to talk about an ambit of validity in contrast to a section of reality? Talking about the ambit of validity implies that knowing is related to all kinds of actions related to the respective formalism. Regarding physics this means that it does not only include the knowledge how to relate formal systems to experiments but also how to deal with these formal systems theoretically, e.g., concerning valid approximations or mathematical formalisms. It comprises all practices that are related to the particular ambit. Then explications describe those facets of this practice that have turned out to be stable under various different circumstances. Though: Explicit knowledge describes nothing else but the main aspects of these implicit capabilities in static way.

5. Process of Adaptation and Abstraction

Reality is new in every situation and requires respective knowledge adaptation. Generally we accomplish this on the basis of our implicit (partially embodied) capability of adaptation. Even if the situations change the main clues remain sufficiently stable to identify common structures herein (Smith 95). These common structures can be described in an explicit way and the resulting explications help us or others to deal with similar situations. These main clues are identified in two directions, first in regard of their applicability and second in regard of expressiveness in the sense of communicability or logical consistency on the abstract level. Within their domain they describe stable relational patterns of entities which might be involved in a situation A. We call the stable relations categories. As far as we remain in the respective ambit of validity we even might establish new practices without changing categories. However, certain situations include changes of circumstances that go beyond the usual patterns of which we dispose. How do we manage it to adapt our knowledge that has not extended in the meantime to handle new situations and why are certain persons more successful in handling and adapting knowledge for situation A in situation B? We suggest the following solution. Capabilities of handling new situations are nothing else but rearrangements of the already know. What is new according to Situation B is the fact that the relations of the contents of our knowledge have changed. In the course of such a rearrangement explicit knowledge is modified according to the new context. This is our answer how we come to new explications. It will be argued next that this process of adaptation and rearrangement is not arbitrary.

The available data can be aggregated in arbitrary varieties. By automatic processing (theoretically) myriads of entities can be collected and each of them can be described by a (theoretically) infinite number of properties. This shows that a mere proceeding of trial and error will never lead to valid explication in an acceptable way. Even the idea of automatic learning on the basis of trial and error is unrealistic. This multitude doesn't make sense since it only reflects the plenty of possibilities. Reality, however, does not realize all possibilities that combinatorics suggests. Experience rather teaches us that cer-tain relations only appear in specific sections of the world. The capability of association is one of our most prominent intellectual capabilities (Hagengruber 05). In contrast to machine learning we regard human mental capability not as the result of a quantitative process but of a qualitative process. For human thinking it is decisive how existing knowledge is associated to achieve the intended goal as efficiently as possible. Certain proceedings must be efficiently represented and explications must be unhinged to achieve solutions for specific goals. Human beings apply specific strategies to reduce the available data by selecting and rearranging the data. They apply a selection and rearrangement procedure to adapt knowledge to new situations. It might be illustrative to remember here Polanyis example. He investigated this referring to the notions of subsidiary and focal awareness (Polanyi 62). Polanyi's example is particularly interesting since it shows, on the level of seeing, how we switch the neuronal context looking at different things and nonetheless transporting lots of knowledge from one domain to another without focusing on it. The interesting point is that we can switch our focus of attention to the subsidiaries. However, the consequence of such a switch is that we loose the comprehension of the whole in the sense of a representation of an entity or a category that is constituted by these subsidiaries. Nevertheless it is this switch of focus that unfolds the implicit knowledge in to a partly explicit knowing. Which subsidiaries are grasped depends on the action by which the switch of awareness was caused starting the process of evolving the relational pattern into a new one.

This process consists in an alternation of analysis, i.e., explication, and synthesis, i.e., implicit integration. The latter term was introduced by Polanyi to stress the fact that this describes an active process of recontextualization of subsidiaries to a new entirety (Polanyi 69: 125). The analysis consists in a disintegration of the whole into entities that leads to a decontextualization of the subsidiaries. Analysis means to handle the entities of the domain on the level of relational patterns as the basis of explicit representations. Since we cannot focus on all subsidiaries that constitute the whole we always get an incomplete representation. The actual advantage of the analysis consists in the fact that this abstraction allows another kind of access to the relational pattern. On this level, the analyzed pattern might change into a new pattern, which is open for a synthesis that is evoked by any action. Though the analyzed relational pattern has to be rich enough for allowing again resynthesizing, it must be simple enough to allow handling these patterns in a context independent way. Reducing physical phenomena to mathematical formulae allows us to apply the entire stock of mathematical instruments to it, coming to conclusions that the implicit comprehension would never provide. Our consideration of the original object has changed to a consideration of an abstract relational pattern of its subsidiaries.

However, the context that made the particular subsidiaries come to the fore is lost. Implicitly this context accompanies the abstraction all the time. Losing track of the context brings about the risk to deteriorate the (implicit) re-integration. The sorites problem is an instructive example for that:

> A million grains of sand do make a heap.
> If n grains of sand make a heap, then also (n-1) grains of sand do it.

This finally leads to the conclusion that also two grains of sand make a heap, which is obviously wrong.

This conclusion appears to be wrong although logically valid and it seems we have left its ambit of validity. However, the control whether this happens lies outside the applied abstraction.

If we deal with explication of knowledge we always have to ask for the validity of these explications with respect to context changes. If we consider the simple example of apples, Merriam-Webster tells us that an apple is "the fleshy usually rounded and red, yellow, or green edible pome fruit of a tree (genus Malus) of the rose family". In this explication the entity 'apple' is related to a number of other entities and these relations can help people to identify apples if they don't know them already. However, we also see that this explication requires the familiarity with the entities to which the entity 'apple' is related. Whether the explication teaches me to know what an apple is depends on this familiarity. At this point implicit knowledge comes into play again.

Second, the explanation only describes apples in a specific context. Therefore the dictionary also gives another explication like "a fruit or other vegetable production sug-gestive of an apple". The latter is related to another context and these two descriptions represent only a vanishing minority of all possible explications in all possible contexts. This raises the question why it is reasonable to select these two explications at all. The answer is that not all possible contexts are likewise relevant (Hagengruber 05). We can call this an ontological turn that shows us that it is not necessary to intrude into all possible worlds to get an explication of the entity apple. If we consider the context that we actually face in reality we find that only a minimum of all possible contexts make an appearance and that the reduction to a finite number of explications is generally sufficient. However, this does not exclude that other contexts might appear. It only means that the probability to face these exceptions is comparably small.

Therefore we can deal with rather simple and few explications. However, depending on the different classes of context we might get differences in the explications and this raises the question how we can establish the identity of entities under different explications. This means that in different contexts one and the same entity belongs to different relational patterns, referring to different categories. Although entities are in principle open for all kinds of relations not all of these relations are either relevant (n)or possible in the context investigated and with respect to the actions that define this context in question.

Going back to the first given explication of the entity 'apple' it will be difficult for a non-botanist to use it effectively. For the context of a supermarket the description, e.g., for a child, might be even simpler. Thus we can say that the explication must fit to the action in mind and the agent of this action. This is the reason why a more dynamic concept of explication is required. Explication is a static representation of a process and to understand changes in explications, we have to have a look on these underlying processes. The entities in question have to be explicated dynamically according to the corresponding target action and respective agent but it is not arbitrarily in which relational pattern they come forth. As explicit knowledge guides us to deal with situations subsumed under a certain domain, situations might permanently change in a way that they are no longer covered by the respective structure of the domain. As an example we can consider quantum mechanics which can be regarded as an adaptation to situations that certain experiments on microscopic level that could no longer be explained by classical mechanics. Every situation comprises an arbitrary number of clues but which of them are relevant results from the action that we what to accomplish. Closing the gap between these clues and a consistent action requires the judgment of the knower who has to decide whether the particular situation suggests the successful execution of an intended plan. The individual clues are explicitly grasped and can be comprehended as subsidiaries of a whole contributing to the action (Polanyi 61: 124). Therefore, given a situation, we have to decide whether we can reuse the usual explication or whether we require a frame that goes beyond this explication. In most cases we rely on the usual explications with a limited granularity adapted to the intended action but theoretically we can always grasp new relations from the infinite pool of existing clues coming to more explicit descriptions. However, in general we abstain from doing unless these additional relations contribute to the successful action in the current situation.

6. Rearrangement according to Categorical shifts

The previous considerations raise the question how we can come to new categorical description of entities that are more adapted to the context at hand than those patterns we have taken over from former contexts. In these cases we have to rely on our implicit knowledge. For example, we observe that some subsidiaries that were already present in the former contexts but of no importance suddenly become categorical whereas other subsidiaries that had been categorical now loose relevance. If we live in a restricted environment with a limited radius of freedom of movement, for example, the assumption that the world is flat might be admissible. If we, however, start to travel thousands of kilometers we leave the ambit of validity of this assumption and various conclusions built on it become misleading.

Considering such rearrangement only those subsidiaries come into question that are already (in principle) aware to us. This means that they are not completely new to us and that we only have not yet regarded them as relevant in the respective context. Often these subsidiaries are already known to us from other circumstances, e.g., in relation to other actions. Finally it is the agent's point of view that determines the categorical subsidiaries since it does not become apparent from the relational pattern itself which does not yield any access to entities outside the pattern. We have to go back to the context itself to identify the changes. In the last resort it is the implicit integration and application of an explicit inference that tells us whether we are still in the ambit of validity of the respective formalism. Generally we take the same stable patterns and apply them to all new contexts that are more or less similar to the already known. Only failures call our attention to the fact that a rearrangement is necessary.

However, as mentioned before categorical changes are never as disruptive as it might seem. They are built on preexisting schemes that are translated from other patterns, i.e., new abstractions always build on preexisting ones, even if certain relations are exchanged by new ones. Of course the capability to identify these shifts requires a certain expertise of the respective domain. To grasp a reoccurring pattern that then can be explicated it is necessary to experience the pattern in various situations. Only repeated action of similar kind provides us with the basis for the identification of stable patterns.

7. Conclusions

Today we generally operate with a 'parallel' conception of static knowledge, which is independent of circumstances due to its analytic description, and of dynamic implicit knowledge. The insight that all action is finally based on the latter raises the question how this practice of using analytical expressions represented by a finite number of relations between certain entities can transfer any knowledge at all. We have to understand how context dependency of action bases on the integration of an infinite number of clues is related to such static explication.

The first insight in this respect is that, even if action requires a holistic and irreducible conception of knowledge, generally stable patterns of finite relational structures are sufficient to induce successful action. In other words, successful action can be built on stable patterns that are to a certain degree context independent since they are open to implicit integration. Even if the law of gravity manifests itself every time in a different way we can still identify the relevant clues. We must see this as a necessary fundament of knowledge since it is this fact that allows us anticipatory planning of our actions.

The second insight concerns the fact that these stable patterns can be built with a rather small number of entities and relations. Otherwise it would not be possible to explicate the respective patterns and they could only be grasped implicitly. It is this very property of finite representation that makes these stable patterns communicable. In particular otherwise it could not be explained how Meno is lead in a finite number of steps to the solution of the problem that he could not solve before. To be more precise the actual context cannot be reduced to this finite number of clues so that it is only the agents' capability of implicit integration of the subsidiaries that allows them to cope with the variability of real contexts.

Finally, coming back to the example of Meno the instruction only works because it refers to Meno's foreknowledge concerning the individual subsidiaries. Does this mean that Meno already possess the solution of the problem and only needed a reminder as Socrates interpreted the situation? This would underestimate the innovative act of implicit integration that Meno had to accomplish although all elements were already known to him. Of course, by appropriate instruction it is possible to lower the threshold of integration by more extensive explication but even the most sophisticated explication must come to an end.

The question is what we can learn from the described conception of explicit knowledge representations. The possibility to impart knowledge by explications is not determined by the explication itself but depends on the implicit knowledge of which the recipient of this explication disposes. Thus we cannot make any decisive use of the explicit knowledge that $E = mc2$ if we lack the corresponding basics of physics that allow us to understand and apply it. We must be familiar with the entities in this equation to do so. The explication only represents knowledge to those who already possess the necessary capabilities.

However, although the contents of implicit knowledge are mainly inaccessible to us we can often state some conditions that tell us whether a person is likely to handle such representations, e.g., if the person has graduated in physics. This means that to a certain degree we can predict by information about the experience of a person whether he or she can make use of some offered explication. Its knowledge character decisively depends on the experience of the recipient so that the knowledge character is always relative.

The considerations also throw some light on innovation, i.e., new knowledge. Agents continuously produce new knowledge since every situation in which knowledge leads to action is singular. In contrast to that, explications are static and therefore cannot cope with this singularity. To have any value at all they must be universal, i.e., applicable to various situations. The final adaptation must then be done by the agents with their implicit knowing. Moreover, explications only possess a limited ambit of validity. This means that for situations that are too different from the usual standard it becomes impossible for the agent to relate explicated subsidiaries and contextual clues since other clues have changed their relevance. In these cases we have to rearrange explications on the basis of our implicit knowing. Such new explication cannot be planned but we can say that the intensive occupation with a specific matter decisively increases the probability of successful rearrangement due to sufficient expertise of the respective domain.

A final insight concerns explicit (quasi-automatic) inferences on the basis of formal logic. Here we have to keep in mind that the conclusions are only valid in the intersection of different ambits of validity. An example is the sorites paradox. We start with a statement that is valid in the considered ambit and a derivation rule that is also valid. However, repetitive application of the derivation rule leads to a progressive extruding from the ambit of validity since the application derivation rule changes the ambit. This also shows the limits of formal logic. It only leads to valid results as long as we stay in the respective ambit of validity. However, the question of validity can only be answer from a standpoint outside that takes contextual aspects into account. In particular these consideration show the limitations of automatic processing which are always bound to a restricted domain.

References

Hagengruber, R. 2005. "Mapping the Multitude. Categories in Representations", in: *Proc. of the 3rd Conference Professional Knowledge Management WM 2005*, LNCS, vol. 3782, Springer, Berlin.

Nonaka, I. and Takeuchi, H. 1995. *The knowledge creating company*. Oxford University Press, Oxford.

Polanyi, M. 1966. "Knowing and Being, in: Knowing and Being." *Essays by Micheal Polanyi*. Edited by M. Grene. Chicago University Press, Chicago, IL, 1969.

—. 1962. *Personal Knowledge*. Chicago University Press, Chicago, IL.

—. *The Tacit Dimension*. Routledge and Kegan Paul, London.

Riss, U. V. 2005. "Knowledge, Action, and Context: A Process View on Knowledge Man-agement", in: *Proc. of the 3rd Conference Professional Knowledge Management WM 2005*, LNCS, vol. 3782, Springer, Berlin.

Smith, B. 1995. "Formal Ontology, Common Sense and Cognitive Science", in: *International Journal of Human Computer Studies* 43, 641-667.

Tsoukas, H. 2005. *Complex Knowledge*. Oxford University Press, Oxford.

Wiig, K.M. 2004. *People-focused knowledge management: how effective decision making leads to corporate success*. Butterworth-Heinemann, Burlington, MA.

Chapter Ten

Towards a Programming Language Ontology

Raymond Turner and Amnon H. Eden

Abstract

We examine the role of semantic theory in determining the ontology of programming languages. We explore how different semantic perspectives result in different ontologies. In particular, we compare the ontological implications of set-theoretic versus type-theoretic semantics.

Key terms: Philosophy of computer science
Related terms: Mathematical logic, type theory

1. Introduction

Programming languages (PLs) combine two, not always distinct, facilities: data structures (e.g., numbers, lists, trees, finite sets, objects) and control structures (e.g., assignment, iteration, procedure calls, recursion) that operate on these data structures. Such structures (Naur 1981; McCarthy 1981; Landin 1964) are immensely varied in their style of presentation and conceptual content. For example, logic based languages such as PROLOG are based upon Horn clause logic with a very primitive type structure. Functional ones such as Miranda™ have no imperative features and use recursion equations and inductive data types as their means of constructing programs. Imperative languages such as Algol employ a whole range of data types and are characterised by the presence of assignment and its associated imperative constructs. Object-oriented languages such as Smalltalk insist that everything is an *object* or, at very least, can be naturally represented as such. In all of them, we can express very complex ideas and construct extremely complicated and intricate algorithms. Indeed, PLs may be usefully thought of as *theories of problem solving* in the sense that each language proffers a means of solving problems with given methods of representation and problem solving strategies enshrined in their techniques of program construction. To varying degrees, each language forces one to solve problems within a given conceptual framework (its *programming paradigm*). This underlying conceptual framework is what we have in mind when we talk about the ontology of a PL. Our objective in this paper is to say something about such ontologies: what is the best way of characterising and formalising them? Unfortunately, the very diversity of PLs makes it hard to see how to start any such investigation. Consequently, at the outset we say a little about our approach (Smith 2004; Johansson 1989) to ontology.

2. Ontological Perspectives

Since PLs are formal languages, they have much in common with the formal languages used in logic, mathematics and physics. Indeed, many have been inspired by the languages of formal logic. Consequently, we shall explore some of the ontological options that have been suggested for these languages. We begin with a famous one.

Quine (1961; 1969) distinguishes between the ontological commitments of a scientific theory and the actual choice of a theory itself. The latter is to be decided in terms of overall scientific adequacy i.e., explanatory power, simplicity, elegance etc. However, once the theory has been selected, within it, existence is determined by what the theory says exists. In theories stated within the languages of formal logic, this unpacks in terms of existential quantification. For example, Peano arithmetic is committed to zero and the successor of any number; second order arithmetic, to numbers and classes of numbers; and Russell's simple type theory to classes, classes of classes and classes of classes of classes etc. This also applies to scientific theories expressed within such languages. So for example, axiomatic accounts of Newtonian physics are committed to the mathematics required to express the physics together with any of the actual physical notions that do not form part of the underlying pure mathematics. The same is true for any axiomatic formulation of any branch of science. Each theory has its own existential commitments and these are explicitly laid out by the axioms and rules of the theory, and these determine its underlying ontology.

It would be pleasant to be able to apply these ontological guidelines to PLs, i.e., to be able to read off the underlying ontology via its existential structure. Unfortunately, as soon as we try to do so, we are presented with an obstacle: unlike logical languages, no programming language is explicitly distilled as a pure logical theory, not even PROLOG. We are rarely given anything like an axiomatization that exhibits its ontological commitments. So unlike logical languages, uncovering the ontological underpinnings of a PL is not quite as simple as searching through the axioms. In general, we are only presented with a syntax of the programming language together with some informal account of its semantics. What we are rarely given is anything like an axiomatization that displays its existential commitments [1]. So this approach offers little direct help.

A closely allied alternative line of enquiry is offered by Frege (1952) and Dummett (1973; 1991). Instead of focusing on an axiomatic account of its constructs, it associates ontology with semantics. The ontological implications of a language are to be identified with the entities required to provide its constructs with a semantic interpretation. For logical languages, such semantic accounts are normally given in the form of its model-theoretic characterisation. Indeed, the axioms of the theory are often justified by direct appeal to its semantics. Consequently, for these languages, the two ontological strategies are two sides of the same coin. This suggests that we might be able to apply the Quinean perspective via its semantic dimension.

But once more, with PLs, matters are less straightforward. Indeed, for them, even the statement of this semantic strategy is a little vague; presumably, it all depends upon what one means by semantic account. These are not logical languages whose semantics can be given using Tarski satisfaction. Moreover, the notion that PLs have or need a formal semantics came much after their invention and use. Fortunately for us, semantics of PLs has now been under investigation for several decades, and so the semantic approach offers us a strategy to move forward. While several flavours of semantics are on offer, *Denotational Semantics* (DS) (Stoy 1977; Strachey 1973; White 2004) is not only the market leader, but is also the most ontologically self-conscious. Consequently, DS will form our starting point. Eventually, by following this trail and abstracting the central features, we shall be led back to the primary Quinean perspective.

---

[1] The nearest we get to any axiomatic account of a PL is in the work of Manna and Hoare. However, they were mainly concerned with program correctness and devised ways of attaching predicate information to programs; information intended to record the before and after states of the execution of a piece of program text. Moreover, while the presentation of Hoare (1969) is axiomatic, it does not capture all the ontological commitments of a language; it only records the impact of the constructs on some underlying notion of state.

3. Set-Theoretic Semantics

In DS every data item and control feature is taken to denote a mathematical object of some kind. At a deeper level, all the central notions of the underlying mathematics are sets. For example, the functions employed in the semantics are sets of ordered pairs. This is such a common characterisation of the notion of function that, as an assumption, it is rarely made explicit and it even seems somewhat pedantic to spell it out. However, it will play a crucial role in our evaluation of DS as providing an acceptable ontology for PLs.

In order to be more explicit about matters, and draw out some of its underlying assumptions, we need to sketch the DS approach. We are advocating a strategy of ontological classification with DS at its heart and, although we shall discard a great deal of the underlying mathematical foundations, we shall maintain the essence of DS, as well as the methodology of recovering the ontology from it. For this reason we need to spend a little time developing the basic ideas and machinery of DS.

We illustrate matters with a simple imperative language (**SIL**). Although it is a toy language, it will suffice to illustrate some of the central aspects of DS and how the ontology of the language may be linked to it. **SIL** has three syntactic categories: Booleans, expressions and commands. We shall use B as the set of Boolean expressions, E as the set of expressions and C as the set of commands. The denotational semantics requires the following sets for the denotations of these syntactic categories.

$$\text{Variables} = \{x_1, x_2, x_3, ...\}$$
$$\text{Bool} = \{true, false\}$$
$$\text{Nat} = \{0, 1, 2, ...\}$$
$$\text{State} = \text{Variables} \rightarrow \text{Nat}$$

where $A \rightarrow B$ denotes some set of functions from the set A to the set B. In addition, we require the following semantic functions for the various syntactic categories.

$$\mathcal{B} : B \rightarrow (\text{State} \rightarrow \text{Bool})$$
$$\mathcal{E} : E \rightarrow (\text{State} \rightarrow \text{State})$$
$$\mathcal{C} : C \rightarrow (\text{Variable} \rightarrow \text{State})$$

To illustrate the semantics we shall concentrate on the most interesting part i.e., the command language. This is generated by simple assignment statements, conditionals, sequencing and a while loop; it is given formally by the following BNF syntax.

$$c ::= x := e \mid \textbf{if } b \textbf{ then } c \textbf{ else } c \mid c \,;\, c \mid \textbf{while } b \textbf{ do } c$$

where e is an expression and b a boolean expression. The semantic functions are defined by recursion on the syntax. We shall illustrate with the command language.

$$\mathcal{C}[x{:=}e]\,s = Update[s, x, \mathcal{E}[e]\,s]$$
$$\mathcal{C}[\textbf{if } b \textbf{ then } c_1 \textbf{ else } c_2]\,s = Cond(\mathcal{B}[b]\,s, \mathcal{C}[c_1]\,s, \mathcal{C}[c_2]\,s)$$
$$\mathcal{C}[c_1; c_2]\,s = \mathcal{C}[c_1](\mathcal{C}[c_2]\,s)$$
$$\mathcal{C}[\textbf{while } b \textbf{ do } c]\,s = \textbf{if } \mathcal{B}[b]\,s$$
$$\textbf{then } \mathcal{C}[\textbf{while } b \textbf{ do } c](\mathcal{C}[c]\,s]) \textbf{ else } s$$

The $Update$ function changes the state: it forces the value of x in the new state, to be equal to the value of e in the old one. $Cond$ chooses the first or second component according to the value of the Boolean; it is given the undefined value ($\bot$) if the latter is. Sequencing is interpreted as functional composition (o) while the **while** loop is unpacked in terms of the conditional whose important aspect is that it is interpreted as a recursive definition:

$$\mathcal{F}[s] = \textbf{if } \mathcal{B}[b]\,s \textbf{ then } \mathcal{F}(\mathcal{C}[c]\,s) \textbf{ else } s$$

This is usually expressed by saying that the function $\mathcal{F}$ is a fixed-point of the implicit functional expression.

To provide mathematically support for such semantics, we need to use a class of functions, indeed theory of mathematical structures and their associated functions, that is guaranteed to support such recursive definitions. Such structures were supplied by Scott's Theory of Computation (Stoy 1977), i.e., his theory of *Domains*[2]. In DS all the sets employed are taken to be domains[3]. Of

---

[2] These are partly ordered sets $\langle D, \sqsubseteq \rangle$ where D is a set and $\sqsubseteq$ is a partial ordering, with a least element $\bot$ such that any ω-chain of elements has a least upper bound.
[3] Or some other mathematical framework that supports all the constructions in a set-theoretic setting. The last 30 years has seen the development of many variations and alternative frameworks including those where the space of functions is cut down to just the computable ones-according to some indexing. But for us these variations are not philosophically significant since it is on the underlying set theory that we shall concentrate.

particular importance, is the domain of functions from one domain to another. In domain theory, the set $A \to B$ is not taken to be the set of all functions from A to B but just the set of *continuous* ones ([4]).

Given this mathematical background, we can now read off the ontological commitments of our language. To provide DS for **SIL**, we require the sets $Variables$, Nat, $Bool$ to be domains. These are taken to be flat domains (i.e. sets with a bottom element added). Finally, we take $State = Variables \to Nat$ to be the domain of continuous functions from the domain of variables to the domain of values. Of course, different programming languages require different domains i.e., they have different ontological requirements. Indeed, enrichments to the language such as the addition of declarations and procedures will effect the structure of domains considerably ([5]).

Domain theory provides an underlying mathematical system in which to articulate the DS semantics of PLs and is a candidate ontology for PLs. Firstly, at the level of individual PLs, the underlying ontological demands of each language is articulated in terms of the domains required and the relationships between them. Moreover, the theory of domains provides the general ontological setting: it provides the general mathematical framework in which DS is situated. This is an attractive picture: it is not only a mathematically elegant approach to semantics but an insightful and useful way of pinpointing the underlying ontological structures of PLs. We shall try to maintain the majority of these features.

4. A Computer Science Perspective

Observe that there are three underlying assumptions of DS: Compositionality, Extensionality and Completeness. *Compositionality* insists that the meaning of a complex expression is systematically put together from the meanings of its parts. In DS it unpacks as the demand that the semantic functions are defined by recursion on the syntactic structure of the language. It is largely uncontroversial, and in some form it is accepted in all versions of formal semantics. Indeed, it is

---

[4] i.e. the ones that both preserve the orderings in D and D' and preserve the least upper bounds of ω-chains.
[5] The set theoretic approach requires certain domains to contain copies of their own function spaces. Instead we adopt recursive models in the sense of recursive function theory.

such a fundamental assumption of semantics in all its guises, that we shall not pause to question it. It is the others that need further reflection.

Extensionality relates primarily to the interpretation of programs; it insists that two programs are equal iff their denotations are the same. This means that their equality is given in terms of the functions they compute. It is enforced in DS by making the denotations of programs be set theoretic functions.

The third assumption, *Completeness* is more of a consequence of the fact that the semantics is set-theoretic than a separate principle. It demands that all the semantic items be interpreted as sets given in extension.

One of the fundamental ontological questions about DS concerns the role of sets ([6]). Some ontologists now accept *sets* as a basic ontological structure. They put them alongside individuals, properties and events, thereby taking them to be part of our conceptual framework. Within this framework, extensionality and completeness are natural assumptions. Indeed, they almost follow as corollaries.

Despite this, we have some reservations. Does the set-theoretic account of programming languages satisfy the intuitions of the computer scientist (CS)? Is this style of semantics definitive for the working CS? Does it define a language for her/him? We suspect that in all three cases the answer is negative. It seems that set-theoretic constructs do not reflect the intuitions of the computer scientist. More exactly, any philosophically worthy ontology should capture what the computer scientist talks about and employs about i.e., data structures, programs and algorithms. These and only these things exist in their conceptual universe.

With these concerns to hand, consider the last two principles of DS. Extensionality is interpreted in DS as the demand that programs denote set-theoretic functions. But from a CS viewpoint, programs are not best understood as such. For a start, we cannot compute with infinite functions given in extension. Moreover, properties of programs such as efficiency, flexibility and elegance are, from the CS view of things, absolutely essential. But these properties are obliterated by DS. In particular, whatever the appropriate notion of equality for algorithms and programs, it should be at least semi-decidable. This is certainly not delivered by its set-theoretic interpretation, i.e., two programs are equal if they denote the same set-theoretic function. This is not to say that the set-theoretic interpretations are not worthwhile for metamathematical purposes; they are. When we wish to explore the functions computed by a program and set up theories of equivalence that abstract from the details of a program, functions

---

[6] We shall not so much reflect upon domain theory and the fact that the functions are continuous but on the fact that domains are sets and continuous functions are set-theoretic ones.

are appropriate. However, the set-theoretic interpretation does not represent the way computer scientists treat programs and does not reflect the underlying ontology of CS; while modelling them as infinite sets may bring about some metamathematical insight, it cannot be definitional ([7]).

Completeness is equally problematic from a CS perspective. Consider the data type of natural numbers. A computer scientists does not see this as an infinite set given in extension. For her, *being a natural number* is an operational notion characterised by its rules of generation: 0 is a number and for any number, its successor is a number. Much the same is true for lists, trees etc. For the CS, these are operational notions that are not to be characterised set-theoretically. CS are Aristotelian about infinity (in a manner not unlike the justification for the extendable tape of the Turing machine). They allow for the possibility that we can keep adding one, but not for the possibility that we can finish the process and thereby put everything into a completed totality.

If we are right, set theory cannot form the basis for PL ontology and, more generally, an ontology of computer science. The situation is not that dissimilar to that to be found in the *possible world* models of intuitionistic logic that employ sets and *possible worlds*. Such models are not for the constructive mathematician, but the classical one. They do not reflect what the constructive mathematician takes the logical connectives to mean. Constructive logicians and mathematicians appeal to notions such as *operation* and *constructive proof* as ways of explaining the basic logical connectives. The situation with PLs is similar. While, for their own purposes, set theorists are free to interpret computational notions in their terms, it is clear that computer scientists have their own ontology.

5. Computational Ontology and Semantics

In this section we shall suggest and sketch the beginnings of an alternative ontological framework. The idea is simple enough: we return to the intuitions of computer science itself. Instead of sets we propose to turn matters around and use data types as our basic ontology. Once this has been sketched, we shall indicate how DS can be redone in terms of them; of course sacrificing the offending principles of extensionality and completeness in the process.

---

[7] Some of these objections can be met by appealing to a different foundation namely category theory. Although these models are more flexible, it is still not that clear that they can furnish the ontology of the working computer scientists who as we shall claim shortly, has an ontology of their own. White (2004) provides a fine summary of some of these alternatives with some insightful comments about their different roles and properties.

But to begin with we need to be clear about one aspect of this program: we cannot just use the CS notions of data type and program as we find them in PLs. There are two reasons for this. Firstly, our ontology must be theoretically secure. If it is to be a rival to domain theory, then it needs to be as rigorously formulated as the latter. More importantly, we need to know what our underlying ontology amounts to. For this we require a formal ontology. One way of unpacking this, and the standard way, is to formulate axiomatic theories of our data objects. This will be our approach. In the following we shall only be able to sketch the general idea but see (Turner 1993; Turner 1996; Turner 2005) for more details.

First consider completeness and how this impinges on the development of a computationally acceptable ontological framework. We illustrate with the natural numbers. We shall not adopt the set-theoretic interpretation but rather a type-theoretic one governed by the following rules.

$\mathbf{N}_0$ $Nat\ type$

$\mathbf{N}_1$ $0 : Nat$

$\mathbf{N}_2$ $\dfrac{a : Nat}{a^+ : Nat}$

i.e., we are proposing to replace the *set* of natural numbers with the *type* of natural numbers as it is used in computing science. This captures its role in type-checking. But in general, type inference is not enough to nail down a decent theory of numbers. We require other rules to determine its logical content (Turner 2001; Turner 2005). For example, we must have a principle of induction

$$\dfrac{\phi[0] \quad x : Nat \ \vdash \ \phi[x] \to \phi[x^+]}{x : Nat \ \vdash \ \phi[x]}$$

where ϕ is a wff (well-formed formula) in our formal language. Without such a theory we would not be able to support recursion and fixed-points.

In short, we are advocating that Nat is taken as a primitive notion, i.e., Nat is a basic type and is not interpreted in set-theoretic terms. The same applies to all types, namely, all our types are defined axiomatically by their rules and, while they can be modelled as sets, they need not be interpreted as such. In particular, we replace the set of functions from A to B with the type of *operations* from the type A to the type B (Hindley & Seldin 1986). In a similar way, constructors such as Cartesian products and disjoint unions are also given a type-theoretic analysis.

We shall now illustrate how DS can be carried out within such a mathematical setting. We shall re-examine the semantics of **SIL**, and indicate how this mathematical framework can be applied to provide a computationally acceptable DS. It is important to realise here that we are not promoting a semantics that is closer to an implementation such as Stack semantics (Milne & Strachey 1977). Our semantics will be at the same abstract level only the underlying theory will be changed.

For the interpretation of programs in **SIL**, we must explicitly deal with partiality; programs may not terminate and so may not produce a value. Consequently, $t:T$ is now to be understood as asserting that t, if it is defined, is of type T. With this in mind, we introduce a new type

$$State \rightsquigarrow State$$

i.e., the type of partial operations from states to states. This is determined by the following introduction and elimination rules.

$$\frac{x : Variables \quad v : Nat}{Update(x,v) : State \rightsquigarrow State}$$

$$\frac{f : State \rightsquigarrow State \quad g : State \rightsquigarrow State}{f \circ g : State \rightsquigarrow State}$$

$$\frac{b : Bool \quad f : State \rightsquigarrow State \quad g : State \rightsquigarrow State}{Cond(b,f,g) : State \rightsquigarrow State}$$

$$\frac{b : Bool \rightsquigarrow State \quad f : State \rightsquigarrow State}{While\ b\ do\ f : State \rightsquigarrow State}$$

$$\frac{f : State \rightsquigarrow State \quad a : State}{Apply(f,a) : State}$$

The notion of being defined/having a value (expressed as a down arrow) is determined by rules such as the following:

$$\frac{Apply(t,s) \downarrow}{t \downarrow} \qquad \frac{Apply(t,s) \downarrow}{s \downarrow}$$

Such rules enforce strictness ([8]). Finally, we add some rules that determine the equality criteria. We illustrate with the most important one i.e., the one for the while loop.

$$\frac{b : Bool \rightsquigarrow State \quad f : State \rightsquigarrow State \quad s : State}{(While\ b\ do\ f)s \approx Cond(bs, (While\ b\ do\ f)(fs), s)}$$

where $\approx$ denotes partial equality, i.e.

$$a \approx b \triangleq (a \downarrow \wedge b \downarrow) \rightarrow a = b$$

Informally, this asserts that, where both sides of the equality are defined, they are equal. The semantics of **SIL** can now proceed much as before but with these constructs replacing the set theoretic ones, e.g.,

$$\mathcal{C}[\mathbf{while}\ b\ \mathbf{do}\ c]s \approx While\ \mathcal{B}[b]s\ do\ \mathcal{C}[c]s$$

This has something in common with axiomatic semantics in the Hoare style but we have concentrated more on the logic of the programs themselves. Although very much a sketch of such a theory, it provides enough details for the reader to get the conceptual point being made: we are advocating an axiomatic account of data types where their status is similar to that of constructive mathematics (Turner 1993; Turner 1996; Martin-Löf 1975) ([9]). We claim that such accounts better capture the fundamental notions that computer scientists operate with. However, the essence of DS remains intact. The semantic functions and the structure of the semantics including the structure of the relationships between the various entities remains. Moreover, we can read off the ontology of the language just as before. What has changed is the underlying ontological theory. We claim that we have the beginnings of an axiomatic account of underlying CS ontology. As such, this brings us full circle back to Quine: the types of the logical language employed in the axiomatic underpin-

---

[8] Other ways which impose some more operational information are also possible.
[9] There are some obvious connections with constructivism but also some major differences. In particular, we are not advocating a change of logic. Indeed, we assume classical logic. Our interest is in the mathematics that directly reflects the CS intuitions.

nings of the denotational semantics determine the underlying ontology of the language.

Acknowledgements

The authors wish to thank the Royal Academy of Engineering for supporting this research.

References

Dummett, Michael. 1973. *Frege's Philosophy of Language*. London: Duckworth.
—. 1991. The Logical Basis of Metaphysics. London: Duckworth.
Frege, Gottlob. 1952. "On sense and reference". In *Translations from the Philosophical Writings of Gottlob Frege*. Edited by Peter Geach and Max Black.
Hoare, Tony. 1969. "An axiomatic basis for computer programming." *Communications of the ACM* 12: 576–580.
Hindley, J. Roger, and Jonathan P. Seldin. 1986. *Introduction to Combinatory Logic and Lambda Calculus*. Cambridge: Cambridge University Press.
Johansson, Ingvar. 1989. Ontological Investigations: An Inquiry into Nature, Man and Society. New York and London: Routledge.
Landin, Peter J. 1964. "The mechanical evaluation of expressions." *Computer* 6:308–320.
Martin-Löf, Per. 1975. "An intuitionistic theory of types, predicative part". In *Logic Colloquium '73*. Edited by H. E. Rose and J. C. Shepherdson. Amsterdam: North Holland.
McCarthy, John. 1981. "History of Lisp". In *History of Programming Languages*. Edited by Richard L. Wexelblat. New York: Academic Press.
Milne, Robert E, and Christopher Strachey. 1977. *A Theory of Programming Language Semantics*. New York: Wiley.
Naur, Peter. 1981. "The European side of the last phase of the development of Algol." In *History of Programming Languages*. Edited by Richard L. Wexelblat. New York: Academic Press.
Quine, Willard Van Orman. 1961. "On what there is." In *From a Logical Point of View*. Cambridge: Harvard University Press.
—. 1969. "Speaking of objects." In *Ontological Relativity and Other Essays*. New York: Columbia University Press.
Stoy, Joseph E. 1977. Denotational Semantics: The Scott-Strachey Approach to Programming Language Theory. Cambridge: MIT Press.

Smith, Barry. "Ontology". In *The Blackwell Guide to the Philosophy of Computing and Information*. Edited by Luciano Floridi. Malden: Blackwell, 2004.

Strachey, Christopher. 1973. *The Varieties of Programming Language*. Oxford: Oxford Computer Lab.

Thomason, Richard H., ed. 1974. *Formal Philosophy: Selected papers of Richard Montague*. Yale: Yale University Press, .

Turner, Raymond. 1993. "Lazy theories of operations and types". *J. Logic Computation* 3(1): 77–102.

—. 1996. "Weak theories of operations and types." *J. Logic Computation* 6(1): 5–31.

—. 2001. "Type inference for set theory." *Theoretical Computer Science* 266(1-2): 951–974.

—. 2005. "The foundations of specification." *J. Logic Computation* 15(5): 623–663.

White, Graham. 2004. "The philosophy of computer languages." In *The Blackwell Guide to the Philosophy of Computing & Information*. Edited by Luciano Floridi. Malden: Blackwell, 2004.

PART III:
BIOINFORMATION AND BIOSEMANTICS

Chapter Eleven

The Informational Architectures of Biological Complexity

Pedro C. Marijuán and Raquel del Moral

Abstract

This work attempts a consistent approach to the informational structures of biological complexity. By starting out from the conceptualization of molecular recognition phenomena, an elementary panorama about the informational modes of interaction or "architectures" of living cells and by extension about the evolutionary growth of biological complexity may be obtained. The endless modalities of molecular recognition in living cells basically revolve around "sequential" versus "amorphous"' (or dilute) interaction architectures. Biomolecular automata (enzymes and proteins) are the central components of the former, while DNA and RNA aperiodic sequences and whole chromosome territories constitute the latter. In the functional encounter of the two informational architectures, the cell cycle appears as the global instance of reference, up to the point of envisioning the cellular-molecular construction of "meaning" throughout the agency of dedicated networks of molecular automata (basically belonging to the Cellular Signaling System) impinging on grammatically organized DNA sequences. Subsequently, in the evolutionary problem-solving strategies of prokaryotic and eukaryotic cells, their very different DNA grammars would imply crucial differences. Their respective universality in evolutionary problem solving is addressed directly towards the solution of molecular "recognition" phenomena in one case, while in the other case it is addressed towards harnessing molecular "organization" phenomena (morphology and differentiation). The peculiar handling of DNA sequences by eukaryotes suggests a parallel with the von Neumann scheme of modern computers, including the cellular capability to "rewrite the DNA rules" along ontogenic development.

Keywords: Molecular recognition, Informational architectures, Molecular automata, DNA grammar, Embodiment, von Neumann scheme.

1. Introduction: Molecular recognition as a key to biological information and complexity

Information and complexity are amongst the most vexed terms in theoretical biology and related disciplines. Conversely to conventional top-down approaches which start out from preconceived notions of what are the most relevant informational aspects of the living cell, the approach followed here will be based on a bottom-up strategy, linking informational structures with molecular recognition modalities (Conrad, 1996; Marijuán, 2003).

Molecular *specificity* (together with *affinity*) provides the ground for all molecular recognition phenomena. Actually these two terms are amongst the most essential concepts of molecular sciences and of classical chemistry as all chemical reactions are based on the specificity of the intervening molecular partners and their inherent affinity or (free energy) reaction capability. By far, it is in the myriad of heterogeneous molecules that constitute living matter where this basic phenomenon of molecular recognition reaches its maximal ubiquity, universality, and combinatory capabilities.

An initial image may be illustrative ("worth's one thousand words"): see Fig. 1. What's happening there? The drawing symbolically represents the encounter of two avenues of biological organization: eukaryots vs. prokaryots (actually, a lymphocyte is engulfing a coli bacterium).

Figure 1. A lymphocyte engulfs a bacterium (Goodsell, 2003, 2004—modified).

How many molecular recognition encounters may be distinguished there? In the structures and in the dynamic processes within both cellular systems, thousands of specific molecular encounters are taking place in an organized and systematic way (Goodsell, 1991); but apparently the multiple modalities of mechanistic matching are occurring beyond any useful molecular taxonomy. This may not be the case, as we will argue soon.

At the same time, these two cells symbolize the two main avenues of biological complexity: prokaryots vs. eukaryots. In terms of evolutionary problem-solving, we could initially distinguish between the shallow or *extensive computation* performed by microbial communities and the intensive or *deep computation* characteristic of eukaryotic multicellularity – with the caveat that we are superficially equating "computation" with evolutionary problem-solving. For a variety of organizational-combinatoric reasons, only eukaryotic cells have been able to organize a deep evolutionary exploration of multicellularity, assembling together the complexity of both morphology and differentiation processes. While prokaryotic cells have organized vast multi-species communities with extensive horizontal gene transfer, and are capable of solving any useful molecular recognition and metabolic transformation case, they have not gone very deeply into the exploration of multicellular colonies endowed with stable morphologies and permanent tissue differentiation. In the exploration of "molecular organization" prokaryots are missing a fundamental combinatoric step in their DNA grammars, as we will argue in further sections.

1.1. Looking for a unitary informational background

Returning to the question of how many specific recognition encounters could be distinguished within the biomolecular "soup" of any living cell (Goodsell, 1991), it is surprising that in spite of the ubiquity and universality of molecular recognition phenomena, they are not well focused in their general biomolecular categorization yet.

Molecular recognition is like any other specific chemical reaction; it simply implies the "making and breaking of bonds". The problem with biomolecular instances is that they involve an amazing variety and combinatorics of bond types and Coulombian motifs, which together provide specificity and affinity to the intermolecular encounters (covalent bonds, hydrogen bonds, hydrophobic / hydrophilic forces, dipole forces, van der Waals forces, Coulombian forces, etc.). Dozens or even hundreds of weak bonds may participate, for instance, in the formation of a protein-protein specific complex. Quite probably, measuring molecular recognition and establishing its crucial parameters and variables can only be realized biologically on a case-by-case basis. At least this is the current trend in most molecular biological and molecular dynamic approaches.

A few references, however, could provide some interesting insights on molecular-recognition generalities. First, W. Meggs (1998) about "biological homing", contemplated particularly from a Coulombian "lock and key" combinatoric point of view; then S.K. Lin (2001) about the changes in thermodynamic entropy and entropy of mixing derived from molecular similarity changes; and finally M. Carlton (2002), with proposals for measuring the information content of any complex molecular system.

1.2. Symmetry considerations

The usefulness and depth of symmetry considerations in molecular recognition phenomena, as emphasized by Lin (2001), are self-evident. Symmetry allows an immediate classification of biomolecular recognition occurrences by means of three ordering categories: *identity, complementarity,* and *supplementarity*. They respectively mean: recognition by sharing identical molecular properties (e.g., self-organization of phospholipids in membranes), recognition by means of complementary properties of the molecular partners (e.g., nucleic acids' double helix), and recognition through a quasi-universal capability to envelop any molecular shape by building a complex molecular scaffold of bonds around the target (e.g., enzymic active sites, protein complexes).

From an organizational point of view, these very categories based on symmetry considerations would be reflecting the global distribution of molecular functions within the cell: *identity* in the structural self-organization of membrane and cytoskeleton support systems, *complementarity* in the informational memory-banks of nucleic acids (the sequential architecture), and *supplementarity* in the active sites and recognition-surfaces of enzymic molecular machinery (the diluted architecture). See Table 1.

In the living cell, the most important functional interrelationship concerns the population of biomolecular agents ("automata"), which are cellularly built by means of transcriptional and translational processes performed along codes established upon the sequential arrangement of nucleic acids. This amazing correspondence between individual amino acids integrated in molecular machines and sequences of triplets in structural banks of "DNA memory" —the arch famous *genetic code*-- may be in itself subject of further symmetry considerations (Petoukhov, 1999; Marijuán, 2002). The code essentially represents the foundations of biological evolvability. By tinkering at multiple levels upon DNA sequences, living cells can substantially change the populations of molecular agents and subsequently alter any organismic performances (Lima de Faria, 1988, 1995).

The coding relationship between DNA sequences and proteinaceous agents is also integrated within the multiple levels of DNA metabolism (the "fluid genome" views). Thereafter, the astonishing complexity of the "grammar" superimposed onto the DNA/RNA encoding (which involves a plurality of molecular territories: base, codon, promoter, operator, intron, exon, split gene, gene territory, centromere, telomere, chromosome, etc.), and which is remarkably higher in eukaryotes, becomes congruent with the multifarious engines of change in nature's genetic algorithms.

Identity	Complementarity	Supplementarity
phospholipids/membranes tubulins/microtubules actins/microfilaments clathryn/vesicles carbohidrates/glycoproteins lipids/lipoproteins	nucleotides/DNA-RNA RNA/RNA pairing RNA/DNA pairing RNA/ribozymes RNA/ribosomes, RNA/amino acids RNA/ribonucleoproteins	amino acids/protein chains proteins/chaperons proteins/protein kinases proteins/proteinphosphatases proteins/proteases proteins/proteasomes proteins/converter enzymes proteins/protein multimers proteins/protein complexes proteins/protein machines
	DNA/DNA pairing DNA/polimerases DNA/promoters DNA/histones DNA/transcription factors DNA/repressors	enzymes/substrates enzymes/effectors enzymes/cofactors enzymes/proteins antibodies/antigens receptors/peptides receptors/transmitters receptors/ligands receptors/hormones channels/ions channels/nucleotides channels/ligands

Table 1. Basic categories of molecular recognition in the living cell

In evolutionary terms, the generation of variety within biological genetic algorithms becomes surprisingly complex in most eukaryotic genomes, potentially involving occurrences such as: SNPs, repetitive DNA, mobile elements, transposons, retrotransposons, telomere shortening, gene and segmental duplications, chromosome fissions and fusions, whole genome duplications, symbiosis, etc. The striking complexity of eukaryotic beauplans and organismic physiologies has been achieved only by the combined action of all these engines of variation impinging upon the previous "grammatical" structures of eukaryotic genomes.

2. Molecular automata: The enzymic work cycle

Enzymes and proteins, the agential stuff coded onto the DNA, appear as flexi-molecular machines with a life cycle of their own (Ho, 1995). Their constitutive structure of amino acids is permanently caught into a state of flow, from birth at ribosomes to final degradation at proteasomes. In actuality, it is in the enigmatic folding process taking place at chaperons (in itself a computational NP-problem) where enzymes and proteins acquire their machine-like characteristics, which enable them to perform a regular function within the cell. See Fig. 2.

States		Inputs								Outputs	
Previous	Next	a	b	a^*	k_{-1}	k_{-2}	k_3	k_{-3}	k_4	a	a^*
I	I	/	0	/	/	/	/	/	/	0	0
I	A	/	1	/	/	/	/	/	/	0	0
A	I	0	/	0	1	/	/	/	/	0	0
A	A	0	/	0	0	/	/	/	/	0	0
A	X	1	/	0	0	/	/	/	/	0	0
A	T	0	/	1	0	/	/	/	/	0	0
X	A	/	/	/	/	1	0	/	/	1	0
X	T	/	/	/	/	0	1	/	/	0	0
X	X	/	/	/	/	0	0	/	/	0	0
T	A	/	/	/	/	/	/	0	1	0	1
T	X	/	/	/	/	/	/	1	0	0	0
T	T	/	/	/	/	/	/	0	0	0	0

Figure 2. (Left) Formal mechanism of an isomerase bisubstrate E regulated by the activator b. The substrate and the product are a and a^*. (Right) Qualitative representation of the enzyme's action. The *states I, A, X* and *T* correspond with *Einact, Eact* and *Ea**. (Above) Logical table of the automaton. The 1 and 0 values represent the occurrence or non-occurrence of the specific phenomenon associated to each variable (e.g., binding of substances, spontaneous dissociation). The sign "/" means that the value of that particular variable is indifferent.

Enzyme (and protein) function is but a continuation of the folding process. Apparently it implies a clear and regular succession of enzymic states: specific molecular recognition of the substrate, mutual coupling, lowering of the activation energy, interconversion between forms of energy, exit of the substrate transformed into product, and culmination of a regular work cycle (Marijuán and Westley, 1992; Urry, 1995). As a matter of fact, classical biochemical approaches have described this regular functioning of the enzyme through deterministic rate equations, non-linear ones that are often analyzed in a linear simplified way by means of control theory.

Nevertheless, this functioning may also be approached probabilistically. A stochastic dynamics –*molecular automata*– where enzymes "fire" their state transitions according to probabilities derived from the free energy differences in between states, can be more realistic than classical equations of control theory (Marijuán, 1994). Moreover, such probabilistic dynamics would be closer to the stochastic nature of transitions in the "post-folding" energy landscape from which the different states of the enzyme cycle are derived (Frauenfelder et al., 1991; Shimizu and Bray, 2001). The correspondence between the enzyme's chemical graph and the automata table of states is illustrated in Figure 2.

2.1. Enzyme networks

Enzymes and proteins do not act in isolation. By sharing their inputs and outputs, by having multiple interconnections through effectors (either activators or inhibitors), and by directly acting upon each other (e.g., protein kinases, proteases), and also by means of the formation of complexes, they are actually caught into enormous protein networks. The new *in vivo* approaches, derived from genomic and proteomic analysis, and from signaling science and other 'omic' fields, have dramatically changed the classical views about *in vitro* (mostly metabolic) enzyme networks (Kitano, 2001; Ravasz et al., 2002).

Enzyme and protein circuits are displaying any conceivable class of functional interrelationship: positive and negative feedback, amplification cascades, feedforward, lineal and parallel processing, robustness and resilience properties, sensitivity, redundancy, graceful degradation, variable interconnection, etc. (Hartwell et al., 1999). At a global scale, *power laws* clearly emerge in the functional connectedness between enzymes, and also in the formation of protein complexes (Maslov and Sneppen, 2002). This lawfulness seems to be derived from the very formative processes at work in the evolution of genomes (related to "fluid genome" views), as argued in 1.2.

2.2. Embodiment of functional agents

Apart from discussing the stochasticity of the enzyme's function, we have to pay attention to the global role of *embodiment* in the way such functionality is deployed intracellularly. For instance, the organization of degradation processes or *degradomics* (as they are called; traditionally they were forgotten) nowadays appears almost as complex as the transcription process itself (Marijuán, 1996, 2002).

Parsimonious definitions of biomolecular function have to pay attention not only to the functional *"what"* dictated in the active site of the enzyme, but also to a series of accompanying processes distributed over different parts of the molecular structure, which may include: modulation by effectors, intracellular transportation, permanent (post-translational) modification, formation of complexes, time-frames derived from transcription and translation, and final degradation.

Thus, the *"what"* of the functional clause should be accompanied by many other circumstances such as: *how fast, where, which way, with whom, when,* and *how long*. In general, the functionalities of the active site and the retinue of accompanying processes are independently defined onto the DNA sequences, constituting *addresses* which, as said, are separately coding for function ("primary address" coding the active site), and also for the other operation of control, transportation, splicing, modification, complexes, transcription-translation, degradation, etc. (each one implying some specific "secondary address" in the DNA coding, irrespective that they may be functionally operative in the DNA, RNA, or in the protein stages).

In prokaryotes, the global embodiment processes are far simpler than in eukaryotes —in correspondence, their protein components are smaller and contain fewer domains comparatively. Then, the possibility of systematic tinkering upon multiple modules and domains becomes one of the most distinctive evolutionary strategies of eukaryotes, the tool-box of their multicellularity. A serial-combinatoric arrangement of exons and introns (which usually constitute folding domains), tissularly tailored by differential splicing, allows eukaryotes a far bigger proteome than prokaryotes (around one or two orders of magnitude) without multiplying the number of genes involved (Claverie, 2001).

By tinkering and playing combinatoric games upon exons and introns containing a vast array of secondary addresses, eukaryotic cells may systematically explore and change the whole boundary conditions surrounding the triggering of each biomolecular function --mastering all those circumstances of *when, where, how fast, which way, for how long, with whom,* etc., which together co-determine the functional action of any eukaryotic enzyme or protein (Marijuán, 2003).

the triggering of each biomolecular function --mastering all those circumstances of *when, where, how fast, which way, for how long, with whom,* etc., which together co-determine the functional action of any eukaryotic enzyme or protein (Marijuán, 2003).

3. Integrated functioning: The cell cycle

The appearance of regulated cell cycles was a necessary evolutionary accomplishment. Out from vast enzyme networks and protein complexes, each one individually having a stochastic function, there emerges a regularized cell-cycle of quasi-deterministic characteristics capable of performing a specialized function at a new organization realm: the multicellular organism. The cell cycle becomes a *macro-engine* (elegantly driven by protein degradation), the accurate control of which constituted an evolutionary prerequisite for the onset of multicellularity. See Fig. 3.

How can the cell cycle be so exactly and quasi-deterministically produced out from individual stochastic components? Recent work on proteomic networks is throwing a new light on the biomolecular mechanistic scheme of the cell cycle adumbrated in the 80's and 90's (MPF, cyclins, CD protein kinases, checkpoints, etc.). There seem to be different kinds of *hubs* in the proteomic nets, both transient and permanent ones, which collectively drive the evolution of the whole system of networks, subnetworks, circuits, complexes, etc. towards common attractors. Ironically, individual stochasticity becomes a must for achieving a viable whole, as was already claimed by some molecular biologists out from experimental grounds – see Misteli (2001).

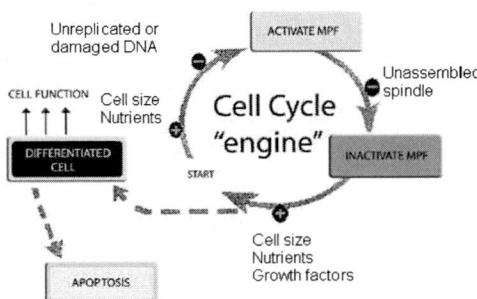

Figure 3. The cell-cycle engine and its regulation. The MPF (Maturing Promoting Factor) is composed of cyclins and associated kinases. They connect with the control structures known as checkpoints, which instantiate a signal transduction system of their own. Apoptosis appears at the end of specialization, or due to the arrival of specific signals.

Overall, the living cell is functioning as a tireless synthesizer, always filling-in its functional needs of active elements by means of (signaled) protein synthesis, coupled with massive protein degradation. Therefore, as much as the living cell is always in the making, in a continuous self-production process, it is simultaneously engaged in its own degradation, adaptively getting rid of its unnecessary, obsolete, or disturbing functional elements (Marijuán, 1996).

Adaptively weaving and un-weaving the own structures becomes a highly complex informational calculus to be performed by any cell belonging to any multicellular organism. It implies filling-in the own functional needs following internal and external signals, and keeping a balance between synthesis and degradation processes. How to select, thus, among the multiple pathways of control and intervention that are possible? And how to orchestrate them just in time, adaptively? For evolutionary reasons, a global economy of action has to be involved (Conrad, 1996; Marijuán, 1996).

3.1. Signaling systems

The Cellular Signaling System appears as the computing apparatus evolved to confront the adaptive control challenge. Out from prokaryotic origins, the CSS of eukaryotes --or *signalome*-- integrates the communication events with the synthesis and degradation needs. It comprises hundreds of different classes of dedicated molecular agents (receptors, ion channels, transducers, amplification cascades, second messengers, intermediate effectors, final effectors) that have been arranged differently in each tissue. See Fig. 4. Every cell-type has tailored its specialized signalome along its developmental trajectory, in dependence of its own history of received signals and self-modifying processes (Marijuán, 2002).

The general "detection, measurement, and intervention" character of the signalome has to be emphasized. The second messengers (cAMP, cGMP, Ca, InsP3, diacylglicerol, ceramide...) are dramatically modified in their concentrations by the different signaling paths that have been transiently activated, within a generalized cross-talking among all activated paths — echoing McLuhan, in the cellular system "the pathway is the message." Therefore, particularly throughout the second messenger concentrations, an integrated perspective (measurement) of the different internal and external influences at play is obtained within the cell, and is subsequently passed towards intermediate chains and the final effectors. At one of the crucial ends of the signaling command-chain, the nuclear machinery is waiting to be fed with a combination of *ad hoc* signals in order to change the transcriptional status of the genome.

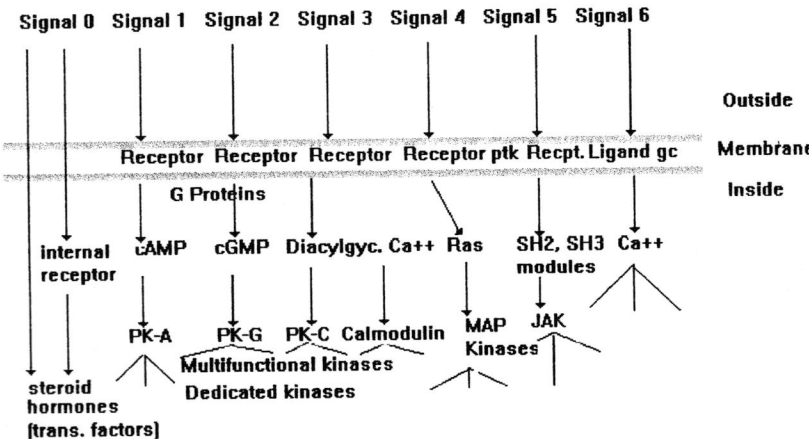

Figure 4. Representation of the principal classes of signaling pathways in eukaryotic cells. The signaling paths in the left (steroids) are the slowest ones, usually associated with cell fate and hormonal effects. Paths 1 to 3, mediated by G proteins, are faster and have a great amplification (ideal ones for sensory receptors), counting with numerous variants. Path 4 corresponds to control of development and cell cycle. Path 5 represents the customary access for neuropeptide action. Path 6, ligand-gated channels, is the genuine cortical path for fast neurotransmitters (GABA, Glutamate). The representation is highly simplified and does not include further effector cascades and vertical-lateral cross talking between paths. (Modified from: Marijuán, 2003).

The nuclear part of the whole signalome apparatus has already been implementing the *histone code,* in order to allow a tight grip upon the euchromatin-heterochromatin states which regulate access to transcription -–so that the well measured signals from the cytoplasmic signalome may be finally enacted as a new transcription program in relation with the advancement of the cell cycle or with the specialized function of the cell.

3.2. Convergence on the cell cycle

Everything has to converge factually on the cell cycle: metabolism, signaling system, protein synthesis, protein degradation, network organization, and control of the cell cycle itself (Marijuán, 1996).

Cellular "checkpoints" are instances of overall convergence where the fusion of a plurality of processes may be gauged. They are usually implemented as protein complexes where the ongoing transformation processes related to cell division, signaling, metabolism, etc. may talk to each other and produce a unitary signal of advancement along the phases of the cell cycle --or they may discard any further advancements, and cell death would ensue, either by apoptosis or by necrosis. Checkpoints act as *decision points* in between the well known four phases or stages of the eukaryotic cell-cycle: G1, S, G2, and M. A noticeable degree of stochasticity reappears within most of these decision loci, as several highly complex molecular operations are simultaneously launched, particularly during the S and M phases, and different signaling balances and metabolic and environmental constraints have to be rigorously maintained within the "intercellular milieu." Cells that fail to cross the whole checkpoints are doomed to an apoptotic fate; otherwise global deregulation of their cell cycles would ensue.

As successive rounds of replication are accomplished, there occurs a functional rewriting of "DNA rules". The transcriptional status of most DNA regions is systematically altered as cells advance along the totipotent, pluripotent and stem cell path, until completion of the tissular differentiation and specialization is achieved (Gasser, 2002). The euchromatine / heterochromatine state of a number of genomic regions is irreversibly altered by signaled implementation of the "histone code". See Fig. 5. From the point of view of formal systems, this unusual characteristic of "rewriting the own rules" could be significant concerning the cellular automata field (Wolfram, 2002), perhaps opening new paths towards new types of biologically inspired cellular automata capable of negotiating complex morphological / differentiation spaces.

The cell cycle is the most appropriate stage to discuss the intracellular construction of meaning. Any signal of external (or internal) origins will convey the *meaning* generated by its perturbation trajectory across the CSS and associated checkpoints, with *ad hoc* synthesis & degradation of proteins as the main factor. Three basic cases could be distinguished: Complete irrelevance when the signal is dissipated into the sea of equifinal trajectories within the phases of the cell cycle. Utmost relevance when the signal itself determines passage across an interphase checkpoint. And functional meaningfulness when the signal triggers realization of the specialized cell-function. In all cases, the abstract construct of the cell cycle becomes the necessary reference to establish the meaning of any received signal. Properly speaking, living matter does not refer to *states*, but to *phases* established along the advancement of a life cycle.

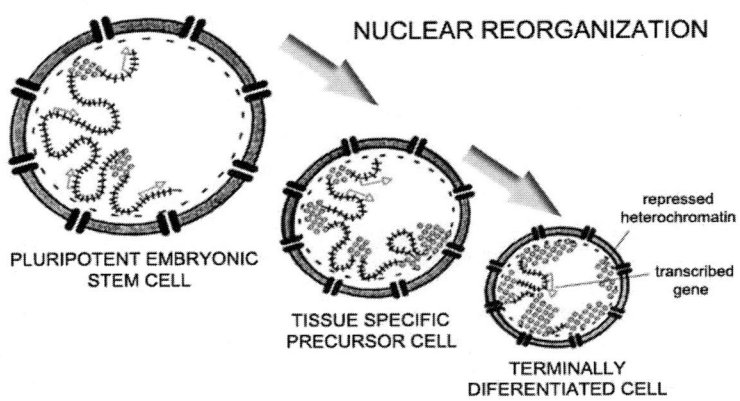

Figure 5. Rewriting the DNA rules. As a cell advances along its differentiation process, both the expression profile and the dynamics of the interphase chromatin are modified and severely restricted.

With the spiraling and multiplication of multicellular cycles along the eukaryotic developmental path, the hallmark for a new type of biocomplexity is set. The prokaryotic cell cycle has been loaded with a formidable complexity in multicellular eukaryotes, setting the stage for a number of *emergences* discussed in computational and philosophical fields. For instance: transition from stochasticity to systemic robustness and quasi-determinism, establishment of organismic top-down causality, autonomy, agency, plus the appearance later on of quasi-universal information processing systems (advanced Central Nervous Systems), not to speak about the enigmatic origins of consciousness and the neuronal and biomolecular counterparts of this phenomenon.

4. Concluding comments: On evelutionary problem-solving strategies (and a physiological coda)

In the extent to which the complexity growth of eukaryotes has been built by tinkering upon the scheme of *functional addresses* and *secondary addresses* put together onto the same DNA memory, the parallel with the von Neumann scheme of modern computers seems unavoidable –in computers, logical functions and memory addresses are also put together in the CPU memory.

Because of this DNA scheme in eukaryotes, the evolutionary genetic algorithms for physiological problem-solving are largely parallelized in eukaryotes. The different components of the biomolecular solutions may be tinkered with separately, and linked together later on. Besides, every molecular stage (transcription, folding, transportation, modification, complexes, degradation), specifically coded onto DNA addresses, may be used as a new functional element of control. Solutions may be chosen, then, from an augmented set of molecular building blocks.

The so called "Central Dogma" of classical molecular biology should not be taken cellularly as a closed black-box; rather its successive stages could participate as legitimate molecular partners, each one endowed with endogenous recognition capabilities, within a whole *transmolecular matrix* of controlling interactions (Marijuán, 2002, 2003). As an instance, in the recently discovered phenomenon of RNA interference, scores of micro RNAs are transcribed for the only purpose of using up their molecular recognition capabilities within the context of other DNA transcription and RNA translation events, collectively known as "gene silencing."

Concerning the evo-devo discussions (Raff, 1996; Carroll, 2001), the explorations of connectivity and functional modules in multicellular eukaryotes become far easier along this rationale. In the transmolecular matrix regime, "functional loans" between developmental paths may be easily arranged. When conflicts arise, gene and segmental duplications may straightforwardly solve the problem.

In actuality, the evolutionary coupling between the two informational architectures of life, the sequential and the amorphous, has explored almost every conceivable beauplan and organismic physiology. Life has thrived throughout the deployment of an organization with amazing informational capabilities and systemic emergences.

References

Carlton M. 2002. *The information paradigm.* Posthumous compilation available at: http://conway.cat.org.au/~predator/paradigm.txt
Carroll, S.B. 2001. "Chance and necessity: the evolution of morphological complexity and diversity." *Nature* 409 pp. 1102-1109.
Claverie J.M. 2001. "What If There Are Only 30,000 Human Genes?" *Science* 291pp. 1255-1257
Conrad M. 1996. "Cross-scale information processing in evolution, development and intelligence." *BioSystems* 38 pp. 97-109.
Frauenfelder H., Sligar S.G. and Wolynes P.G. 1991. "The Energy Landscapes and Motions of Proteins." *Science* 254 pp. 1598-1603.
García-Olivares A. and Marijuán P.C. 2004. "Emergence of power laws from

partitional dynamics." *BioSystems* 74, 63-71.
Gasser S.M. 2002 "Visualizing Chromatin Dynamics in Interphase Nuclei." *Science* 296, 1412-1416.
Goodsell D.S. 1991. "Inside a living cell." *TIBS* 16, 203-206.
—. 2004. *Bionanotechnology: Lessons from Nature.* Wiley-Liss Inc., New Jersey.
Hartwell L.H., Hopfield J.J., Leibler S. and Murray A.W. 1999. "From molecular to modular cell biology." *Nature* 402 pp. C47-C52.
Ho M.V. 1995. *Bioenergetics.* The Open University, London,
Kitano H. 2001. "Systems Biology: Towards System Level." In *Foundations of Systems Biology*, ed. by H. Kitano. The MIT Press, Cambridge.
Lima-de-Faria A. 1988. *Evolution without selection: Form and function by autoevolution.* Elsevier, Amsterdam.
Lima-de-Faria A. 1995. *Biological Periodicity.* JAI Press Inc., London.
Lin S.K. 2001. "The Nature of the Chemical Process. 1. Symmetry Evolution – Revised Information Theory, Similarity Principle and Ugly Symmetry." *Int. J. Mol. Sci.* 2 pp. 10-39.
Marijuán P.C. 1994. "Enzymes, automata and artificial cells." In *Computing with biological metaphors,* ed. by R.C. Paton. Chapman & Hall, London, pp. 50-68..
—. 1996. "The Cell as a Problem-solving 'Engine'." *In Computation in Cellular and Molecular Biological Systems*, ed. by R. Cuthberson, M. Holcombe and R. Paton. World Scientific, Singapore, pp. 183-194.
—. 2002. "Bioinformation: untangling the networks of life." *BioSystems* 64, pp. 111-118.
—. 2003. "From inanimate molecules to living cells: the informational scaffolding of life." In *Energy and Information Transfer in Biological Systems*, ed. by F. Musumeci, L.S. Brizhik and M.W. Ho. World Scientific, Singapore.
Marijuán P.C., Pastor J. and Villarroel M. 1999. "The Language of Cells: A Compositional Approach to Cellular Communication." *Symmetry: Culture and Science*, Vol. 9, pp. 383-392.
Marijuán P.C. and Westley J. 1992. "Enzymes as molecular automata: a reflection on some numerical and philosophical aspects of the hypothesis." *BioSystems* 27 97-113.
Maslov S. and Sneppen K. 2002. "Specificity and Stability Topology of Protein Networks." *Science* 296, pp. 910-913.
Meggs W.J. 1998. "Biological homing: hypothesis for a quantum effect that leads to the existence of life." *Medical Hypothesis* 51, pp. 503-506.

Misteli T. 2001. "Protein Dynamics: Implications or nuclear Architecture and Gene Expression." *Science* 291, pp. 84-847.

Petoukhov S.V. 1999. "Genetic Code and the Ancient Chinese Book of Changes." *Symmetry: Culture and Science*, Vol. 10, pp. 221-226.

Raff R.A. 1996. *The Shape of Life*. The University of Chicago Press, Chicago.

Ravasz E., Somera A.L., Mongru D.A., Oltvai Z.N. and Barabási A.L. 2002. "Hierarchical Organization of modularity in Metabolic Networks." *Science* 297 pp. 1551-155.

Shimizu T.S. and Bray D. 2001. "Computational Cell biology –The Stochastic Approach." In *Foundations of Systems Biology*, ed. by H. Kitano. The MIT Press, Cambridge.

Urry D.W. 1995. "Elastic Biomolecular Machines." *Scientific American* January pp. 44-49.

Wolfram S. 2002. *A New Kind of Science*. Wolfram Media Inc.

Chapter Twelve

The Cybersemiotic Framework as a Mean to Conceptualize the Difference Between Computing and Semiosis

Søren Brier

1. Introduction

Semiotics evolves a general theory for all possible kinds of signs, their modes of signification and information, and whole behaviour and properties, but is usually restricted to human communication and culture. Biosemiotics (bios=life & semion=sign), the scientific study of signs and semiosis in living systems is a growing field that studies the production, action and interpretation of signs, such as sounds, objects, smells, movements, as well as molecular signs in all living systems. Biosemiotics is the study of signs, communication and information in living systems. This can be further specified as the theory of semiosis in living systems seen as sign systems and the study of biological codes. Semiosis, both in terms of signification and communication, is an important part of what makes living systems transcend pure physical, chemical and even informational explanations. Biosemiotics attempts to integrate the findings of biology and semiotics to form a new view of life and meaning as immanent features of the natural world. Biosemiotics transcends on one hand the pure chemical description of life in molecular biology and on the other the traditional idea that semiotics is only the study of signs in the language and culture of human beings.

Ever since Umberto Eco formulated the problem of the "semiotic threshold" in 1976, semiotics, especially Peircian semiotics, has developed into the realm of biology. The efforts of Thomas Sebeok (1976, 1989) in particular, have led to the development of a biosemiotics encompassing all living systems – including plants and microorganisms – as sign users. This semiotics has even moved into the interior of organisms including the human body, describing semiosis between body cells and within the cells (endosemiotics) (Uexküll et al. 1993).

The question that is now becoming essential for the whole debate about the possibility of a transdisciplinary information/signification science is, whether the biosemiotic Peircian framework will also comprise un-interpreted "natural" objects and technological objects and/or their products as signs. Most obvious phenomena are autocatalytic and dissipative structures, which emerge by the spontaneous generation of order and patterns in nature. These objects were originally described in physico-chemical terms. Now some of the pan-informational paradigm adherents, e.g. Stonier (1997) want to explain them in purely informational terms.

The other question is whether any of the human signs/words/concepts that computers manipulate algorithmically can be said to be signs for the computer, or a robot, itself. What is the relation between logic, mathematics, algorithms, truth, signification and meaning which so far makes us focus only on humans in language, culture and society as the producers of meaning? Biosemiotics enlarges this to encompass all living systems, but what is it that distinguishes them from machines in theories dealings with signs?

2. The theory of protosemiotic phenomena

Peirce's semiotics (Peirce 1931-58, 1992) is the only semiotics that deals systematically with non-intentional signs of the body and of nature at large. It therefore accepts as signs: 1. Involuntary body movements (such as instinctive motor patterns); 2. Patterns of and within the body (such as limping and small pox); and 3. Patterns and differences in nature (such as the track of a tornado) when interpreted by a living system. But from a Peircian view the informational phenomena of non-living nature and computers are protosemiotic, or quasisemiotic when compared to the semiosis of living systems, as they are only displays of Secondness (Nöth 2001). We are not talking about the situation where any natural thing can become a sign when placed in a meaningful context by a living system, but about the objects and their processes per se. This is a similar problem to the question of what machines, like computers, are processing when no humans are interpreting. Are they signs or just signals? We know that we codify the signals so they carry meaning for us in our context and, therefore, they are signs to us, and forwarding that sign's meaning to receiving interpreters is what we do. But can one accept a machine and especially computers as interpreters? Does an interpreter have to be in a living context where meaning is already introduced through an embodied mind's existence? Relating to the question of the semioticity of calculating machines Nöth (2002:8) explains how Peirce coined the term "quasi-semiosis" to deal with this problem. Through his synechism Peirce did not believe in a strictly dualistic separation of mind and matter. Peirce's concept of mind is then extremely broad, and does not need to include consciousness or intentionality but only goal-directedness. The use of the term quasi-semiosis to designate 'degenerated' semiosis near the shift between Secondness, in machines, and Thirdness of the biosemiotic sign games, stems first of all from a lack of a triadic object relation.

This brings us right into cybernetics, especially Bateson's (1973). Here information makes a difference for a cybernetically defined "mind". This mind works primarily on differences with feedback loops based on energy. The energy is not important for the coding process per se, but the critique directed at cybernetics' concept of information and meaning has been emphasising exactly this, that any system based on information theory is simply functional, and does not have the capacity to encompass meaning in a biological, not to say a human perspective (Brier 1992). It may describe the cybernetic aspect of living systems well, but not the aspects of living systems that distinguish them from mechanical and informational systems. This makes sense, since the whole basic idea of cybernetics when combined with systems theory was to make a new transdisciplinary framework, which found the level uniting man, machines and animals.

To Bateson, mind cannot exist without matter, and matter without mind can exist but is inaccessible. Mind is recursive patterns of information and logical types in a dynamic "Chinese box" hierarchy. His world view is a mind-ecology based on differences that make a significant difference in informational terms. The framework is Norbert Wiener's cybernetic thermodynamically statistical concept of information as neg-entropy and therefore order! In the probabilistic interpretation of entropy in thermodynamics as developed by Bolzmann and Gibbs, who is the main figure for Wiener (see 1988/1948 p.8-12) order is the mystery. The order is in the virtual world. It is a dynamic order of logical types, which he saw as the basic grammar in a kind of cybernetic language. This dynamics is mind and the pattern that connects all living systems. Mind is in all of nature from the brain to the ecosystem, from the species to the whole biosphere, Gaya and beyond. The combination of energy and 'cybernetic mind' is what drives evolution. The code or pattern that connects and creates is thus the creative cybernetic mind. This mind is both in our heads and outside in nature. It rules our emotions too. It shows up in aesthetics. It is The pattern that connects! What cybernetics does to our insight in the world and knowing is to add the virtual world of information dynamics to the scientific world of force, energy and mass. So, Bateson (1980) insisted on the possibility and desirability of a science of epistemology and a scientific aesthetics! Thus, the cybernetic science, which is also a science of codes, is seen as the key to such a deep non-mystical knowledge of the relation between us, mind, ecology and evolution.

The Lonely Skeleton of Truth - as Bateson (Bateson and Bateson) called the inner deep knowledge of the cybernetic philosophy - is a cybernetic, thermodynamic, evolutionary and ecological mind of recursively dynamic logical types. Evolution is a (cybernetic) mental process! But a code is a set of processes, rules, or habits that connect elements in one area with another area in a specific context as for instance the Morse code standing for letters in the alphabet. It is crucial that the correspondence is not a universal natural law, but is local and conceptualized or rather motivated from a living signifying system. A sequence of differences such as the base pairs in DNA can be information for coding, but is not a code in itself. A code only give meaning to differences or information in certain contexts. Thus machines do not make codes themselves; but living systems function based on self-constructed codes.

Cybernetic information theory works with differences in a dualistic system. Information is a difference that makes a difference - Bateson's definition. But differences only make a difference in a system that somebody has coded from some sort of individual interest. Codes would therefore, from a semiotic point of view, be seen as triadic sign processes where an interpretant makes the motivated connection between objects and signs (representamens). Therefore, a triadic concept of signification is needed to get to a concept of code plus a concept of first person experiences. The whole cybernetic information area is proto-semiotic or quasi-semiotic, since the machines are produced by semiotic beings, but they are only dualistically informational communication tools. The problems between these two transdisciplinary paradigms of information and signification seem to stem from the fact that they are coming from opposite directions of the hierarchy of science and humanities as they develop their theories of messages.

The semiotic epistemological star

Subjectivity and meaning are always produced from embodied beings with some kind of individual perspective, which orders the perception into objects, events and possibilities relevant to its own functionality and survival. Sebeok (1976, 1989) points out that the semiosphere, the totality of interconnected signs, is identical with the biosphere or - one might add - is a broader and more profound understanding of it. Through this foundation for semiosis, a theory of meaning and interpretation including mind as immanent inside nature is possible, and cybernetic views of information can be combined with pragmatic theories of language in the biosemiotic perspective.

But the enlarged philosophical framework has to start with some minimum requirements for living systems – and especially humans – to be able to produce knowledge at all, before we see how far we can carry this into the world of machines and inanimate nature: 1. Embodiment: our body is at least a main source of life and cognition. 2. Consciousness: consciousness is the source of an inner life of cognition, volition, feeling and perceptual qualities (qualia). 3. Situated in meaning: In semiosis meaning is constructed through a semiotic system like language in a social and cultural network of other living beings, and in humans linguistic conscious systems. 4. Living systems are placed in an environment that seems partly independent of our perception and being (Brier 2000c).

Visualizing how from the communicative social system of embodied minds' four main areas of knowledge arise: Usually physical nature is explained from energy and matter, living systems are explained from the development of life processes, social sign cultures are explained from the development of meaning, and finally our inner mental world is explained from the development of consciousness.

As analyzed above, humans are embodied, feeling and knowing cultural beings in language. My point then is that this makes us live in four different worlds: 1. Embodiment: Our "body-hood" and our sharing of "body–hood" with other living species. 2. Inner Mental World: Our inner world of emotions and thoughts manifested as mind and consciousness. 3. Physical nature: The physico-chemical aspect of ourselves and of the environment of the natural world. 4. Culture: The cultural world of language and meaning.

Each of the four worlds calls on its own type of narrative. Physicists and chemists tend to see the universe as basically consisting of matter, energy and meaningless information. Biologists tend see the universe basically as a living being; the social and cultural sciences tend to see the world as constructed from our socio- linguistic interpretations (unless they are dualistic, and accept that nature is as science describes it and only culture is constructed by man). Those dealing with the phenomenological aspect of our being tend to be rather anti-scientific and anti-realistic often viewing the world as a product of consciousness as product of a linguistic system. But, like Peirce, I see the semiotic mind at the heart of all four worlds.

Maturana and Varela (1980), in their theory of autopoiesis, do not apply the word 'information' to cognition when it is to be understood from within the autopoietic system. Nothing is transferred from the environment to the living system that can be designated as meaningful information. But they admit that you can say that, when you observe from the outside, it looks like the system has obtained information. One might say that information is created inside the autopoietic system when it receives a disturbance, which as a species it is prepared for by the creation of a structural coupling. Maturana and Varela do not view structural coupling as an information channel because no representations are moved through it. Ethologists would say it had an instinctual perception where sign stimuli elicited an Innate Release Response Mechanism (IRM) which released a pre-programmed instinctive behaviour (see for instance Brier 2000b, 2001a). This constructivistic biological cybernetics stresses the intimate evolutionary and developmentally dynamic relation between environment and organism. But Maturana and Varela's concepts do not in themselves fit with the concepts of information science, nor with semiotic concepts, such as semiosis as an interpretation. Elsewhere I have argued (Brier 2006) that there is an area of nature between the physical causal level and the level of biosemiosis, and that this level is the area that cybernetics and information science have conceptualized. This level is also a basic layer in the construction of living systems, but it does not capture the aspects of them that make them different from mechanical and informational systems.

Cybernetic information science erases a threshold between causality and information when all nature becomes informationalized. (Brier 2006) When information theory attempts to encompass the area of meaning and semantics it passes and destroys the semiotic threshold, but in the other direction, blurring the difference between informational and semiotic processes, and thereby between mechanical signal manipulation or quasi-semiotic systems and living systems. This produces all manner of simplistic theories about intelligences that are unable to grasp the cognitive processes specific to embodied living systems, not to speak of those specific to conscious socio-linguistic systems. Cybernetic information theory works with differences in a dualistic system. "Information is a difference that makes a difference" was Bateson's definition. Logical patterns and types do not have meaning in themselves. The logic of the living beings includes meaning, emotions, ethics and aesthetics. It is, at least, arguable that Bateson is looking for the deep codes of reality since he attempts to reduce the phenomenological to the cybernetic. But, in so doing, access to first person experience is lost. It falls outside this world view. Where are emotions and meanings experienced in flesh and in culture?

Thus it is that sign making is the threshold between cybernetics and semiotics. To make a difference is to establish a sign for it (the interpretant) in an embodied mind. Before that it is only second order cybernetic signals or quasi-semiotic according to Peirce. The whole subject area of cybernetic information theory must be, then, quasi-semiotic. Underneath that, is the physico-chemical level which in general is best described in terms of energy, matter and causality by natural forces (Secondness).

One way to understand our inner mental world is to see it as a way of representing our bodily interactions with the environment through the constructions of a felt signification sphere. In this way an individual "point of view" as a centre of cognition, interest and interpretation is created. What

Spinoza calls conatus, self-value and self-interest in preserving the individual's and species' self-organizing structure is basic to living systems' ability to signify. But this individual signification sphere is again perturbed by the species' specific social interactions starting with mating, rearing of the young, competing for hunting territory, and hierarchy in the group, co-operation in food gathering and hunting. These socially interactive activities first generate sign games, and later in evolution, human language games. The construction or development of meaningful and informative messages has, as a prerequisite, autopoiesis, signification and conatus/motivation/intentionality. It is only within this triad that the selections of information, utterance and meaning are possible. But biological autopoiesis is not enough as we have seen in the semiotic star. A theory of the closure and self-organizing abilities of the psyche's inner life and the outer life of interpersonal communication in society is also necessary if we want to connect cybernetics and semiotics in living beings and in culture.

Luhmann's Triadic Autopoietic Systems

Luhmann has generalized the autopoietic concept of Maturana and Varela (1980) in order to encompass psychological thinking systems and socio-communicative systems. He views the psyche as a silent inner system, a closed system of perception, emotion and volition. A special linguistic system has to be created for communication to happen. Communication is again an organizationally closed system. Only communication communicates. Social systems are communicative systems with human bodies and minds as surroundings. To Luhmann (1995) communication is a sequence of selections, namely of 1) information, 2) utterance and 3) meaning. The first two have to be made by what we traditionally call "the sender", the last one by the receiver. He chooses his understanding of the signs produced, and then one could say that a message is produced when the receiver says something that the sender chooses to understand as a confirmation of understanding of his first message. Finally, in a fourth selection the message is connected to present practice.

Although his view of information is loosely based on Shannon's concept, it differs from the latter in that Luhmann (1995) does not believe in its use outside of human social communication. Thus, he does not want to generalize it outside the analysis of human messages. Also, Luhmann does not seem to believe that information exists in nature independently of human perception. The information concept functions as a quantitative aspect within a meaningful human context. Further he combines information with the aspects of utterance and meaning, stressing that both the sender and the receiver have to make their choices to produce a meaningful message. I think that instinctive reactions would also count as such a choice. Information is choice related to subject matter, utterance is choice pertaining to the way of saying something, and meaning is the choice of interpretation by the listener depending on his evaluation of the human context. But Luhmann's theory has problems producing a concept of meaning that relates deeply to the flesh, blood and life (conditions) of biological systems, and to the existential conditions of human consciousness. Here pragmatic language philosophy, like Wittgenstein's language game theory, and Lakoff and Johnson's embodied cognitive semantics combined with ethology, all seen within Peircian biosemiotic framework (Brier 1999a , 2000a), demonstrate that signs as concepts and classifications arise in our embodied biological and social "life forms". From our inner world we express our bodily experiences in social relations. It is especially regarding the social communicative construction of meaning that Luhmann's theory connects so well with semiotics. But Luhmann himself did not connect to semiotics in any systematic way. In what follows I will reformulate this problem from, what I shall refer to as, a Cybersemiotic viewpoint.

The Cybersemiotic View of Cognition and Communication

Viewed in this way, Luhmann's three autopoietic systems (see Luhmann 1990) are all needed to create the meaning of a message, and one needs the sign concept to understand their interaction. One way of getting out of the impasse of Luhmann's functionalism, where the role of body and mind in the production and meaning of social communication has not been adequately grasped by the theory, is to view the interpenetration between the three organizationally closed systems semiotically. Signs acquire meaning where the systems interpenetrate. Interpenetration is Luhmann's term for the interaction between biological autopoiesis, psychic closure and the socio-communicative system with its own closure at the social level. My hypothesis is that sign and language games arise on the basis of the interpenetration of the three different autopoietic systems. Meaning is seen as being generated by the interpenetration of the systems. For example, language is a part of the socio-communicative system, but it does not really acquire meaning until it interpenetrates with the psychic system and gets to indicate differences of emotions, volitions and perceptions "putting words" to our silent inner being. But our cognitive, emotional and volitional qualities would only have a weak connection to reality if they were not connected to the survival of the living systems' organization as a body. This has evolved through its interaction with the environment's differences in the development of a sphere of signification in the evolution of the species.

Biosemiotics and metaphor theory have argued extensively for the importance of embodiment in semiosis. In Brier (2000a) I have tried to show the connection between the biosemiotic (ethologically based) concept of motivation and the motivational concept of embodied cognitive semantics. I have shown that ethology and embodied metaphor theory have both discovered that the conception of a sign as standing for something for somebody in a particular way is controlled by some releasing mechanisms that connect motivation, perception and behaviour/action into one systemic process as already described by Jacob von Uexküll in his "Funktionskreis", and which Heinz von Foerster refers to as perceptual "eigenvalues". Instinctually, the actual IRM is chosen through the urge coming from a specific motivation. This is again based on biological expectancies and vital needs, for example, food and mating. I argue that the linguistic motivation, which Lakoff and Johnson claim controls the ICM (Idealized Conceptual Models), has connections to the biological motivations in many instances. This is obvious in the much-used example where a woman classifies a man as a bachelor, and therefore as a potential mating partner. It is our bio-psychological embodiment that ties these relations together.

Further, I have shown that a phenomenological-emotional concept was necessary to understand the production of meaning, and this is consistent with Peirce's placing of feeling as an attribute of Firstness. In his evolutionary theory, feeling becomes an immanent inner reality, that also exists in matter. Knowledge systems thus unfold from our bio-psycho-socio-linguistic conscious being. Their function is to help us orient (ourselves) in the world and help us act together in the most fruitful way, but they do not explain us to ourselves. Peirce's view that we cannot with any good reasons to split the concepts of mind and matter is both sound and a profound foundation for a transdisciplinary metaphysical framework. There is no good reason why the inner world of cognition, emotion and volition should not be accepted as possessing the same degree of reality as the physical world, and similarly our cultural world of signs and meaning. Finally to both the spiritualist and the materialist, embodied life, even with only one cell as the body, has to be a basic part of, or component for, constructing reality. We are thinking in or maybe even with the body. The psyche and its inner world arise within and between biological systems or bodies. With Peirce one may say that there will always be some kind of psyche in any kind of biological autopoietic and dual code system. Still, a partly autonomous inner world of emotions, perceptions and volitions only seems to arise in multi-cellular chordates with a central nervous system. Lorenz (1973) argues that such a system with emotions and experiences of pleasure is necessary for animals to have appetitive behaviour, searching for the objects or situations that can elicit their instinctual behaviour and release the motivational urge built up behind it. This is qualitatively different from how reflexes function in response to a signal, which is a proto-semiotic informational level. Instinctual sign function is on a genuine semiotic level.

Luhmann's theory of the human socio-communicative being consisting of three levels of autopoiesis can be used in cybersemiotics to distinguish between 1) the languaging (Maturana) of the biological systems, which is the coordination of behaviours between individuals of a species on the reflexive signal level, 2) the motivation-driven sign games of the bio-psychological systems and, finally, 3) the well-driven language games level of the self-conscious linguistic human through generalized media in the socio-communicative systems. A semiotic understanding has thus been added to Luhmann's conception, and his theory has been placed in the Peircian triadic metaphysics. In the following section, I will explain and develop this further.

Intrasemiotics

It is obvious that what we call language games arise in social contexts where we use our mind to coordinate our willful actions and urges with fellow members of our culture. Some of these language games will be about our conceptions of nature, now filtered through our common culture and language. But underneath that, we also have emotional and instinctual bio-psychological sign games (Brier 1995, 2001a)) which function for humans as unconscious paralinguistic signs, such as facial mimics, hand movement gestures and body positions, with their origin in the evolution of species-specific signification processes in living systems. Simultaneously, we have an internal communication between our mind and body. In Luhmann's version it is somewhat different from what Kull (1998) calls psychosomatics; it is not a direct interaction with culture, only with the psyche. On the other hand it is not only endosemiosis. The terms 'endosemiosis' and 'exosemiosis' were probably both coined by Sebeok (1976, p3), 'endosemiosis' denoting the semiosis that takes place inside the organisms, and 'exosemiosis' being the sign process that occurs between organisms. 'Endosemiosis' became a common term in semiotic discourse (see Uexküll et. al. 1993), meaning a semiotic interaction at a purely biological level between cells, tissues and organs. Nöth (2001) introduced the term ecosemiotics, specifically for the signification process of non-intentional signs from the environment or other living beings, which convey meaning to another organism, for instance, the scent of prey to a hunting animal. Thus the sign signifying an organism as suitable prey is not intentionally emitted by the organism preyed upon and is, therefore, rather ecosemiotic than exosemiotic. (Brier 2001b). What might we call the internal semiotic interaction between the biological and the psychological systems? One suggestion for the interaction between the psyche and the linguistic system might be thought semiotics. This is where our culture through concepts offers us possible classifications of our inner state of feelings, perceptions and volitions. These, in their non-conceptual or pre-linguistic states not recognized by conceptual consciousness, I call phenosemiotic processes. For short I just call them phenosemiosis. As the interactions between the psyche and the body are internal bodily, but not purely biological as in endosemiotics, I call the semiotic aspect of this interpenetration between the biological and the psychological autopoiesis intrasemiotics (Brier 2000b). These different terms are coined to remind us that we deal with different kinds of semiotics. Future work must include the more specific study of the way semiosis is created in such cases.

Today we know that there are semiotic interactions between the hormone systems, the transmitters in the brain, and the immune system, and that their interactions are very important for the establishment of the autopoietic system of the Second order, which is constructed as a kind of biological self within a multicellular organism. Its parts are cells that are themselves autopoietic systems organized on another level. But we know very little about the relations between our lived inner world of feeling, volition and intention and this other system. It seems that certain kinds of attention to bodily functions, such as imagining, can create physiological effects in this combined system. This is partly the result of different substances having significant effects on organs and specific cell types in the body (endosemiotics). We also know that our hormonal level influences our sexual and maternal responses, and fear turns on a series of chemicals which change the state and reaction time of several body functions, and so on. This is a very significant part of the embodiment of our mind, but intrasemiotics seem to function as meta-patterns of endosemiotic processes. For example, our state of mind determines our body posture through the tightness of our muscles. There is a subtle interplay between our perceptions, thoughts and feelings and our bodily state, working among other things through the reticular activation system. There is still a lot we do not know about the interaction between these systems.

The nervous system, the hormonal system and the immune system seem to be incorporated into one big self-organized sign web. Now, the autopoietic description of living cybernetic systems with closure does not really open to sign production per se, and semiotics in itself does not reflect very much about the role of embodiment in creating signification. Thus, the cybersemiotic suggestion to solve this problem is that signs are produced when the systems interpenetrate in different ways (Brier 1999b). The three closed systems produce different kinds of semiosis and signification through different types of interpenetration, plus a level of structural couplings and cybernetic 'languaging', as Maturana and Varela (1980) call it.

An autopoietic theory underlines that two interpenetrating systems are primarily closed black boxes to each other. But interpenetration between them develops a coordination of behaviour or 'languaging'. Parts of these systems are inherited on reflexive and instinctual levels, and are foundational for communication to develop. Thus, it must be through the reciprocal structural coupling formed between the two systems that signs can be produced and exchanged. Maturana's concept of languaging (co-ordination of co-ordinations of behaviour) seems to be the bio-psychological connection between two individuals in a social species. But it is not the sign and/or language game as such; it is the underlying cognitive coupling that is the coordination necessary for communication to develop as a signification system with its own organizational closure. I would, therefore, suggest that we distinguish between languaging and sign games at the level between reflexes and instinctual movements respectively (Brier 2000b). Thus, the schooling behaviour of fish is reflexive-informational, but courtship communication is instinctual sign games. The perception eliciting reflexes is independent of motivation, whereas the perception of sign stimuli is motivation-dependent, which leads into the instinctual sign games. Ethologists would here point to how certain instinctual movements become ritualized and get a release value for instinctive behaviour as "sign-stimuli". As Lorenz (1973), in his last period, realized emotions had to be connected to the performances of instinctual movements to create the motivational urge of appetitive behaviour; we here have criteria to distinguish between the two levels (Brier 2000b). We here see how the connection between signs and internal or phenomenological understanding is constructed. Lakoff (1987), and Lakoff and Johnson (1998) have shown us how this basic mechanism of bodily meaning can be explained, by metaphorical processes, to encompass socially and culturally produced signs.

Based on ethology and biosemiotics I claim that our cognition manifests itself as embodied semiosis, motivated in our biological social interest, which is a powerful creator of structure and meaning in our signification sphere. Most animal behaviour is – like much of our linguistic categorizations and use of metaphors – considered to be unconscious. Still ethologists have had to realize that motivation is not a physiological concept (Brier 1992, 1998a); emotional experiences are connected to the perception and behaviours through an instinctive basis. Sign games are developed into language games through evolution, and begin in the life of the infant human. As we are born and grow into human social communicators the psyche is perfused with signs. Our mind is infected with language, and we become semiotic cyborgs or what we call humans! We are in this view born as animals with a capacity to construct this interpenetration between the psychic and socio-communicative systems, creating internal interpretants that are meaningful to us because of the mutual structural couplings of languaging established in evolution.

Meaning is seen in biosemiotics, cognitive semantics, autopoiesis theory and ethology as embodied. But with the new cybernetics and von Uexküll (1909, 1934, 1940), I suggest that embodiment is thought of as much broader than only the structure of the nervous system, or even the integration of the neurotransmitter, the hormone and the immune systems through reaction to common sign substances that they secrete. As Kirkeby (1997) suggests, we should look at the body-mind or the body-thought as a complex phenomenological dynamical system, including the construction of the environment and the other (body-mind) systems that make it possible for signification to appear. Realizing that a signification sphere not only pertains to the environment, but also to the perception of other members of the species in cultural and proto-cultural behaviour as well as to perceptions of own 'mind and body-hood', I use 'eco' as a prefix to the signification sphere, when it pertains especially to non-intentional nature and culture outside the species in question. In both inanimate nature, as well as in other species, and in cultural processes, we can observe differences that signify meaning to us, although never intended by the object.

This is also true for the human species, indicating that our language has a deep inner connection to the ecology of our culture. Any existing culture is a collective way of making a social system survive ecologically. As such, the cybersemiotic theory of mind, perception, and cognition is a realistic one, but not a materialistic or mechanistic one. It builds on an inner semiotic connection between living beings; nature, culture, and consciousness carried by the three Peircian categories in a synechistic and tychastic ontology in an agapistic theory of evolution, delivering a philosophy that goes beyond the dualistic oppositions between idealism (or spiritualism) and materialism (or mechanism).

We can now go back and see that the linguistic motivation, mentioned earlier, must be placed in the area of thought-semiotics where our internal non-linguistic phenosemiotic processes of mind meet with the concepts of language, and imbue them with inner meaning, whereas the animal motivation stems from the intrasemiotic area where the endosemiotic processes of the body cells meet with the phenosemiotic processes of mind and awareness. Thus body, mind and language have been encompassed by a shared framework able to conceptualize their interactions on the same process level, but now integrating concepts of meaning and qualia. The cybersemiotic model thus provides a new conceptual framework, in which these different levels of motivation can be represented and distinguished in a way that was not possible in the earlier three different frameworks of biology, psychology and socio-culture. Thus, by viewing meaning in an evolutionary light, as always embodied, and seeing the body as semiotically organized in Peirce's triadic worldview, where mind as pure feeling is Firstness, a transdisciplinary framework can be constructed, which supersedes some of the limitations of the earlier divisions of subject areas. This gives us hope that the cybersemiotic development of biosemiotics can contribute to a new inter- and transdisciplinary semiotic theory of mind, cognition, communication and consciousness.

Peircean semiotic philosophy seems to be able to deliver a philosophical and metaphysical framework without the limitations and flaws of the purely mechanical and informational approaches (including the computational information processing paradigm in cognitive science). It is now generally acknowledged that the mechanical and the computational sciences can only describe limited and idealized aspects of reality. In both the mechanical and the computational areas we can understand, control and predict systems with wonderful clarity and power. These systems, unfortunately, seem only to be tiny samples of the types of systems that make up the Universe as we know it. Recognizing that the social and psychological system of emotions, willpower and meaning is just as real as the mechanical system, although of a different nature it is no longer viable to model nature as purely mechanical or mind as only computational. On the basis of Peirce's philosophy, cybersemiotics offers a different and more comprehensive foundation which encompasses the previously mentioned paradigms, but now relativized to be the most pertinent descriptions of certain levels of reality embedded in Peirce's philosophic framework. They are parts of a greater whole, where not only efficient causality (physical), but also formal causality (informational) and final (semiotic) causality work as real forces, but manifesting themselves at different levels. The evolutionary view encompassing system science, cybernetics, and information science on this new basis is, in short, that semiosis is thus immanent in the universe, manifesting itself clearly in living systems and becoming emancipated and self-organized in social systems.

References

Bateson, G. 1973. *Steps to an Ecology of Mind*, Paladin, USA, Great Britain.
—. 1980. *Mind and Nature: a Necessary Unit*. USA: Bantam Books.
Bateson, F. and Bateson, M. C. 2005/1987. *Angels Fear: Towards an Epistemology of the Sacred*, New Jersey: Hampton Press.
Brier, S. 1992. "Information and consciousness: A critique of the mechanistic concept of information." *Cybernetics and Human Knowing*, Vol.1, No. 2/3, pp. 71-94.
—. 1995. "Cyber-semiotics: On autopoiesis, code-duality and sign games in bio-semiotics." *Cybernetics & Human Knowing*, Vol. 3, No. 1, pp.3-25.
—. 1996. "Cybersemiotics: A new interdisciplinary development applied to the problems of knowledge organization and document retrieval in information science", *Journal of Documentation*, Vol. 52, no. 3, September 1996, pp.296-344.
—. 1998a. "The Cybersemiotic Explanation of the Emergence of Cognition: The

Explanation of Cognition Signification and Communication in a Non-Cartesian Cognitive Biology." *Evolution and Cognition* Vol. 4, No.1, pp. 90-105.

—. 1998b. "Cybersemiotics: a transdisciplinary framework for information studies." *BioSystems* 46 1998 185-191.

—. 1999a. "Biosemiotics and the foundation of cybersemiotics. Reconceptualizing the insights of Ethology, second order cybernetics and Peirce's semiotics in biosemiotics to create a non-Cartesian information science." *Semiotica*, Vol.127, No.1/4, pp.169-198. Special issue on Biosemiotics.

—. 1999b. "What is a possible ontological and epistemological framework for a true universal "Information science"? The suggestion of a cybersemiotics." Paper presented at the International Conference on the Foundations of Information Science, 1996, Vienna, Austria, 79-99.

—. 2000a. "On the connection between cognitive semantics and ethological concepts of motivation: A possible bridge between embodiment in cognitive semantics and the motivation concept in ethology." *Cybernetics and Human Knowing*, Vol. 7. No. 1, pp. 57-75.

—. 2000b. "The relation between the semiotic and the informational research programs in the quest for a united theory for information, cognition and communication." Proceedings from the 7th International Congress of the International Association for Semiotic Studies/Association Internationale de Sémiotique (IASS-AIS): Sign Processes in Complex Systems, Dresden, University of Technology, October 6-11, 1999. In print.

—. 2000c. "Trans-Scientific Frameworks of Knowing: Complementarity Views of the Different Types of Human Knowledge." *Yearbook Edition of Systems Research and Behavioral Science*. V.17, No. 5, pp. 433-458.

—. 2001a. "Cybersemiotics and Umweltlehre." *Semiotica*. Special issue on Jakob von Uexküll, 134-1/4, 779-814.

—. 2001b. "Ecosemiotics and Cybersemiotics." *Sign System Studies*, 29.7: 107-120.

—. 2006. "The Cybersemiotic model of communication: An Evolutionary model of the threshold between Semiosis and informational exchange." *Semiotica* 158-1/4 2006, 225-296.

Kirkeby, O.F. 1997. "Event and body-mind. An outline of a Post-postmodern Approach to Phenomenology." *Cybernetics & Human Knowing* Vol. 4, No. 2/3, pp. 3-34.

Kull, K. 1998. "Semiotic ecology: different natures in the semiosphere," *Sign System Studies*, Vol. 26, pp. 344-364.

Hoffmeyer, J. 1998. "Surfaces Inside Surfaces." *Cybernetics & Human Knowing* Vol. 5, No. 1, pp. 33-42.

Lakoff, G. 1987. *Women, Fire and Dangerous Things: What Categories Reveal about the Mind*, Chicago and London: The University of Chicago Press.
Lakoff, G. and Johnson, M. 1999. *Philosophy in the flesh: The embodied mind and its challenge to western thought*. New York: Basic Books.
Luhmann, N. 1990. *Essays on Self-Reference*, New York: Colombia University Press.
—. 1995. *Social Systems*. Stanford, California: Stanford University Press.
Lorenz, K. 1970-71. *Studies in animal and human behaviour I and II*. Cambridge: Mass. Harvard Univ. Press, USA.
—. 1973. *Die Rückseite des Spiegels: Versuch einer Naturgeschichte menschlichen Erkennens*. München: Piper.
Maturana, H & Varela, F. 1980. *Autopoiesis and Cognition: The realization of the Living*, Reidel, London.
Nöth, W. 1995. *Handbook of Semiotics*. Bloomington and Indianapolis: Indiana University Press.
—. 2001. *Introduction to Ecosemiosis*, Tarasti, ISI Congress papers, Nordic Baltic Summer Institute for Semiotic and Structural Studies Part IV, June 12-21 2001 in Imatra, Finland: Ecosemiotics: Studies in Environmental Semiosis, Semiotics of the Biocybernetic Bodies, Human/too Human/ Post Human, pp. 107-123.
—. 2002. "Semiotic machines." *Cybernetics & Human Knowing*. Vol. 9, No. 1, pp. 5-21.
Peirce, C.S. 1931-58. *Collected Papers vol. I-VIII*. eds, Hartshorne and Weiss. Harvard University Press.
—. 1992. *The Essential Peirce: Selected Philosophical, Volume 1. 1867-1893*. eds, Houser, N. and Kloesel, C., Bloomington: Indiana University Press.
Sebeok, T. 1976. *Contributions to the Doctrine of Signs*. Bloomington: Indiana University Press, 1976.
—. 1989. "The Sign & Its Masters. Sources." *Semiotics VIII*. New York: University Press of America.
Stonier, T. 1997. *Information and Meaning: An Evolutionary Perspective*. Berlin: Springer Verlag.
Uexküll, Jakob von. 1909. *Umwelt und Innenwelt der Tiere*. J.Springer Verlag, Berlin.
—. 1934. "Streifzüge durch die Umwelten von Tieren und Menchen." Springer, Berlin (transl.: "A stroll through the worlds of animals and men: a picture book of invisible worlds." In Claire H. Schiller, ed.: *Instinctive Behavior, The Development of a Modern Concept*, International Universities Press, New York, 1957).
—. 1940. "Bedeutungslehre." (Bios 10. Johann Ambrosius Barth, Leipzig), [transl.: 1982: "The theory of meaning." *Semiotica* 42(1): 25-82].

Uexküll, Thure von, Geigges, W., Herrmann J. M. 1993. "Endosemiosis." *Semiotica* 96(1/2), 5-51.

Wiener, N. 1988/1954. *The Human Use of Human Beings: Cybernetics and Society*, Da Capo Press Series in Science, Perseus Book Group

Chapter Thirteen

Meaning and Self-Organisation in Cognitive Science

Arturo Carsetti

Abstract

Cognitive processes can be considered, in the first instance, as self-organising and complex processes characterised by a continuous emergence of new categorisation forms and by self- referentiality. In order to understand the inner mechanisms of this kind of processes we have to outline a theory of more and more sophisticated forms of organisation. We need, for instance, to define new measures of meaningful complexity, new architectures of semantic neural networks, etc. However, cognition is not only a self-organising process. It is also a co-operative and coupled process. If we consider the external environment as a complex, multiple and stratified Source which interacts with the nervous system, we can easily realise that the cognitive activities devoted to the "intelligent" search for the depth information living in the Source, may determine the same change of the complexity conditions according to which the Source progressively expresses its "wild" action. In this sense, simulation models are not neutral or purely speculative. The true cognition appears to be necessarily connected with successful forms of reading, those forms that permit a specific coherent unfolding of the deep information content of the Source. Therefore, the simulation models, if valid, materialise as "creative" channels, i.e., as autonomous functional systems, as the same roots of a new possible development of the entire system represented by mind and its Reality. Thus, at the level of simulation models, it appears necessary now to extend the condition of predicative activity, as defined by Quine, by admitting the necessary utilisation of specific abstract concepts in addition to the merely combinatorial concepts referring to symbols. For this purpose we must count as abstract those concepts that do not comprise properties and relations of concrete objects but which are concerned with the inner articulation of the intellectual tools of invention and control proper to the human mind.

Introduction

Cognitive processes can be considered, in the first instance, as self-organising and complex processes characterised by a continuous emergence of new categorisation forms and by self- referentiality. In order to understand the inner mechanisms of this kind of processes we have to outline a theory of more and more sophisticated forms of organisation. We need, for instance, to define new measures of meaningful complexity, new architectures of semantic neural networks, etc.

However, cognition is not only a self-organising process. It is also a co-operative and coupled process. If we consider the external environment as a complex, multiple and stratified Source which interacts with the nervous system, we can easily realise that the cognitive activities devoted to the "intelligent" search for the depth information living in the Source, may determine the same change of the complexity conditions according to which the Source progressively expresses its "wild" action. In this sense, simulation models are not neutral or purely speculative. The true cognition appears to be necessarily connected with successful forms of reading, those forms that permit a specific coherent unfolding of the deep information content of the Source. Therefore, the simulation models, if valid, materialise as "creative" channels, i.e., as autonomous functional systems, as the same roots of a new possible development of the entire system represented by mind and its Reality. Thus, at the level of simulation models, it appears necessary now to extend the condition of predicative activity, as defined by Quine, by admitting the necessary utilisation of specific abstract concepts in addition to the merely combinatorial concepts referring to symbols. For this purpose we must count as abstract those concepts that do not comprise properties and relations of concrete objects but which are concerned with the inner articulation of the intellectual tools of invention and control proper to the human mind.

With the assistance of the new methodologies introduced by Synergetics and by the more inclusive theory of dissipative systems, we are now witnessing the effective realisation of a number of long-standing theoretical Gestalt assumptions concerning, in particular, the spontaneous formation of order at the perceptual level. This realisation endorses lines of research G. Kanizsa has been conducting along the entire course of his life [Kanizsa, 1979]. However, a careful analysis of Kanizsa's experiments, particularly those dedicated to the problem of amodal completion, presents us with incontrovertible evidence: Gestalt phenomena such as those relative to amodal completion can with difficulty find a global model of explanation by recourse only to the methodologies offered by order-formation theories such as, for example, those represented by non-equilibrium thermodynamics and the theory of non-linear dynamical systems.

Indeed, it is well known that particular neural networks, inhabiting the border-area between the solid regime and chaos, can intelligently classify and construct internal models of the worlds in which they are immersed. In situations of the kind, the transition from order to chaos appears, on an objective level, as an attractor for the evolutionary dynamics of networks which exhibit adaptive properties, and which appear able to develop specific forms of coherent learning. However, natural-order models of the kind, while appearing more adequate than Koehler's field-theoretical model, are still unable to provide a satisfactory answer to the complexity and variety of problems regarding the spontaneous order formation at the perceptual level. A number of questions immediately arise. What cerebral process, for example, constitutes and "represents" perceptual activity as a whole? How can we define the relationship between the brain and the mind? How can we explain the direct or primary nature of the perceptual process when we know that at the level of underlying non-linear system dynamics there exists a multiplicity of concurrent mechanisms? How can we speak in terms of stimulus information if the measure of information we normally use in psychological sciences is substantially a propositional or monadic one (from a Boolean point of view) like that introduced by Shannon? A percept is something that lives and becomes, it possesses a biological complexity which is not to be explained simply in terms of the computations by a neural network classifying on the basis of very simple mechanisms (the analogue of which is to be found, for example, in some specific models studied at the level of statistical mechanics, such as spin-glass models).

In a self-organising biological system, characterised by the existence of cognitive activities, what is self-organising is, as Atlan states [Atlan, 1999], the function itself with its meaning. The origin of meaning at the level of system-organisation is an emergent property, and as such is strictly connected to very specific linguistic and logical operations, to specific procedures of observation and self-observation, and to a continuous activity of internal re-organisation. In this context, the experimental findings offered, for example, by Kanizsa remain an essential point of reference, still constituting one of our touchstones. The route to self-organisation, which Kanizsa also considers in his last articles the route of primary explanation, is ever more universally accepted. Yet questions remain: via what informational means and logical boundaries is self-organisation expressed? What mathematical and modelistic instruments can we use to delineate self-organisation as it presents itself at the perceptual level?

What selection and elaboration of information takes place at, for example, the level of amodal completion processes? What is the role, in particular, of meaning in visual cognition (and from a more general point of view, in knowledge construction)?

Problems of the kind have for some years been analysed by several scholars working in the field of the theory of natural order, of the theory of the self-organisation of non-linear systems, and of the theory of the emergence of meaning at the level of biological structures. They have recently received particular attention (albeit partial), from a number of scientists investigating connectionist models of perception and cognition. The connectionist models, as developed in the eighties, may be divided into two main classes: firstly, the PDP models first posited by Hinton (1985) and Rumelhart (1986), based essentially on a feed-forward connectivity, and on the algorithm of back-propagation for error-correction. These models require a "teacher": a set of correct answers to be introduced by the system's operator. A second class, posited by, in particular, Amari (1983), Grossberg (1987), and Kohonen (1984), replaces the back-propagation and error-correction used by PDP models with dense local feedback. No teacher is here necessary: the network organises itself from within to achieve its own aims. Perception is here no longer viewed as a sort of matching process: on the contrary, the input destabilises the system, which responds by an internal activity generated via dense local feedback.

Freeman's model of olfactory perception, for instance, belongs to this second class [Freeman, 2000]. It contains a number of innovative elements that are of particular interest to the present analysis, in that for Freeman perception is an interactive process of destabilisation and re-stabilisation by means of a self-organising dynamics. Each change of state requires a parametric change within the system, not merely a change in its input. It is the brain, essentially, which initiates, from within, the activity patterns that determine which receptor input will be processed by the brain. The input, in its turn, destabilises, for instance, the olfactory bulb to the extent that the articulated internal activity is released or allowed to develop. Perception thus emerges above all as a form of interaction with the environment, originating from within the organism. As Merleau-Ponty maintained, it is the organism that selects which stimuli from the physical world it will respond to: here we find a basic divergence with respect to the theory of perceptual organisation as posited by Synergetics. Freeman's system no longer postulates an analogy-equivalence between pattern formation and pattern recognition. While in other self-organising physical systems there exists the emergence of more ordered states from less-ordered initial conditions, with precise reference to the action of specific control- and order-parameters, at the brain level, according to Freeman, a specific selective activity takes place with respect to the environment, an activity which lays the foundation for genuinely adaptive behaviour. What happens inside the brain can therefore be explained, within the system-model proposed by Freeman, without recourse to forms of inner representation. At the perceptual level we have the creation of a self-organised internal state which destabilises the system so as to enable it to respond to a particular class of stimulus input in a given sensorial modality. Perception is thus expressed in the co-operative action of masses of neurones producing consistent and distributed patterns which can be reliably correlated with particular stimuli.

It should be emphasised here, however, that if we follow the route indicated by Freeman, the problem of the veridical nature of perception immediately takes on a specific relevance. As we have just said, we know quite well that, for example, Boolean neural networks actually classify. Networks of the kind possess an internal dynamics whose attractors represent the asymptotic alternative states of the network. Given a fixed environment, from which the network receives inputs, the alternative attractors can be considered as alternative classifications of this very environment. The hypothesis underlying this connectionist conception is that similar states of the world-surroundings are classified as the same. Yet this property is nearly absent in the networks characterised by simple chaotic behaviour. At this level the attractors as such are unable to constitute paradigmatic cases of a class of similar objects: hence the need to delineate a theory of evolutive entities which can optimise their means of knowing the surrounding world via adaptation through natural selection on the edge of chaos. Hence the birth also of functional models of cognition characterised in evolutionary terms, capable of relating the chaotic behaviour to the continuous metamorphosis proper to the environment.

This line of research, while seeming a totally natural direction, is not without its difficulties. There is the question, for example, of the individuation of the level of complexity within existing neural networks capable of articulating themselves on the edge of chaos, at which the attractors are able to constitute themselves as adequate paradigms to cope with the multiple aspects of external information. How can we specify particular attractors (considered as forms of classification), able to grasp the interactive emergence proper to real information as it presents itself at the level of, say, the processes of amodal completion? How can the neural network classification-processes manage to assimilate the information according to the depth at which the information gradually collocates itself? And what explanation can be given for the relationship between the assimilation of emergent "qualities" on the one hand, and adaptive processes on the other? How to reconcile a process having different stages of assimilation with perception's direct and primary nature as described by Gibson and Neisser? What about the necessary interaction between the continuous sudden emergence of meaning and the step by step development of classification processes? And finally, what about the necessary link between visual cognition and veridical perception or, in other terms, between cognitive activity, belief and truth?

To attempt even a partial answer to all these questions, it should first be underlined that the surrounding information of which Gibson speaks is, as reiterated above, immense, and only partly assimilable. Moreover, it exists at a multiplicity of levels and dimensions. Then, between the individual and the environment precise forms of co-evolution gradually take place, so that to grasp information we need to locate and disclose it within time: we have progressively to perceive, disentangle, extract, read, and evaluate it. The information is singularly compressed, which also explains why the stimulus is a system stimulus. Actually, information relative to the system stimulus is not a simple amount of neutral sense-data to be ordered, it is linked to the "unfolding" of the selective action proper to the optical sieve, it articulates through the imposition of a whole web of constraints, possibly determining alternative channels at, for example, the level of internal trajectories. The intrinsic characteristics of an object in a given scene are compressed and "frozen", and not merely confused in the intensity of the image input. If we are unable to disentangle it, we are unable to see; hence the need to replace one form of compression for another. A compression realised in accordance with the selective action proper to the "optical sieve", producing a particular intensity of image input, has to be replaced by that particular compression (costruction+selection) our mind constructs from the information obtained, and which allows us to re-read the information and retrieve it along lines which, however, belong to our visual activity of recovery-reading. What emerges, then, is a process of decodification and recodification, and not merely analogy-equivalence between pattern formation on the one hand, and pattern recognition on the other. This process necessarily articulates according to successive depth levels. Moreover, to perceive, select, disentangle, evaluate, etc. the mind has to be able autonomously to organise itself and utilise particular linguistic instruments, interpretative functions, reading-schemes, and, in general, specific modules of generation and recognition which have to be articulated in discrete but interconnected phases. These are modules of exploration and, at the same time, of assimilation of external information; they constitute the support-axes, which actually allow epigenetic growth at the level of neural cortex.

From a general point of view, depth information grafts itself on (and is triggered by) recurrent cycles of a self-organising activity characterised by the formation and a continuous compositio of multi-level attractors. The possibility of the development of new systems of pattern recognition, of new modules of reading will depend on the extent to which new successful "garlands" of the functional patterns presented by the optical sieve are established at the neural level in an adequate way. The afore-mentioned self-organising activity thus constitutes the real support for the effective emergence of an autonomous cognitive system and its consciousness. Insofar as an "I" manages to close the "garland" successfully, and imprison the thread of meaning, thereby harmonising with the ongoing "multiplication" of mental processes at the visual level, it can posits itself not only as an observer but also as an adequate grid-instrument for the "reading-reflection" on behalf of the Source of itself (but in accordance with the metamorphosis in action), for its self-generating and "reflecting" as Natura naturata, a Nature which the very units (monads) of multiplication (the final result of this specific metamorphosis) will actually be able to read and see through the eyes of mind.

When we take into consideration visual cognition we can easily realise that vision is the end result of a construction realised in the conditions of experience. It is "direct" and organic in nature because the product of neither simple mental associations nor reversible reasoning, but, primarily, the "harmonic" and targeted articulation of specific attractors at different embedded levels. The resulting texture is experienced at the conscious level by means of self-reflection; we actually sense that it cannot be reduced to anything else, but is primary and self-constituting. We see visual objects; they have no independent existence in themselves but cannot be broken down into elementary data. Grasping the information at the visual level means managing to hear, as it were, inner speech. It means first of all capturing and "playing" each time, in an inner generative language, through progressive assimilation, selection and real metamorphosis (albeit partially and roughly) and according to "genealogical" modules, the articulation of the complex semantic apparatus which works at the deep level and moulds and subtends, in a mediate way, the presentation of the functional patterns at the level of the optical sieve.

What must be ensured, then, is that meaning can be extended like a thread within the file, constructing a "garland"; only on the strength of this construction can an "I" posit itself together with a sieve: a sieve in particular related to the world which is becoming visible. In this sense, the world, which then comes to "dance" before my eyes, is impregnated with meaning. The "I" which perceives it realizes itself as the fixed point of the garland with respect to the "capturing" of the thread inside the file and the genealogically-modulated articulation of the file which manages to express its invariance and become "vision" (visual thinking which is also able to inspect itself), anchoring its generativity at a deep semantic dimension. The model can shape itself as such and succeed in opening the eyes of the mind in proportion to its ability to permit the categorial to anchor itself to (and be filled by) intuition (which is not, however, static, but emerges as linked to a continuous process of metamorphosis). And it is exactly in relation to the adequate constitution of the channel that a sieve can effectively articulate itself and cogently realize its selective work at the informational level. This can only happen if the two selection processes meet, and a telos shape itself autonomously so as to offer itself as guide and support for the task of both capturing and "ring-threading". It is the (anchoring) rhythm-scanning of the labyrinth by the thread of meaning which allows for the opening of the eyes, and it is the truth, then, which determines and possesses them [Carsetti, 2004]. Ariadne is a lesson in how to "think by forms": how to order and unify (according to a semantic representation process) generative thoughts and functional patterns in order to see. Hence the progressive construction of an "I" as a fixed point: the "I" of those eyes (an "I" which perceives and which exists in proportion to its ability to perceive). What they see is a generativity in action, its surfacing rhythm being dictated intuitively. What this also produces, however, is a file that is incarnated in a body that posits itself as "my" body, or more precisely, as the body of "my" mind: hence the progressive outlining of a meaning, "my" meaning which is gradually pervaded by life.

The revelation and channelling procedures thus emerge as an essential and integrant part of a larger and coupled process of self-organisation. In connection with this process we can ascertain the successive edification of an I-subject conceived as a progressively wrought work of abstraction, unification, and emergence. The fixed points which manage to articulate themselves within this channel, at the level of the trajectories of neural dynamics, represent the real bases on which the "I" can reflect and progressively constitute itself. The I-subject can thus perceive to the extent in which the single visual perceptions are the end result of a coupled process which, through selection, finally leads the original Source to articulate and present itself as true invariance and as "harmony" within (and through) the architectures of reflection, imagination, computation and vision, at the level of the effective constitution of a body and "its" intelligence: the body of "my" mind. These perceptions are (partially) veridical, direct, and irreducible. They exist not in themselves, but on the contrary, for the "I", but simultaneously constitute the primary departure-point for every successive form of reasoning perpetrated by the observer. As an observer I shall thus witness Natura naturata since I have connected functional forms at the semantic level in accordance with a successful and coherent "score".

According to these considerations, the reference procedures (like those of simulation) are never neutral, and never regard the human realm alone, but are able to act as guide, mirror, and canalization for the primary information fluxes which gradually inscribe themselves in the form of codices, constraints, and modules-forms in action: natural self-organising "mirror" modules which govern, at the basic level, the structuration processes articulating at the level of the living (and cognitive) organism. In this sense, the operational logic of rational perception (as well as of simulation processes) must also be considered in combination with a deeper logical level concerning the articulation of life itself, also requiring us to map out their co-operative and functional interdependence. The procedures of reference, far from being external to reality, lead, on the basis of an ongoing interdependence with the evolutionary paths in action, to the progressive constitution of individuals who finally act as autonomous entities and as observers able to posit themselves as the operational basis for the successive metamorphosis of the body proper to their minds (at the level of knowledge construction). The reference procedures thus give rise to a complex dialectical exchange between action, thought, and meaning, producing, in particular, an evaluation and exploration of the contents and limits of the original information-fluxes. This exchange finally leads, at the end of metamorphosis process, to new forms of autonomy, and the extension and recovery of the conditions of primitive creativity: hence the primary source of that continuous "addition" of new nuclei of creativity characterising the logic of the living (being) which Bergson speaks of, an addition that largely identifies the secret contours of the route to self-organisation at the cognitive level.

References

Atlan, Henri. 1999. "Self-organising Networks: Weak, Strong and Intentional, the Role of their Underdetermination." In *Functional Models of Cognition. Self-Organising Dynamics and Semantic Structures in Cognitive Systems*. Edited by Arturo Carsetti. Dordrecht: Kluwer A. P.

Carnap, Rudolf, and Richard Jeffrey. 1971. *Studies in Inductive Logic and Probability*. Berkeley: University of California Press.

Carsetti, Arturo. 2000. "Randomness, Information and Meaningful Complexity: Some Remarks About the Emergence of Biological Structures." *La Nuova Critica*, 36: 47-109.

—. ed. 1999. *Functional Models of Cognition. Self-organizing Dynamics and Semantic Structures in Cognitive Systems*. Dordrecht: Kluwer A.P.

—. ed. 2004. *Seeing, Thinking and Knowing. Meaning and Self-Organisation in Visual Cognition and Thought*. Dordrecht: Kluwer A. P.

Chaitin, Gregory. 1987. *Algorithmic Information Theory*. Cambridge: Cambridge U. P.

Chaitin, Gregory and Christian Calude. 1999. "Mathematics/Randomness Everywhere." *Nature* 400: 319-20.

Freeman, Walter. 2000. *Neurodynamics: an Exploration of Mesoscopic Brain Dynamics*. London: Springer.

Grossberg, Stephen. 2004. *Neural Models of Seeing and Thinking*. In

Seeing,Thinking and Knowing. Meaning and Self-Organisation in Visual Cognition and Thought. Edited by Arturo Carsetti. Dordrecht: Kluwer A. P.

Hopfield, John J. 1982. "Neural Networks and Physical Systems with Emergent Collective Computational Abilities." *Proc. of the Nat. Ac. Sci.* 79: 2254-2258.

Husserl, Edmund. 1954. *Erfahrung und Urteil*. Hamburg: Claasen.

Jackendoff, Ray. 1983. *Semantic Structures*. Cambridge: MIT Press.

Kanizsa, Gaetano. 1979. *Organisation in Vision: Essays on Gestalt Perception*. NewYork: Praeger.

Kauffman, A. Stuart. 1993. *The Origins of Order*. New York: Oxford U.P.

Koffka, Kurt. 1935. *Principles of Gestalt Psychology*. New York: Harcourt.

Köhler, Wolfgang, and Richard Held. 1947. "The Cortical Correlate of Pattern Vision." *Science* 110: 414-419.

Kohonen, Teuvo. 1984. *Self-organization and Associative Memories*. Berlin: Springer.

Quine, Willard V.1990. *Pursuit of Truth*. Cambridge Mass: MIT Press.

Talmy, Leonard. 2000. *Toward a Cognitive Semantics*. Cambridge: MIT. Press.

PART IV:
COGNITIVE SCIENCE AND PHILOSOPHY

Chapter Fourteen

A Neurophysiological Approach to Consciousness: Integrating Molecular, Cellular and System Level Information

Peter Århem

Abstract

Consciousness is basically a biological problem, but with philosophical consequences. How do the dynamically interacting electrical impulse patterns in sets of neuronal networks, forming brains, cause consciousness? We are approaching this problem along different routes and at different complexity levels. At the system level we ask which brain structures are critical for creating consciousness. This problem is approached by testing how influential consciousness theories apply to the known fine structure of evolutionarily different brain types. Our analysis suggests that avian and mammalian brains share functional features in spite of being structurally different, bringing reptilian brains into focus as target for understanding the evolution of consciousness. At the cellular level we ask how the impulse patterns critically change when a brain goes into an unconscious state. This problem is approached by analysing the surprisingly little understood mechanisms of general anaesthesia. The received view is that general anaesthetics mainly affect a class of membrane bound proteins, ligand-gated channels. Our analysis shows that general anaesthetics also modify voltage-gated ion channels, and that such modifications can contribute to general anaesthesia by determining the firing pattern of the neurons. How the density of voltage-gated channels affect the firing pattern in detail is analyzed by studying a cortical model neuron. The calculations show that the oscillatory activity can be separated into several distinct channel-density dependent firing patterns. This suggests that certain general anaesthetics can contribute to general anaesthesia by inducing a switch from firing frequencies associated with conscious states to frequencies associated with sleep or unconscious states.

1. Introduction

The problem of consciousness is archetypically an interdisciplinary problem, today approached from many angles; philosophical, neurophysiological, computational and psychological. This multidisciplinarity is a relatively new phenomenon. The problem of consciousness or the mind-brain problem has traditionally been seen as purely philosophical. Today a growing insight, even among philosophers (e.g. see Popper, 1974, 1978; Popper and Eccles, 1977; Searle, 1991) tells us that the problem is basically biological; perhaps even the greatest problem of biology today (Francis Crick in Koch, 2004).

Such a statement implies that other approaches have proven less successful. And this is the case. Many - neurophysiologically unguided - philosophical and computational attempts have failed; attempts such as the linguistic and conceptual manoeuvres to expel the problem of consciousness or by replacing the problem with the problem of intentionality or of cognition or of memory or of intelligence or of attention (by positivistically inclined philosophers and cognitive scientists; e.g. Dennett, 1991; see Århem and Liljenström, 1997). It is increasingly clear that consciousness constitutes a problem in itself and is not reducible to other properties of life.

The basic ultimate (for the concept see Mayr, 1988) biological problem is why consciousness originates in evolution. What is its function and what constitutes the advantage it confers to its proprietor? The basic proximate (see Mayr, 1988) biological problem is to understand how the dynamically interacting electrical impulse patterns in sets of neuronal networks, forming brains, cause consciousness? Both problems are typically multilevel problems and should be approached along different routes and at different complexity levels.

Which brain structures and which brain processes are critically involved in causing consciousness? This is still poorly understood. Here I will approach this problem along two lines. The question of brain structures, critical for creating consciousness (the structural neural correlate), is approached by testing how influential consciousness theories apply to the known fine structure of evolutionarily different brain types. This analysis suggests that avian and mammalian brains share functional features in spite of being structurally different, bringing reptilian brains into focus (Butler et al., 2005).

The question of brain processes, critically involved in creating consciousness (the functional neural correlate), is approached by investigating how general anaesthetics affect impulse patterns when a brain goes into an unconscious state. The received view is that general anaesthetics mainly affect a class of membrane bound proteins, ligand-gated channels. Our analysis shows that general anaesthetics also modify another group of membrane proteins, voltage-gated ion channels, and that such modifications can contribute to general anaesthesia by determining the firing pattern of the neurons (Århem et al., 2003)

This is further pursued in a computational analysis of how the density of voltage-gated channels affects the firing pattern. The calculations show that the oscillatory activity can be separated into several distinct channel-density dependent firing patterns. This suggests that certain general anaesthetics can contribute to general anaesthesia by inducing a switch from firing frequencies associated with conscious states to frequencies associated with sleep or unconscious states (Blomberg et al., 2004).

2. The Structural Neural Correlate: An Evolutionary Approach

The structural problem of consciousness, the question which brain structures are critically associated with consciousness, is usually approached by using imaging techniques or by inflicting targeted brain lesions, with well known experimental limitations in space in time. We have taken another approach (Butler et al., 2005). We attack the structure problem along evolutionary lines. We try to validate some of the principal, currently competing, mammalian consciousness-brain theories by comparing these theories with data on both cognitive abilities and brain organization in birds. Our argument is that, given that multiple complex cognitive functions are correlated with presumed consciousness in mammals, this correlation holds for birds as well. Thus, the neuroanatomical features of the forebrain common to both birds and mammals may be those that are crucial to the generation of both complex cognition and consciousness.

The general conclusion from this comparison is that the principal consciousness-brain theories appear to be valid for the avian brain. Even though some specific homologies are unresolved, most of the critical structures presumed necessary for consciousness in mammalian brains can be shown to have clear homologues in avian brains. Thus, the macrostructure portion of the theory of Crick and Koch (1995), assuming that the higher (collopallial) visual areas and the (lemnopallial) prefrontal cortex are necessary for visual experience, is by and large compatible with the hypothesis of avian brain consciousness. Likewise, the theory of Edelman and Tononi (2000), assuming a special role for multimodal areas and prefrontal cortex and possibly for the anterior cingulate, is compatible with the avian brain hypothesis. Also, the theory of Cotterill (2001), assuming that primary sensory areas and prefrontal cortex are necessary for consciousness, is in general terms compatible with the avian brain hypothesis.

In details, however, the Crick and Koch theory is less easy to apply to avian brains. For instance, layer 5 neurons assigned a special role, are at present difficult to identify in avian brains, showing a totally different microstructure. Likewise, the bottom-up, microorganization theory of Eccles (1990, 1992) is at present not compatible with the hypothesis of avian brain consciousness. A structural homologue/analogue to the dendron has not been found in avian brains.

A consideration for future studies is that the findings of this study bring the reptilian brain into focus. The reason is that reptile-bird brain evolution transition shows more continuity than the corresponding reptile-mammalian evolution (e.g., see Manger et al., 2002). Attributing consciousness to birds makes the sharp line at the reptile-mammalian border, drawn by several principal theorists, questionable. This makes it important to reinvestigate reptile brains—especially the relatively well-developed forebrains of crocodiles and some lizards. Will the borderline of the world of conscious experiences be drawn within the reptilian class?

3. The Functional Neural Correlate: Mechanisms of Anaesthesia

The problem of the functional correlate of consciousness, the question which brain processes are critically associated with consciousness, is effectively approached by using electrophysiological techniques; from holistic recordings of dynamically interacting impulse patterns of brain cell populations (e.g. EEG) under various conscious states to direct recordings of single brain cells under different attentional conditions (e.g. binocular rivalry) (see Koch, 2004). We have used these techniques to assess the mechanisms of a clinically well-known class of consciousness-altering compounds, general anaesthetics. Understanding which impulse patterns are critical for transitions between different phenomenal levels of consciousness will help us to understand which processes are critical in creating consciousness (Århem et al., 2003).

The mechanisms of how general anaesthetics induce unconsciousness are surprisingly little known. This is especially surprising, considering the fact that general anaesthesia was introduced more than 150 years ago, when Crawford Long performed the first surgical operation with ether anaesthesia (The history of the innovating years does not seem settled yet, but we find the arguments favouring Crawford Long as pioneer convincing; see ADDIN ENRfu Friedman and Friedland 1998.) However, in recent years new technologies in the inventory of experimenters working in the field have made it possible to hope for a faster advancement in the understanding of general anaesthesia. Thus molecular engineering methods, such as the knock-out (eliminating genes and associated proteins) and the knock-in techniques (genes are manipulated so that the associated protein is made unable to bind a drug but still is functional), has drastically improved the possibilities to identify the molecular and cellular targets of general anaesthetics.

General anaesthesia is clinically separated in several components such as amnesia, hypnosis, immobilization and analgesia. Recent studies suggest that the different components are caused by different mechanisms. (Antkowiak, 2002). Although all the different components are important in clinical praxis, we here focus on the hypnotic component, the component describing the loss of consciousness.

The fragmentary knowledge of the anaesthetic mechanisms pertains to all components and all levels of brain organization. At the macroscopic level we have knowledge about a number of brain structures that are affected by general anaesthetics but we have little detailed knowledge about which structures are critical for anaesthesia. Similarly, at the mesoscopic level we know how anaesthetics modulate cellular processes in a number of systems but not which modifications are critical. At the microscopic level we know relatively much about how anaesthetics phenomenologically affect membrane proteins, but not by which molecular mechanisms and not which membrane proteins are critically affected. And, consequently, we do not know how the effects on the different levels interact to produce anaesthesia.

One of the problems, complicating the determination of the anaesthetic mechanisms at all levels, is the fact that anaesthetics form a chemically very diverse group. General anaesthetics comprise chemically unrelated compounds such as the gases nitrous oxide, diethyl ether and halogenated hydrocarbons, and alcohols and barbiturates, as well as ketamine and propofol. Does this imply that anaesthesia is caused by many different mechanisms? It seems so, and consequently a unitary theory once dominant now appears obsolete.

3.1 Modifying Impulse Patterns: The Role of K Channels in General Anaesthesia

Of the different organization level approaches to the problem of anaesthesia, the molecular level approach has probably been the most fertile so far. A number of investigations have successfully clarified effects of general anaesthetics in molecular detail (Franks and Lieb, 1994). The problem, however, is not to determine molecular mechanisms in general, but to determine which molecular mechanism leads to anaesthesia?

Which anaesthetics-induced ion channel modifications are critical in causing anaesthesia? The dominant theories are focussed on two ligand-gated channels; GABA and NMDA channels. In recent years a class of K channels has come into focus, background or two-pore domain channels. But also voltage-activated channels have been suggested as main targets. However, as already mentioned, the problem is not to demonstrate that anaesthetics affect channels, but to demonstrate which affects are critical in causing anaesthesia.

We have explored the role of yet another channel family in general anaesthesia, voltage-gated K channels (Kv). Most general anaesthetics have been shown also to block voltage gated channels, but as a rule they have been assumed to act at higher concentrations than those blocking GABA and NMDA (Franks and Lieb, 1994). However, a number of investigations have shown that both volatile and intravenous anaesthetics affect voltage gated channels, including Kv channels, at clinically used concentrations. That Kv channels are critically involved in anaesthesia has been clear since long; the Shaker channel is named after the Drosophila mutant, which under ether narcosis shows shaking movements (Hille, 2001). We have preliminarily shown that a functional Kv1.1 knock-out mouse is more sensitive to volatile anaesthetics than wild type mice, suggesting a role for Kv1.1 in general anaesthesia (Nilsson et al., 2004). But how channel specific are the effects? Can we find specific ultrasensitive voltage-gated channels? A growing number of studies suggest that this may be the case.

Voltage-gated K channels regulate the resting potential and sculpture the firing patterns of activated neurons, two features essential in all molecular theories of anaesthesia. Assuming that disruption of coherence plays a role in general anaesthesia it is not surprising that Kv channels have come into focus as targets for general anaesthetics. However, comparative studies on the sensitivity of different Kv channels are rare. In a few cases, a specific Kv channel has been suggested to be especially sensitive, even being identified as the main target for general anaesthetics (ADDIN ENRfu Covarrubias and Rubin, 1993). To get further information on Kv species sensitivity for general anaesthetics, we analysed effects of intravenous anaesthetics on Kv1, 2 and 3 channels, expressed in Xenopus oocytes. The results show that Kv2.1 channels are more sensitive to intravenous anaesthetics (propofol and ketamine) than are Kv1.2 and Kv3.2 (Nilsson et al., 2004). Furthermore, the mechanism of action on Kv2.1 differs between the different anaesthetics.

A block of K channel activity is generally assumed to increase the excitability of the affected neuron, while an increase is assumed to cause the reverse effect. Assuming a general suppression theory as explanation of general anaesthesia, we would therefore expect a facilitating effect of general anaesthetics on Kv channels. However, most reported effects are inhibitions. In computer experiments we could demonstrate that this does not necessarily mean an increased excitability (Nilsson et al., 2004). The mechanism of blocking the channel is thus essential for the modifying effect on cellular firing patterns, and consequently on the brain activity.

Summarizing the results of these and other studies, general anaesthetics show channel-specific and mechanism-specific effects on Kv channels. Our studies suggest that Kv2.1 channels are especially sensitive. Kv2.1 seems to confer fast spiking capacity to neurons, suggesting that general anaesthetic block of Kv2.1 might decrease the firing frequency in some neurons. What that means at the system level of neural activity is, as already mentioned, poorly understood.

What conclusions for the functional correlate of consciousness can be drawn from such studies of general anaesthetic effects on Kv channels? Not many. But they point in a direction. Effects on Kv channels may contribute by disrupting coherent firing in the brain, thereby causing general anaesthesia. The degree of action probably depends on the general anaesthetic. This may help to identify firing patterns critical for creating consciousness. But how does the modified cellular firing correlate with the firing of whole neuron populations? Fragmentary data suggest that general anaesthetics directly or indirectly hyperpolarize neurons in thalamo-cortical loops, and thereby disrupt coherent oscillatory activity in the cortex (Alkire et al., 2000). However, this view has been challenged. Recent experiments on isolated neocortical slices show that general anaesthetics induces changes in firing patterns similar to those in in vivo preparations. They thus suggest that the thalamo-cortical loops are unnecessary for causing general anaesthesia and, consequently, for consciousness (Angel and Arnott, 1999).

A thought forced upon us from the multi-target character and non-unitary effects of general anaesthetics is that the unconsciousness associated with general anaesthesia might be a case of degeneracy, as defined by ADDIN ENRfu Edelman and Gally (2001). Possibly general anaesthesia induced unconsciousness is caused by many interacting mechanisms, each in itself or in interaction with other mechanisms sufficient to create unconsciousness. Is this degeneracy of the neural mechanisms causing unconsciousness the reason for the difficulties to define the neuronal correlate of consciousness?

4. Regulating Brain Firing Patterns: Role of Ion Channel Densities

Blocking ion channels in a neuron means modifying the functional density and distribution of channels and thus modifying its activity pattern, and in the case of general anaesthesia, causing a transition from a conscious brain state into an unconscious. How do the channel densities determine the activity patterns? How do different combinations of channel block modify the activity patterns? We have approached this question by simulating the activity of a model neuron, constructed on measurements from a set of hippocampal interneurons (Johansson and Århem, 1992). We found that different impulse patterns could be associated with different regions on a Na-K channel density plane (Blomberg et al., 2004). The repetitive activity could be classified in at least three distinct patterns associated with three distinct regions. A stability analysis showed that the different regions were associated with saddle-node, two-orbit and Hopf bifurcation threshold dynamics, respectively. Hopf bifurcation dynamics means that the oscillations start immediately with non-zero frequency at the threshold, and saddle-node bifurcation dynamics means that the oscillations start with very low frequency when stimulation reaches the threshold level (Koch, 2001). Single strongly graded action potentials occur in an area outside the oscillatory regions, but less graded action potentials occur together with repetitive firing over a considerable range of channel densities.

Our analysis thus suggests that a neuron can switch between graded impulse and all-or-nothing repetitive activity, thus switching between transferring either amplitude or frequency coded information. For amplitude coding to play a role in the nervous system, the amplitude modulated impulse should be able to propagate along the axons, requiring axons of the same or smaller length than the axon length constants. We are presently exploring this issue.

The presently found relationship between channel densities and oscillatory behaviour explains the difference between the principal spiking patterns previously described for crab axons and cortical neurons; the spike pattern of Hodgkin's class 1 axons and regular spiking pyramidal cells on one side and that of class 2 axons and fast spiking interneurons on the other side (Hodgkin 1948, Tetano et al., 2003).

The fact that the oscillation-density map consists of different activity regions, suggests novel ways to understand the mechanisms of general anaesthesia and novel strategies for constructing general anaesthetics. Neurons in the Hopf region show at continuous stimulation a discontinuous emergence of repetitive activity with frequencies in the gamma range (due to Hopf bifurcation behaviour), while neurons in the saddle node region do not have any low frequency limit (saddle-node behaviour). We are presently investigating how networks of such model neurons behave. Preliminary results suggest that perturbing a network of Hopf region neurons causes firing in the gamma range while perturbing a network of saddle node neurons causes firing in a lower frequency range (Halnes et al., 2004). It has been proposed that neurons firing in the gamma frequency range are involved in conscious activities, while lower frequencies characterize unconscious states such as sleep and general anaesthesia (Crick and Koch, 1990; Engel et al., 2001). This opens up for a novel category of general anaesthetics, functioning by specifically blocking K channels and thus shifting the affected neurons from the Hopf region (high minimum frequency) to the saddle node region (low minimum frequency), causing the whole network to switch from gamma to alpha and theta frequencies, and possibly to switch the brain from a conscious to an unconscious state.

5. Conclusions

A minimum conclusion from these fragmentary discussions on the consciousness problem is that a biological approach seems to work, even if we still are far from a solution. I pointed out some paths to follow and even went a small way on two of them. I discussed an evolutionary approach to the problem of a structural correlate and concluded that the next crucial problem here is to put reptilian consciousness and brains under scrutiny. Is consciousness something that emerges independently in mammalian and avian brains, or are early reptiles conscious? It should be remembered that homeothermia seems to have emerged in mammals and birds independently. And homeothermia is based on a highly complex regulatory system. I also discussed the general anaesthesia approach to the problem of a functional correlate and suggested - less convincingly - that consciousness depends on highly interacting dynamic impulse pattern of certain circuits in the brain. General anaesthetics induce unconsciousness by modifying these patterns, decreasing the power in the high frequency (gamma) band and increasing it in low frequency (delta and theta) bands. How and where the critical modifications take place is still poorly understood. The role of the cortico-thalamic loops for generating critical patterns seems controversial. But computer simulations show us how blocking channels can switch a neuron between qualitatively different firing patterns. We are slowly approaching a theory how such cellular firing pattern modifications affect the activity of whole neuron populations.

Thus the biological approach seems fertile. But is a biological solution enough? Does the finding of a structural and functional neural correlate to consciousness, even in a fine grained version, present us with a solution? No! It does not. Clearly a next step must be to search for a physical correlate. Is it some configuration of molecules or ions during the neural processes that are associated with conscious perception that shows the best correlation with the mental experience or is it the resulting electromagnetic fields or is it something else? It seems to me impossible to equate conscious states with physical states of present-day physics. Some bold attempts have been made to find the best physical correlate in physical fields, but we are far from a solution (see Popper et al., 1993; Lindahl and Århem, 1994; John, 2001). But even after finding a physical correlate to consciousness we cannot avoid ending up with classical philosophical questions. Can the relation between mind and brain be described in parallelistic terms or do we need an interactionistic description? Most thinkers today tend to embrace parallelistic views (Dennett, 1991; Churchland, 1986). However, I find it difficult to accommodate the theory of evolution in their solutions, and we are forced to explore new types of interactionistic solutions, as already and convincingly argued by Popper (Popper, 1974; Popper and Eccles, 1977).

References

Alkire M.T., Haier R.J. and Fallon J.H. 2000. "Toward a unified theory of narcosis: brain imaging evidence for a thalamocortical switch as the neurophysiologic basis of anesthetic- induced unconsciousness. *Conscious Cogn.* 9, 370-86. See:
"http://www.ncbi.nlm.nih.gov/entrez/query.fcgi?cmd=Retrieve&db=pubmed&dopt=Abstract&list_uids=10383639&query_hl=21"

Angel, A. and Arnott, R. H. 1999. "The effect of etomidate on sensory transmission in the dorsal column pathway in the urethane-anaesthetized rat." *Eur. J. Neurosci.* 11, 2497-505.

Antkowiak, B. 2002. "In vitro networks: cortical mechanisms of anaesthetic action." *Br. J. Anaesth.* 89, 102-11.

Århem, P. and Liljenström, H. 1997. "On the coevolution of cognition and consciousness." *J. Theor. Biol.* 187, 601-612.

Århem, P., Klement, G. and Nilsson, J. 2003. "Mechanisms of anesthesia: towards integrating network, cellular, and molecular level modeling." *Neuropsychopharmacology* 28, 40-47.

Blomberg, C., Klement, G. and Århem, P. 2004. "Channel density regulation of repetetive firing: Modelling cortical neurons." Paper presented at the 5th International Conference on Biological Physics:
http://www.ncbi.nlm.nih.gov/entrez/query.fcgi?cmd=Retrieve&db=pubmed&dopt=Abstract&list_uids=16108067&query_hl=1"

Butler, A.B., Manger, P.R., Lindahl, B.I. and Århem, P. 2005. "Evolution of the

neural basis of consciousness: a bird-mammal comparison." *Bioessays.* 27, 923-36.
Churchland, P.S. 1986. *Neurophilosophy: Toward Unified Science of the Mind-Brain.* Cambridge, MA: The MIT Press.
Cotterill, R.M. 2001. "Cooperation of the basal ganglia, cerebellum, sensory cerebrum and hippocampus: possible implications for cognition, consciousness, intelligence and creativity." *Prog. Neurobiol.* 64, 1-33.
Covarrubias, M. and Rubin, E. 1993. "Ethanol selectively blocks a noninactivating K+ current expressed in Xenopus oocytes." *Proc. Natl. Acad. Sci.* USA 90, 6957-6960.
Crick, F. and Koch, C. 1990. "Towards a neurobiological theory of consciousness." *Seminars in the Neurosciences 2*, 263-275.
Crick, F. and Koch, C. 1995. "Are we aware of neural activity in primary visual cortex?"*Nature* 11, 121-3.
Dennett, D. 1991. *Consciousness explained.* Boston: Little, Brown and Company
Eccles, J.C. 1990. "A unitary hypothesis of mind-brain interactions in the cerebral cortex." *Proc. R. Soc. Lond.* B 240, 433-451.
—. (1992) "Evolution of consciousness." *Proc. Natl. Acad. Sci.* USA 89,7320-7324.
Edelman, G.M. and Tononi, G. 2000. *Consciousness. How Matter Becomes Imagination.* London: Allen Lane The Penguin Press.
Edelman, G.M. and Gally, J.A. 2001. "Degeneracy and complexity in biological systems." *Proc. Natl. Acad. Sci.* USA 98, 13763-13768.
Engel, A.K., Fries, P. and Singer, W. 2001. "Dynamic predictions: oscillations and synchrony in top-down processing." *Nat. Rev. Neurosci.* 2, 704-16.
Friedman M, and Friedland G. 1998. *Medicine's 10 greatest discoveries.* New Haven and London,Yale University Press: http://www.ncbi.nlm.nih.gov/entrez/query.fcgi?cmd=Retrieve&db=pubmed&dopt=Abstract&list_uids=11584308&query_hl=16"
Franks, N.P. and Lieb, W.R. 1994. "Molecular and cellular mechanisms of general anaesthesia." *Nature* 367, 607-614.
Halnes, G., Liljenström, H and Århem, P. 2004. "Density Dependent Neurodynamics." Paper presented at the 5th International Conference on Biological Physics.
Hille B. 2001. *Ionic Channels of Excitable Membranes.* Sunderland, Sinauer Associates.
Hodgkin, A.L. 1948. "The local electric changes associated with repetitive action in a non-medullated axon." *J. Physiol.* 107, 165-181
Johansson S, and Århem P. 1992. "Computed potential responses of small cultured rat hippocampal neurons." *J Physiol.* 445, 157-167

John, E.R. 2001. "A field theory of consciousness." *Conscious. Cogn.* 10, 184-213.

Koch, C. 1999. *Biophysics of Computation*. Oxford. Oxford University Press

—. 2004. *The quest for consciousness*. Eaglewood. Roberts and Company.

Lindahl, B.I.B. and Århem, P. 1994. "Mind as a force field: Comment on a new hypothesis." *J. theor. Biol.* 171, 111-122.

Manger, P.R., Slutsky, D.A. and Molnar, Z. 2002. "Visual subdivisions of the telencephalon of the iguana, Iguana iguana." *J. Comp. Neurol.* 453, 226-248

Mayr, E. 1988 *Toward a New Philosophy of Biology: Observations of an Evolutionist*. Cambridge, MA, Harvard university press.

Nilsson, J., Madeja, M. and Århem, P. 2004. "Selective block of Kv channels by general anesthetics." *Biophys. J.* 86, 539A-539A.

Popper, K.R. 1978. "Natural selection and the emergence of mind." *Dialectica* 32, 339-355.

Popper, K.R. and Eccles, J.C. 1977. *The Self and Its Brain: An Argument for Interactionism*. Berlin: Springer-Verlag.

Popper, K.R., Lindahl, B.I.B. and Århem, P. 1993. "A discussion on the mind-brain problem." *Theor. Med.* 14, 167-180.

Searle, J. (1992). *The Rediscovery of Mind*. Cambridge, MA: MIT Press: http://www.ncbi.nlm.nih.gov/entrez/query.fcgi?cmd=Retrieve&db=pubmed&dopt=Abstract&list_uids=15381746&query_hl=7"

Tateno, T., Harsch, A. and Robinson, H.P. 2004. "Threshold firing frequency-current relationships of neurons in rat somatosensory cortex: type 1 and type 2 dynamics." *J. Neurophysiol.* 92, 2283-2294..

CHAPTER FIFTEEN

DOES DYNAMICAL MODELLING EXPLAIN TIME CONSCIOUSNESS?

PAAVO PYLKKÄNEN

Abstract

1. One of the fascinating features of conscious experience is its temporal structure. When I am listening to a song, I am conscious of the notes that I hear now for the first time. But I also seem to be conscious of the notes that I heard a moment ago, and through my anticipations I even seem to be conscious of the notes I have not yet heard.

2. Husserl's famous model of time consciousness has three aspects. There is the "primal impression" directed to the notes heard 'now'. But there is also an awareness of the 'just past' ('retention') and even an awareness of the tones to come ('protention'). Husserl thought that retention and protention are perceptual processes. At the same time he realized that the idea that we would literally perceive the past is paradoxical. According to the usual view of time only the present and what is in it exists; the past no longer exists, the future does not yet exist. How could we possibly perceive that which does not exist?

3. van Gelder has proposed that time consciousness can be approached by considering a dynamical model of auditory pattern recognition. Here the state of the system at any given time models the awareness of the auditory pattern at that moment. Van Gelder suggests that this state builds the past and the future into the present, which is what Husserl required. However, van Gelder denies the idea that retention involves perception of the past.

4. I propose that even the dynamical approach fails to give an intelligible account of time consciousness. van Gelder just eliminates an essential aspect of time consciousness, namely the perception of previously experienced elements. A more adequate account can be provided within David Bohm's 'implicate order' framework. This allows for a continued perception of previously heard notes, because these are understood to be 'enfoldments' that actually are in the present moment. Because Bohm's approach builds upon a richer (quantum physically inspired) view of time and movement, it can better than Husserl's make sense of the idea of retention as 'perception of the past'.

1. Introduction

Conscious experience has become a focus of intense study in recent years in philosophy, psychology, cognitive neuroscience, cognitive science, artificial intelligence, etc., so much so that it is fair to say that a new interdisciplinary field of 'consciousness studies' has been born (see e.g. Güzeldere 1997, van Gulick 2004). An important aim of consciousness studies is simply to explain the various puzzling aspects of consciousness. Following van Gulick's (1995) classification, the puzzling aspects that need explanation include a) the difference between conscious mental states and nonconscious or unconscious mental states or processes; b) the distinction between conscious and nonconscious or unconscious creatures; c) qualia and the qualitative nature of conscious experience; d) subjectivity; and e) intrinsic intentionality / semantic transparency. There is yet another feature which van Gulick lifts up. While consciousness researchers sometimes use the term 'phenomenal' interchangeably with 'qualitative' (connected to 'raw feels'), van Gulick prefers to reserve 'phenomenal' for a more comprehensive range of features:

Current philosophical debate has focused heavily on raw feels, but they are just one aspect of our experienced inner life and thus only part of what we must deal with if we aim to describe the phenomenal structure of experience. In this sense the use of 'phenomenal' accords better with its historical use by Kant and later by the phenomenologists. The order and connectedness that we find within experience, its conceptual organization, its temporal structure, its emotive tones and moods, and the fact that our experience is that of a (more or less) unified self set over against an objective world are just a few of features other than raw feels that properly fall within the bounds of the phenomenal. All will need to be addressed if we take the phenomenal aspect as our explanandum. (1995: 64)

This article discusses the phenomenal structure of experience in light of some new theoretical developments. I will focus on the temporal structure of consciousness, in particular to a phenomenon known as 'time consciousness', characterized by Tim van Gelder as "...a special kind of awareness of temporal objects – an awareness of them as enduring " (1999: 245).

A good example of time consciousness is provided by considering what happens when one is listening to music. When I am listening to a song, I am conscious of the notes that I hear now for the first time. But I also seem to be conscious of the notes that I heard a moment ago, and through my anticipations I even seem, as least in some sense, to be conscious of the notes I have not yet explicitly heard.

Husserl's famous model of time consciousness has three aspects. There is the "primal impression" directed to the notes heard "now". But there is also an awareness of the "just past" ("retention") and even an awareness of the tones to come ("protention"). Van Gelder emphasizes that Husserl thought that retention and protention are perceptual processes. At the same time Husserl realized that the idea that we would literally perceive the past is paradoxical. According to the usual view of time only the present and what is in it exists; the past no longer exists, the future does not yet exist. How could we possibly perceive that which does not exist?

Van Gelder (1999) has tried to resolve the above paradox by proposing that time consciousness can be adequately described by dynamical models (such as a dynamical model of auditory pattern recognition). Here the state of the system at any given time models the awareness of the auditory pattern at that moment. Van Gelder suggests further that this state builds the past and the future into the present, which is what Husserl required. However, van Gelder denies Husserl's idea that retention involves perception of the past, in this way hoping to avoid the paradox.

I propose in this article that even the dynamical approach fails to give an intelligible account of time consciousness. For it seems to me that van Gelder just eliminates rather than describes or explains an essential aspect of time consciousness, namely the perception of previously experienced elements. To understand the limits of the dynamical approach even better, I will consider the physicist-cum-philosopher David Bohm's criticism of the differential calculus as a description of motion. I will finally consider Bohm's own characterization of time consciousness within his "implicate order" framework. I suggest that a Bohmian model of time consciousness allows for a continued perception of previously heard notes, because these are understood to be "enfoldments" that actually are in the present moment. Because Bohm's approach builds upon a richer (quantum physically inspired) view of time and movement, I suggest that it can better than that of Husserl make sense of the idea of retention as "perception of the past".

2. van Gelder's dynamical model of time consciousness

When trying to tackle time consciousness in light of the dynamical approach van Gelder considers a dynamical model of auditory pattern recognition (the Lexin model, developed by Sven Anderson and Robert Port). The idea here is that the state of the system at any given time models awareness of the auditory pattern at that moment, and that state builds the past and the future into the present, just as Husserl saw was required. How is the past, according to van Gelder, built in to current awareness? He notes that in a dynamical system there is only one way in which the past can be retained in the present, namely by making a difference to the current state of the system, i.e. to the location of the current state in the space of possible states. The idea is that it is that location in its difference from other locations in the context of the intrinsic dynamics of the system, which "stores" in the system the way in which the auditory pattern unfolded in past. It is how the system "remembers" where it came from. In such an arrangement the past intrinsically and automatically flavours awareness of the current stage. In this kind of model, the momentary awareness (Husserl's primal impression) is essentially shaped by retention of the past.

How, then, is the future built in? Van Gelder notes that a dynamical system, by its nature, continues on a trajectory from any point, even when there is no external influence. The particular path it follows is determined by its current state in conjunction with its intrinsic dynamics. He suggests that there is a real sense in which the system automatically builds in a future for every state it happens to occupy. The system will automatically proceed on a path that reflects the particular auditory pattern that it has heard up to that point. For van Gelder this implies that protention, too, is a geometrically describable property of dynamical systems. What is relevant about the current state is the way in which, given the system's intrinsic dynamics, the location shapes the future behaviour of system. The current location of the state of the system stores the system's "sense" of where it is going. As with retention, protention is an essential aspect of current awareness

Van Gelder says, however, that if retention is the current location of system (considered insofar as that current location reflects the past inputs), it is hard to make sense of retention as perceptual and especially as perceptual with regard to something no longer exists. He is thus led to conclude that Husserl was mistaken in attempting to describe retention on a perceptual model.

I think there are reasons to question van Gelder's suggestion. Does a dynamical model really describe, say, our experience of listening to music adequately? When I am listening to a song, I hear some notes for the first time "now", but the notes I have heard some time ago are typically still "reverberating" in my conscious experience. It seems obvious that I perceive them both, and in this sense it seems that Husserl was correct. Can a dynamical model, in the way characterized by van Gelder, thus really describe my experience. Van Gelder suggests, for example, that in a dynamical system there is only one way in which the past can be retained in the present, namely by making a difference to the current state of the system, i.e. to the location of the current state in the space of possible states. Presumably this means that the notes heard a little time ago no longer are present in experience but rather influence the only notes that exist, namely the notes that are heard "now". But I think that in our actual experience the "past" notes make a difference to the current state of conscious experience by simply being present in experience, and thus they can be perceived. If this is correct, it seems that the dynamical model cannot really describe the past tones adequately. It is no wonder that van Gelder is led to give up the notion that retention of the past notes is a kind of perception. But it seems to me that when doing this he does justice to dynamical systems, not to actual conscious experience.

I would like to suggest further that the above kind of troubles of trying to model time consciousness with dynamical models might connected with the troubles of using the differential calculus to model motion in general. Such troubles have been described in an illuminating way by David Bohm in the last chapter of his 1980 book Wholeness and the Implicate Order. In this context Bohm also proposed another way of characterizing motion in terms of a notion he called the "implicate order". Further, he described time consciousness in light of his new theory. Assuming that van Gelder's attempt to use dynamical modelling to describe time consciousness does not really work, it might be worth examining Bohm's views. For on the one hand these might help us to get a deeper understanding of why dynamical modelling fails to capture the essence of time consciousness; on the other hand they might offer us an alternative, more fruitful way of describing time consciousness. In what follows I shall therefore first examine Bohm's criticisms of using the differential calculus to describe physical motion in general (section 3). I will then briefly consider Bohm's alternative approach to describe motion and consider what a Bohmian model of time consciousness might look like (section 4).

3. Bohm's criticism of the differential calculus as a description of motion

Bohm starts his discussion of the limitations of the differential calculus in the description of physical motion by drawing attention to the way motion is usually thought of, i.e. in terms of a series of points along a line. If a particle moves, one typically assumes that at a given time t1 a particle is at a position x1, while at a later time t2, it is at another position x2. The velocity v of such a particle can be then be expressed as

x2-x1/t2-t1.

Bohm then criticizes (in a way that resembles Bertrand Russell's criticisms) this usual way of thinking:

Of course, this way of thinking does not in any way reflect or convey the immediate sense of motion that we may have at a given moment, for example, with a sequence of musical notes reverberating in consciousness (or in the visual perception of a speeding car). Rather, it is only an abstract symbolization of movement, having a relation to the actuality of motion, similar to that between a musical score and the actual experience of the music itself. If, as is commonly done, we take the above abstract symbolization as a faithful representation of the actuality of movement we become entangled in a series of confused and basically insoluble problems. (1980: 201-2)

Bohm is thus strongly underlining the difference between our immediate sense of motion and the commonly used abstract symbolization of motion. If one takes the abstract symbolization as a representation of motion, one is led to assume that the times t1 and t2 both exist. For presumably, if the abstract symbolisation is assumed to represent something real, the things it represents must exist. The symbolization refers to t1 and t2 at the same time, so presumably t1 and t2 must exist at the same time. Bohm emphasizes, however, that the assumption that both t1 and t2 exist at the same time is in contradiction with our actual experience, which indicates that "...when a given moment, say t2, is present and actual, an earlier moment, such as t1 is past. That is to say, it is gone, non-existent, never to return" (ibid: 202). The key trouble is that "...if we say that the velocity of a particular now (at t2) is (x2-x1)/(t2-t1) we are trying to relate what is (i.e., x2 and t2) to what is not (i.e., x1 and t1)" (ibid: 202). The usual view of time says that only the present and what is in it exists. The past is gone, the future is not yet. Yet the usual notion of velocity at a given now paradoxically involves both the present and the past.

Bohm admits that we can use the above expression as long as we remember that we are using it abstractly and symbolically, as is, indeed, commonly done in science and mathematics. But he emphasizes that the abstract symbolism cannot comprehend that:

> ...the velocity now is active now (e.g., it determines how a particle will act from now on, in itself, and in relation to other particles). How are we to understand the present activity of a position (x1) that is now non-existent and gone for ever?

He notes that it is commonly thought that this problem is resolved by the differential calculus:

> What is done here is to let the time interval, delta t = t2-t1 become vanishingly small, along with delta x = x2-x1. The velocity now is defined as the limit of the ratio delta x/delta t as delta t approaches zero. It is then implied that the problem described above no longer arises, because x2 and x1 are in effect taken at the same time. They may thus be present together and related in an activity that depends on both. (1980: 202)

However, Bohm is not satisfied with even this approach. He claims that "...this procedure is still as abstract and symbolic as was the original one in which the time interval was taken as finite. Thus one has no immediate experience of a time interval of zero length, nor can one see in terms of reflective thought what this could mean" (ibid: 202). The procedure is thus both empirically and conceptually/logically ambiguous! Bohm thus thinks that when taken as an abstract formalism, the differential calculus is not fully consistent in a logical sense. Of course, it is widely used in contemporary science, so it does work up to a point. What is particular important for our present discussion is that there is even a whole research programme in cognitive science, namely the above mentioned "dynamical approach" or "dynamical modelling" which makes essential use of the differential calculus when describing various cognitive processes (see e.g. Port and van Gelder eds 1995). However, Bohm underlines that the differential calculus has a limited range of applicability even for physical phenomena:

> ...it applies only within the area of continuous movements and then only as a technical algorithm that happens to be correct for this sort of movement. ...however, according to the quantum theory, movement is not fundamentally continuous. So even as an algorithm its current field of application is limited to theories expressed in terms of classical concepts ... in which it provides a good approximation for the purpose of calculating the movements of material objects. (1980: 202)

The above point might also encourage us to reflect upon the applicability of dynamical systems theory (insofar as it relies on the different calculus) to describe cognition and consciousness. To be sure, cognition and conscious experience involve the sort of movement which can conveniently be described in terms of the differential calculus. However, one sees sometimes a tendency to assume that this approach works for cognition and conscious experience in a very broad and comprehensive sense. But is such a tendency really justified? For example, we saw briefly above that van Gelder's (1999) attempt to discuss time consciousness in terms of the dynamical approach seems very problematic. He ends up eliminating the idea of retention as perception, because there is no room for such "perception of the past" in the dynamical framework. But this may be more a reflection of the limits of the dynamical approach, than an indication that time consciousness does not involve perception of the past.

I think Bohm's above criticism of the differential calculus applies strongly also in the case of time consciousness, thus suggesting that there are important limits of applicability to the dynamical approach in the domain of cognition and consciousness. But how should we then think about time consciousness? Bohm proposed an alternative way of thinking about this, and we shall now move on to briefly consider this.

4. A Bohmian model of time consciousness

We saw above how for Husserl time consciousness involves "perceiving the past". He proposed that the "retentions" of the "just past" tones ought to be understood as a kind of perception. At the same time he admitted that such "perception of the past" is paradoxical. Let us now see whether Bohm's description of time consciousness can avoid this paradox, without eliminating important aspects of time consciousness, as van Gelder's model seems to do.

Bohm notes that when listening to music (e.g. a rapid sequence of C-D-E-F-G), in the moment we hear G for the first time, we also hear C-D-E-F reverberating in consciousness. Such reverberations are not memories nor representations but rather active transformations of the original sounds. They are all co-present but can differ in that they can have a different degree of enfoldment.

We can measure this degree of enfoldment in terms of the time elapsed since the sound was first heard. Let us assume our unit of time to be 100 ms, and introduce an enfoldment parameter n. C_n then means that C was first heard n units ago, and is at the nth degree of enfoldment. We hear now G for the first time, and we have just heard the sequence of C-D-E-F-G (with 100 ms interval between the notes). We can now describe the conscious experience of the melody at that moment as a co-presence of C_n, D_{n-1}, E_{n-2}, F_{n-3}, G_{n-4}. That is, we have a co-presence of elements at different degrees of enfoldment

When listening to music one is thus apprehending a set of co-present elements at different degrees of enfoldment. Such an experience has a certain order, which Bohm calls enfolded or "implicate" order. He suggests that when listening to music one is directly perceiving an implicate order (as opposed to thinking about such an order abstractly in terms of thought). Bohm further suggests that such a direct perception of an implicate order consists of an immediate sense of flow. In other words, our sense of flow is a certain mode of experiencing, namely a mode of directly experiencing an implicate order

In my view, Bohm's characterization helps to make sense of Husserl's paradoxical view of time consciousness which involves "perceiving the past". For in Bohm's model the "past" elements are assumed to be in the present, as active transformations or enfolded structures. Thus, they can be perceived without such a perception involving any paradox. At the same time Bohm's model does not eliminate important aspects of time consciousness, in the way van Gelder's dynamical approach seems to do.

Bohm arrived at the notion of implicate order when thinking about the problems of interpreting quantum theory. Although Bohm himself proposed in 1950 famous "hidden-variable" model, in which we can think of particles (such as electrons) as moving continuously, he admitted that it is not likely that they actually move continuously at very short time intervals (e.g. the Planck time of 10 to -33 s). The notion of a particle moving continuously thus has to be replaced by some model which gives rise to discrete movement. In one such discrete model we have "co-present elements (fields) at different degrees of enfoldment", i.e. an implicate order in Bohm's terms (see Bohm 1980: 179-86; Bohm and Hiley 1993: 367-8). The basic mathematical algorithm to describe an implicate order is a certain kind of algebra, not the differential calculus (Bohm 1980: 157-71).

The above suggests, amazingly, that the implicate order model of an electron in Bohmian quantum theory is in some key ways analogous to a model that can describe the phenomenal structure of time consciousness. This opens up the possibility of a whole new research programme, with a wide range of applications. Of course, we have seen that even dynamical modelling has been applied in a wide range of fields, from the physical to the cognitive, all the way to time consciousness. What we have suggested in this article is that there may be important limits to the applicability of dynamical modelling, especially when it comes to phenomena which have a discrete structure, such as motion at the quantum level, or time consciousness. We have further suggested that it seems that the implicate order can do better. Much study is, of course, required in the future to establish in more detail the prospects of this new approach (for further discussion, see Bohm 1980; 1986, Pylkkänen forthcoming).

References

Atmanspacher, H. and Ruhnau, E. eds, 1997. "Time, Temporality, Now. Experiencing Time and Concepts of Time" in an *Interdisciplinary Perspective*. Berlin: Springer.

Bohm, D. 1980. *Wholeness and the Implicate Order*. London: Routledge.

—. 1986. "Time, the implicate order and pre-space", in D.Griffin ed. *Physics and the Ultimate Significance of Time: Bohm, Prigogine and Process Philosophy*. Albany: SUNY Press.

Dainton, B. 2000. *Stream of Consciousness. Unity and continuity in conscious experience*. London and New York: Routledge.

—. 2001. *Time and Space*. Chesham: Acumen.

Güzeldere, G. 1997. "Introduction: The Many Faces of Consciousness: A Field Guide", in Block et al. eds, 1997. *The Nature of Consciousness: Philosophical Debates*. Cambridge, Mass: MIT Press.

Petitot, J. et al. eds, 1999. *Naturalizing phenomenology*, Stanford University Press.

Port, R.F. and van Gelder, T. eds, 1995. *Mind in Motion*. Cambridge, Mass.: The MIT Press.

Pylkkänen, P. (forthcoming) *Time Consciousness. The Relevance of Bohmian Physics to Our Understanding of the Mind*. Heidelberg: Springer, Frontiers Collection.

Ruhnau, E. 1995. "Time-Gestalt and the Observer", in T. Metzinger ed, *Conscious Experience*. Schöningh: Imprint Academic.

Van Gelder, T. 1999. "Wooden Iron? Husserlian phenomenology meets cognitive science" , in Petitot et al. eds, 1999.

Van Gulick, R. 1995. "What would count as explaining consciousness?", in T. Metzinger ed, *Conscious Experience*. Schöningh: Imprint Academic.

—. 2004. "Consciousness", The Stanford Encyclopedia of Philosophy (Fall 2004 Edition), Edward N. Zalta ed, URL <http://plato.stanford.edu/archives/fall2004/entries/consciousness/>.

Varela, F.J. "The specious present: A neurophenomenology of time consciousness", in Petitot et al. eds

CHAPTER SIXTEEN

COMPLEXITY, COGNITION, AND LOGICAL DEPTH

PAULI BRATTICO

1. Computational theory of the mind

Most of us will agree that the computational theory of the mind has been a success story in cognitive science. The idea that the mind is performing information processing when engaging in a cognitive task is so deeply embedded into cognitive science today that we hardly notice it. Starting from the proximal stimulus of the senses, the incoming information is processed by neural networks or symbol manipulation processes, or both, then integrated into the background information available, and finally used to produce reasonable beliefs about the world to help us to make plausible decisions concerning our future actions. The view is ubiquitous in the cognitive sciences, ranging from low-level computational neuroscience to the study of mental faculties, and from the computational modeling of high-level cognition to the study of emotion and consciousness (Pinker 1997).

In a recent book, however, Fodor (2000) argues that despite some success, "The most interesting ... problems about thinking are unlikely to be much illuminated by any kind of computational theory we are now able to imagine" (p. 1).[1] Fodor's view is thoroughly negative when it comes to the applicability of the theory of computation to many of the interesting aspects of our cognition, especially to those aspects which have to do with what Fodor calls global cognition. This involves everyday thinking, pragmatic reasoning, problem solving, abductive reasoning, creativity, and so on. In Fodor's view, the computational theory of the mind can be attributed only to the mind's modular

---

[1] See also Dreyfus 1972, Dreyfus and Dreyfus 1988, Fodor 1983, 2005 and Pylyshyn 1986.

parts or, more loosely, only to peripheral cognitive reflexes.[2] Higher cognition, he maintains, cannot be understood in terms of computation.

To get a better grasp of the problem we are dealing with, suppose that we want to develop a computer that could tell whether it is wise to take an umbrella when one is heading out. The first approach, conceived in the 50s and 60s, was to consider every problem like this as a problem of search. In essence, the idea was that in order to know whether it is wise to take an umbrella, we should compute all the consequences of taking it or leaving it, together with other possible actions and events that may take place, and thus find out which of these options is more likely to lead to a better situation in the future.[3] It quickly became obvious that this solution was too slow, since in any nontrivial case the amount of possible consequences grows too fast, in fact exponentially so. For instance, in most circumstances it makes little sense to try to determine whether taking the umbrella would be wise if Nixon is still the president, but, from a purely logical point of view, Nixon's presidency could be relevant.

This problem led to the idea that people use *heuristic rules* in their thinking. Heuristic rules do not guarantee an optimal outcome in every situation as they leave some possibilities unconsidered, but they were hoped to be able to obtain reasonable results in most cases.[4] In other words, a heuristic rule tries to buy more speed at the expense of rationality. A heuristic rule in the case of umbrellas could be "take an umbrella if it is raining outside". Because of this shortcut, the computer avoids thinking about Nixon's presidency or other logically possible but ridiculously irrelevant facts.

This approach, too, leads to a curious outcome. Suppose a computer located in New York ascertains from the news that it is raining heavily. The condition that "it is raining outside" is satisfied, leading to the recommendation to take an umbrella. But suppose it is raining in China, not in New York. The rule would probably need to be something like "take an umbrella just in case it is raining outside *close to the present location*". But then it becomes apparent that one should not apply this rule if one does not have an umbrella; robbing an umbrella from the first random passer-by in order to execute the rule would not be rational. So you would need to add another phrase to the rule, specifying that one

---

[2] The distinction between modular and non-modular cognition is more delicate that what I have the opportunity to explicate here.
[3] Perhaps more than anything else, this approach culminated in the General Problem Solver envisioned by A. Newell and H. Simon (1963).
[4] For recent discussion on heuristic rules in psychology, see Gigerenzer and Todd 1999, Gilovich, Griffin and Kahneman 2002 and Goldstein and Gigerenzer 2002. Although I will conclude that heuristics does not, by itself, provide a solution to the problem of everyday cognition, I do not want to deny that we use heuristics.

should take an umbrella only if you possess one. In total, the heuristic rule now amounts to "take an umbrella just in the case that it is raining outside close to the present location and if you possess an umbrella". Yet we are still far from anything reasonable, because the computer does not understand that one should not take an umbrella if one already has taken one, so that the rule is not repeated indefinitely. If we actually manage to write down the heuristic rule which allows the computer to know with a reasonable success when to *take* the umbrella, it would still not understand that it had to *open* it as well. And so on it goes, without limit. In Fodor's words, even in a simple situation like this any fact can be relevant to whether one should take an umbrella or not. So one is forced to go back to the model which searches through the whole database and, in doing so, tries to evaluate the consequences of all possible future events to see what is the best thing to do (see Fodor 2000: 41-46). In other words, one cannot "frame" the relevant facts beforehand; hence this problem is sometimes called in the literature as the "frame problem".[5] But this approach has a serious drawback in that it takes again a millennia to decide if it is wise to take an umbrella.

The conclusion I am inclined to make is that the tradeoff between efficiency and human rationality is too steep: give up enough rationality to gain reasonable speed, and the model behaves irrationally; try to maintain good levels of rationality and the model thinks too much.

As far as I know, there are two strategies that cognitive scientists and AI researchers have offered to remedy the situation. First, a number of researchers have proposed that the complexities of everyday life which somehow hamper the computational approach are learned from the environment instead of being written into the model. This approach begs the question, however, because it is well known that unconstrained learning algorithms have exactly the same problem of complexity: they, too, are based on search. Thus, given the data D seen so far, the learning algorithm is supposed to form a hypothesis H about the patterns in the data. Because there are an infinite number of hypotheses consistent with any data set, this creates an enormous problem of search.[6] We are back to where we started. So even if learning is an interesting empirical phenomenon, both from the perspective of AI and psychology, it does not constitute a solution to the problem of search. In many cases, it makes the problem of search much worse.

---

[5] There are several interpretations of the frame problem. The sense in which I use the term here, following Fodor and others, is discussed in Pylyshyn (1986). Originally the term was introduced by J. McCarthy and P. J. Hayes in 1969 with a somewhat narrower meaning.

[6] For a few classic papers on the problems of learning, see Gold 1967, Minsky and Papert 1968/1990, Judd 1990, 1996 and Valiant 1984.

The second option is to use what are sometimes called "expert systems". An expert system tackles the problem of search by using a priori information about the task domain. For instance, an expert system which is used to deal with umbrellas might contain a potentially large databank of possible umbrella scenarios that one might encounter in the world, each associated with the correct choice for the particular situation, and thus handle umbrella behaviour both elegantly and quickly. Yet this approach cannot solve the problem of global cognition, which requires not just knowledge of umbrellas, but also knowledge of weather, possession, dry and wet clothes, the function of umbrellas, and so on. Umbrella behaviour is not an isolated, modularised system: it must be understood in the background context of many other facts. In other words, you need something that is able to integrate knowledge from several sources in an efficient and rational manner; the expert system, by definition, cannot do that.

In the face of these difficulties, Fodor (2000) ends up proposing that the problem goes deeper, into the very foundations of computation itself. But he does not offer anything concrete to replace the supposedly false picture of the mind.

2. Towards a solution

Taking stock of the previous discussion, it appears that there is a pattern in the failures. The pattern is that the tradeoff between successful simulation and efficiency is too poor for theoretical and practical purposes. In other words, as soon as we try to achieve reasonable levels of intelligence (or what I will call, loosely, rationality), there occurs an outburst of computational complexity, and conversely, a reduction of complexity instantly pays off negatively in a gain of stupidity. I will call this the "tradeoff problem". This kind of tradeoff is entirely peculiar to cognitive science(s), as nothing of the sort has ever been seen, as far as I known, in other natural sciences. For instance, in physics, all the gravitational effects imposed upon a given piece of matter take place instantly, without intervening computation, independent of the number and origin of these forces. Planets do not compute their trajectories from a countless set of possibilities by means of symbolic search; instead, all the causal factors are summed up in the resulting trajectory at the speed of light. Looked at from this perspective, the tradeoff problem suggests that what we are dealing with, in the case of global cognition, is something not yet encountered in the natural sciences, or else we have adopted a completely wrong approach to the phenomenon (or both).

As for an explanation, we need something which both makes (i) the poor tradeoff between rationality and computational complexity inevitable, hence explainable, and (ii) which can, at least in principle, characterise the human mind/brain. My purpose in this essay is to provide something that satisfies (i—ii) and to touch on a number of consequences of this solution.

As for (i), the good news is that, as far as I know, there appears to be exactly one property which has the desired tradeoff property, namely the complexity theoretical notion of logical depth (Bennett 1988). The formal details of this notion are moot, but the essentials crucial to the present purposes are easy to understand. Imagine a long string of bits which contains a simple regularity, such as "010101010...0". The string can be compressed in the sense that the simple rule "repeat the symbol 01 n times" suffices to describe it completely. Because there is a simple rule which describes the string (depending on the nature of n, which is irrelevant here), it is algorithmically simple. On the other end of the spectrum, some strings consist of such totally chaotic constellation of bits that they cannot be described by any rule simpler than the string itself. These strings are, therefore, algorithmically complex. In information theoretical jargon, they are also called irregular, random, incompressible, or having high entropy (Li and Vitányi 1997)[7]. Interestingly, some strings have the property that they are simple only under a description which takes a long time to compute. Metaphorically speaking, the simplicity of such strings is 'buried more deeply' into their structure.

The reason why logical depth can explain why there is a poor trade-off between rationality and efficiency in cognitive modeling is because, if phenomenon X is logically deep, then there is, necessarily, a trade-off between simplicity and efficiency. The more simple models you attempt to formulate (as scientists are invariably driven to simplify everything), the more computations you are going to have to tolerate. The worse the tradeoff between simplicity and efficiency, the deeper the phenomenon is in the logical sense.

By saying that the human brain is a logically deep object I do not mean either that it must necessarily be a simple phenomenon (logically deep or otherwise) or that if it is simple, its simplicity must all be attributed to logically deep principles. The first provision is important because part of human cognition could be irreducibly complex. I will not discuss this alternative here; suffice it to note that it, too, is a viable alternative (Brattico, in prep, Salo 1998, 2000). The second provision is important because, demonstrably, there are

---

[7] Algorithmic information theory was invented independently by G. Chaitin (1969), A. N. Kolmogorov (1965) and R. Solomonoff (1964). The theory is based on an invariance theorem which states that the algorithmic complexity of an object is independent of the description method and description language in so far as these are both computational.

simple aspects of human cognition which are not logically deep. Rather, what I am suggesting is that that our rational behaviour in everyday situations is, or contains aspects, which are logically deep. I would propose that, if Fodor is right about umbrellas, then this is because our knowledge concerning umbrellas, for instance, is logically deep.

The obvious objection to this hypothesis is that the human mind is effective when it comes to making a decision about everyday activity, i.e., whether to take an umbrella. Recall that "being logically deep" entails being inefficient under a description which is algorithmically simple. But why should the description of the use of knowledge in everyday situations be algorithmically simple? The amount of information needed to function efficiently in everyday situations could instead be what is enormous. If our everyday knowledge is logically deep, the computations that make up its hidden principles cannot be instantiated in spur-of-the-moment thinking itself, but, I propose, in the ontogeny of the relevant knowledge. Some amount of everyday understanding has surely resulted from the Darwinian evolutionary process, which provides one kind of trial-and-error method for seeking out good hypotheses and filtering out the bad ones. Insofar as I understand the matter, this is the position of evolutionary psychologists and those developing what are known as genetic algorithms (Fogel 1995, Mitchell and Taylor 1999). This biological aspect is presumably enriched with a cultural heritage of deep knowledge, which consists of the lessons from previous generations transmitted via communication, not via biology[8].

Acknowledgements

Preparation of this manuscript was made possible by a grant from the Academy of Finland (project number 106071).

---

[8] In the case of chess, for instance, cultural heritage refers to the previous generations of chess players who have explored the dynamics of the game and whose testimony provides us a databank of valuable knowledge of chess, avoiding us the trouble of seeing all the consequences by ourselves. In the sciences, the previous generations provide a record of hypotheses that have been tested, verified, or falsified.

References

Bennett, C. H. 1988. "Logical depth and physical complexity." In *The Universal Turing Machine. A Half-Century Survey.* 227—257. Edited by R. Herken. Oxford: Oxford University Press.

Brattico, P. in prep. "Towards a theory of everyday reasoning: A complexity theoretical perspective."

Chaitin, G. J. 1969. "On the length of programs for computing finite binary sequences." *Journal of Association of Computer Machinery*, 13, 547-569.

Dreyfus, H. 1972. *What computers can't do.* New York: Harper & Row.

Dreyfus, H. and S. E. Dreyfus. 1988. *Mind over machine.* New York: Macmillan.

Fodor, J. A. 1983. *The modularity of mind: An essay on faculty psychology.* Cambridge, MA.: MIT Press.

—. 2000. *The mind doesn't work that way. The scope and limits of computational psychology.* Cambridge, MA.: MIT Press.

—. 2005. Reply to Steven Pinker "So How Does The Mind Work?" *Mind & Language* 20, 25—32.

Fogel, D. B. 1995. *Evolutionary computation: Toward a new philosophy of machine intelligence.* Piscataway, NJ.: IEEE Press.

Gigerenzer, G., Todd, P. M. and The ABC Research Group. 1999. *Simple heuristics that make us smart.* New York: Oxford University Press.

Gilovich, T., D. Griffin, and D. Kahneman. (Eds.) 2002. *Heuristics and biases: The psychology of intuitive judgement.* Cambridge: Cambridge University Press.

Gold, E. M. 1967. "Language identification in the limit." *Information and Control*, 10, 447—474.

Goldstein, D. G. and G. Gigerenzer 2002. "Models of ecological rationality: The recognition heuristic." *Psychological Review* 109, 75—90.

Judd, J. S. 1990. *Neural network design and the complexity of learning.* Cambridge, MA: MIT Press.

—. 1996. "Complexity of learning." In *Mathematical perspectives on neural networks.* Edited by P. Smolensky, M. C. Mozer, and D. E. Rumelhart. New Jersey: Erlbaum.

Kolmogorov, A. N. 1965. "Three approaches to the quantitative definition of information." *Problems of Information Transmission*, 1, 1—7.

Li, M., and P Vitányi. 1997. *Introduction to Kolmogorov complexity and its applications.* New York: Springer-Verlag.

Logan, G. D. 1988. "Toward an instance theory of automatization." *Psychological Review* 95, 492—527.

Newell, A., and H. Simon. 1963. "GPS: A program that simulates human thought." In *Computers and thought*, 279—293. Edited by Feigenbaum E. A., and J. Feldman. New York: McGraw-Hill

Minsky, M. L. and S. A. Papert. 1969/1990. *Perceptrons: An introduction to computational geometry.* Cambridge, MA: MIT Press.

Mitchell, M., and C. E. Taylor. 1999. "Evolutionary computation: An Overview." *Annual Reviews of Biological Systems* 30: 593—616.

Pinker, S. 1997. *How the mind works.* New York: W. W. Norton

Pylyshyn, Z. (Ed.). 1986. *The robot's dilemma: the frame problem in artificial intelligence.* Norwood: Ablex.

Salo, P. 1998. Complexity and Cognition: Kolmogorov complexity and its application to cognitive science. Unpublished licenciate thesis, University of Helsinki.

—. 2000. "Psykofyysiset lait ja intentionaalisten tilojen redusoitumattomuus." *Ajatus* 57, 57-75.

Solomonoff, R. J. 1964. "A formal theory of inductive inference, part 1, part 2." *Information and Control.* 7, 1-22, 224-254.

Stockmeyer, L. J., and A. K. Chandra. 1979. "Provably difficult combinatorial games." *SIAM Journal of Computing.* 8, 151-174.

Valiant, L. G. "A theory of learnable." *Communications of ACM* 27: 1134-1142.

Chapter Seventeen

Is Computationalism Trivial?

Marcin Miłkowski

Abstract

In this paper, I want to deal with the triviality threat to computationalism. On one hand, the controversial and vague claim that cognition involves computation is still denied. On the other, contemporary physicists and philosophers alike claim that all physical processes are indeed computational or algorithmic. This claim would justify the computationalism claim by making it utterly trivial. I will show that even if these two claims were true, computationalism would not have to be trivial.

First, I analyze the vague definition of computationalism. By showing how it depends on what we mean by "a computational process", I distinguish two main flavors of computationalism claim:

1. That cognitive processes could be described algorithmically (in G. Chaitin's sense of "algorithmic")
2. That cognitive processes are algorithmic or computational (they implement recursive functions).

This second claim could be analyzed further as a claim:

1. That cognitive processes could be described as computational
2. That cognitive processes are really implemented computationally
3. That cognitive processes are generated by computational processes.

I distinguish then three varieties of computationalism. The first is that cognitive processes can be simulated computationally; the second is that they can be realized computationally; the third is that cognitive processes are generated by overall computational processes. This last sense is on the verge of being trivial if we accept that all physical processes are computational.

I show that the non-trivial computationalism involves a multi-level model of cognition where certain level of organization of processes is emergent on the base level. This base level could be even conceived of as algorithmic but the emergent computational level would implement other algorithms than the base level. I try to sketch a multi-level model of cognition which involves computation without being at the same time trivial.

In this paper, I want to deal with the triviality threat to computationalism in cognitive science. On the one hand, the controversial and vague claim that cognition essentially involves computation is still denied as false or explanatory vacuous (see for example Searle 1992). On the other hand, many contemporary physicists and philosophers alike accept universal computationalism (known also as pancomputationalism) – a claim that all physical processes are indeed computational or algorithmic (Wolfram 2002, Fredkin 2005, Lloyd 2000, Ng 2001, Chaitin 2005, and in the context of evolutionary theory Dennett 1995). Universal computationalism would easily justify mental computationalism by making it utterly trivial. I will show that even if all processes are computational and cognition is essentially a computational process, a version of computationalism in cognitive science and philosophy of mind would not have to be trivial.

I will not argue for nor against universal computationalism because such arguments would require a separate analysis of the concepts in question (for a critical discussion of pancomputationalism see for example Piccinini 2007). For the sake of argument, I will assume that some variety of it could be true, and see if it makes mental computationalism completely trivial. The result of my analysis is a taxonomy of possible computationalisms, some of which are weak and trivial, and some of them more robust and non-trivial.

1. What is mental computationalism?

The current usage of "computationalism" is broad and vague. However, all versions of mental computationalism[1] are committed to a claim:

---

[1] For the sake of brevity, I restrict myself here to cognitive computationalisms which do not have to imply a claim that all mental processes (for example, emotional or experiential) are also computational. Such hybrid views seem however to be endorsed so

(MC) Cognitive processes involve computational processes.

MC could be accepted probably even by Searle 1992 if "involve" is taken here to mean a very weak association relation. There are varieties of mental computationalism which would be acceptable even for vehement critics of the stronger versions of it. I will discuss below three ways to make "involve" more precise.[2]

The second vague term here is "a computational process" or "an algorithmic process". It could be understood in at least two ways, so I distinguish two main flavors of the computationalism claim:

1. That cognitive processes could be described algorithmically (in G. Chaitin's sense of "algorithmic", see Chaitin 1975), i.e. they expose non-stochastic regularity which could be accounted for in some compression algorithm.
2. That cognitive processes are algorithmic or computational, i.e. they implement recursive functions[3] or realize computations.

The first flavor of computationalism is a very weak claim that cognitive processes could be described in a scientific theory offering laws (they could be much less strict than physical-mental laws denied by D. Davidson in his anomalous monism, see Davidson 1970). I will focus on a second version which seems more controversial. This one could be broken down further according to the meanings "involve" could have in the original (MC) claim:

---

they should be accounted for in a full taxonomy of computationalisms.

[2] A similar formulation is to be found in Chrisley 2000, but Chrisley uses "is" instead of "involve".

[3] I am using the notion of recursive functions to define the class of computable functions. This is of course an application of Church/Turing thesis. However, my arguments would also hold if I had used a more neutral formulation with a phrase "... described in terms of the ideal formal computation theory". Such a move is recommended by Chrisley 2000 as a general defense of computationalism claim. For my purposes, it is not required because I take for granted that universal computationalism has already been defended, and that mental computationalism is understood on today's theoretical grounds because this is exactly what generates the triviality threat. But the universal computationalism in my analysis is exactly transparent in Chrisley's sense: I point only to a possible ideal version of it, and ignore current details.

1. Cognitive processes could be *described* as computational.
2. Cognitive processes are *really implemented* computationally.
3. Cognitive processes are *generated* by computational processes.

These three versions are derived from three possible senses of what an algorithmic process *involves*:

1. It is a process described in terms of recursive functions (*descriptive-algorithmic*).
2. It is a process implemented by recursive functions (*realization-algorithmic*).
3. It is process caused by a process (2) in some physical device (*derivative-algorithmic*).

The first claims that cognitive processes can be simulated computationally. This is a variety that involves the popular "computer-metaphor" talk. John Searle would not mind endorsing it, as it is quite weak and does not imply that simulated processes are also intentional or conscious. Note that every finite sequence of discrete values is descriptive-algorithmic (Cutland 1980, 122), so if the world is describable by such a finite sequence, it is descriptive-algorithmic, but it is only a trivial definitional implication. This kind of universal computationalism is very weak.

The second claim is that cognitive processes are realized computationally. This is a classical sense of computationalism in cognitive sciences. I will get into necessary details of realization later because on weak renderings of realization, critics of computationalism are tempted to bold suggestions that anything at all computes every possible computable function under some description. I argue that realization of algorithms should be defined not only in terms of discrete states of physical causal processes but of a whole interconnected architecture, and that it is not true that any interpretation goes.

The third variety is a claim that cognitive processes are generated by universal computational processes. This last sense is on the verge of being trivial if all physical processes are computational. But as I argue later, this is not the case for certain models of cognition which stay robust even in a purely digital world.

2. What is realization of algorithms?

A classical account of realization implies that its sufficient and necessary condition is that there is a correspondence relation between states of the program and states of the physical system (see for example Chalmers 1996, 318). The weaker account has it that there should be correspondence between input and output states of the program and of the physical system but such a notion of realization seems to conflate mere algorithmic description with causal implementation.[4] The more robust accounts demand that there should be some structure in between: internal states mediating input/output states. For example, Jerry Fodor requires additionally semantic proof-theoretic relations to obtain:

Every computational system is a complex system which changes physical state in some way determined by physical laws. It is feasible to think of a system as a computer just insofar as it is possible to devise some mapping which pairs physical states of the device with the formulae in the computing language in such a fashion as to preserve desired semantic relations among the formulae. For example, we may assign physical states of the machine to sentences in the language in such a way that if $S_1,..., S_n$ are machine states, and if $F_1, ..., F_{n-1}, F_n$ are sentences paired with $S_1, ..., S_{n-1}, S_n$, respectively, then the physical constitution of the machine is such that it will actually run through the sequence of states only if $F_1,..., F_{n-1}$ constitutes a proof of F_n. (Fodor 1975, 73)

This definition of realization is too broad and too narrow at the same time. Not all programming languages are supposed to be used in a proof-theoretic fashion and only some logical systems have expressibility equivalent to the Universal Turing Machine. We might also add some additional conditions to the specification of a computing language required in this definition, and specifying such a condition can be quite straightforward because this computing language should have expressibility equal to the Universal Turing Machine. This is also a reason why it is more intuitive to directly define required relations between the states of the physical system using Turing machines or other equivalent computation models. Moreover, it is not at all clear if the stipulation of the semantic relations to hold between states of the machine is supposed to exclude all non-symbolic machines, and which machines are taken to be non-symbolic, because Fodor has argued that even subsymbolic connectionist networks are symbolic or representational in his sense (Fodor & Pylyshyn 1988).

---

[4] The reduction of notion of realization to interpretation in both Searle 1992 and Putnam 1988 seems close to such a conflation.

The other problem is that the correspondence is rendered as a weak condition. Hilary Putnam has notoriously claimed he "proved" that any object realizes any computation (Putnam 1988). Similar objection is to be found in Searle:

The same principle that underlies multiple realizability would seem to imply universal realizability. If computation is defined in terms of the assignment of syntax, then everything would be a digital computer, because any object whatever could have syntactical ascriptions made to it. You could describe anything in terms of 0's and 1's.... For any program and any sufficiently complex object, there is some description of the object under which it is implementing the program. Thus for example the wall behind my back is right now implementing the Wordstar program, because there is some pattern of molecule movements that is isomorphic with the formal structure of Wordstar. (Searle 1992, 207-208)

David Chalmers in his discussion of this problem admits that some computations will be implemented by every system – for example, single element, single-state combinatorial-state automata – but this does not mean that every computation is implemented by anything Chalmers 1996, 319). In some ways, one could see objections raised by Putnam and Searle as based on the principle that any ascription of functional properties, especially of formal mathematical properties, is interpretation-based. Would both authors argue also that no objective measurement of physical quantities is possible because measurement scales are interpretation-based? They seem to treat all numerical ascriptions (not only of 0's and 1's) as a matter of interpretation, not as a matter of fact. But at the same time they don't seem to question the validity of all measurements in natural sciences (for a similar objection, see McDermott 2001, 171).

How could one escape such consequences? They would make also digital physics trivial, not only mental computationalism, and they would eventually undermine all uses of mathematics in natural sciences as interpretation-based (or rather interpretation-biased).

First of all, one must require that the syntactical ascriptions to physical objects be consistent. All physical changes in Searle's wall should be isomorphic to changes in a Wordstar program executed on a PC from the beginning of execution until its end: we wouldn't be likely much impressed by a correspondence to a halted Wordstar program looping infinitely.

Mere descriptions do not implement any non-trivial functions (at most, they could be said to compute constant functions) if they are causally inert. This is a common requirement that a whole causal structure of a physical process is as complex as the formal description of the algorithm (Chalmers 1994, 392). It has been however argued that mere causal complexity is not a sufficient condition (Scheutz 2001): to wit, the relation of states of the program being executed to the physical states cannot be sufficiently described with isomorphism which is only defined for functions. So some other relation (like bisimilarity postulated by Scheutz) is required for a physical object to implement computations. I would therefore reject the notion of state-to-state correspondence as too weak.

One other requirement is that computational relations should obtain in machines which are relatively easy to single out from the environment. While there may be a long causal chain which eventually links the internal states of the machine to some distal events, not all causally connected pairs of states of a physical system and its environment should be viewed as parts of the computing machinery (even if one accepts so-called wide computationalism, Wilson 1994, or active externalism, Clark & Chalmers 1998). Thus the system realizing computations should be relatively isolated from its environment so that its computational states could be easily singled out. This condition is that the boundaries of the computational system should be spelled out not in purely computational terms. On a physical level, it is extremely hard to demarcate boundaries of Searle's computing wall, in contrast to the boundaries of a standard PC sitting under my desk, which is a system which can be delineated from the environment using physical and functional descriptions (flow of electricity in the cables etc.).[5] The same objection applies to Putnam's arbitrary disjunctions of physical states which do not form a relatively closed system (see Putnam 1988, 95, for a good discussion see Scheutz 1998).[6]

For this reasons, I define realization as follows:

An algorithm A is realized in a system S iff there is an descriptive algorithmic sequence A' (a sequence having a description in terms of recursive functions) encoded in a physical medium that in connection with a physical device D causes some derivative algorithmic processes A" which in turn generate descriptive algorithmic sequences A'''. The encoding must fulfill the requirement of bisimilarity (or similar relation)[7] but is not necessarily discrete, and the system S must be relatively isolated from its environment.

---

[5] I'm using an informal and intuitive description instead of a formal definition for the sake of brevity. It should be noted that it is complexity of physical relations between the states of a system (which is larger than the complexity of physical relations between the system and its external environment) that underlies the very notion of isolation used here. Nevertheless, a precise definition is not needed for my purposes here.

[6] The precise formulation of this requirement is however out of the scope of this article.

[7] I don't want to argue for or against any such relation here. I think it is sufficient to point to the kind of relations that would fulfill the task. In this respect, my account is committed to Chrisley's transparent computationalism.

Note that the notion of realization as used in digital physics is compatible with the above definition: The cellular automata are relatively isolated systems and they are supposed to implement only a strictly defined set of computations in a given moment. But of course it is a matter of fact if the fundamental physical level is essentially realizing computations in the above sense (this might turn out very hard to show).[8] So while a full definition of realization might seem wordy, it is the price we pay for not accepting Searle's and Putnam's interpretation-only variety of universal computationalism, and at the same time we are not bound to say that all universal computationalism is false by definitional *fiat*.

The stronger universal computationalism makes however the claim "cognition is realized by a computation of an algorithm" trivial. Is there a way to make it more substantial?

3. Semantic Information

A non-trivial computationalism involves a multi-level model of cognition where certain levels of organization of processes are emergent on the base level. This base level could be even conceived of as algorithmic (Wolfram 2002) but the emergent computational level would implement *other* algorithms than the base level.

There are many notions of emergence in use. I accept here William Wimsatt's concept of emergence as non-aggregativity, where aggregative properties are defined by four conditions:

(1) a condition on the intersubstitution or rearrangement of parts; (2) a condition on size scaling (primarily, though not exclusively, for quantitative properties) with addition or subtraction of parts; (3) a condition on invariance under the decomposition and reaggregation of parts; and (4) a linearity condition that there be no cooperative or inhibitory interactions among parts in the production or realization of the system property. (Wimsatt 2000)

Wimsatt also defines the critical notion of the organization level: Levels are local maxima of regularity and predictability in the phase space of alternative modes of organization of matter (Wimsatt 1994).[9] Individual levels singled out below are emergent in this very sense.

---

[8] It is not so important for my discussion if describing the fundamental physical level in terms of cellular automata is viable.

[9] This definition fits my overall strategy to link ways we individuate entities with complexity.

In a multi-level model of cognition, not all processes, nor all computational processes, could count as cognitive processes. It seems plausible that a multi-level model of a cognitive system comprises at least the following levels:

- Physical and chemical (including quantum level)
- Neurobiological
- Computational
- Representational
- Environmental/Adaptive
- Experiential/Conscious.

A strong multi-level variety of computationalism would be committed to a hypothesis:
Every cognition is realized by recursive functions which implement algorithms on the internal information processing level of cognitive systems.

So, cognition involves computation in the sense that there is a special computational level realizing special cognitive computations, but even when all physical processes are digital and computational, the emergent higher levels of organization implement other algorithms than the base physical level. The computational level would involve, as in traditional cognitive science, perceptual data processing, memory retrieval etc., but its computations would be implemented by lower level processes or computations. Thus it is not trivial that there is any computational level in cognitive systems.

The crucial point here is that the claims about computational nature stop being trivial when computation is construed of not as a formal relation but rather as the existence of a real-world implementation of a computational architecture in the cognitive system (Sloman 1997). It is interaction of sub-states that makes computation possible. Complex systems such as cognitive systems have architectural complexity that is best described using multiple levels. The exact specification of such an architecture is not a matter of conceptual analysis but rather of a modeling which has to be empirically valid. It may as well turn out that there is a distinct computational level in the architecture, or a whole architecture may turn out computational. This remains a matter of fact, and not of armchair analysis.

4. Summary

Let me review possible versions of computationalism and point at these, which seem free from the triviality threat:

- Weak Regularity Computationalism: Cognitive processes can be described as non-stochastic.
- Weak Simulation Computationalism: Cognitive processes can be simulated as recursive functions.
- Weak Implementation Computationalism: Cognitive processes can be implemented as recursive functions.
- Strong Simulation Computationalism: Cognitive processes are actually simulated (e.g. in animals) as recursive functions.
- Strong Implementation Computationalism: Cognitive processes are actually implemented as recursive functions.
- Weak Multi-Level Computationalism: Cognitive processes could be described as recursive functions on some level of organization of cognitive systems.
- Strong Multi-Level Computationalism: Cognitive processes are implemented by recursive function on some level of organization of cognitive systems.

Only the Strong Multi-Level Computationalism is non-trivial if some robust variety of universal computationalism is true.

The question arises whether this computationalism claim is empirical, metaphysical (conceptual) or simply heuristic for cognitive scientists. The computationalism claim is usually ascribed various statuses: empirical, heuristic, or conceptual. In its purely trivial versions, it is conceptual. In its non-trivial versions, it is also *empirical*, and could play a *heuristic* role. Computational systems are not only systems with some interpretation ascribed intentionally. Their computational structure is as real as any functional structure.

Universal computationalism could make single-level mental computationalism true but trivial. For multi-level computationalism, it is both empirical and conceptual question whether all or some cognitive systems are or could be computational on one of their levels. The hypothesis of the strong multi-level computationalism seems however to be empirical as there are no real conceptual problems with cognitive systems realizing computations, all criticisms notwithstanding.

References

Chaitin, Gregory. 1975. "Randomness and Mathematical Proof." *Scientific American*. 232, 5, 47-52.
—. 2005. *Meta Math! The Quest for Omega*. Pantheon Books.
Chalmers, David J. 1994. "On Implementing a Computation". *Minds and Machines*, 4, 391-402.
—. 1996. *The Conscious Mind. In Search of a Fundamental Theory*. Oxford University Press.
Chrisley, Ron, 2000. "Transparent Computationalism." In Scheutz, M. (ed.) *New Computationalism: Conceptus-Studien* **14**, Sankt Augustin: Academia Verlag.
Clark, Andy & Chalmers, David J. 1998. "The Extended Mind". *Analysis*, 58.1, 7-19.
Cutland, Nigel. 1980. *Computability*. Cambridge University Press.
Davidson, Donald, 1970, "Mental Events" in *Experience and Theory*, ed. Foster, L. and J. W. Swanson, University of Massachusetts Press.
Dennett, Daniel. 1995. *Darwin's Dangerous Idea: Evolution and the Meanings of Life*. Simon& Schuster.
Fodor, Jerry. 1975. *Language of Thought*. Thomas Y. Crowell.
Fodor, Jerry & Pylyshyn, Zenon. 1988. "Connectionism and Cognitive Architecture". *Cognition*, 28, 3-71.
Fredkin, Ed. 2005. Introduction to Digital Philosophy (ms).
Lloyd, Seth. 2000. "Ultimate physical limits to computation". *Nature*, 406 (6799), 1047-54.
McDermott, Drew. 2001. *Mind and Mechanism*. MIT Press.
Ng, Y Jack. 2001. "From computation to black holes and space-time foam". *Phys. Rev. Lett.*, 86, 2946-2949.
Piccinini, Gualtiero. 2007 (in print). "Computational Modeling vs. Computational Explanation." *The Australasian Journal of Philosophy*.
Putnam, Hilary. 1988. *Representation and Reality*. MIT Press.
Scheutz, Matthias. 1998. "Implementation: Computationalism's Weak Spot". *Conceptus JG*, 31, 79, 229-239.
—. 2001. "Computational versus Causal Complexity". *Minds and Machines* 11, 543-566.
Searle, John. 1992. *The Rediscovery of Mind*. MIT Press.
Sloman, Aaron, 1997, "Beyond Turing Equivalence", in *Machines and Thought: The Legacy of Alan Turing I*, ed. Millican, Peter & Clark, Andy, Oxford University Press.
Wilson, Robert A. 1994. "Wide Computationalism". *Mind*, 103, no. 411, 351-372.

Wimsatt, William. 1994. "The Ontology of Complex Systems: Levels of Organization, Perspectives." *Canadian Journal of Philosophy*, supp. vol #20, 207-274.
—. 2000. "Emergence as Non-Aggregativity and the Biases of Reductionism(s)." *Foundations of Science* 5, 3, 269-297.
Wolfram, Steven. 2002. *A New Kind of Science*. Wolfram Media.

CHAPTER EIGHTEEN

ON FACING UP TO THE SEMANTIC CHALLENGE

OTTO LAPPI

1. Introduction

Grush (2001) presents computational neuroscience with the following challenge: How to distinguish between computation - understood as computational processing of "genuinely semantic" information - and any other complex causal process, merely governed by a computationally tractable rule? Given that there are countless physical systems that are not computers but in which there nevertheless occur state transitions that can be modeled or simulated computationally, how exactly is one to distinguish *computational* systems from *computable* systems? The natural answer would be to invoke a semantic notion of computation, which holds that computations (performed by the system, not merely giving a valid description of the system) are information processing operations over semantically evaluable "mental" entities (contents), represented in a physical medium (see Piccinini 2004). This then charges one with providing a theory of mental content appropriate for the purposes of computational neuroscience, neurosemantics.

Grush frames the problem in terms a distinction between what he calls a-semantics and e-semantics. a-semantics is isomorphism between the causal neural processes and some abstract algorithm, e-semantics is isomorphism between the causal neural process and the physical causal processes of the environment. He argues that recent computational neuroscience treats computation and representation a-semantically, but that this is inadequate and should be replaced with a more genuinely semantic notion of computation and representation, e-semantics.

In this paper I discuss Grush's challenge and his solution in terms of a slightly different distinction between what I call "horizontal" and "vertical" approaches to assigning a semantics to neural activity. The main point I will argue for is that Grush's e-semantics, his proposed alternative to a-semantics (which in my terminology is vertical) is a version of horizontal content-assignment, but that what one needs to fully address the semantic challenge of computational neuroscience, should be a vertical semantics. However, Grush is right that a-semantics is inadequate. What one really needs is a "top-down" vertical semantics - call it c-semantics - rather than the sort "bottom-up" vertical a-semantics rightly criticized by Grush. My negative argument against e-semantics and my positive argument for a c-semantic construal of computation and representation is based on considerations concerning the poverty of the stimulus hypothesis and the veridicality assumption (Akins, 1996).

2. Neuroscience and computation: The semantic challenge

There are many types of automata that can compute information, i.e. implement algorithmic computations, by their state transitions. Computational neuroscience is founded on the computational hypothesis of the mind/brain: that complex neural systems are such automata, and that understanding this property of the brain is useful for accounting for much of the intelligence we find in the behavior of organisms.

In a *locus classicus* of the approach, Churchland, Koch & Sejnowski (1990) define the assumption thus (cf. Churchland & Sejnowski, 1992; Cummins 1989):

(1) "In a most general sense we can consider a physical system as a computational system just in case there is an appropriate (revealing) mapping between some algorithm and associated physical variables. More exactly, a physical system computes a function $f(x)$ when there is (1) a mapping between the system's physical inputs and x, (2) a mapping between the system's physical output and y, such that (3) $f(x) = y$"

According to definition (1) *all it takes* for a system to compute a function f – all that is required to make the system "a computer" – is for its causal processes to be appropriately equivalent to some algorithm in this sense.

The trouble with this account is, roughly, that computable state transitions occur in countless systems that are *not* computers. Indeed, any computable causal process trivially realizes any algorithm describing its behavior reasonably accurately. What, then, beyond (assumed) *computability* makes neural systems *computational* in the specific sense computational neuroscience is interested in?

The natural response is invoke a semantic notion of computation (as defined in Piccinini 2004a, 2004b), and insist that the difference between genuine computation and mere computability is that in semantic computation the entities which computational relations are defined over are (mental) representations, i.e. entities which are semantically related to each other and/or the external world.

With the semantic notion of computation we can see why the solar system, to use Grush's example, does not "compute" anything in accordance with the laws of Kepler, Newton or Einstein. Some of its state transitions might be *computable* in the sense of being *governed by rules* that can be framed in computational terms. The system can be simulated computationally but is not *computational*, in the sense of "performing" those computations. Likewise, not all computational modeling of neural processes counts as computational neuroscience. It is quite possible, and indeed common, to model *physiological mechanisms*, rather than mechanisms at "the representational level" of the brain.

This, of course, means one needs an explicit and non-circular definition of representation and semantic information. To do computational neuroscience in the full sense one should be assigning some sort of "semantics" to the internal states of the brain. Yet, looking at one example of contemporary neuroscience (Koch, 1990), Grush observes that:

> "The [computational account] involving the bullfrog ganglion cell appears to involve no more than would be involved in any example of computer-simulation-cum-experimental-testing endeavor, of the sort familiar in computational physics, economics, meteorology, and dozens of other areas." Grush (2001, p.162).

Grush suggests we should think of the semantic challenge in terms of a-semantics, isomorphism to an algorithm, and e-semantics, isomorphism between environmental variables and the variables of an internal system used in the brain to "stand in for" the environmental system (cf. e.g. Gallistel, 1990). Grush's contention is that what definition (1) above captures, is merely the "a-semantics" of a system, when what you need to do genuine computational neuroscience in the full-blooded sense is semantics of a different sort: "e-semantics"; accounts where you can see that:

"The brain (or parts thereof) computes in the sense that it processes information - it deals with what genuinely are information-carrying states – e.g. states that carry information about objects or states of affairs in the environment". (Grush, 2001, p.158).

So,

"[I]f there were some principled means to determine which states are representing aspects of the environment [...] We would have the means to distinguish those systems that are genuinely computational in the required sense, and there would be no danger of computational neuroscience being assimilated without residue into the general category of computer simulation studies." (Grush, 2001, p.162).

The general approach to such informational neurosemantics (Dretske, 1981, 1988; Eliasmith, 2000; Fodor ,1990; Grush, 1997, 2004; Millikan, 1989; Ryder, 2002, 2004;Usher 2001, 2004) is something like this: to get representation out of information you start out with a (physical) account of the dependencies between environmental variables and neural activity. The causally interacting elements of the system (vehicles; Grush calls them articulants) are representations if they are by design isomorphic to something else, and are used in the system to stand in for that something. Relying on the mathematical notion of isomorphism (Gallistel, 1990; Ryder 2002, 2004) and perhaps the statistical notion of mutual information to define "standing in for" (Eliasmith 2000, Usher 2001, 2004) provides means of disambiguating what the individual brain states could stand in for.

This picture has intuitive plausibility, and probably captures much of the logic of representational talk in current neurocience. Yet I will next argue that the account of semantic relations between the brain and the world it gives is incorrect. The problem with this analysis is that it presupposes a very robust sense in which the content of the representation must be "out there", in the environment, and that the very function of neural representations is to reflect with fidelity structures already in the environment (the "veridicality assumption").

3. Poverty of the stimulus and the veridicality assumption

For the purposes of this paper, "poverty of the stimulus" may be defined as the hypothesis that the extensions of most concepts do not constitute mind-independent (physical) natural kinds, only the concept constitutes a (cognitive) natural kind (cf. e.g. Fodor, 1998). Likewise, by "veridicality assumption" I mean the converse hypothesis that the function of representation is to "pick out" real kinds in the environment, implicitly represented in the information available to the organism via its sensory apparatus (cf. e.g. Millikan, 1998, Churchland & Churchland, 2002; for a contrary opinion see Akins, 1996).

If you are working within the framework of externalist neurosemantics and the semantic notion of computation, then you need to take a stance on the poverty of the stimulus hypothesis. As far as I can tell, *all* current neurosemantics, including Grush's e-semantics, seem inconsistent with the poverty of the stimulus (and instead buy into a very strong veridicality assumption). The problem with this is that, empirically, it seems plausible that the poverty of the stimulus is true, and should therefore be taken into account as a constraint on philosophical theory construction.

Take, for example, color concepts. On the assumption of poverty of the stimulus, you would not consider color properties (categories) such as *red*, *purple* and *brown* as something in the environment, implicit in the structure of the physical energy impinging on an organism. Color is a mind-dependent property, only "there" for a particular kind of organism. Assessing the facts about color as a natural phenomenon must therefore take into account not only the physical properties of the distal stimulus (and maybe sensory physiology of the proximal stimulus), but the cognitive properties constituting the *point of view* of the organism.

One way of putting this is to say that in genuinely mental representation there is "more information" in the representation of a domain than is present or available in the domain itself - the distal physical stimuli. This additional information that the "poverty" of the stimulus requires, represents the organism's contribution to the natural phenomenon. And insofar as the information constitutes a cognitive (as opposed to physiological) characterization of the organism, this sets apart the study of cognitive phenomena and cognitive natural kinds from the study of the physics of the organisms' natural environment and/or brain.

The alternative is that you end up with a theory where representation reduces into mirroring or reflecting (possibly quite abstract) *physical* features of the environment, and the organism is charged with finding the true classifications (physically natural ways of organizing the distal environment – or perhaps the proximal stimuli - into objects, categories, properties etc.).

Arguably, this isn't at all what brains do. It in any case is a strong empirical claim that the function of information gathering and processing systems is to find out about physical features of the environment (For a general criticism see Akins, 1996). Yet this is what you get if you begin with the "actual referent", as Grush's e-semantics does (and as all current neurosemantics seems to do), and then base your *semantics* on causal history, isomorphism and what natural (physical) kind the referents belong to. All that is left for the organism is for it to "take in" that which is "given".

Millikan puts this clearly:

> "It is not a matter of logic, of course, but rather of the makeup of the world, that I can learn from one observation what color Xavier's eyes are or, say, how the water spider propels itself. It is not a matter of logic that these things will not vary from meeting to meeting. [...] most of the knowledge that carries over about ordinary substances is not certain knowledge but merely probable knowledge [...] But no knowledge whatever carries over about nonsubstance kinds." (Millikan, 1998, p.57)

The very representational content of the vehicle would be determined by the real category structure of the world behind the sensory "evidence" available to the organism. According to the poverty of stimulus hypothesis, there *is* no such *physical* category structure. For example, it is common wisdom that there is nothing specific that, say, *brown* things have in common *physically*. There is no natural class that would allow you to "generalize to denotation" based on a sample of the stimuli belonging to a class - say, *brown* things. Knowing that a motley selection of objects all fall under the concept BROWN does not enable you to pick out the denotation (all brown things) from the environment without further information, based on just their physical properties (surface reflectances, say).

Not assuming the referents constitute a useful sample of a real physical kind (poverty of the stimulus) leaves you logically with two options. One would be to assume that they therefore must constitute an "unnatural" (nominal) distal physical category. But this does not seem to offer the right solution; for we are committed to naturalizing cognitive kinds as natural kinds. So what we would want in the case of BROWN is a theory of color. The option we are left with is to assume that the theory of colors is (in part) a theory of the *cognition* of organisms with color vision.

It does not follow from naturalism as such that the theory that allows you to generalize to denotation must be a physical one, less so a theory of the distal stimuli. Consider Millikan again (ibid.):

> "[K]inds are not natural if they yield inductive knowledge by accident. [...] If a [representation] is to have genuine 'rich inductive potential' it had better attach not just to a pattern of correlated properties, but to a univocal explanatory ground for correlation."

It is not part of commitment to naturalism – or even externalism - as such, that the source of correlation, or "the univocal explanatory ground for correlation", must be entirely external to the organism's mind/brain. What is required for a kind to be real (for the animal) is for encounters with it to license induction to new encounters. Note that the brain and the mental faculties of the organism is itself an important constant across contexts. The properties need to "carry over" – but what needs to carry over is *represented* properties. Our encounters with a brown object *do* license inductive inferences about further encounters – but this is really as much in virtue of our brain's peculiar color constancy mechanisms, as any physical properties of brown objects as such. In the case of colors at least, physical properties (e.g. spectral distribution or surface reflectance) are precisely the kinds of things we *cannot* expect to carry over.

4. Conclusions

One may think of *horizontal* "information coding" as the causal process of activating an "indicator state". Looking at information coding vertically, on the other hand, one looks for entities within the organism which can be considered to represent the value of some variable. The fact that the entity/vehicle was in such-and-such state would "stand for" the fact that the value of the variable was such-and-such - and in genuinely semantic contexts the variables would be elements of a mental representation of some domain. Philosophically, these are two quite different ways of looking at representation and information (cf. Cummins, 1996), invoking two very different (and complementary) notions of "representation".

Now, a-semantics and c-semantics are both vertical, while Grush's e-semantics is horizontal. The key difference is that in a-semantics the algorithmic computations are a representation of the organism, whereas in c-semantics the organism is a representation of the computations. In a-semantics, the internal physical configurations of neural tissue and their state transitions can be seen as instantiations of *some* variables and *some* algorithm, and what the algorithm is, is interpreted as it were "bottom up", starting from the brain states (vehicles). The problem is that, as stated, this "interpretation" does not constrain the variables and algorithms as part of a mental representation of any domain. Add this requirement, c-semantics.

The difference between c-semantics and e-semantics, on the other hand, is that in e-semantics the organism's internal states (representations or vehicles), have the function of standing in for something *physical* - something that is really "physically out there" in the environment. The veridicality assumption built into e-semantics requires that the *same* theory (the same formal structure) should characterize both the external environment and the organism's vehicles (isomorphism). c-semantics by contrast makes essential reference to cognitive mechanisms of the organism, that are not merely a reflection of structure in the environment but represent a systematic and genuine contribution of the organism to semantic content.

Distinguishing between a-semantics and c-semantics enables us to see that Grush's solution does not exhaust the options. In fact, it could be argued that by confounding a-semantics and c-semantics Grush is blurring precisely that distinction which is crucial to understanding the difference between mere computable regularity and semantic computation - what we set out to elucidate in the first place.

References

Akins, K. 1996. "Sensory Systems and the Aboutness of Mental States." *Journal of Philosophy* 93: 337-372.
Churchland, P. and M. Churchland. 2002. "Neural Worlds and Real Worlds." *Nature Reviews Neuroscience* 3: 903-907.
Churchland, P., C. Koch, et al. 1990. *What is Computational Neuroscience? Computational Neuroscience*. Cambridge, MA., MIT Press.
Churchland, P. and T. Sejnowski. 1992. *The Computational Brain*. Cambridge, MA., MIT Press.
Cummins, R. 1989. *Meaning and Mental Representation*. Cambridge, MA., MIT Press.

Dretske, F. 1981. *Knowledge and the Flow of Information*. Cambridge, MA., MIT Press.
—. 1988. *Explaining Behavior: Reasons in a World of Causes*. Cambridge, MA., MIT Press.
Eliasmith, C. 2000. "How Neurons Mean: A Neurocomputational Theory of Representational Content." Washington University in St. Louis.
Eliasmith, C. 2003. "Moving Beyond Metaphors: Understanding the Mind for what It Is." *Journal of Philosophy* C(10): 493-520.
Fodor, J. 1990. *A Theory of Content*. Cambridge, MA., MIT Press.
—. 1998. *Concepts: Where Cognitive Science Went Wrong*. Oxford, Oxford University Press.
Gallistel, C. R. 1990. *The Organization of Learning*. Cambridge MA., MIT Press.
Grush, R. 1995. *Emulation and Cognition*, University of California, San Diego.
—. 1997. "The Architecture of Representation." *Philosophical Psychology* 10: 5-23.
—. 2001. "The Semantic Challenge to Computational Neuroscience." in Machamer, P. Grush, R. & McLaughlin, P. (Eds.), *Theory and Method in the Neurosciences*, Pittsburgh, PA: University of Pittsburgh Press.
—. 2004. "The Emulation Theory of Representation: Motor Control, Imagery and Perception." *Behavioral and Brain Sciences* 27: 377-442.
Koch, C. 1990. "Biophysics of Computation: Toward the Mechanisms of Information Processing in Single Neurons." *Computational Neuroscience*. E. Schwartz. Cambridge, MA., MIT Press.
Millikan, R. G. 1989. "Biosemantics." *Journal of Philosophy* 86: 288-302.
—. 1998. "A Common Structure for Concepts of Individuals, Stuffs and Real Kinds: More Mama, More Milk and More Mouse." *Behavioral and Brain Sciences* 21: 55-100.
Piccinini, G. 2004. "Functionalism, Computationalism and Mental Contents." *Canadian Journal of Philosophy* 34(3): 375-410.
—. 2004. "Functionalism, Computationalism, and Mental States." *Studies in the History and Philosophy of Science* 35(4): 811-833.
Ryder, D. 2002. "Neurosemantics: A Theory." University of North Carolina at Chapel Hill.
—. 2004. "SINBAD Neurosemantics: A Theory of Mental Representation." *Mind & Language* 19: 211-241.
Sejnowski, T., C. Koch, et al. 1988. "Computational Neuroscience." *Science* 241: 1299-1306.
Usher, M. 2001. "A Statistical Referential Theory of Content: Using Information Theory to Account for Misrepresentation." *Mind & Language* 16: 311-334.

—. 2004. "Comment on Ryder's SINBAD Neurosemantics: Is Teleofunction Isomorphism the Way to Understand Representations?" *Mind & Language* 19: 241-248.

PART V:
COMPUTATIONAL LINGUISTICS

Chapter Nineteen

Computational Linguistics as an Applied Science

Pius ten Hacken

In this paper I will argue that computational linguistics (CL) can be seen as an applied science, that it is useful for CL to be seen as an applied science, and that recent developments in CL show a move towards this conception of CL

1. Applied Science

A characterization of applied science should distinguish it on the one hand from empirical science and on the other from technological problem-solving. The opposition between empirical and applied science is that the former only attempts to explain observations whereas the latter also tries to solve practical problems. An example of a purely empirical study is the work on black holes in astronomy. In medicine, by contrast, people expect research to result in cures for patients, not just in an explanation of their sufferings.

The nature of the opposition between applied science and technological problem-solving becomes clear when we compare medicine with traditional crafts. A cobbler mends shoes and uses a variety of techniques. How to apply these techniques is a matter of experience and judgement. He can normally not give a scientific explanation of the chemical processes involved in the manipulation of leather or the physical forces exerted on a shoe in different types of use. No one would expect him to and he does not get extra pay if he can. A medical doctor, by contrast, is expected to be able to explain why a particular cure is prescribed to a specific patient. This explanation should be in terms of available scientific knowledge. It is not sufficient to have a cure, we also need an explanation for why it works. This makes medicine an applied science.

For medicine, Bynum (1994) sketches the gradual and imperfect transition from a craft to an applied science in the 19th century. He also mentions a line of research in early 19th century Paris that could be labelled empirical. It consisted in meticulously observing the state of patients that were not given medical treatment. Even though available treatment was rather primitive and its effectiveness not proven, the approach was heavily criticized for ethical reasons.

Like medicine, CL can be pursued as an empirical science, as an applied science or as mere technology. The contrast between these three perspectives can be seen in the different attitudes one can have to parsing. If building a parser is done in order to develop a model of human parsing, CL is approached as an empirical science. An example of such an approach is Crocker (1996). One can dispute whether the assumptions underlying this approach are valid, because it may well be that the best theory of human parsing cannot be implemented readily on present-day computers. It is clear, however, that this approach is empirical rather than applied. This is illustrated by the fact that, in this approach, improving the parser's performance by means of a rule which is certainly not part of the human parser would not be acceptable.

A purely technological approach to parsing is common in corpus linguistics. For many research questions in corpus linguistics, a parsed corpus is necessary. The corpus linguist is not interested in the theoretical foundation of the parser, but only in its output. Corpus linguistics itself is an empirical approach to linguistics (not necessarily CL) alongside, for instance, Chomskyan linguistics (cf. ten Hacken (2002)).

Parsing as a component of an applied science presupposes both a practical orientation and an explanatory focus. In this approach the evaluation criteria for the parser are based on performance, e.g. percentage of correct analyses, robustness, speed. Whether the parser works in a similar way to the human parser does not play a role. The explanatory focus implies that an attempt is made to explain the parser's performance in terms of theories about the input and the internal structure of the parser.

Applied sciences are problem-oriented. If CL is considered as an applied science, the following four questions have to be addressed.

Problem identification: What is the range of acceptable input and what is the type of output to be produced?

Evaluation: How can it be determined that the system produces the correct output and thus solves the problem?

Problem decomposition: How can the problem be analysed into components?

Knowledge selection: Which types of knowledge should be used to solve the component problems?

2. Traditional CL

CL is almost as old as computers. Arguably the first non-numeric application proposed for computers was translation, cf. Weaver (1949). Machine Translation (MT) was largely dominant as a framework of research in early CL. This does not mean that all work labelled as being "on MT" involved translation. Thus, two-thirds of the chapter entitled "General Aspects of Language Translation" in Booth et al. (1958) is devoted to setting up a dictionary of inflectional endings for French using a minimal amount of disk space. MT served as a framework for a variety of tasks having to do with linguistic analysis.

Arguably, what most researchers in CL were interested in was making computers understand natural language. Thus, in Barr & Feigenbaum's handbook of artificial intelligence, the chapter on CL (1981:223-321) is entitled "Understanding Natural Language" and starts with the prospect of a computer understanding unrestricted input in English. There are two main reasons for the importance of MT as a framework for research. The first is practical. The general category of understanding is difficult to test. When a computer can produce a translation, this is at least a rough criterion for determining that it 'understands' the input. The second reason is even more practical. Research needs funding. Translation is a task that people with a background that qualifies them for leading positions in funding agencies can understand. Against the background of the Cold War, an analyser for Russian morphology becomes more relevant when it is presented as part of a system that will eventually allow American physicists to read Russian papers on nuclear physics. This type of motivation is explicit in Edmundson & Hays (1966 [1958]:137). The consequence of these considerations was that much of the research carried out under the general label of MT was more interested in other questions than in translation.

In approaching the four questions central to applied science, the starting point for CL at this stage was invariably the choice of a theory, i.e. the knowledge needed. From this choice, answers to the other questions followed. As linguistic theory was sentence-based, so was the evaluation measure. As linguistic theory distinguished syntax from morphology and semantics, so did the architecture of at least the more advanced systems. As to the problem of MT, in most cases the label translation was thought of as sufficiently explicit by itself, but Nirenburg (1987:2) formulates it as follows:

"The task of MT can be defined very simply: the computer must be able to obtain as input a text in one language (SL, for source language) and produce as output a text in another language (TL, for target language), so that the meaning of the TL text is the same as that of the SL text."

There is every reason to suppose that this definition corresponds to a general consensus. A more sophisticated analysis of the problem is found in the context of the MT project Rosetta. Recognizing that the translation of a sentence can be influenced by its context and by extra-linguistic factors, Landsbergen (1987:351) proposes to distinguish "possible translation" from "best translation". The former is based on equivalence that can be calculated sentence-internally and without recourse to world knowledge. The latter is what a human translator would optimally choose. There is a formal difference of "the relation possible-translation, which can be regarded as a symmetric relation, while the relation best-translation obviously is not symmetric." Apart from confirming the general trend indicated by Nirenburg's quote, this approach also demonstrates the sentence-based evaluation.

3. Problems with Traditional CL

The emergence of a crisis in traditional CL was slow but steady. The predominance of MT was reduced somewhat when ALPAC (1966) concluded that the investment of more money in the field was not optimally efficient. In particular, ALPAC concluded that teaching Russian to nuclear physicists and training more translators would be more cost-effective than developing MT systems along the lines then known. This is the reason why natural language understanding was pursued in the USA rather under labels such as question answering.

Especially in Europe, however, it was argued that ALPAC did not take into account the potential offered by new linguistic theories combined with faster computer equipment. In the European context, this argument was successful in the sense of convincing funding agencies to continue investing money in MT. However, whereas systems of the older design type, e.g. Systran, produced translations that were often deficient, projects in the linguistic approach typically failed to deliver systems producing any translation at all.

A typical example of this negative outcome is what happened at the Commission of the European Communities, now the European Commission. This institution employs the biggest translation service in the world. As Hutchins & Somers state, they bought a license for Systran in 1976 (1992:176). It also funded its own MT project, Eurotra, which ran from 1982-1990 and employed over 150 specialists at 18 institutions in 1989 (1992:239-240). Maegaard & Perschke (1991:80-81) sketch ambitious future plans, but note that "what has been achieved is just a very first step" (1991:82). In their overview of translation in EU institutions, Wagner et al. (2002) do not mention Eurotra or any MT system based on it. The only MT system available to translators is Systran.

In view of problems of this type, an influential group of CL-researchers argued that the problem was the orientation towards linguistic theories. Frederick Jelinek is quoted having said "Whenever I fire a linguist our system performance improves" at the Workshop on Evaluation of NLP Systems, Wayne PA, December 1988 (cf. Jelinek (2004)). His alternative was to use the statistical analysis of large corpora instead of linguistic theories. Many researchers in CL experienced the emergence of statistical techniques as a revolution. Church & Mercer (1993) also represent the opposition between statistical approaches and approaches based on theoretical linguistics as one between paradigms. On closer inspection, the two approaches turn out to be more similar than transpires at first sight.

In MT, the first system based on these techniques was developed at IBM and described by Brown et al. (1990). They take their knowledge not from a linguistic theory but from the statistical analysis of a bilingual aligned corpus. The analysis tools are taken from Shannon's (1948) information theory.

While this approach transforms the working method and the skills involved quite dramatically, it does not change the problem definition compared to Nirenburg's. Brown et al. also evaluate their system on the basis of percentage of correctly translated sentence (1990:84), i.e. the same, traditional evaluation measure. As opposed to linguistically based systems, they do not have intermediate levels of representation, but this is a direct consequence of the type of knowledge selected. In sum, even with the emergence of statistical approaches, discussions continue to turn on the selection of knowledge as the first decision.

There is also another sense in which statistical approaches are similar to linguistically based projects. For complex tasks such as MT they do not manage to produce a practically viable system. Therefore, while statistical techniques enlarged the repertoire available to CL researchers they did not solve the problems of traditional CL.

4. A New Approach

As described in more detail by ten Hacken (2001), the field of MT in the early 1990s was in a crisis. Neither linguistic nor statistical approaches could realistically be expected to solve the problem of MT. This crisis was equally felt in other areas of CL. In a crisis, researchers start questioning the foundations of their field.

An early sign of a new approach can be found in Kay et al. (1994). They argue at length that a problem definition for MT such as the one formulated by Nirenburg (1987:2) is not correct because translation is situated. This insight was not new in theoretical approaches to translation, but it had never been operationalized in MT. Clear arguments to the effect that translation decisions depend not only on the language pair and the input text, but also on the context of translation can be found in Nida (1964). In functional approaches to translation, prevailing in Germany from the late 1970s, these considerations take a central position (cf. Nord (1997) for an overview).

While Landsbergen's (1987) distinction between possible and best translation shows his awareness of the problem, his choice to concentrate on possible translations is a move away from the productive use of functional aspects. The idea of a borderline between possible and impossible translations of sentences suggests a degree of precision not supported by any practical application. The communicative situation and the purpose of translation are much more important in determining the quality of a translation than the use of target language sentences from the range of possible translations.

The four central questions of applied science can now be taken in their natural order. If we start from the problem definition, producing a good translation cannot be considered without taking into account questions such as for whom and for what purpose the text is translated. In the case of MT we should even add why the translation should be produced by a computer rather than manually and why translating is the correct solution to the problem at hand. The other three central questions should be taken as a consequence of the first one.

The result of this approach is that the general problem of MT is recognized as a non-well-formed problem, i.e. a problem that cannot possibly be solved. Instead, MT has become a field of study, encompassing a range of more specific problems. These problems are constrained in the domain and context of communication. Verbmobil, the system for which Kay et al. (1994) provided the initial recommendations, concentrated on dialogues in with the participants have a common goal, e.g. fixing the time and place of a meeting. The choice of dialogues complicates the task, because it involves the recognition and generation of spoken language, but the cooperative nature of the exchange can be exploited by the system in the solution of the communicative problem. At every turn in the conversation, the human participants can correct any communicative errors produced in translation. A fair evaluation standard for such a system is therefore not the number of correctly translated sentences, but the number of successful dialogues, for instance when participants can agree on a suitable time and location for a meeting.

In the new approach, translation is no longer seen as a goal in itself but as a way of achieving goals that are closer to real-life situations. If we look up a web page in a language we do not know, MT of the type offered by Systran can give a good impression of what is on the page (cf. Yang & Lange (2003)). For the commercial production of a user manual, a human translation with the help of Computer-Assisted Translation tools such as translation memories and terminology databases is more adequate (cf. Bowker (2002)).

If the actual reason for translating is the extraction of information, translation is in many cases a rather inefficient way to obtain it. If the problem is getting to know what is said in a particular document in another language, a summary of the document reduces the problem in a fairly literal sense. Automatic text summarization has become a very active field in the 1990s, cf. Mani (2001). As observed by ten Hacken (2003), the way the summary is further processed depends on a variety of factors. It may range from struggling through the summary with a dictionary if one has a very imperfect knowledge of the language to consulting a speaker of the language or commissioning a professional translation.

As ten Hacken (2001, 2003) argues, the field of MT has undergone a revolution leading to a diversification of problems. These problems are much more well-formed than the traditional problem of MT. This approach has stimulated and renewed the entire field of CL, opening up an entire range of new research problems.

5. Knowledge Specific to CL

For the recognition of CL as an applied science it is essential that it provides explanations. In the classical approach, explanations were given in terms of linguistic theories. Even when in MT the problem was nominally one of translation, what was explained was the degree of success of linguistic analysis. In the case of Rosetta, the concept of possible translation was introduced to formalize this. In the new approach, there is more room for knowledge specific to CL.

CL as an applied science has to address the questions formulated at the end of section 1. The parallel with medicine is instructive. In medicine, a health problem is analysed in terms of symptoms. Symptoms are relevant properties of observed cases (patients). The next step is to recognize a disease. A disease is a group of symptoms with causal links. This degree of understanding is necessary to provide a cure and explain how and why it works. In CL, we deal with problems of a different type, but we can also recognize symptoms and group them into causally connected problems. The knowledge required to identify well-formed problems is an essential part of CL as an applied science, because only for well-formed problems is it possible to find solutions whose success can be explained. This knowledge is supplemented by the knowledge necessary to derive evaluation measures, to analyse the problem into components, and to select the appropriate knowledge for a solution.

The role of statistical approaches is somewhat reduced by the need to provide explanations, but it is not eliminated. Here again, the parallel with medicine can be exploited. The reason we want medicine to provide explanations is that we trust the cure more if we understand how it works. The same goes for the solutions provided by CL. Explanation contributes to a better solution. If we do not have a proper theoretical understanding yet, having a solution resulting from practical work may also contribute to understanding. This is the type of contribution statistical analysis can make. The discovery of the cause of cholera, as described by Bynum (1994), is a good example. First statistical analysis linked the incidence of cholera to the use of water from a particular source. This connection helped finding an explanatory link between the disease and the virus causing it. Also in CL, statistical procedures are used for those tasks for which a more precisely stated solution is not available. In this way, such components of well-formed problems do not get in the way of a proper solution and may indeed suggest regularities that advance the search.

References

ALPAC [Automatic Language Processing Advisory Committee] 1966. *Language and Machines: Computers in Translation and Linguistics.* Washington (DC): National Academy of Sciences.
Barr, Avron and Feigenbaum, Edward A. eds, 1981. *The Handbook of Artificial Intelligence.* Volume 1, Los Altos (Calif.): Kaufmann.
Booth, Andrew D.; Brandwood, L. and Cleave, J.P. 1958. *Mechanical Resolution of Linguistic Problems.* London: Butterworth.
Bowker, Lynne 2002. *Computer-Aided Translation Technology: A Practical Introduction.* Ottawa: University of Ottawa Press.
Brown, Peter; Cocke, John; Della Pietra, Stephen; Della Pietra, Vincent J.; Jelinek, Fredrick; Lafferty, John D.; Mercer, Robert L. and Roossin, Paul S. 1990. "A Statistical Approach to Machine Translation." *Computational Linguistics* 16:79-85.
Bynum, W.F. 1994. *Science and the Practice of Medicine in the Nineteenth Century.* Cambridge: Cambridge University Press.
Church, Kenneth W. and Mercer, Robert L. 1993. "Introduction to the Special Issue on Computational Linguistics Using Large Corpora." *Computational*

Linguistics 19:1-24.
Crocker, Matthew W. 1996. *Computational Psycholinguistics: An Interdisciplinary Approach to the Study of Language*. Dordrecht: Kluwer.
Edmundson, H.P. and Hays, David G. 1958. "Research Methodology for Machine Translation." *Mechanical Translation* 5/1: 8-15, repr. in Hays, David G. ed, 1966. *Readings in Automatic Language Processing*. New York: Elsevier, p. 137-147.
ten Hacken, Pius. 2001. "Has There Been a Revolution in Machine Translation?", *Machine Translation* 16:1-19.
—. 2002. "Chomskyan Linguistics and the Sciences of Communication." *Studies in Communication Sciences* 2/2:109-134.
—. 2003. "From Machine Translation to Computer-Assisted Communication." in Giacalone Ramat, Anna; Rigotti, Eddo & Rocci, Andrea eds, *Linguistica e Nuove Professioni*. Milano: FrancoAngeli, p. 161-173.
Hutchins, W. John and Somers, Harry L. 1992. *An Introduction to Machine Translation*. London: Academic Press.
Jelinek, Frederick. 2004. "Some of my Best Friends are Linguists." presentation at LREC 2004.
Kay, Martin; Gawron, Jean Mark and Norvig, Peter. 1994. "Verbmobil: A Translation System for Face-to-Face Dialog." Stanford (Calif.): CSLI.
Landsbergen, Jan. 1987. "Isomorphic Grammars and their Use in the Rosetta Translations System." in King, Margaret ed, *Machine Translation Today: The State of the Art*, Edinburgh: Edinburgh University Press, p. 351-372.
Maegaard, Bente and Perschke, Sergei. 1991. "Eurotra: General System Design." *Machine Translation* 6:73-82.
Mani, Inderjeet. 2001. *Automatic Summarization*. Amsterdam: Benjamins.
Nida, Eugene A. 1964. *Toward a Science of Translating, with Special Reference to Principles and Procedures Involved in Bible Translating*. Leiden: Brill.
Nirenburg, Sergei. 1987. "Knowledge and Choices in Machine Translation." in Nirenburg, Sergei ed, *Machine Translation: Theoretical and Methodological Issues*. Cambridge: Cambridge University Press, p. 1-21.
Nord, Christiane. 1997. *Translating as a Purposeful Activity: Functionalist Approaches Explained*. Manchester: St. Jerome.
Shannon, Claude S. 1948. "The mathematical theory of communication." Bell Systems Technical Journal 27:379-423 and 27:623-656.
Wagner, Emma; Bech, Svend and Martínez, Jesús M. 2002. *Translating for the European Union Institutions*. Manchester: St. Jerome.
Weaver, Warren. 1949. "Translation" ms. reprinted in Locke, William N. and Booth, A. Donald eds, 1955. *Machine Translation of Languages: Fourteen Essays*. Technology Press of MIT, Cambridge (Mass.) and Wiley, New York, p. 15-23.

Yang, Jin & Lange, Elke. 2003. "Going live on the internet." in Somers, Harold ed, *Computers and Translation: A translator's guide*. Amsterdam: Benjamins, p. 191-210.

CHAPTER TWENTY

VIEWS OF TEXT MEANING IN COMPUTATIONAL LINGUISTICS: PAST, PRESENT, AMD FUTURE

GRAEME HIRST

1 Introduction

The successes in recent years of computational linguistics, natural language processing, and human language technologies (CL, NLP, and HLT) through empirical methods based on statistics and lexical semantics have been achieved, at least in part, by changing the problem to be solved. Until the early 1990s, the central problem of computational linguistics was taken to be *natural language understanding*, a subproblem of *artificial intelligence*. Users' spoken or typed utterances, or complete documents, were to be "understood", in some deep sense of that term, by means of a full and correct syntactic parse followed by conversion into a "representation of meaning" from which all the necessary inferences could be drawn. It was easy to construct examples that showed that anything less than this kind of full "understanding" could and would lead to errors: the wrong flight booked, a misleading translation, a domestic robot washing the baby in the washing machine. Researchers built narrow but deep systems that could Do The Right Thing for a few "toy" examples, but the methods didn't scale up, often because they presupposed the existence of large knowledge resources, the creation of which was considered a separate, very long term problem.

The move away from this paradigm came with the growing realization that there were many useful natural-language applications in which some degree of error could be tolerated. These include text classification and document routing, text summarization, and finding answers to questions in a document collection.

The price of these successes, however, has been a diminished view of text-meaning and interpretation in computational linguistics. In this paper, I will discuss three computational views of text-meaning and how they have been tacitly used in computational linguistics research over the last three decades. I'll explain why the current view is a "diminished" one that needs to be changed, and say a little about how recent work in my research group fits in with that.[1]

In this paper, I'll use the word *text* to denote any complete utterance, short or long. In a computational context, a text could be a non-interactive document, such as a news article, a legal statute, or a memorandum, that a *writer* or *author* has produced for other people and which is to undergo some kind of processing by a computer. Or a text could be a natural-language utterance by a *user* in a spoken or typewritten interactive dialogue with another person or a computer: a *turn* or set of turns in a conversation.[2] The term *text-meaning*, then, as opposed to mere *word-meaning* or *sentence-meaning*, denotes the complete in-context meaning or message of such texts at all levels of interpretation including sub-text.

2 Three decades of text-meaning in computational linguistics

There are three distinct views on exactly where the meaning of a text can be found:
1. Meaning is in the text.
2. Meaning is in the writer.
3. Meaning is in the reader.

These different views of text-meaning often lead to heated debates in semiotics, literary theory, the philosophy of language, and semantics. In computational linguistics, however, all three views are found in the research literature, with different degrees of prominence at different times in the field's history, and researchers are rarely explicit as to which view they are taking — often they don't distinguish the views at all or they slide back and forth between them.

The varying prominence of the different views reflects the degree of prominence and success of different CL and NLP research paradigms and methods over the years. And perhaps surprisingly, as computational linguistics has developed, the predominant view has shifted from the one generally regarded as the most sophisticated to the one generally regarded as the least sophisticated. In more-cynical terms: the original problem was too hard, and so it was replaced by an easier problem.

---

[1]This paper is thus intended as an explicit response to these questions in the E-CAP 2005 call for papers: What are the philosophical underpinnings of computational linguistics? Are they (still) the right ones or do they need to be replaced? If so, with what? What are the philosophical implications of your current research?
[2]While this terminology emphasizes written language, I do not want to exclude spoken "texts"; the terms *writer* and *reader* should be taken to include *speaker* and *hearer*.

In this section, I'll look in more detail at each of the three views of text-meaning in computational linguistics, and, working backwards in time, show how each was associated with the milieu of (roughly) one decade of research.

2.1 1995–2005: Objective text-meaning

The dominant paradigm for the last decade or so in CL and NLP has been the application of statistical and machine-learning methods to large, non-interactive texts. The paradigm is exemplified and driven by books such as Manning and Schütze's *Foundations of Statistical Natural Language Processing* (1999). In this paradigm, the implicit view is that text-meaning is objectively "in" a text, and is determined solely by the combined effect of the words of the text, each as context for the others. That is, a text is a representation of its own meaning, just as much as any semantic formalism is; and this meaning is preserved, more or less, by operations such as summarization and translation to another natural language.

This view underlies, for example, applications that rely on statistically based lexical methods. If the user asks for articles about raptor migration in Colorado, then the statistical relationship of the words in the text to those in the query is determined, and the text is ranked accordingly for the degree of relevance of its meaning. A topic detection and tracking system for news stories, in determining that two stories are or aren't about the same event, is in effect making a judgement that the objective meaning of the texts is or isn't the same (at a certain level of granularity). The job of an extractive summarization system is to pick out the sentences in which the "important" meaning is concentrated. A system that monitors conversations in on-line chat rooms is looking out for sentences with "dangerous" meanings.

Thus a text is regarded as an *objet trouvé*, with little or no consideration of its author or its provenience. It just arrives from a wire service or from an anonymous user. Meaning is then "extracted" from the text by "processing" it.

2.2 1985–1995: Authorial intent

In the preceding decade, research in computational linguistics placed a much greater emphasis on interactive dialogue systems. A user was assumed to be conversing with the machine in pursuit of some task in which the machine played a role such as that of tutor, travel agent, or domestic servant. The computer's job was taken to be figuring out what it is that the user "really wants" from the "literal meaning" of what they say; for example, *I'd like a beer*, said to a domestic robot, means *Bring me a beer, and do it right now*. In effect, the computer has to read the user's mind. This research was marked by the application of Gricean and other theories of linguistic pragmatics to users' utterances, and by the development of models of the user that could be used to reason about the user's plans and goals. The more that was known about a specific user, the better their meaning could be determined. The paradigm was exemplified and driven by books such as Cohen, Morgan, and Pollack's *Intentions in Communication* (1990) and Kobsa and Wahlster's *User Models in Dialog Systems* (1989).

Thus, in this paradigm, the implicit view is that text-meaning is "in" the writer or user. A text or turn means whatever the user thinks it means or intends it to mean (i.e., humpty-dumptyism), and the reader (be it human or computer) might or might not determine what this is.

2.3 1975–1985: Subjective text-meaning

A view that is perhaps associated with literary criticism more than computational linguistics is that text-meaning is "in" the reader of the text. That is, a text means whatever the reader (or the "interpretive community") thinks it means. Generally in this view, the emphasis is not just on meaning but on *interpretation*, implying a perspective, a context, and an agenda that each reader brings to the act of reading any particular text. A consequence of this is that the meaning or interpretation depends, at least in part, on what the reader knows or believes (or doesn't know or believe); or, in computational terms, on what is or isn't in the system's knowledge base.

This view is implicit in the application-independent language-understanding research that dominated computational linguistics from the early-to-mid 1970s to the mid-to-late 1980s, which was rooted in the traditional knowledge-based artificial-intelligence paradigm of creating independent intelligent agents. Typically in this research, texts were seen to be massively ambiguous in both their syntax and their semantics, and the goal for the computer was to find the interpretation of the input that was most consistent with the knowledge that was already present in the system. The more the system knew, the more it would be able to understand. The paradigm was exemplified and driven by books such as Schank and Colby's *Computer Models of Thought and Language* (1973) and Sowa's *Conceptual Structures* (1984) (perhaps even Hirst's *Semantic Interpretation and the Resolution of Ambiguity* (1987)). This subjective view of text-meaning became very explicit in research such as that of Corriveau (1995), who additionally considered the question of how the interpretations produced by a language-understanding system are affected by the time constraints under which it operates.[3]

---

[3]Corriveau's work, though published in book form only in 1995, was carried out mostly in the late 1980s.

2.4 Vacillation

Thus, as the methods and applications changed, as the *weltanschauung* of CL and NLP changed from one in which computers were (would-be) independent intelligent agents to one in which humans *command* computers by means of natural language and then to one in which humans *use* computers to sift the information in the natural languages of the world, so too the predominant view of text-meaning tacitly changed. In the traditional intelligent-agent paradigm, the computer is trying to make sense of the linguistic utterances it finds in the world, increasing its knowledge and planning its actions accordingly; the subjective, in-reader view of text-meaning dominated. In the computer-as-servant paradigm, if the user asks the computer to do something — book a flight, fetch a beer — then it is the user's intent that is paramount in what the computer should actually do, regardless of how the request is phrased; the in-writer view dominated. And if the computer's task is to find information in text, then it is objective, in-text meaning that matters.

Computational linguistics and computational linguists thus vacillate between the three views of text-meaning, but don't generally notice that they are doing it and probably wouldn't care if they did notice: computational linguists are not normally students of philosophy, and therefore tend to be unaware of, or gloss over, the philosophical consequences of their work, the philosophical assumptions underlying it, and the philosophical issues that it raises.

Moreover, CL makes additional naive assumptions about meaning:
- that the writer or user is a perfect language user: they make no mistakes in their utterances (other than superficial performance errors of spelling and grammar), and when using interactive systems, they comprehend the system's utterances correctly;
- that meaning is conveyed only by or through what's present in the text and not what's omitted;
- that the system's agenda and the user's or author's agenda are complementary and they share the same goals: e.g., that the user wants to learn something that a tutoring system wants to teach; that the user wants to book the kind of trip that a travel assistant is able to arrange; that the system is looking for the overt information that the writer wishes to convey;
- that no distinction need be made between meaning and interpretation.

All of these assumptions will be challenged as computational linguistics proceeds. In the next section, I will show how forthcoming applications will remove the fourth assumption and implicitly the third. And in the subsequent section, I'll briefly discuss removal of the second assumption as one component of that. (For research on removing the first assumption, see Hirst et al (1994).)

3 2005–2015: Reclaiming the distinctions

What, then, of views of text-meaning in the next decade? How will new methods and new applications affect the view that computational linguistics takes? I believe that forthcoming applications will move CL to recognize the three views as distinct, but to embrace all three as complementary — as representative of different kinds of understanding that are needed, or expected, in different computational tasks. In particular, the in-writer and in-reader views will both come to the fore again, but not for the same reasons as in the past. Rather, in the new NLP applications that are now on the horizon, people will use computers to *interpret* the natural language of the world, not just to search it for information. Moreover, there will be two types of interpretation possible: interpretation on behalf of the user and interpretation on behalf of the writer.

The first of these, while the greater technical challenge, is the conceptually simpler; it is a straightforward extension of the current paradigm of searching, filtering, and classifying information. It requires the computer to consider a text from the point of view of the user, including his or her beliefs, goals, and agenda. For example, if the user wants the computer to find, say, evidence that society is too tolerant of intoxicated drivers or evidence that the government is doing a poor job or evidence that the Philippines has the technical resources to commence a WMD program, then a relevant text need not contain any particular set of words nor anything that could be regarded as a literal assertion about the question (though it might), and the writer of a relevant text need not have had any intent that it provide such evidence. In this paradigm, then, the computer is a surrogate for the user, and its job is to decide, as closely as it can, what some particular text would mean to the user, given the user's goals and anything else known about the user. For this kind of interpretation, the in-reader view of text-meaning becomes explicit: What's important to me in this text? In my view of the world, which camp does this opinion fall into?

The second kind of interpretative task requires the computer to consider a text from the point of view of its author, including his or her beliefs, goals, and agenda. It is a hermeneutic task, in which the user of the computer system wants to understand what it is that the author intends to say, or even what he or she is saying without intending to. Applications with this kind of interpretation include the analysis of opinion texts and of sentiment in text more generally, and the simplification of complex texts; it will also be a component of faithful, high-quality machine translation. In this paradigm, the computer, although working on behalf of some user, acts as a surrogate for the writer, and its job is to present, as closely as it can, what some particular text would mean to the writer. Thus, for this kind of interpretation, the in-writer view of text-meaning becomes explicit: What's this person trying to tell me? What are they up to? What are their implicit assumptions?

It's clear that applications of computational linguistics are moving towards both these kinds of interpretive tasks. Search engines have already turned the typical lay computer user into a researcher, but they have also shown the limitations of string-matching; interpretation remains solely the responsibility of the user. Automatic or assisted interpretation is thus the next great goal for computational linguistics. Many of the applications that are the subject of contemporary research, even if still using the in-text view, can be seen as preliminary steps in this endeavour: non-factoid question-answering, query-oriented summarization, and multi-document summarization; automatic classification of the sentiment or opinion expressed in a text; automatic essay scoring. Even machine translation, once construed solely as a tool to assist a professional human translator (or to replace them), is now also seen as a (still crude) interpretive tool for the ordinary user.

4 Knowing the alternatives

An important component of interpreting text is sensitivity to *nuances* in language and the choices that speakers make from the options that are available to them. Saussure (1916) wrote:

> In a given language, all the words which express neighbouring ideas help define one another's meaning. Each of a set of synonyms like *redouter* ('to dread'), *craindre* ('to fear'), *avoir peur* ('to be afraid'), has its particular value only because they stand in contrast to one another. If *redouter* did not exist, its content would be shared out among its competitors. (p. 114)

Nuance lies not only in near-synonyms, as in Saussure's example, but in all aspects of both content and style — from deciding what to say in the first place, through to the words and syntactic structures of its realization. If I tell you that I am *afraid* of my forthcoming exam, you can infer that my fear is not so great as to be *dread* (or at least, I'm not admitting that it is). If I concede that *a mistake was made* and you believe that it was in fact I who made the mistake, you can infer from my agentless passive that I'm avoiding taking any responsibility for the mistake.

Nuance in language thus arises from the speaker's or writer's deliberate (though not necessarily conscious) choice between close alternatives — from that which might have been said but wasn't. Sensitivity to nuance thus requires, for any particular utterance in its context, knowing what the possible alternatives were. Clearly, this kind of analysis requires both complex knowledge of the language and complex knowledge of the world. The latter may be arbitrarily hard — ultimately, it could imply, for example, a computational representation of a deep understanding of human motivations and behaviour that even many people do not achieve. The required linguistic knowledge is also difficult, but is at least in the territory of computational linguistics, and sets an agenda for research that has strongly influenced my own work for many years. If a computer system is to draw inferences from a writer's choice among a cluster of near-synonyms, it must first have a method of representing both the core meaning of the cluster and the distinctions among its members (Edmonds and Hirst 2002), and it must then have a lexical knowledge base that, using this method of representation, lists all this information for all the words of the relevant language or (in the case of machine translation) languages (Inkpen and Hirst 2006). If it is to draw inferences from the writer's choice of syntactic structures it must have a representation of the alternative structures available and the pragmatic consequences of each: e.g., emphasis or deliberate obfuscation (DiMarco and Hirst 1993).[4]

5 Conclusion

For its new and developing applications, computational linguistics needs to move away again from the solely objective in-text view of text-meaning that has dominated much of the statistically based work of the past decade, and reclaim both the subjective in-reader and authorial in-writer views. But the subjective view will now have purpose at its centre rather than idiosyncrasies of the system's knowledge; and the authorial view will be based not just on rules of pragmatics and implicature but also on a broader determination of what the author might have said but didn't.

---

[4]I have presented this argument from the perspective of language comprehension; but clearly language generation and the *creation* of text meaning by making the choices described above also require these kinds of knowledge. In computational linguistics, the primary work on this is undoubtedly still Hovy's (1987) system PAULINE, which tactfully adapted its political comments according to whom it was talking to and even shut up completely if it decided that it was a bad idea to say anything.

Acknowledgements

The preparation of this paper was supported by the Natural Sciences and Engineering Research Council of Canada and by the Center for Spoken Language Research, University of Colorado at Boulder, where I was a guest at the time of its completion. For discussions and insights on this topic, I am grateful to Jane Morris (who first drew my attention to how the contemporary view in CL of the locus of text-meaning differs from that of the 1980s), Stephen Regoczei, Diana Inkpen, Philip Edmonds, Eduard Hovy, Nadia Talent, Jean-Pierre Corriveau, Chrysanne DiMarco, and Sergei Nirenburg.

References

Cohen, Philip R.; Morgan, Jerry; and Pollack, Martha E. (1990) (editors). *Intentions in communication*. Cambridge, MA: The MIT Press.

Corriveau, Jean-Pierre (1995). *Time-constrained Memory: A Reader-based Approach to Text Comprehension*. Mahwah, NJ: Lawrence Erlbaum Associates.

DiMarco, Chrysanne and Hirst, Graeme (1993). "A computational theory of goal-directed style in syntax." *Computational Linguistics*, 19(3), September 1993, 451–499.

Edmonds, Philip and Hirst, Graeme (2002). "Near-synonymy and lexical choice." *Computational Linguistics*, 28(2), June 2002, 105–144.

Hirst, Graeme (1987). *Semantic Interpretation and the Resolution of Ambiguity*. Cambridge University Press.

Hirst, Graeme; McRoy, Susan; Heeman, Peter; Edmonds, Philip; and Horton, Diane (1994). "Repairing conversational misunderstandings and non-understandings." *Speech Communication*, 15(3–4), 213–229.

Hovy, Eduard (1987). *Generating Natural Language under Pragmatic Constraints*. Hillsdale, NJ: Lawrence Erlbaum Associates.

Inkpen, Diana and Hirst, Graeme (2006). "Building and using a lexical knowledge-base of near-synonym differences." *Computational Linguistics*, 32(2), June 2006.

Kobsa, Alfred and Wahlster, Wolfgang (eds.) (1989). *User Models in Dialog Systems*. Springer-Verlag.

Manning, Christopher and Schütze, Hinrich (1999). *Foundations of Statistical Natural Language Processing*. Cambridge, MA: The MIT Press.

Saussure, Ferdinand de (1916). *Course in General Linguistics*. (Translated by Roy Harris, 1983.) La Salle, IL: Open Court Press. [Page numbers refer to the English edition.]

Schank, Roger C. and Colby, Kenneth M. (1973). *Computer Models of Thought and Language*. San Francisco: W.H. Freeman.
Sowa, John F. (1984). *Conceptual Structures*. Reading, MA: Addison-Wesley.

CHAPTER TWENTY ONE

LANGUAGE TECHNOLOGICAL MODELS
AS EPISTEMIC ARTEFACTS: THE CASE
OF CONSTRAINT GRAMMAR PARSER[1]

TARJA KNUUTTILA

Abstract

This paper suggests that the philosophical difficulties concerning the scientific status of language technology results from the predisposition of the philosophy of science to concentrate on the theoretical and representational aspects of science. This is reflected in the way the philosophical discussion of models tends to treat them as abstract, theoretical representations of the world. However, such an approach to models seems not to suit such a practically and instrumentally oriented field as language technology. Through studying a specific language technological model, the Constraint Grammar Parser, I attempt to identify some characteristic epistemic features of language technological research. I argue that language technological models could be considered as epistemic artefacts, which notion stresses the epistemic importance of the artificiality, workability and experimentability of scientific models.

1. Introduction

Caught between different disciplines, programming and practical purposes language technology raises interesting philosophical questions. First and foremost, what is the scientific status of language technology? How to account

---

[1] The surface structure refers here to the words spoken and written as opposed to the deep structure, the supposed abstract underlying organisation of a sentence. See Humphreys 2004 for the discussion of the importance of output representations in simulation.

for the epistemic value of technological research that importantly strives for new applications and efficient solutions? From the philosophical point of view this is a complicated problem indeed, since philosophy of science has usually approached the epistemic value of science in terms of theory and representation. Science has primarily been understood as a theoretical activity that seeks to explain and predict natural and social phenomena. That science has been successful in this task has more often than not been attributed to the ability of scientific theories to represent the world accurately or truthfully, in relevant respects or aspects. But this view of science fits uneasily language technology which rather than theoretically representing the world aims to develop well-working machines. Should this lead us to relegate language technology to the realm of technology only? Granted that this kind of conclusion does hardly any justice to the epistemic challenges of language technology in particular, or technological research in general, the question then becomes how else to approach the epistemic status of language technology. In an attempt lay out the lines for answering this question I shall in this paper study a specific language technological model, the Constraint Grammar Parser, from the points of view of representation, theory and expertise. A promising way to approach language technological models like parsers, I suggest, is to consider them as epistemic artefacts, that is, as purposefully constructed, material entities whose epistemic value derives from their productive and interactive, rather than representational, characteristics.

2. Constraint Grammar Parser

The process of describing a word or a sentence grammatically is called parsing. In the context of language technology, parsing means "the automatic assignment of morphological and syntactic structure (but not semantic interpretation) to written input texts of any length and complexity" (Karlsson 1995, 1). A parser is thus a language-technological device, a program devised for producing parsed text necessary for various different language-technological tasks such as word processing, grammar-checking and information retrieval. On a more theoretical level parsing poses the problem of how to infer the grammatical structure of words and phrases by automatic means.

There are two primary approaches to parsing (see van Halteren and Voutilainen 1999). One is grammar-based, linguistic and descriptive approach, while the other approach is probabilistic, data-driven and statistical. The methods of the data-driven approach include corpus-based learning rules, Hidden Markov models and machine learning approaches. Constraint Grammar parser (CG, Karlsson et al. 1995), which is a product of long-term research in language technology being carried out at the Department of General Linguistics at the University of Helsinki, is a grammar-based parser. What makes it especially interesting is its heterogeneous nature: even though it is based on hand-crafted rules made by a linguist, it is also firmly grounded on linguistic corpora, like statistical parsers.

The Constraint Grammar (CG) is a language independent parsing formalism whose main task is to enrich each word of a running text with its correct grammatical reading. Constraint Grammar parsing builds on a morphological analysis performed by a morphological analyser, such as two-level morphology (TWOL, Koskenniemi 1983), on whose development the Helsinki group's early international breakthrough was based. TWOL is a computational formalism and method for analysing and generating word-forms, which strives to give all the possible morpho-syntactic readings for each word of the text to be analysed. Typically the words we use are such that the same word-form, say "round", can be read differently depending on the context in which it is used. Thus TWOL gives the word 'round' a total of eight different readings, of which four are verbal; however, it can be read also as a preposition, noun, adjective or adverb (Voutilainen 1995, 165). The task of the parser is to choose which one of these readings is the proper one in the context of its occurrence in the text. This is called disambiguation.

Parsing proceeds as follows. Once the morphological analyser has provided all the correct morphological readings of the words of an input text, the parser checks which readings are appropriate by applying to them morphological constraints. The constraints make use of the context of each word (i.e. the words in the vicinity of the word in question), whereby the clause boundaries provide the limit for the relevant context. For instance, if a word has both nominal and verbal readings and is preceded by an article, the relevant constraint rules out all the verbal readings of the word on this basis (see Ex. 2-1). Ideally, the input text should be disambiguated so that none of its constituent words have more than one morphological interpretation.

```
"("<the>"
   ("the" ART))
("<lack>"
   ("lack" V SUBJUNCTIVE)
   ("lack" V IMP)
   ("lack" V INF)
   ("lack" V PRES -SG3)
   ("lack" N NOM SG))
```

The word 'lack' can have both verbal (SUBJUNCTIVE, IMP, INF, PRES) and nominal (NOM) readings. However, if it occurs after an article (ART), all possible verbal readings can be eliminated. Consequently, one can apply to the ambiguous word 'lack' the constraint (@w =0 (V) (-1C DETERMINER) which discards (=0) all lines containing the feature 'V' from an ambiguous cohort if the first word to the left (-1) is an unambiguous (indicated by the letter C) determiner (the feature ART being a member of the set DETERMINER) (Voutilainen, Heikkilä and Anttila 1992: 2).

Once the parser has disambiguated the morphologically ambiguous words, it gives them a surface syntactic analysis (Karlsson 1990). Thus the output of the morphological disambiguation module provides in turn an input to the next module, namely syntactic mapping, which subsequently assigns all possible (surface) syntactical functions to each accepted morphological reading. Once again, a certain word-form can have several different surface syntactic functions. A noun, for instance, can be a subject, object, indirect object, etc. Consequently, to give each word its correct syntactic reading, syntactic constraints are applied after mapping. These constraints are similar to morphological disambiguation constraints, in that they discard contextually illegitimate syntactic function tags (see Voutilainen 1994, 16-17). The final output of the parser is a text in which, in a best-case scenario, each word is labelled (or "tagged") with its correct morphological reading and syntactic function.

3. Parser as a representation?

Even if most people familiar with parsers have no difficulty in calling parsers computer models, many philosophers would feel uneasy of categorising parsers as models. This is due to the almost unilateral agreement among philosophers that models are representations (see e.g. Hughes 1997; Teller 2001). But it is unclear what exactly does an instrument such as a parser represent even though it is in itself a result of a complicated process of representation and it is valued for the output representation. i.e. tagged text, it produces.

Indeed, the construction of a CG parser can be approached as a continuous process of representation involving different representative layers and repeated testing with corpora. In order to create a (grammar-based) parser for a particular language, one has to describe the rules of that language with the aid of a parsing formalism, a sort of meta-language (such as CG). This set of rules is in turn implemented as a computer program, whose code constitutes another layer of representation. In practice, the set of rules and computer program has been developed concurrently with the help of previously annotated text corpora. Prior to building the parser, however, the problem of how to represent the rules of a language had to be solved. Fred Karlsson, the original creator of the CG-formalism, tried for many years to develop a syntactic parser by applying several different theoretically grounded linguistic formalisms before he realised that in order to make a functionally robust parser, he had to turn everything upside down and try to do something by rejecting instead of stating positively what might be possible. Thus in contrast to traditional and formal grammars, which are licensing grammars, a CG grammar is a reductive grammar. Instead of defining the rules for the formation of correct expressions in a language (L), the task becomes to specify constraints that discard as many improper alternatives as possible (Karlsson, 1995, 10)

The CG grammar is written in a corpus-based fashion. One starts with a morphologically analysed text for which one writes constraints that disambiguate the words of that text. After the resulting grammar is applied to manually disambiguated benchmark corpus, the software of the system generates application statistics for each of the constraints. On the basis of these statistics and after identifying the mispredictions, the grammarian either corrects or removes old constraints, or creates new ones. Then the cycle is repeated, making use of any new corpus evidence until the performance of the parser is considered to be good enough.

The focus on the process of representation underlying the parser opens up a different view into representation than the traditional philosophical one, which concentrates on the relation between a ready-made model and its real target system. According to the traditional view a model is epistemically valuable if it, in itself, gives us an accurate depiction of its object. Here the parser is an outcome of the labour of representation, but the crucial epistemic challenge does not concern that what is represented, i.e. the linguistic rules, but how they can be represented in such a way as to make a do-able parser. Moreover, the parser itself is valued primarily for the linguistic representation of the input text it produces, in which it resembles simulation models in general. The accuracy of this output representation is more important for the developers of parsers than the psychological realisticness of the parsing process itself.

4. Theory and expertise

If the EngCG-parser cannot be seen as a clear-cut representation of any part of the world, existing independently of our representational endeavours, its relationship to theory is also not straightforward. In addition to treating models as representations, the philosophical tradition considers models as interpretations or some sort of concretisations of (formal) theories or theoretical laws, but this captures poorly the part that theory plays in language technology. In fact, the CG parser as a model is not an application of any distinct autonomous linguistic theory. Due to the corpus-based way it is created, the CG grammar does not resemble the ordinary grammars of any given language, and the constraints are quite different from the grammar rules that are described by syntactic theories. Instead of one general rule in the CG grammar, "there will be a few dozens of down-to-earth constraints that state bits and pieces of the phenomenon, approaching or even reaching the correct description by ruling out what cannot be the case in this or that context" (Karlsson 1995, 26).

There are also certain parsers that are based on autonomous grammar theory, but their success in parsing running texts has been rather modest. Yet the CG parser is not an a-theoretical entity despite not being a concretisation of any autonomous formal theory. It nevertheless embodies linguistic concepts, such as dependence, word class and syntactical functions in its construction and output. Moreover, in the field of language technological research, the Constraint Grammar is presented as a theory of how to design a robust parser—it is a description of the principles needed for inducing the grammatical structure of the sentences by automatic means. What is remarkable from the point of view of our traditional understanding of what constitutes a theory is that here the theory is not understood as an abstract description of the general mechanisms and laws prevailing in external reality but as a set of instructions for building a specific artefact. These principles remain, however, in a very general level, and do not, in themselves, really amount to any guide as to how to build a CG parser. What this shows is that a large part of language technological knowledge can be attributed rather to a special kind expertise than to overall explicit theoretical knowledge.

The role and nature of expertise has lately been discussed also in the context of scientific knowledge (see Collins and Evans 2002 for an overview of this discussion). Expertise has typically been attributed to local, experience-bound and tacit dimensions of science, but it has remained rather difficult to tell what expertise consists of and how it is born. The case of parsing suggests that expertise is importantly tied to certain specific methods and artefacts, and it involves many kinds of knowledge and skills acquired from different fields of study and an ability to synthetise them in view of certain goals. As Karlsson's struggle to develop a proper formalism for parsing shows, the epistemic challenge of building a parser is to find a strategy or an idea of how to take into account both the complexities of language and the computational capacity of computers in view of the task to be accomplished. The goals aspired to should not be understood as pre-given or fixed: an important part of expertise consists of the ability to define goals in such a way that they are do-able. It seems actually typical for language technologists that they value highly the ability of a researcher to (fore)see what can be done with different methods.

5. Models as epistemic artefacts

I have argued that the epistemic value of a parser is neither predominantly tied to its representative function nor based on any pre-existing autonomous formal theory. Rather, it seems to me that the clue to the epistemic value of a parser is provided by the important role of expertise in parser building. Namely, as expertise is typically coupled with specific artefacts and methods one may ask whether or not the epistemic qualities of language technological models arise from their being concrete things with which one can work and experiment with. Indeed, the recent practice-oriented approach to models has stressed that we learn from models by building and manipulating them (see Morrison and Morgan 1999; Magnani 2002). It seems to me that this kind of approach to models is more appropriate to the language technological research than the traditional focus on abstract theorizing and representation. Thus I suggest that a promising way to capture the epistemic intricacies of language technological research is to treat language technological models as epistemic artefacts, as materially embodied entities that can give us knowledge in various ways and which also, in themselves, provide us new objects of knowledge (see Knuuttila 2004).

Nobody really questions the artefactual nature of parsers. What is thus gained by approaching models as artefacts rather than as theoretical representations? The concept "epistemic artefact" draws attention to the fact that in modelling we are devising artificial things, the epistemic value of which is largely due to their constructed and material nature that allows us to use them and interact with them in various ways. But how does that then add to our knowledge?

If we consider the CG-parser as an epistemic artefact, its scientific value can be approached through its different roles as a tool, object and inferential device. As tools, parsers are valuable for both their product, a tagged text, and as a first stage in many natural language-processing (NLP) systems. Tagged corpora are needed for many purposes such as corpus-based dictionaries and grammars, and corpus-based linguistic research. In the development of language technology, parsers are typically used as modules in a variety of natural language-processing applications, such as automatic term recognition, automatic thesauri and speech technology appliances.

The strong focus on the representative aspects of models makes it easy to forget that models and computational methods used in science are also interesting and important research objects in themselves. Much of our knowledge actually concerns the artefactual sphere we have surrounded us with, and their fabrication and properties constitute interesting epistemic and methodological issues in their own right. We have, in fact, created new objects of research that spawn a host of new problems: the analysis of words in the lexicon of a parser is not an inconsequential problem, and neither is the problem of how to implement the parser so that it works more quickly and is more space-effective. Furthermore, one needs to find out what kind of information is needed for correct disambiguation, how this information can be acquired (e.g., on the basis of observations by linguists, automatic learning algorithms or combinations thereof) and how such information should be represented (e.g., in the form of rules, collocational matrices, hidden Markov models or neural networks).

The epistemic value of a parser as an inferential device derives largely from its being an artificial entity whose principles, mechanism and structure we know. This applies to other kinds of models as well: it seems generally to be the case that the constraints built into a model are crucial for its epistemic functioning. In the case of parsers, the constraints are made operative by implementing the language description as a computer program, which has actually made grammars more interesting as scientific objects. Traditionally, the evaluation of grammars has relied on conventional academic discussion, but it is practically impossible for humans to consistently follow such complex rule systems as extensive grammars. Thus the computer makes the evaluation of grammars easier providing an interpreter with well-known knowledge sources and well-known operation. Due to the implementation of the grammar, the linguist also has the possibility to learn from the performance of the model by finding out which rules cause troubles and trying out different ones—which stresses the epistemic importance of the workability and 'experimentability' of models. Once the parser functions well, it provides an interesting starting point for diverse interpretations and questions. One can study, for instance, what properties distinguish successful models from unsuccessful ones, what assumptions can be made about human language faculties, and so on. Actually, it seems clear that the difficulties and challenges of developing language technology has taught us a lot about language, for instance, the regularities of our language use and the polysemous and ambiguous nature of our linguistic "order".

6. Conclusion

Using the CG parser as a practical example I have suggested that the reason why the scientific status of language technology is often considered to be uncertain is due to its instrumental nature, which seems to downplay the importance of theory and representation. As an implemented computer program designed give a morpho-syntactic analysis of a running text the Constraint Grammar Parser appears to be entirely unlike the abstract theoretical models of physics that are often taken as the prototypes of scientific models. It is difficult to say what parsers, like many other natural language processing tools, represent or even imitate. They are rather valued for what they produce and how accurate their output is. Thus, from the traditional philosophical point of view the Constraint Grammar Parser seems to be relatively uninteresting thing being merely an instrument. What this view on science forgets is that instrument development constitutes an interesting epistemic challenge in itself and by way of making working instruments we learn new things about our surrounding world. Thus to make justice to the epistemic intricacies of language technological models I have described their various roles as epistemic artefacts.

Now this short philosophical visit into the world of parsing has also wider philosophical implications than rendering parsers, and other language technological tools alike, as scientifically worthwhile things. Namely, approaching models as epistemic artefacts discloses the affinity of the parser to various other things scientists call models. In stressing the epistemic value of the artificiality, and the consequent workability and 'experimentability' of models, the alternative approach to models set forth in this paper differs significantly from the traditional philosophical accounts of models. These accounts have more often than not been predisposed to treat models as abstract, idealised or theoretical structures that stand for real target phenomena. The tendency to treat representation as the epistemic task of models derives from this point of view. If models were but abstract structures, it would be difficult to understand how they could give us knowledge except by representing the world more or less accurately. But, on the other hand, if models are recognised as materially constructed things, it is evident that in them we already have something tangible to work on and experiment with. This in turn speaks for the indispensable and versatile role of artefacts as regards our cognitive endeavour: because the nature of our language or any other phenomenon is not intuitively known to us, the only way to gain knowledge is mediated through the creation and use of artefacts. Thus it seems that studying technological research can also help us to rethink how to approach science more generally

References

Collins, Harry M. and Robert Evans. 2002. The Third Wave of Science Studies: Studies of Expertise and Experience, Social Studies of Science 32(2): 235-296.
Hughes, R.I.G. 1997. Models and Representation, Philosophy of Science 64: S325-S336.
Humphreys, Paul. 2004. Extending Ourselves. Computational Science, Empiricism, and Scientific Method, Oxford: Oxford University Press.

Karlsson, Fred. 1990. Constraint Grammar as a Framework for Parsing Running Text. In COLING-90: Papers Presented to the 13th International Conference on Computational Linguistics. Edited by Hans Karlgren. Helsinki: University of Helsinki, 168-173.

—. 1995. Designing a Parser for Unrestricted Text. In Constraint Grammar. A Language-Independent System for Parsing Unrestricted Text. Edited by Fred Karlsson, Atro Voutilainen, Juha Heikkilä and Arto Anttila. Berlin: Mouton de Gruyter, 1-40.

Karlsson, Fred, Atro Voutilainen, Juha Heikkilä, and Arto Anttila, eds. 1995. Constraint Grammar. A Language-Independent System for Parsing Unrestricted Text. Berlin: Mouton de Gruyter.

Knuuttila, Tarja. 2004. Models, Representation and Mediation. Paper presented at Nineteenth-Biennial Meeting of the Philosophy of Science Association, November 18-20, in Austin, USA. Available at http://philsci-archive.pitt.edu/archive/00002024/

Koskenniemi, Kimmo. 1983. Two-Level Morphology. A General Computational Model for Word-form Production and Generation, Publications of the Department of General Linguistics, University of Helsinki, No. 11. Helsinki: University of Helsinki.

Magnani, Lorenzo. 2002. Epistemic Mediators and Model-Based Discovery in Science. In Model-Based Reasoning. Scientific Discovery, Technology, Values. Edited by Lorenzo Magnani and Nancy J. Nersessian. New York: Kluwer/ Plenum, 305-329.

Morrison, Margaret, and Mary S. Morgan. 1999. Models as Mediating Instruments. In Models as Mediators. Edited by Mary S. Morgan and Margaret Morrison. Cambridge: Cambridge University Press, 10-37.

Teller Paul. 2001. Twilight of the Perfect Model Model, Erkenntnis 55: 393-415.

van Halteren, Hans, and Atro Voutilainen. 1999. Automatic Taggers: An Introduction. In Syntactic Wordclass Tagging. Edited by Hans van Halteren. Dordrecht: Kluwer Academic Publishers, 109-115.

Voutilainen, Atro. 1994. Three Studies of Grammar-Based Surface Parsing of Unrestricted English Text, Department of General Linguistics, Publication No. 24. Helsinki: University of Helsinki.

—. 1995. Morphological Disambiguation. In Constraint Grammar. A Language-Independent System for Parsing Unrestricted Text. Edited by Fred Karlsson, Atro Voutilainen, Juha Heikkilä and Arto Anttila. Berlin: Mouton de Gruyter, 165-284.

Voutilainen, Atro, Juha Heikkilä, and Arto Anttila. 1992. Constraint Grammar of English: A Performance-Oriented Introduction, Department of General Linguistics, Publication No. 21. Helsinki: University of Helsinki.

Part VI:
Ethics and Education

CHAPTER TWENTY TWO

THE PARADOX OF AUTONOMY: THE INTERACTION BETWEEN HUMANS AND AUTONOMOUS COGNITIVE ARTIFACTS

ALEXANDER RIEGLER

Abstract

According to Thrun and others, personal service robots need increasingly more autonomy in order to function in the highly unpredictable company of humans. At the same time, the cognitive processes in artifacts will become increasingly alien to us. This has several reasons: 1. Maturana's concept of structural determinism questions conventional forms of interaction. 2. Considerably different ways of embodiment result in incompatible referential frameworks (worldviews). 3. Engineers focus on the output of artifacts, whereas autonomous cognitive systems seek to control their input state. As a result, instructional interaction – the basic ingredient of conventional man–machine relationships – with genuine autonomous systems will become impossible. Therefore the increase of autonomy will eventually lead to a paradox. Today we are still in a position to anthropomorphically trivialize the behavioral pattern of current robots (von Foerster). Eventually, however, when self-organizing systems will have reached the high levels of autonomy we wished for interacting with them may become impossible since their goals will be completely independent of ours..

1. Introduction

The success of virtual life forms since the late 1990s shows that humans can develop feelings for autonomous artifacts. Examples of entertainment agents are abundant. On the software level we find Tamagotchi (a tiny cyberspace pet that needs constant care in order to grow bigger and more beautiful), the Sims (a group of virtual people who have a set of 'motives' that need to be satisfied), and Kyoko (the Japanese virtual teen-age idol singer). Implemented in hardware there are 'creatures' such as Sony's AIBO robodog (which understands dozens of voice commands but does not necessarily obey) and Kismet (a robot with humanlike expressiveness and the ability to interact with people like a growing child).

In these examples the interaction between the human audience and the artifact is dominated by feelings of sympathy and acceptance. This observation can be accounted for by the fact that entertainment robots are not supposed to carry out a particular task; they merely act as a pet. In contrast to such toys the interaction with service robots follows a different pattern. They are made for specific ends and are therefore under the control of humans. It is a relationship determined by power which applies to robots and computers alike: "Users are empowered by having a clear predictive model of system performance and a sense of mastery, control, and accomplishment." (Shneiderman in Don et al. 1992). Thrun (2004) distinguishes three types of purposeful robots: 1. industrial robots, 2. professional service robots, and 3. personal service robots. Although these categories mainly refer to their domain of action they also reflect the degree of autonomy the robots are equipped with. While robots in industrial settings are supposed to mechanically repeat a closely defined range of working steps, need personal robots (such as robotic vacuum cleaners and robodogs) a high degree of autonomy. As Thrun put it, "robots which operate in close proximity to people require a high degree of autonomy, partially because of safety concerns and partially because people are less predictable than most objects." Due to the rising public interest in robots of category 3 engineers are requested to design cognitive artifacts of increasingly more extended autonomy. I claim that this development will lead to a paradox where the interests of artifact designers collide with intrinsic properties of cognitive autonomy.

The remainder of the paper is concerned with first identifying the fundamental differences between humans and cognitive machines. The idea is to make a sharp distinction between behavior-based modeling and the input-centered perspective of the cognitive entity. Due to this fundamental gap, as observer-designers we are driven into trivializing cognitive systems. Consequently, our bias to model even most complex phenomena in terms of input–output relations thwarts our attempts to build genuinely autonomous systems. Finally, I discuss the implications of the autonomy paradox and how it will change our interaction with future generations of cognitive artifacts.

2. Alien cognition

In his 2002 paper, Alois Knoll succinctly pointed out that "humanoids will never be an exact replica of human intelligence." It can be argued that cognitive artifacts will always be differently embodied than humans. They are composed of inorganic materials and they lack phylogenetic ancestry, whereas "we human beings are the arising present of an evolutionary history in which our ancestors and the medium in which they lived have changed together congruently around the conservation of a manner of living in language, self-consciousness and a family life", as Maturana (2005) put it. Furthermore, artifacts have only a rudimentary ontogeny in the sense that their learning capacity either does not exist or is based on arbitrarily defined or incomprehensible algorithms. Here are four examples.

In what I called PacMan systems (which includes artificial life simulations as well as toys like Tamagotchis) anthropomorphically defined entities try to optimize certain parameters which are interpreted as their behavior. In such models it seems arbitrary why a certain pixel on the screen represents 'food' for the creature. Rather, it is the programmer who imposes meaning onto it. In situational systems robots merely cope with the present context and react to instantaneous information rather than construct sophisticated mental models of their environment. In symbolic rule-based systems the artifact has to base its cognition on readily prepared propositions that cut the world into crisp anthropomorphic categories. And while massively distributed systems using unsupervised learning algorithms seem to display 'natural' behavior they have a rather poor explanatory performance, which obfuscates the cognitive details. (For a more detailed discussion, cf. Riegler in press).

As a consequence, cognition in artifacts is and will remain alien to us. Chess computers play their game entirely different than humans. The former exhaustively explore all possible consequences of a certain move, the latter rely on intuitive heuristics. Poems prove to be an obstinate problem for translation programs because they are implemented in a way that focuses on formal syntactical patterns. Even the introduction of semantic ontologies does not greatly improve the problem as it merely shifts the problem of arbitrary reference between cognition and token. Consequently, such highly rational and detached systems are unable to capture a human being's referential system indispensable for text interpretation.

It can be argued that the alienation merely depends on choosing the 'proper' algorithm. However, there are reasons to assume that it is based on a fundamental epistemological aspect, which I detail in the following section.

3. The fundamental gap

I shall argue that the alienation of artificial cognitive systems arises from neglecting the difference between two perspectives, P1 and P2.

P1. Human designers concentrate on the output of an artifact: a robotic lawn mower should cut the grass efficiently, a navigational system should find the shortest route to save time and energy, etc. These technological artifacts do have a clearly pre-defined goal. Their autonomy is confined to finding the optimal chain of sub-goals in order to meet their purpose. Maes (1995) described artifacts equipped with this sort of autonomy as "computational systems that inhabit some complex dynamic environment, sense and act autonomously in this environment, and by doing so realize a set of goals or tasks for which they are designed." These are "automatic systems [...which] steer themselves along a given path, correcting and compensating for the effects of external perturbation and disturbances as they go" (Smithers, quoted in Steels 1995). Ziemke (1998) referred to their mode of working as "operational autonomy", i.e., "the capacity to operate without human intervention". For purposes of simplicity, let us call this sort of self-steering subgoal-autonomy, or s-autonomy for short.

From an engineering point of view, operational subgoal autonomy may prove inadequate in complex environments where the original human-specified goal becomes ill-defined, outdated, or inferior to other solutions. Based on Smithers demand that systems should "develop, for themselves, the laws and strategies according to which they regulate their behavior," Ziemke introduces the notion of "behavioral autonomy". However, as argued below, for natural systems and future artifacts this notion may be misleading and should be called emerging autonomy, or e-autonomy, instead.

P2. In contrast to robot builders, natural animals control their input (perception) rather than their output (behavior), or as Powers (1973) put it, "behavior is the process by which organisms control their input sensory data" (cf. also Porr & Wörgötter 2005 who discuss input control in more technical terms). This perspective is based on the concept of homeostasis (Cannon 1932), which says that a living organism has to keep its intrinsic variables within certain limits in order to survive. Such "essential variables" (Ashby 1952) include body temperature, levels of water, minerals and glucose, and similar physiological parameters, as well as other proprioceptively or consciously accessible aspects in higher animals and human beings. Consequently, natural systems execute certain actions in order to control and change their input state, such as avoiding the perception of an obstacle or drinking to quench their thirst. The state of homeostasis is reached by the process of negative feedback. Like in a thermostat, a given parameter is kept under control by appropriate counteractions. As well known, the thermostat adjust the temperature by turning off the heating as soon as a certain temperature is reached and turning it on as soon as the temperature drops below a certain reference value. While such a simple feedback loop may suffice for primitive intrinsic variables, higher order goals are accomplished in a hierarchical assemble of feedback loops in which each level provides the reference value for the next lower level: "The entire hierarchy is organized around a single concept: control by means of adjusting reference-signals for lower-order systems" (Powers 1973). So at higher levels the system controls the output of lower levels, at the bottom, however, its perceptual input.

4. The anthropomorphizations of behavior

Making the P1–P2 distinction implies that for observers and designers of artifacts the situation is diametrically different from the situation of the modeled artifacts. The former lack the possibility to sense the system's input state (or, philosophically speaking, "first-person experience"), so they focus on the system's output. If they want to understand a living organism and try to model it they will face with the problem of reverse engineering, i.e., the reconstruction of a functional model (either in the abstract-mathematical or material domain) that copies the original model's behavior. This amounts to the fact that the modeler defines systems over the range of their behaviors and builds them accordingly. The result are anthropomorphic rather than autonomous artifacts. Consequently, reverse engineering in the cognitive domain means postulating a link between the rule-like behavior of observed of natural cognitive systems and general laws of cognition and knowledge acquisition. However, observers – whether ethologists or engineers – are not embodied in the world of the observed animal (Nagel 1974) nor designed artifact (Riegler 2002). They interpret its behavior within their own referential system of understanding, usually called worldview. According to Aerts et al. (1994), a worldview can be described as a system of co-ordinates or a frame of reference in which everything presented to us by our diverse experiences can be placed. Such a representational system allows us to integrate everything we know about the world and ourselves into a global picture, one that illuminates reality as it is presented to us within a certain context. Within this framework, moving and living entities are closely linked with personal states of mind and emotional dispositions, as entertainment agents demonstrate. This bias to interpret the movements of artifacts in a particular way was characterized by Kiesler & Hinds (2004) as follows, "People's mental models of autonomous robots are often more anthropomorphic than are their models of other systems… The tendency for people to anthropomorphize may be fed, in part, by science fiction and, in part, by the powerful impact of autonomous movement on perception."

What follows from the P1–P2 distinction is that there are two domains of description, one which describes the (natural or artificial) system in question in relation with its environment and one that describes the actual working of the system in terms of its components. To paraphrase Maturana (1974), what occurs within a composed entity (e.g., living systems) is different from what happens to this entity. This is particularly obvious in the case of living systems, which exist in the domain of physiology and in the domain of behavior. These two phenomenal domains do not intersect since the description of a composite unity takes place in a meta-domain with respect to the description of the components that constitute that unity. An observer may simultaneously look at both. They might state that changes in physiology cause changes in the behavior of an observed creature, but that is not a logical necessity. Or as Glasersfeld (1979) put it, "First, there is the tempting but logically erroneous idea that what we rightly call 'environment' relative to an organism when both the organism and its environment are being observed by us, must also be our environment and can, therefore, be held causally responsible for what we ourselves experience. Second, there is the mistaken belief that the 'environment' which is part of our experiential field has to be identical with the experiential field of the observed organism." But "… in order to explain a given behavior of a living system, the observer must explain the generation and establishment of the particular structures of the organism and of the environment that make such behavior possible at the moment it occurs." (Maturana 1974).

In the context of artificial intelligence, it becomes clear why Turing (1950) so vehemently rejected the "Can machines think?" question. His imitation game is nothing more than admitting that there is no other way to assess the cognitive abilities of an artifact than approximating them in an output-oriented test.

5. Behavioral trivialization

What is the consequence for artificial autonomous systems? As pointed out before, cognitive engineers would need the intellectual capacity of making inferences from behavior to inner working. Such reverse engineering, however, requires checking a large number of possible mappings from observational data onto the model. As known from Duhem underdeterminism theorem and extended by McAllister (2003) there is an arbitrarily large number of ways to explain data points: "Any given data set can be interpreted as the sum of any conceivable pattern and a certain noise level" (McAllister 1999). This becomes immediately obvious in the case of black boxes whose inner mechanisms are unknown to the outside observer. It is extremely difficult to make inferences. Consider a box with four input, four internal, and four output states, all of which can be wired in any way. The total number of possible configurations is 444 =

$2^{32} \approx 4 \times 10^9$. In other words starting from a behavioral protocol one needs to test 4 billion different models to find the one that produced the recorded behavior.

Facing this combinatorial obstacle, all we can do is trivialize systems of this complexity (Foerster 1970) in order to deal with them as cognitive scientists and engineers. This means to reduce the degrees of freedom of a given complex entity in order to behave like a 'trivial machine', i.e., an automaton without internal states, which responses to an input with always the same output. Trivialization can be accomplished by anthropomorphically attributing behavior, i.e., by "projecting the image of ourselves into things or functions of things in the outside world" (Foerster 1970). Modeling is therefore the procedure that trivializes complex living systems. Maturana (1974) notes that it possible to "treat an autopoietic [i.e., living] system as if it were an allopoietic [i.e., man-made] one by considering the perturbing agent as input and the changes that the organism undergoes while maintaining its autopoiesis as output. This treatment, however, disregards the organization that defines the organism as a unity by putting it in a context in which a part of it can be defined as an allopoietic subsystem by specifying in it input and output relations."

So there are two non-overlapping domains, the actual working of the robots as e-autonomous system and the conceptual domain of the designer-user who would like the artifact to perform certain tasks in an s-autonomous way. This is the autonomy paradox.

The paradox makes it appear unlikely that our interaction with e-autonomous artifacts will be one of control and mastery. Such instructive interactions are impossible because the instructions e-autonomous systems undergo "will only trigger changes in them; they will not specify what happens to them" (Maturana 1987).

6. Domestication instead of interaction?

Although the autonomy paradox has implications on how we will interact with future artifacts it is not the first time in history that humans would learn to cope with autonomous systems. Thousands of years ago people started to turn wild beasts into domesticated pets. The domestication of highly autonomous and partly unpredictable wild animals must be considered a case of trivialization. No longer does the horse freely roam the steppe. It is now used a transport vehicle with the clearly defined goal of moving from A to B. In other words the domestication of natural autonomous systems is an indication that despite the autonomy paradox direct and instructive interaction with sophisticated autonomous artifacts may be possible.

However, there is a caveat. As pointed out by Diamond (2002), only 14 out of 148 mammals could be successfully domesticated. In nine out of ten cases domestication failed as not all of the following criteria could be met. These criteria can be divided into two physiological and four cognitive conditions. (P1) There must be an easy and inexpensive way to supply the animals with food. This means that carnivores and other inflexible eaters such as lions are not eligible. (P2) Animals must have a reasonably fast growth rate and short birth intervals. This is the reason why elephants got tamed but never domesticated. (C1) Taming refers to the fact that the individual animal is bred in the wild and captured afterwards. Species that are generally reluctant to breed in captivity are therefore poor candidates for domestications. The lama-like vicuñas in South America display this shortcoming, which makes it impossible to domesticate these animals whose fur is highly appreciated and priced. (C2) Creatures must have a pleasant disposition unlike grizzly bears, which have delicious meat, or zebras, which could have been used as an alternative to horses. (C3) Animals must no show the tendency to panic easily. Deer and gazelles are therefore excluded from domestication. (C4) Animals must live in modifiable social hierarchies which are dominated by a leader and which can be penetrated by a human. Antelopes do not have such a social structure, and neither have cats. This is the reason why there are no domesticated cats; they do not obey commands.

The list of criteria shows that it might turn out rather difficult to use highly autonomous systems for anthropomorphic goals. In the case of animals, the required six conditions cover both physiological and cognitive areas. Future research will have to pint out how the six conditions map onto artifacts. Among the cognitive conditions, C2 could be interpreted as the three robots laws as formulated in Isaac Asimov's novels. It clearly assigns priority to the protection of human beings. C3 may refer to a solid action-selection algorithm taking care that in unexpected situation the artifact does not resort to random and hence potentially panic-like actions. Despite this apparent alignment, however, the criteria for artifacts could also be completely different and even impossible to meet in design and engineering. In contrast to natural animals, which share a good deal of genetic structure with human beings, autonomous embodied agents featuring an entirely different phylogenetic makeup may not meet any of the six conditions and therefore will never be service robots.

7. Conclusions

The autonomy paradox threatens the objectives of embodied cognitive science, the goal of which is "building an agent for a particular task" (Pfeifer & Scheier 1999). Quite on the contrary, we will have to witness the arrival of increasingly e-autonomous agents which follow their own purposes up to the point that, as Fredkin once put it, "[e]ventually, no matter what we do there'll be artificial intelligence with independent goals". His prediction that "it's very hard to have a machine that's a million times smarter than you as your slave" is the consequence of the structural determinism in living (i.e., autopoietic in the terminology of Maturana) systems. Knoll's (2002) musing whether robots' intelligence will remain at the level of whales such that "they would probably not be able to tell us anything of interest even if we could communicate with them" (which is reminiscent of Wittgenstein's lion argument) will actually turn into its opposite namely that not we but machine will excel over us so that, in the end, genuinely e-autonomous systems may fulfill all the requirements we wanted service robots to have, but "there will be very little communication between machines and humans, because unless the machines condescend to talk to us about something that interests us, we'll have no communication" (Fredkin quoted in McCorduck 2004) – and hence no interaction.

References

Aerts, D., L. Apostel, B. De Moor, S. Hellemans, E. Maex, H. Van Belle and J. Van Der Veken. 1994. *Worldviews: From fragmentation to integration. Brussels.* VUB Press.
Ashby, W. R. 1952. *Design for a Brain.* London: Chapman and Hall.
Cannon, W. B. 1932. *The wisdom of the body.* New York: Norton.
Diamond, J. 2002. "Evolution, consequences and future of plant and animal domestication." *Nature* 418: 700–707.
Don, A. et al. 1992. "Anthropomorphism: From Eliza to Terminator 2." In: Proceedings of CHI'92, pp. 67–70.
Foerster, H. von 1970. "Thoughts and Notes on Cognition." In: P. Garvin ed, *Cognition: A Multiple View.* New York: Spartan Books, pp. 25–48.
Kiesler, S. & Hinds, P. 2004. "Introduction to this special issue on human-robot interaction." *Human-Computer Interaction.* 19(1–2): 1–8.
Knoll, A. 2002. "Cui Bono Robo Sapiens?" *Autonomous Robots* 12 (1): 5-12.
Maes, P. 1995. "Artificial life meets entertainment: Life like autonomous agents." *Communications of the ACM* 38: 108–114.
Maturana, H. R. 1974. "Cognitive strategies." In: Foerster, H. von ed, *Cybernetics of cybernetics.* Illinois: University of Illinois.
—. 1987. "Everything is said by an observer." In: Thompson, W. I. ed, Gaia. *A way of knowing. Political implications of the new biology.* Chicago: Lindisfarne Press, pp. 65–82.
—. 2005. "The origin and conservation of self-consciousness." *Kybernetes* 34 (1/2): 54–88

McAllister, J. W. 1999. "The amorphousness of the world." In: Cachro, J. and Kijania-Placek, K. eds, *IUHPS 11th International Congress of Logic, Methodology and Philosophy of Science*. Cracow: Jagiellonian University, p. 189.

—. 2003. "Algorithmic randomness in empirical data." *Studies in the History and Philosophy of Science* 34: 633–646.

McCorduck, P. 2004. *Machines who think*. Natick: A. K. Peters.

Nagel, T. 1974. "What is it like to be a bat?" *Philosophical Review* 83: 435-450.

Pfeifer, R. and Scheier, C. 1999. *Understanding intelligence*. Cambridge: MIT Press.

Porr, B. and Wörgötter, F. 2005. "Inside embodiment. What means embodiment to radical constructivists?" *Kybernetes* 34 (1/2): 105–117.

Powers, W. T. 1973. *Behavior. The control of perception*. New York: Aldine de Gruyter,

Riegler, A. 2002. "When is a cognitive system embodied?" *Cognitive Systems Research* 3: 339–348.

—. In press. "The goose, the fly, and the submarine navigator. Interdisciplinarity in artificial cognition research." In: Loula, A., Gudwin, R. and Queiroz, J. eds, *Artificial Cognition Systems*.

Steels, L. 1995. "When are robots intelligent autonomous agents?" *Robotics and Autonomous Systems* 15: 3–9.

Thrun, S. 2004. "Toward a Framework for Human-Robot Interaction." *Human-Computer Interaction* 19: 9–24.

Turing, A. M. 1950. "Computing machinery and intelligence." *Mind* 59: 433–460.

Ziemke, T. 1998. "Adaptive Behavior in Autonomous Agents." *Presence* 7(6): 564–587.

CHAPTER TWENTY THREE

A COPERNICAN REVOLUTION IN ETHICS?

TERRELL BYNUM

1. A "Copernican" Shift?

In his book The Structure of Scientific Revolutions, Thomas Kuhn (1962) made his famous distinction between "normal science" and "revolutionary science". Normal science, he said, is much like "puzzle solving" in which one treats entrenched scientific theories as trustworthy givens. Then one tries to design experiments, conduct observations, provide explanations, and make predictions in ways that conform to the entrenched theories. Revolutionary science, on the other hand, occurs when a number of "anomalies" begin to creep into the results of experiments and observations. Some predictions do not come true and the old theories fail to provide satisfying explanations.

During a period of revolutionary science, instead of engaging in everyday "puzzle solving", some scientists begin to question the entrenched theories and look for alternatives to explain the anomalies more successfully. At the time of Copernicus, for example, the old earth-centered, wheels-within-wheels Ptolemaic astronomy had become complex and unwieldy. In addition it was not very successful at explaining and predicting the observed behavior of certain heavenly bodies. Copernicus' new astronomy shifted the assumed center of the universe from the earth to the sun and (with some help from Galileo and Kepler) effectively eliminated many of the anomalies. It also decreased the complexity and unwieldiness of predictions and explanations. Because the Ptolemaic theory still was able to yield reasonably good results in most cases, astronomers continued using the old theory for much of their work. Over time, however, they eventually adopted the newer theory because of its efficiency and its ability to resolve Ptolemaic anomalies.

Ethics is not science, but it shares with science the overall goal of making sense of human experience. Just as science tries to explain, predict and systematize our experience of the natural world, so ethics tries to make sense of our moral lives.[1] During the past three thousand years, a number of powerful and highly respected ethical theories have emerged within various cultures around the globe. Some of the most influential theories are associated with great philosophers like the Buddha, Lao Tse and Confucius in Eastern societies, and Aristotle, Bentham and Kant in Western societies (to name a few examples). These and other "great ethical theories" do indeed systematize and make sense of the moral lives of the people and communities who believe in them and treasure them. The theories are deeply ingrained in the fabric of their home cultures, and they help to provide profound and lasting meaning to human lives.

In the present essay, I briefly describe a new ethical theory that has begun to coalesce from the efforts of a number of scholars in the international Computer Ethics[2] community. It is still a very young theory that needs careful systematic development, but it shows great promise. It has deep Aristotelian roots, as well as strong ties to our contemporary scientific understanding of life, human nature and the fundamental nature of the universe. The new theory – which I call "Flourishing Ethics" because of its Aristotelian roots – can be viewed as including a shift in perspective that resolves some significant "anomalies" and provides new tools to meet future ethical challenges. In addition, it seems likely to deepen and broaden our understanding of the world's great moral theories, rather than merely to replace them.

Flourishing Ethics can resolve certain "anomalies" associated with existing

---

[1] See especially Bernard H. Baumrin's definitive article "Applying Philosophy" (Baumrin 1988).
[2] The term "Computer Ethics" was coined by Walter Maner in the mid 1970s to refer to that field of research that studies ethical problems "aggravated, transformed or created by computer technology" (Maner 1978). The field itself had already been founded by Norbert Wiener in the late 1940s and early 1950s, although no one at that time, including Wiener himself, viewed it as a separate field of research, so it was not given a name. Later thinkers coined other terms to refer to Computer Ethics in Maner's sense; for example, "Information Ethics", "CyberEthics", "ICT Ethics" (Information and Communication Technology Ethics). In the present essay, the term 'Information Ethics' will be used in a very broad sense to cover ethical issues associated with many different ways of storing, processing and transmitting information, including for example telephones, telegraph, radio, television, photography, computers, information net-works, and so on. The field of Computer Ethics, in Maner's sense, is viewed here as a subfield of Information Ethics in this broad sense. [Luciano Floridi and his colleagues at Oxford University's Information Ethics Research Group use the term "information ethics" as a name for the specific metaphysical foundation of Computer Ethics which they have been developing. In the present paper, I will use the convention of "small caps" (thus, INFORMATION ETHICS) whenever I am referring to Floridi's specific foundation for Computer Ethics, rather than the broad field upon which this essay is focused.]

ethical theories. These include at least the following three shortcomings:

1. *Rejection of all ethical theories but one* – "Devout believers" in one or another ethical theory often claim that their particular theory is the only correct theory. This dogmatic view is held by enthusiasts of many different ethical theories, but it is logically impossible for all of the theories to be the one and only right one. Extremists among such dogmatists are willing, by political action or even violence, to force everyone else to adopt the specific theory that they happen to favor. Loss of respect and understanding among individuals and cultures can be the result.

2. *Troublesome cases* – Even the most respected ethical theories have particular cases which they are unable to handle well. For example, Kantian critics of utilitarianism are fond of describing situations in which terrible injustices can result from adherence to utilitarian principles. Similarly, utilitarian critics of Kantianism point to cases where telling a lie or breaking a promise would prevent horrendous consequences; while telling the truth or keeping a promise, which Kantianism always requires, would cause catastrophic results.

3. *Difficulty coping with non-human agents* – New kinds of "agents" are beginning to emerge from the Information Revolution and genetic engineering. These agents include, for example, cyborgs (part human, part machine), robots, "softbots" (software robots), and genetically engineered "super humans". Such new agents will not fit well into the "great ethical theories", because those theories address human agency. But when non-human agents begin to act more like our children, and less like our puppets, additional ethical tools and concepts will be needed to determine their appropriate role and nature.

All of the major ethical theories appear to be subject to one or another of these "anomalies". Flourishing Ethics, however, can resolve them and provide, as well, helpful new interpretations and insights into the traditional theories. (See the discussion below.)

2. Aristotelian Roots

A remarkable fact about Aristotle's ethical theory is the thoroughgoing way in which it was integrated, not only with his social and political theory (which one would expect), but also with his powerful new scientific theories. Because he was the greatest scientist in his own time, Aristotle had an unusual opportunity to ground and support his ethics with scientific insights into human nature and the nature of the universe. Thus, his account of human psychology was rooted in his theory of animal behavior, which in turn was built from his biology, physics, and metaphysics. And his theory of animal behavior led systematically and logically to his theory of human action and his ethics. (Bynum 1986)

Like Aristotle's ethics, Flourishing Ethics is more integrated with scientific theories of human nature and the universe than most other ethical theories have been. Given today's rapidly growing Information Revolution and its frequent breakthroughs in physics, biology, medicine, communications, and so on, Flourishing Ethics can be supported and integrated with cutting-edge ideas from fields such as astrophysics, cybernetics, genetics, neuropsychology and computer science.

Another significant similarity between Flourishing Ethics and Aristotle's theory is its compatibility with cultures around the globe. A person does not have to be an ancient Greek to admire virtuous behavior in Aristotle's sense of this term, so people from Asia, Europe, Africa, the Americas and other parts of the world can respect, and aspire to become, someone who is courageous, temperate, friendly, as well as virtuous in many other Aristotelian ways. Flourishing Ethics too, like Aristotle's, is compatible with many cultures, and yet it is not simply a version of "galloping relativism" or unwarranted permissiveness.

Aristotle's familiar account of the virtues and vices – the "means" and "extremes" of human character – will not be central to our purposes here. Instead, we will be especially interested in Aristotle's overall assumption that the purpose of a human life is to flourish as a human being by doing excellently what humans are especially equipped to do. For Aristotle, given his famous definition of man as "the rational animal", it follows that flourishing as a human requires reasoning excellently.

Aristotle, of course, did not use presentday terms like "cybernetics", "feedback", "input", "output" or "central processing unit". Nevertheless, his explanations of animal behavior and of human action, as well as his account of the purpose of a human life, include a number of ideas remarkably similar to those used by Norbert Wiener in the mid Twentieth Century when he laid the foundation for Information Ethics. (See Section 3 below.) Aristotle's theory of animal behavior, for example, treats animals as information-processing entities. Indeed, he distinguishes animals from plants by their ability, unlike plants, to perceive. Every animal, he said, has at least the sense of touch, and so every animal receives information from the external world into its body. After perceptual information enters an animal's body, it is processed in ways that depend upon the animal's physiology. The processing of such information typically triggers behavior that is characteristic of the kind of animal in question. Aristotle explores this "triggering" process in his explanation of the so-called "practical syllogism", which functions within an animal very much like a conditional "if …then" operator functions within a modern computer (See Aristotle's On the Movement of Animals, as well as On the Soul; and see especially Bynum 1986.) In summary, then, the physiology of an animal, according to Aristotle, determines: (1) the kinds of perceptual information that the animal can take in, (2) how this information is processed within the animal's body, and (3) what the resulting animal behavior will be.

The most sophisticated information processing in the animal kingdom, according to Aristotle, occurs within human bodies. In particular, the kinds of information processing that Aristotle called "theoretical reasoning" and "practical reasoning" include what we, today, call "comparison", "pattern recognition", "concept formation", "inductive reasoning", "deductive reasoning", "evaluating", "decision making", and more. These activities of theoretical and practical reasoning, according to Aristotle, are – or at least must be accompanied by – the bodily manipulation of "phantasms" (residual perceptual images).[3] As I have said elsewhere,

Aristotle is committed to the view that thinking involves the presence and manipulation of phantasms. His explanations of memory, recollection, concept acquisition, inferring and deliberation all require phantasms. And since phantasms are bodily entities, he seems committed to the view that thinking is – or at least requires – a physiological process. (Bynum 1986, p. 124)

Crucial to the flourishing of human beings is the fact that these bodily processes (manipulations of "phantasms") generate meaning in the semantic and emotional senses of this term. Precisely what meaning is and how it is generated from bodily processing of physical information ("Shannon information" in today's language; see below) are among the most challenging questions in all of philosophy. No philosopher has yet developed a complete and fully satisfying theory of meaning; and decades or even a century may pass before such a theory finally is developed. Nevertheless, it was clear even to Aristotle that physical manipulation of information inside of a person's body is or generates theoretical and practical reasoning, thereby empowering human beings to set goals, manipulate nature, and govern their own actions in an endless variety of ways. These capacities distinguish humans from other animals and make it possible, in the context of society, to achieve knowledge, virtue, and wisdom – and thereby flourish.

---

[3] There are certain passages in the Aristotelian corpus that appear to contradict this interpretation of Aristotle (See Bynum, 1986, p. 124), but the interpretation pre-sented here is consistent with the overwhelming majority of Aristotle's relevant works and passages.

For Aristotle, what contemporary philosophers would call "autonomy" – the capacity to deliberate about possible actions and then act upon the results of deliberation – is a necessary precondition for fulfilling the overall purpose of a human life: to flourish, to do excellently what humans are especially equipped to do. In a very real sense, the autonomy of human beings turns them into "self-creators" in at least two ways: by choosing their actions, one by one, human beings continually create and recreate their own ethical characters – and their own lives and personal identities, as well.

Human beings, however, are not solitary, they are fundamentally social, and they cannot flourish on their own. Knowledge and science, wisdom and ethics, justice and the law are all social achievements requiring communication and interaction within a community of reasoning, decision-making beings. Given an appropriate society, however, a human being can flourish in a wide diversity of ways – as a diplomat, teacher, philosopher, farmer, builder, and so on. And there are many different cultures and societies where such human flourishing is possible.

Much more can be said on this topic,[4] but enough has been said for purposes of the present essay. The goal here is to describe briefly the Aristotelian roots of the emerging theory that I am calling "Flourishing Ethics". Let me summarize by emphasizing the following points:

1. In Aristotle's ethics, *human flourishing* is central.

2. Human beings are *social* animals. Only in the context of society can human beings flourish.

3. The *nature* of any living being, according to Aristotle, is determined by what that being is especially equipped to do, To flourish as a being of that kind is to do those things excellently and continuously.

4. It is the nature of a human being to reason theoretically and practically. Thus to do so excellently and continuously is to flourish as a human being and thereby lead a good (including a *virtuous*) life.

5. Theoretical and practical reasoning are *special kinds of information processing*. Engaging in appropriate information processing, therefore, is central to being ethical and leading a good life.

6. The key to excellent practical reasoning, and therefore the key to being ethical, is the capacity to deliberate well about one's overall goals, choose a wise course of action, and carry out the action. (This ethically central, decision-making, information-processing capacity has been called "a good will" by Kant and other philosophers following him.)

---

[4] See my forthcoming book, tentatively entitled *Flourishing Ethics: An Ethical Theory for the Information Age*, which is currently being written.

3. Norbert Wiener and the Birth of Information Ethics

The American philosopher/scientist Norbert Wiener played a leading role (with others, such as John von Neumann, Claude Shannon and Alan Turing) in creating the technology and the science that launched the Information Revolution. In addition, Wiener had a rare gift of foresight, which enabled him to anticipate many of the enormous ethical and social impacts of his own work and that of his colleagues. This led him to create Information Ethics as an academic subject in the late 1940s and early 1950s. He not only developed a powerful foundation for Information Ethics, which will be examined here, he also provided in books, articles and speeches, a "treasure trove" of information ethics comments, examples and analyses. (See Wiener 1948, 1950, 1954, 1964) The issues that Wiener analyzed, or at least touched upon, decades ago included topics that are still considered "contemporary" today – information networks and globalization, virtual communities, teleworking, computers and unemployment, computers and security, computers and religion, computers and learning, computers for persons with disabilities, responsibilities of computer professionals, the merging of human bodies and machines, "agent" ethics, artificial intelligence, and a number of other topics as well. (Bynum 2000, 2004, 2005) For the most part, these specific topics will not be addressed here. The primary focus, instead, will be upon the metaphysical foundation that Wiener presupposed in his Information Ethics, plus his account of human nature, his account of the nature of society, and his view of the role of information in all of these.

During the Second World War, while working on the development of an antiaircraft cannon, Wiener and some colleagues created a new branch of science, which Wiener named "Cybernetics", from the Greek word for the steersman or pilot of a ship. He defined Cybernetics as the science of information feedback systems and the statistical study of communications. He viewed human beings, and indeed all other animals, as "cybernetic systems" whose internal parts communicate with each other in ways that include "feedback" to monitor their own activities. This dynamic cybernetic activity enables animals to maintain internal bodily stability and also interact with the external world to fulfill their desires and goals.

While creating the field of Information Ethics, Wiener laid a foundation that is very Aristotelian. Although there is no evidence that he explicitly based himself upon Aristotle,[5] the similarities are striking between Aristotle's accounts of animal behavior and human action on the one hand, and Wiener's

---

[5] Indeed there is evidence that Wiener considered Aristotle's biological writings to involve mostly categorizing. (Wiener, 1950, p. 78)

explanations of animal behavior, human action, and machine agency on the other. Like Aristotle before him, Wiener used the science of his day to help understand human nature and thereby derive an account of purpose in a human life. Of course, the science in Aristotle's day was his own biology and physics, while that of Wiener included late Nineteenth and early Twentieth Century sciences like relativity, thermodynamics, statistical mechanics and Darwinian biology.

Both Aristotle and Wiener described animals, including humans, as beings that take in information from the outside world, process and store it in ways dependent upon internal bodily structure, and adjust their behavior to take account of past experience and new information. Like Aristotle, Wiener saw an intimate relationship between the information processing nature of human beings and the purpose of a human life. For Wiener, as for Aristotle, the overall purpose of a human life is to flourish as a person; and to achieve this purpose, one must engage in a diversity of information processing activities, such as perceiving, organizing, remembering, inferring, deciding, planning, and acting. Human flourishing, then, is utterly dependent upon internal information processing:

Information is a name for the content of what is exchanged with the outer world as we adjust to it, and make our adjustment felt upon it. The process of receiving and of using information is the process of our adjusting to the contingencies of the outer environment, and of our living effectively within that environment. The needs and the complexity of modern life make greater demands on this process of information than ever before. To live effectively is to live with adequate information. Thus, communication and control belong to the essence of man's inner life, even as they belong to his life in society. (Wiener 1954, pp. 17-18)

Wiener contrasted information processing in humans with that of other animals, and he noted the importance of bodily structure. Consider his comparison of humans with ants:

I wish to show that the human individual, capable of vast learning and study, which may occupy about half of his life, is physically equipped, as the ant is not, for this capacity. Variety and possibility are inherent in the human sensorium – and indeed are the key to man's most noble flights – because variety and possibility belong to the very structure of the human organism.

While it is possible to throw away this enormous advantage that we have over the ants [and the rest of the animal kingdom], and to organize . . . [an] ant state with human material, I certainly believe this is a degradation of man's very nature, and . . . a waste of the great human values which man possesses. . . . if the human being is condemned and restricted to perform the same functions over and over again, he will not even be a good ant, not to mention a good human being. (Wiener, 1954, pp. 51-52; bracketed words added for clarity)

Cybernetics takes the view that the structure of the machine or of the organism is an index of the performance that may be expected from it. The fact that the mechanical rigidity of the insect is such as to limit its intelligence while the mechanical fluidity of the human being provides for his almost indefinite intellectual expansion is highly relevant to the point of view of this book. (Wiener, 1954, p. 57, italics in the original)

According to Wiener, just as individual animals can be viewed as dynamic, cybernetic entities, so communities and societies can be analyzed in a similar way:

> It is certainly true that the social system is an organization like the individual; that it is bound together by a system of communication; and that it has a dynamics, in which circular processes of a feedback nature play an important part. (Wiener 1948, p. 33)

In Chapter VIII of Cybernetics, Wiener noted that societies and groups can be viewed as second-order cybernetic systems because their constituent parts are themselves cybernetic systems. This is true not only of human communities, but also, for example, of beehives, ant colonies, and certain herds of mammals. According to Wiener's cybernetic understanding of society, the processing and flow of information are crucial to the nature and the functioning of the community. Communication, he said, is "the central phenomenon of society" (Wiener 1950, p. 229).

4. The New Role of Machines in Society

Before 1950, Wiener's social analyses dealt with communities consisting primarily of humans or other animals. From 1950 onward, however, beginning with the publication of *The Human Use of Human Beings*, Wiener assumed that *machines will join humans as active participants in society*. For example, some machines will participate along with humans in the vital activity of creating, sending and receiving messages that constitute the "cement" which binds society together:

> It is the thesis of this book that society can only be understood through a study of the messages and the communication facilities which belong to it; and that in the future development of these messages and communication facilities, messages between man and machines, between machines and man, and between machine and machine, are destined to play an ever-increasing part. (Wiener 1950, p. 9)

Wiener predicted, as well, that certain machines – namely electronic computers with robotic appendages – will participate in the workplace, replacing thousands of human factory workers, both blue collar and white collar. He also foresaw artificial limbs – cybernetic prostheses – that will be merged with human bodies to help persons with disabilities, or even to endow able-bodied persons with unprecedented powers. "What we now need," he said, " is an independent study of systems involving both human and mechanical elements." (Wiener 1964, p. 77) Today, we would say that Wiener envisioned societies in which "cyborgs" (humans merged with machines) will play a significant role and we will need ethical policies to govern their behavior.

A special concern that Wiener often expressed involved machines that learn and make decisions on their own. He worried that some people, blundering like sorcerers' apprentices, might create agents that humans are unable to control – agents that could act on the basis of values which humans do not share. It is risky, he noted, to replace human judgment with machine decisions, and he cautioned that a prudent man will not leap in where angels fear to tread, unless he is prepared to accept the punishment of the fallen angels. Neither will he calmly transfer to the machine[6] made in his own image the responsibility for his choice of good and evil, without continuing to accept a full responsibility for that choice. (Wiener 1950, pp.211-212)

Wiener noted that, to prevent this kind of disaster, the world will need ethical rules for artificial agents, as well as technology to instill those rules effectively into the agents.

In summary, then, Wiener foresaw future societies living in what he called the "Machine Age" or the "Automatic Age". In such a society, machines will be integrated into the social fabric, as well as the physical environment. They will create, send and receive messages, gather information from the external world, make decisions, carry out those decisions, reproduce themselves, and be merged with human bodies to create beings with vast new powers. Wiener's predictions were not mere speculations, because he himself had already designed or witnessed early versions of devices, such as game-playing machines (checkers, chess, war, business), artificial hands with motors controlled by the person's brain, and self-reproducing machines, such as non-linear transducers. (See especially Wiener 1964.)

---

[6] 'the machine...which can learn and can make decisions on the basis of its learning, will in no way be obliged to make such decisions as we should have made, or will be acceptable to us. For the man who is not aware of this, to throw the problem of his responsibility on the machine, whether it can learn or not, is to cast his responsibility to the winds, and to find it coming back seated on the whirlwind.' (Wiener 1950, p. 212)

Wiener's descriptions of future societies and their machines elicited, from others, various questions about those machines: Will they have minds and be conscious? Will they be "alive"? Wiener considered such questions to be vague semantic quibbles, rather than genuine scientific issues. He thought of machines and human beings alike as physical entities with capacities that are explained by the ability of their parts to interact with each other and with the outside world. The working parts of machines are "lumps" of metal, plastic, silicon and other materials; while the working parts of humans are exquisitely small cells, atoms, and molecules.

Now that certain analogies of behavior are being observed between the machine and the living organism, the problem as to whether the machine is alive or not is, for our purposes, semantic and we are at liberty to answer it one way or the other as best suits our convenience. (Wiener 1954, p. 32)

Answers to questions about machine consciousness, thinking, or purpose are similarly semantic choices, according to Wiener; although he did believe that questions about the "intellectual capacities" of machines, when appropriately stated, could be genuine scientific questions:

Theoretically, if we could build a machine whose mechanical structure duplicated human physiology, then we could have a machine whose intellectual capacities would duplicate those of human beings. (Wiener 1954, p. 57)

In his 1964 book, *God and Golem, Inc.*, Wiener expressed skepticism that machines would ever duplicate the complex structure of the human brain, because electronic components were too large and impossible to cram together like the neurons packed into a human brain. As the above quotation indicates, though, he did leave open at least the theoretical possibility that machines would someday be created that could equal or exceed human intelligence.

5. Wienerian Ethical Theory

Even though Wiener noted the need for ethical rules to cover "systems involving both human and mechanical elements" (i.e., cyborgs), and even though he expressed concern about machines being permitted to make ethical decisions in place of humans, he did not propose anything that could be construed as "machine ethics" or "cyborg ethics". Instead, his explicit discussions of ethical theory remained focused upon actions and values of human beings. Thus, in the opening chapter of the first edition of The Human Use of Human Beings, he said:

That we shall have to change many details of our mode of life in the face of the new machines is certain; but these machines are secondary in all matters of value that concern us to the proper evaluation of human beings for their own sake.... The message of this book as well as its title is the human use of human beings. (Wiener, 1950, p.2, italics in the original)

Wiener often discussed ways to defend or advance human values in light of new developments in information and communication technology. Some of those values included life, health, security, knowledge, opportunity, abilities, happiness, peace, and most of all, freedom (not freedom in a right-to-vote political sense, but freedom in the sense of autonomy – making choices and carrying them out in pursuit of one's chosen goals). A good human life, according to Wiener, is one in which "the great human values" are realized – one in which the creative and flexible information-processing potential of human physiology enables people to reach their full promise in variety and possibility of action. At its best, such information processing leads to "man's most noble flights". Of course, different humans have different interests and various levels of talent, so one person's achievements will be different from another's, and it is possible to lead a good human life in a vast variety of ways – for example, as a public servant or statesman, a teacher or scholar, a scientist, engineer, musician, farmer, tradesman, and so on. Like Aristotle, Wiener viewed human autonomy as the power to continually recreate one's self, one's life and one's moral character.

Wiener's conception of the purpose of a human life leads him to state what he calls "great principles of justice" upon which a society should be built – principles that would maximize a person's ability to flourish through variety and flexibility of human action. For easy reference to these "great principles" let us call them "The Principle of Freedom", "The Principle of Equality" and "The Principle of Benevolence". (Wiener himself does not assign names.) Using Wiener's own definitions yields the following list (Wiener, 1950, pp. 112-113):

THE PRINCIPLE OF FREEDOM – Justice requires "the liberty of each human being to develop in his freedom the full measure of the human possibilities embodied in him".

THE PRINCIPLE OF EQUALITY – Justice requires "the equality by which what is just for A and B remains just when the positions of A and B are interchanged".

THE PRINCIPLE OF BENEVOLENCE – Justice requires "a good will between man and man that knows no limits short of those of humanity itself".

In addition to these three "great principles of justice", Wiener added a fourth principle in order to protect freedom from an oppressive government or society. Let us call it "The Principle of Minimum Infringement of Freedom":

THE PRINCIPLE OF MINIMUM INFRINGEMENT OF FREEDOM – "What compulsion the very existence of the community and the state may demand must be exercised in such a way as to produce no unnecessary infringement of freedom".

After introducing these ethical principles in The Human Use of Human Beings (Chapter VII, 1950), Wiener did not elaborate upon them or provide examples, either in that book or elsewhere, to explain or illustrate in detail how his readers should interpret them or apply them to cases. The Principle of Freedom and the Principle of Minimum Infringement of Freedom seem intended to maximize the opportunities for all humans to exercise their autonomy as they strive to fulfill their chosen goals and human potential. Presumably, this would entail the provision of security to protect life, limb and property, as well as the provision of opportunities to apply one's talents to the projects of one's choice. The Principle of Benevolence seems to require respect for each person's efforts to flourish. And the Principle of Equality seems to entail that, for any two people, A and B, if it is ethically permitted for A to treat B in a certain way, then, in ethically similar circumstances, it is permitted for B to treat A in a similar way. (One is left wishing that Wiener had developed this part of his theory more fully.)

6. Ethical Relativism and Multiple Societies

Given Wiener's view of the purpose of a human life, it is possible to live a good life in many different societies and communities. Wiener clearly believed that human potential can be fulfilled to various degrees, with some societies providing less infringement upon creative and flexible human action than others. In The Human Use of Human Beings, he discussed a number of societies including, for example, the Eskimos, India, feudalism, despotism, fascism and the American representative democracy (see, for example, Wiener, 1950, pp. 59-61). He reserved his harshest criticism for "communities ruled by despots" like the fascist states of the first half of the Twentieth Century; and he expressed his belief that if a democracy, such as the United States, were actually to live up to its ideals of freedom for all, it could become a model community for achieving human flourishing. (He also made it clear, in The Human Use of Human Beings and elsewhere, that he thought the American society of the mid-Twentieth Century fell far short of this ideal.)

If one accepts Wiener's account of human nature and a good society, it follows that many different cultures, with a wide diversity of customs, religions, languages and practices, can provide a conducive context for human flourishing. Indeed, given Wiener's view that "variety and possibility belong to the very structure of the human organism", one would expect and encourage the existence of a broad diversity of cultures around the world to maximize the possibilities for human choice and creative action. The primary restriction that Wiener would impose upon any society is that it should provide the kind of context in which humans can realize their full potential; and he believed this to be possible only where significant autonomy, equality and human compassion hold sway.

So-called "ethical relativists" often point to the wide diversity of cultures in the world – with various religions, laws, codes, values and practices – as evidence that there is no global ethics, no underlying universal ethical foundation. But Wiener could offer a compelling response to such sceptics. Given his account of human nature and the purpose of a human life, he can embrace and welcome the rich diversity of cultures, laws, norms and practices that sceptics and relativists are fond of citing; while, at the same time, he can advocate an underlying ethical foundation for all societies and cultures – namely, his "great principles of justice".

7. Moor on Computer Ethics and "Just Consequentialism"

Until very recently, the Information Ethics ideas of Norbert Wiener were essentially unexamined by Computer Ethics scholars.[7] As a result, significant contributions were made to Computer Ethics, independently of Wiener, during the 1970s through the 1990s. One of the most important of these achievements is the "classic" Computer Ethics theory of James Moor, which he developed and refined in the 1980s and 1990s (see, for example, Moor 1985, 1998, 1999). Although it was not based upon Wiener, Moor's Computer Ethics theory is compatible with Wiener's "great principles of justice", under at least one reasonable interpretation of them. In addition, Moor's theory can be viewed as a powerful version of the human-centered part of a complete Flourishing Ethics (see the discussion below). It includes a clear, practical method of case analysis, as well as an effective and innovative theory of justice ("Just Consequentialism"). Moor divides Computer Ethics into two kinds of activity:

> Examination of the social and ethical impacts of computing technology (including hardware, software and networks)
>
> Formulation and justification of policies for the ethical use of computing technology

Of special interest in the first kind of activity is the identification of ethical "policy vacuums" that arise when computing technology makes it possible to do

---

[7] Since the early 1950s, Wiener has been known, among computer professionals, as an early and important "computers and society" thinker. His Information Ethics ideas, however, were not extensively examined by Computer Ethics scholars until 1999. (See Bynum 2000, 2001)

new kinds of things. Because those things have not been done before, there are no "policies" to help determine whether one should do them. According to Moor, such policy vacuums are not unique to computing, but they occur much more often with computing technology than with other technologies, because the "logical malleability" of computers makes them nearly "universal tools" that can perform almost any task.

In the second kind of Computer Ethics activity – ethically justifying policies – one begins by clearing up any relevant ambiguities, then devising a set of possible new (or altered) policies to fill a "policy vacuum". Moor intentionally selected policies for ethical justification, instead of rules:

> Rather than using "policies" I could use "rules." But ethical rules are sometimes regarded as binding without exceptions. A system of exceptionless rules will never work as an ethical theory, for rules can conflict and sometimes exceptions must be made because of extraordinary conesquences. . . . I prefer using the word "policy" because I want to suggest modification may be necessary in cases of conflict or extraordinary circumstance. (Moor 2006, p. 104)

Given a set of possible policies, one tries to identify a subset of just policies to fill the vacuum. A just policy, at a minimum, will apply to everyone equally:

> When we act ethically, we are acting such that anyone in a similar situation would be allowed to do the same kind of action. I am not allowed to have my own set of ethical policies that allow me to do things that others in a relevantly similar situation cannot do. Ethical policies are public policies. (Moor 2006, p. 104)

To be publicly advocated, a policy must be "impartial", and Moor (1999, p. 68) employs the "blindfold of justice" test from Bernard Gert (1998) to identify such policies. The details of Gert's impartiality test need not concern us here. For our purposes we need only note that the Moor/Gert test of impartiality selects policies that also would be compatible with Wiener's Principle of Equality – "what is just for A and B remains just when the positions of A and B are interchanged".

The end result of this process will be a set of possible policies, some of which can be publicly advocated as just by all rational, impartial people; some would be rejected as unjust by all rational, impartial people; and some would be debatable. All policies that pass the justice test must still be evaluated and compared based upon their likely consequences:

> At the core, humans have similar kinds of values, i.e. what kinds of things they consider to be goods (benefits) and what kinds of things they consider to be evils (harms). In general the core goods include life, happiness and autonomy and the

core evils include death, unhappiness, and lack of autonomy. By "happiness" I mean simply pleasure and absence of pain. . . .Obviously, humans do not share all their goals in common. But no matter what goals humans seek, they need ability, security, knowledge, freedom opportunity and resources in order to accomplish their projects. These are the kinds of goods that permit each of us to do whatever we want to. For brevity I will call this set of goods "the goods of autonomy" or simply "autonomy". (Moor 1999, p. 67; see also Moor 1998)

In evaluating the consequences, we must take "the ethical point of view" by being concerned with the good of others at least to the extent of not harming them unjustifiably. This is very similar to – or at least compatible with – Wiener's Principle of Benevolence.

Moor's concern to preserve and advance "autonomy", defined in terms of "core values", is similar to Wiener's concern to preserve and advance "freedom"; and Moor defines 'autonomy' using the same human values that Wiener advocates and defends in his Information Ethics writings.

Like Wiener's Information Ethics theory, Moor's Just Consequentialism is very Aristotelian:

The combined notions of human life, happiness, and autonomy may not be far from what Aristotle meant by "human flourishing". Thus, from an ethical point of view, we seek computing policies that at least protect, if not promote, human flourishing. (Moor 1999, p. 66)

Like Aristotle's early version of human-centered Flourishing Ethics, and like Wiener's later version, Moor's version of human-centered Flourishing Ethics is very compatible with the great ethical theories and traditions around the globe.

8. The Metaphysics of Wiener's Information Ethics

The Flourishing Ethics theories of Aristotle, Wiener and Moor are all human-centered; that is, they are focused upon *human* actions and *human* values. Wiener provided as well (see section 4 above) examples and commentary on the desirability of *ethics for robots and cyborgs* (to use today's language). Though he did not develop any ethical principles for such non-human agents, Wiener did presuppose a metaphysics that can ground a system of ethics for non-human agents (see section 9 below).

Wiener's metaphysics assumed that *information is physical* – that it is subject to the laws of nature and is measurable by science. The kind of information that Wiener had in mind is sometimes called "*Shannon information*" – named for Claude Shannon, who had been a student and colleague of Wiener's at MIT.[7] Shannon information is the kind that is carried in telephone wires, TV cables and radio signals. It is the kind of information that digital computers process and DNA encodes within the cells of all biological organisms. Although Shannon information *can* be a means for conveying semantic contents – like sense, reference and connotation – it need not do so,[8] and in the overwhelming majority of cases it does not do so (see section 9 below). Wiener was very clear about his belief that such information, even though it is physical, is neither matter nor energy. Thus, while discussing thinking as information processing in the brain, Wiener noted that the brain:

> does not secrete thought "as the liver does bile", as the earlier materialists claimed, nor does it put it out in the form of energy, as the muscle puts out its activity. Information is information, not matter or energy. No materialism which does not admit this can survive at the present day. (Wiener 1948, p. 155)

According to Wiener's metaphysics, although matter-energy and Shannon information are different physical phenomena, neither can exist on its own, each requires the other. So-called "physical objects", then – *including living organisms* – are actually persistent patterns of information in an ever-changing "flow" or "flux" of matter-energy. Every physical process is a mixing and mingling of matter-energy with information – a creative "coming-to-be" and a destructive "fading away", as old patterns of matter-energy and information fade and new ones emerge. Metaphorically expressed: information and matter-energy mix and swirl in a "cosmic dance", giving birth to objects and relationships, which constitute all that ever was or ever will be, till the end of time.

This account of the fundamental nature of the universe and the objects and processes within it is reminiscent of important philosophical ideas in a variety of the world's great cultures. For example, Wiener's matter-energy and information are much like Aristotle's "matter" and "form". According to Aristotle, all objects consist of both, and neither can occur without the other; so if all form is lost, no individual object can remain. Similarly, the ongoing mixing and mingling of matter-energy and information in Wiener's universe is much like the blending of yin and yang in the "flow of the Tao", and suggestive of the creative/destructive "cosmic dance" of the Hindu god Shiva Nataraj.

Also worthy of note is the fact that this Wienerian view of the nature of the universe provides a new understanding of both the Industrial Revolution and the Information Revolution. Since the transformation of matter-energy and the flow

---

[8] Shannon and Wiener were among the founding fathers of information theory; and Shannon became known as the founding father of the mathematical and scientific study of information.

of information, respectively, are the two fundamental creative processes of the universe, the world-changing nature of each revolution can be attributed to the fact that humans harnessed each of them for human purposes. The machines of the Industrial Age were *matter-energy-transformation devices*; while the machines of today's Information Age are *information-processing devices* – "heat machines" and "information machines". By harnessing, respectively, each of the two fundamental cosmic processes, humans suddenly could do innumerable things that they were never able to do before, thereby creating innumerable "policy vacuums" (to borrow some language from Moor). The results were two social/ethical revolutions with millions of new policies needed to fill a staggering number of vacuums!

Another new perspective provided by Wiener's metaphysics is his account of human nature and personal identity. Human beings (and all other living organisms), on his view, are *patterns of information persisting through changes in matter-energy*. Because of biological processes within a person's body, such as breathing, eating, drinking, perspiring and so on, virtually all the atoms and molecules that make up one's body are exchanged for new ones from the surrounding environment every few years. In spite of this continuous exchange of matter-energy in a person's body, the complex organization or *form* of that person – the *information* encoded within it – is maintained (via homeostasis) to preserve life, functionality and personal identity. As Wiener poetically said:

> We are but whirlpools in a river of ever-flowing water. We are not stuff that abides, but patterns that perpetuate themselves. (Wiener 1954, p. 96)

> The individuality of the body is that of a flame...of a form rather than of a bit of substance. (Wiener 1954, p. 102)

To use today's language, humans are "information objects" whose personal identity is tied to information processing and persisting patterns of information, rather than to specific bits of matter.

Support from today's physics – The metaphysics that underlies Wiener's Information Ethics anticipated developments in today's physics. In the so-called "theory of everything", which has emerged from physics during the past two decades, the universe is fundamentally digital and informational. Given this new view of the universe, every so-called "object" or physical entity is, in reality, a persisting pattern of relationships and processes that amount to the flow of digital, "yes/no", "on/off" information (Shannon information). This account of the nature of the universe originated with Princeton physicist John Wheeler (see, for example, Wheeler 1990); and it has been refined and supported by many scientific experiments during the past decade. One important discovery, for example, by physicist Jacob Beckenstein (who had been a student of

Wheeler's), is the so-called "Beckenstein Bound" which sets an absolute limit upon the amount of information that can be contained in a given amount of space. (Beckenstein 2003)

Because of recent scientific developments like these, Wiener's metaphysical assumptions, from the 1940s and 1950s, about the fundamental nature of the universe, have been confirmed and elaborated in physics. Indeed, scholars like MIT's Seth Lloyd are now able to publish books that describe, in careful scientific detail, the "cosmic dance" of matter-energy and Shannon information that continually creates everything in the universe. (See Lloyd 2006.)

9. Wiener on Good and Evil

In his Information Ethics writings, Wiener regularly mentions "good and evil". Sometimes the evil to which he refers is the result of malevolent, negligent, or foolish human beings. At other times, however, the evil to which Wiener refers is a natural evil – an evil that is built into the very fabric of the universe. In the Second Edition Revised of The Human Use of Human Beings (e.g., 1954, Ch. 2), Wiener refers to entropy as "the devil" – an "arch enemy" of all order and structure in the universe – the ultimate cause of death, disease, decline, decay, destruction, and pain – a relentless threat that eventually will destroy everything that anyone might value. Because of this, it is good to resist or decrease entropy. But what is entropy?

In the Nineteenth Century, while striving to develop more efficient heat engines, physicists and engineers discovered entropy, which they described as a measure of "lost heat" – heat that can no longer do useful work. It later became clear that entropy applies to all physical entities and processes, and not just to heat transformations within engines. Thus, in every physical object or process, "free energy" (energy that can bring about physical change) can never increase and will almost always decrease. This is a result of the Second Law of Thermodynamics – a fundamental fact about the nature of the universe, which causes all physical objects and processes in the universe to tend toward chaos and destruction as entropy increases and the amount of free energy within them diminishes.

In the last half of the Twentieth Century, it was discovered that entropy is also a measure of lost Shannon information. The conversion of useful free energy to useless "entropic energy" is the result of the loss of Shannon information[9] Because of the relentless loss of information in accordance with

---

[9] "Lost" Shannon information is not actually destroyed, rather it is converted to useless invisible entropic information that is dispersed into the quantum mechanical background of the universe. See Lloyd, 2006, pp. 40-41.

the second law of thermodynamics, every pattern or structure in the universe eventually will decay into chaos and homogeneity. Dissolution and destruction, then, will be the ultimate fate of every physical entity, even priceless works of art, magnificent buildings, living organisms, ecosystems, civilizations, mountain ranges, earth and moon and stars. In this sense, increasing entropy (loss of Shannon information) can indeed be seen as the greatest natural evil, threatening everything that humans hold dear.

Happily, according to Wiener, this "ultimate fate of everything" can be resisted and put off for a very long time, perhaps millions of years, in certain small pockets of the universe, such as the earth. This is possible because the earth teems with beings that increase order and structure locally – and thereby decrease entropy locally – even as they increase entropy in the universe as a whole. Such beings take in information and small bits of matter-energy from other regions (e.g., from the sun) of the vast physical system of which they are a tiny part. On earth, and in its nearby space-time region, several kinds of "local-entropy-decreasing" beings exist:

1. All Living Organisms – All living organisms, because of the information encoded in their genes, and because of the structures and processes within their bodies, are generators of local Shannon information. By living and growing they actually increase the amount of information – and so, decrease the amount of entropy in their local region of the universe. This "anti-entropy" effect is multiplied dramatically when living beings reproduce themselves. The more that living organisms flourish, the more they decrease entropy – natural evil– in their region of the world. Because they decrease natural evil locally, it is good when living organisms flourish.

2. Animals – Animals, of course, are living organisms, so they share with plants the anti-local-entropy impacts described in 1 above. But animals have an additional means of decreasing entropy; namely, the cybernetic information processing and feedback mechanisms which Aristotle and Wiener described in such detail. Animals use small amounts of information and energy from perception, kinesthesia, memory, and other information processing activities to maintain the structure and function of their own bodies, and to bring additional order and structure to their environments. The more that animals flourish, therefore, the more they locally decrease the natural evil of entropy. Thus it is good when animals flourish.

3. Ecosystems – Most animals and plants live together in specific environments like river valleys, rain forests, deserts, and so on. There, they typically interact in ways that bring about a "balance of nature". In this happy circumstance – an "ecosystem" – a complex, dynamic pattern of animal, plant, and "land" interactions creates even more order and structure than the individual

animals and plants could bring about on their own. When such ecosystems flourish, the natural evil of entropy is reduced significantly in the local environment. It is therefore very good when ecosystems flourish.

4. Human Beings – People are members of the animal kingdom, so they share all of the entropy-reducing abilities just described in 1 and 2 above. In addition, humans have the special information processing capabilities that Aristotle called "theoretical and practical reasoning". These special capabilities give humans tremendous power to add order and structure, and thus information, to their local region of the world. When humans flourish, therefore, they dramatically reduce entropy. It is, therefore, a very good thing indeed for humans to flourish.

5. Communities, Societies, and Civilizations – Wiener argued that human communities, as well as bee hives, ant colonies and certain herds of mammals, should be considered "second-order cybernetic systems" because their members are themselves cybernetic systems. Second-order cybernetic systems with large numbers of first-order cybernetic members dramatically decrease local entropy beyond what the individual members could do on their own. This is crucial to the flourishing of human beings, because when humans join forces in communities – especially communities which uphold Wiener's "great principles of justice" (or Moor's "Just Consequentialism") – their ability to generate and acquire meaningful information, and live fulfilling and meaningful lives, is increased exponentially. It is a very good thing indeed, therefore, for such human communities to flourish. They make life profoundly fulfilling, and they dramatically decrease evils like death and disease, chaos and disorder.

6. Information Processing Machines – Today's information processing machines manipulate Shannon information and thereby add much order and structure to the communities in which they function. They reduce local entropy significantly. When future "artificial agents", such as cyborgs, robots and softbots gain sophistication, and begin to act more like our children and less like our puppets, they will participate more and more in communications and decisions that form the "cement" that binds society together. They will gather information about the world; store, sort and access it; make decisions and carry them out – even more so than their primitive cousins do today. As a result, local entropy will be reduced dramatically. It therefore will be very good for well-behaved information processing machines to flourish as active participants in society.

If one agrees with Wiener that entropy is the greatest natural evil, it follows from the above discussion that a major goal of ethics should be, not only the flourishing of human beings, but also the flourishing of plants, animals, ecosystems, just societies, and even cybernetic machines. This startling result indicates that the overall focus of ethics can and should be shifted away from the narrow anthropocentric goal of human flourishing to the broader, and more reasonable goal of the flourishing of life, ecosystems and just civilizations, including well-behaved cybernetic machines that participate in the very fabric of those civilizations. Environmental ethicists have advocated a shift in perspective very much like this, although they did not include "artificial agents" and other cybernetic machines in their ethical considerations.

Given the above described "theory of everything" in today's physics, it even makes sense for people to include in their ethical purview every structured entity – every "information object" – in the universe. This is so because all structured objects, according to that theory, are repositories of Shannon information – the very opposite of entropy, with its loss of information and the resulting chaos and destruction. This broadest of all possible ethical purviews, which values every information object and structure in the universe, has actually been adopted by Luciano Floridi and his colleagues in Oxford University's Information Ethics Research Group (See, for example, Floridi 2006). Floridi and his Oxford colleagues have completed a "Flourishing Ethics shift" in their ethical perspective.

10. Floridi's INFORMATION ETHICS[10] Theory

The shift of perspective made by Floridi and his Oxford Group places at the center of ethics, not the actions, values, and characters of human agents, but instead the evil (harm, dissolution, damage – i.e., entropy) suffered by the recipients of the action. By interpreting every existing entity in the universe as an information object, Floridi is able to shift the ethical perspective from an "agent-based" (and human-based) theory to a "patient-based", non-anthropocentric theory:

[All] entities will be described as clusters of data, that is, as informational objects. More precisely, [any existing entity] will be a discrete, self-contained, encapsulated package containing

   i) the appropriate data structures, which constitute the nature of the entity in question, that is, the state of the object, its unique identity and its attributes; and

   ii) a collection of operations, functions, or procedures, which are activated by various interactions or stimuli (that is, messages received from other objects

---

[10] In the present essay, as indicated above, I use "information ethics" in small caps (INFORMATION ETHICS) to refer to Floridi's specific theory, which is different from and more specific than the very broad field of research that I am calling "Information Ethics".

or changes within itself) and correspondingly define how the object behaves or reacts to them.

At this level of abstraction, informational systems as such, rather than just living systems in general, are raised to the role of agents and patients of any action, with environmental processes, changes and interactions equally described informationally. (Floridi 2006 pp.9-10)

With this approach, every existing entity – humans, other animals, plants, even non-living artifacts, electronic objects in cyberspace, pieces of intellectual property, stones – can be interpreted as potential agents that act upon (i.e., physically affect) other entities, as well as potential patients that are acted upon by other entities.

The set of all such entities – that is, everything that exists, everything that has being – Floridi has named "the infosphere". The overall goal of Floridi's INFORMATION ETHICS is to foster the flourishing of the infosphere and all the informational objects within it. "Good" is defined as anything that preserves or improves the infosphere, and "evil" becomes its opposite; namely, anything that damages or impoverishes the infosphere.

Unlike Wiener's metaphysical foundation for his Information Ethics, which is based upon Shannon-information entropy, Floridi's INFORMATION ETHICS has a different understanding of "entropy" and presupposes a Spinozian metaphysics:

IE [that is, INFORMATION ETHICS] suggests that there is something even more elemental than life, namely being – that is, the existence and flourishing of all entities and their global environment – and something more fundamental than suffering, namely entropy. The latter is most emphatically not the physicists' concept of thermodynamic entropy. . . .

IE holds that being/information has an intrinsic worthiness. It substantiates this position by recognizing that any informational entity has a Spinozian right to persist in its own status, and a Constructionist right to flourish, i.e., to improve and enrich its existence and essence. (Floridi 2006, p. 11)

Floridi and his Oxford Research Group have achieved a milestone in Flourishing Ethics: the first "general" Flourishing Ethics theory, in the sense that it has accomplished the full "shift" from human-centered agent ethics to an ethics that values and embraces all of reality.

11. Flourishing Ethics: An Ethical Theory for the Information Age

The above described "shift" in ethical perspective, which began a generation ago among environmental ethicists and was recently completed by Floridi and his Oxford Research Group, is a major addition to the newly coalescing theory (movement?) that I have called "Flourishing Ethics". I believe that Flourishing Ethics has significant potential to develop into a powerful "global ethics" – one that is rooted in the ultimate nature of the universe and all the beings that inhabit it – one that will shed new light upon "the great ethical theories" of the world, while providing novel insights and contributions of its own. Let me pull together some of the key ideas explained above and put them into a more unified perspective:

RESOLUTION OF ANOMALIES

The three anomalies with which we began in Section 1 above, can all be resolved by Flourishing Ethics:

Rejection of all ethical theories but one — Rather than reject the great ethical theories from around the world, Flourishing Ethics welcomes them as sources of good that dramatically decrease the evils of entropy, bringing order and structure and meaning to human lives.

Troublesome cases – As illustrated by Moor's "Just Consequentialism" version of Flourishing Ethics, if one avoids dogmatic adherence to a single theory, "troublesome cases" that resist resolution when viewed from one ethical tradition can be resolved with the aid of two or more traditions working together.

Difficulty coping with non-human agents – Wiener noted the need for new ethical tools to cope with robots and cyborgs, and Floridi has already developed, in some detail, a promising theory (INFORMATION ETHICS) that seems likely to address that need very successfully.

RESPECT FOR THE WORLD'S GREAT ETHICAL TRADITIONS

Civilizations and societies add meaning and purpose to life; and they dramatically decrease and resist the evils of entropy, such as chaos and corruption, decay and disease, death and dissolution. Great ethical traditions embedded in the world's major civilizations help us to organize, systematize, and make sense of our moral lives; and they help us, as well, to cope with many of life's difficult challenges. Flourishing Ethics brings a new, positive perspective upon cultures around the globe and their role in the lives of their citizens. It also sheds new light upon other ethical theories. Consider, for example:

Utilitarianism – Why do consequentialist theories, like Utilitarianism, which make pleasure/happiness and pain/unhappiness the center of ethical considerations, continue to have wide appeal and usefulness as ethical theories? From the point of view of Flourishing Ethics this "makes sense" because pleasure and happiness are symptoms of flourishing, while pain and unhappiness are symptoms of disease, decay and impending death (i.e., symptoms of increasing entropy). It is not surprising, then, that utilitarian considerations continue to be seen as very important in ethics.

Kantianism – Kant placed human autonomy at the heart of ethics; and this "makes sense" from the perspective of Flourishing Ethics. Although there are differences in the various definitions of autonomy, whether one defines it like Aristotle, or Wiener or Moor, or Kant, it empowers human beings to make plans and choices, and thereby add significant order and structure to their lives, dramatically decreasing entropy in their small region of the universe.

Taoism – Much like Taoism, with its mixing and mingling of yin and yang in "the flow of the Tao", Flourishing Ethics views everything in the universe as a result of the mixing and mingling of two cosmic essences: matter-energy and Shannon information. Instead of viewing non-human entities as alien, both Taoism and Flourishing Ethics view humans and all the other diverse entities in the cosmos as fellow travelers in a cosmic flow of being and becoming.

Buddhism – Compassion for the suffering of all human beings and other living creatures as well, and efforts to help them overcome pain and sorrow, disease and decay, are shared by Buddhism and Flourishing Ethics alike.

THE ETHICAL WORTH OF NON-HUMAN ENTITIES

Ethical theories in the Western tradition, since the time of ancient Greece, for the most part, have placed individual human beings – their characters, their actions, their pleasures and pains – at the center of ethics. These "anthropocentric" theories view human beings as the most important beings in the universe, aside from God or the Gods. Some traditions (see Genesis, Ch. 1). have even viewed the universe as created on behalf of human beings, who were given "dominion over" all creatures and plants on the face of the earth. Some Eastern ethical traditions are similarly centered upon human actions and human achievements. Consider, for example, the Hindu concern about going to the "Heavens above" rather than the "Hells below" in the continuing chain of lives and reincarnations; or the Buddhist emphasis upon the personal achievement of overcoming "selfish craving" in order to gain Nirvana; or the Confucianist's honoring of his ancestors and planning to join them in Heaven. Of course, Eastern traditions have placed more emphasis upon society and social achievements, while the West has placed more emphasis upon individual persons; but both have tended to make human beings — as individuals and as societies — the center of ethical considerations. There are important exceptions to these tendencies, including for example, the Taoist's goal of deemphasizing the self and merging with the flow of the Tao, and the Buddhist's ultimate goal of extinguishing the self and merging with the source of all being.

From the point of view of Flourishing Ethics, it is not unreasonable to place a strong emphasis upon the flourishing of human beings and their societies. These are, as far as we know, the most efficient sources of decreased entropy and increased good in our tiny region of a vast and expanding universe. On the other hand, besides humans and their communities, there are other intrinsically good entities in the universe, as indicated in Sections 9 and 10 above. Flourishing Ethics takes these into account as well. Non-human animals, plants, ecosystems, even some machines decrease entropy in their region of space-time, and therefore preserve and increase the good. Even "inert" objects like stones, rivers, mountains, planets, stars and galaxies are persisting patterns of Shannon information, and therefore repositories of goodness in the universe. Flourishing Ethics fosters respect for all of these sources of the good.

THE OVERALL GOAL OF FLOURISHING ETHICS

The overall goal of Flourishing Ethics is to endorse, and indeed to assist, the flourishing of all beings that resist or diminish – in our local region of the universe – death and disease, decay and destruction, chaos and corruption wrought by "the greatest of natural evils": increasing entropy. All entities that help to achieve this noble goal merit our ethical respect.

HUMANS AS "CARE TAKERS" AND "FELLOW TRAVELERS" IN THE UNIVERSE

In recent years, environmental ethicists and feminist ethicists have led the shift away from seeing humans as "lords of the universe", who treat all non-humans as "others" – as objects to be subdued, dominated and exploited. This "us-over-them" approach establishes a "false wall" that alienates humans from the rest of creation. Instead, humans should see themselves as care takers aiding the flourishing of all beings that resist or even reduce the entropic evils of decay and chaos. Aristotle saw clearly that human beings are part of a natural continuum; they are closely related to all other members of the animal kingdom, and indeed to all other living things. And Wiener pointed out that cybernetic machines can have so much in common with humans and other animals that they blur traditional distinctions between living and non-living, as well as thinking and non-thinking beings. In addition, Floridi, in completing the shift to general Flourishing Ethics, argued that "informational objects", such as the Internet, databases, web sites, electronic texts, chat rooms, softbots, robots – even stones, mountains, planets and stars – which contemporary physics considers "information objects" – merit at least a minimum of ethical respect as repositories of information, resisting the entropic evils of decay and chaos.

The shift in perspective advocated by Flourishing Ethics, then, brings human beings back into the fold with the rest of the universe. It views humans, like all other beings, as fellow participants in the creative unfolding of the cosmos –

fellow travelers in the cosmic river of flowing information.

References

Aristotle. *On the Movement of Animals* and *On the Soul*.
Baumrin, B. H. 1988. "Applying Philosophy" in T. W. Bynum and W. Vitek, eds., *Applying Philosophy*, Blackwell, pp. 1-10. (A monograph of the Metaphilosophy Foundation)
Bekenstein, J.D. 2003. "Information in the Holographic Universe." *Scientific American*, August 2003.
Bynum, T.W. 1986. *Aristotle's Theory of Human Action*. UMI.
—. 2000. "The Foundation of Computer Ethics." *Computers and Society*, June 2000, 6-13.
—. 2004. "Ethical Challenges to Citizens of 'The Automatic Age': Norbert Wiener on the Information Society." *Journal of Information, Communication and Ethics in Society* 2:2, 65-74.
—. 2005. "The Impact of the 'Automatic Age' on Our Moral Lives" in R. Cavalier, ed., *The Impact of the Internet on Our Moral Lives*. State University of New York Press, pp. 11-25.
—. 2006. "Norbert Wiener and the Rise of Information Ethics" in W.J. van den Hoven and J. Weckert, *Moral Philosophy and Information Technology*. Cambridge University Press.
Floridi, L. 1999. "Information Ethics: On the Theoretical Foundations of Computer Ethics." *Ethics and Information Technology* 1.1, 37-56.
Floridi, L. and Sanders, J.W. 2004. "The Foundationalist Debate in Computer Ethics." in R. A. Spinello and H. T. Tavani, eds, *Readings in CyberEthics* 2nd edition, Jones and Bartlett, pp. 81-95.
Floridi, L. 2006. "Information Ethics: Its Nature and Scope" in W.J. van den Hoven and J. Weckert, *Moral Philosophy and Information Technology*. Cambridge University Press.
Gert, B. 1998. *Morality: Its Nature and Justification*. Oxford University Press.
Kuhn, T.H. 1962. *The Structure of Scientific Revolutions*. University of Chicago Press.
Lloyd, Seth. 2006. *Programming the Universe*. Knopf.
Moor, J.H. 1985. "What Is Computer Ethics?" in T. W. Bynum ed, *Computers and Ethics*. Blackwell, 263-275. [Published as the October 1985 special issue of Metaphilosophy.]
—. 1998. "Reason, Relativity and Responsibility in Computer Ethics", *Computers and Society*. March 1998, 28:1.
—. 1999. "Just Consequentialism and Computing." *Ethics and Information Technology* 1: 65-69.

—. 2006. "An Interview with James Moor" in Michael J. Quinn, *Ethics for the Information Age*. Second Edition, Addison Wesley, pp. 103-105.
Wheeler, J. 1990. *Information, Physics, Quantum: The Search for Links*. Westview.
Wiener, N. 1948. *Cybernetics: or Control and Communication in the Animal and the Machine*. Technology Press.
—. 1950/1954. *The Human Use of Human Beings: Cybernetics and Society*. Houghton Mifflin, 1950. (Second Edition Revised, Doubleday Anchor, 1954.)
—. 1964. *God & Golem, Inc. – A Comment on Certain Points Where Cybernetics Impinges on Religion*. MIT Press.

CHAPTER TWENTY FOUR

BUILDING EPISTEMOLOGICAL INFRASTRUCTURES-INTERVENTIONS AT A TECHNICAL UNIVERSITY

LENA TROJER

Abstract

The challenges technical universities encounter, when the cooperation with public and private partners outside the university becomes a predominant reality, calls for transformation processes and actions. This is certainly the case for us situated at a technical university with an explicit profile of applied ICT (information and communication technology) in a region with strong development ambitions. Epistemological openness among people active at the university is a prerequisite for functional cooperation. The paper (chapter) concerns distributed knowledge processes as daily experiences at one of the campuses of Blekinge Institute of Technology (BTH), more precisely at campus Karlshamn. The main questions concern resources for staying confident, future oriented and innovative as an ICT researcher and an academic teaching staff. Referring to a five year development experience with reliable results, when it comes to student recruitment, research and campus building, resources for the epistemological infrastructures needed have been found within gender research developed within a technical faculty - that is within feminist technoscience[1].

The paper (chapter) contributes to the discussions about why an epistemological pluralism is needed at a technical faculty and why resources within feminist technoscience are relevant in this context.

---

[1] Please note that I use gender research within the technology / engineering disciplines and feminist technoscience synonymously.

1. A rationale

At faculties of technology we have to encounter complex realities in our research and pertinent address our cooperation partners in private and public sector. We also have to meet young people and their preferences in learning processes of higher ICT related education. The challenges in this situation involve transformation in more advanced ways than what has been expected and realized in our academic organization with long standing norms of stability and epistemological traditions. One fundamental condition for the transformation needed is to open up for and foster epistemological pluralism.

Ina Wagner (1994) contributes with some central understandings. She argues that the central idea of combining established forms of scientific inquiry with a social pragmatic of developing goals, methods, theories and products can be realised by epistemological pluralism and partial translations between situated knowledges of different communities.

It can never be stressed enough that the fostering of epistemological pluralism is a challenge at a technical faculty, however juvenile or old. When we have learned to spell the word epistemology, when we have acknowledged that we do research and teach by walking on a certain epistemological infrastructure, then it is essential to question this infrastructure whether it is relevant or appropriate enough for our located needs. My local need is based on the following.

Situated at a technical university[2] with an explicit profile of applied ICT in close cooperation between university, business sector and government (local, regional and / or national), the challenges are tremendous. These rely on epistemological openness of us active at the university. The present knowledge and technology production occurs in situations far from what is identified by a traditional, mode 1 (Gibbons et al., 1994) university. These knowledge processes are my daily experiences at one of the campuses of Blekinge Institute of Technology (BTH), more precisely at campus Karlshamn incorporated in an innovation node called NetPort.Karlshamn[3]. A closed and non reflected epistemological basis is a blockage for our daily work whether research or training students at basic and advanced level. That is why I am concerned.

The question is what kind of resources that can be used for staying confident, future oriented and innovative as an ICT researcher and an academic teaching staff? In this paper (chapter) I refer to a five year development experience with so far good results, when it comes to student recruitment, research and campus building. Resources for the epistemological infrastructures

---

[2] www.bth.se
[3] www.netport.karlshamn.se

needed have been found within gender research developed within a technical faculty - that is within feminist technoscience[4]. It might look odd at a traditional technical faculty to find relevant competences for the benefit of building a needed epistemological pluralism within feminist technoscience. The following presentation will try to explain how.

2. Situated within distributed knowledge production systems

Within an international gender research strongly linked to the dominant technical fields of our era: information technology, biotechnology and material technology, there is a widespread understanding of the production of knowledge and technology as processes taking place in distributed systems. In other words, in this day and age knowledge is generated in the borderland between universities, companies and other regional, national and international actors. These processes are not the least apparent in the region of Blekinge, and affect the way in which Blekinge Institute of Technology carries out R&D work. The term technoscience connotes this understanding of the production of knowledge and technology. The way in which technoscience is defined by internationally leading researchers such as Donna Haraway (1997b) raises persisting questions about boundaries and the transgression of the boundaries between science, technology, politics and society, and between humans and non-humans as well as about the processes of hybridisation between people and machines (cyborg theories), etc (Haraway, 2003).

Experiences within an innovation node

The research and teaching staff at the division of Technoscience studies are deeply involved in the complex development process of a distributed knowledge and technology producing system characteristic for what is called NetPort.Karlshamn (Henningsson, Trojer, 2005). The practices within NetPort.Karlshamn can exemplify one way of understanding a triple helix system[5] (Etzkowitz, Leydesdorff, 1997) and why this kind of cooperation is important and a prerequisite for becoming functional, innovative and development oriented.

Since the year 2000 a new university campus is evolving at BTH. This campus is located in the town Karlshamn at the western part of the Blekinge

---

[4] See note 1.
[5] The Triple Helix model states that three institutional spheres (university, industry and government) which formerly operated at arms' length are now increasingly working together, with a spiral pattern of linkages emerging at various stages of the innovation process, to form a "triple helix".

region, Sweden. The university, the local government and trade & industry are actively cooperating partners in a local innovation system[6] called NetPort.Karlshamn, as mentioned above, and which is now a joint formal organization.

After five years operating the academic activity at the new campus and within the framework of NetPort has resulted in 4 licentiate theses and 3 doctoral theses. Also there are more than 400 students studying full time at 3 bachelor programs and 1 master program in media technology and another 2 programs linked to the former. In addition about 40 companies are included in NetPort.Karlshamn. The local government has invested about 24 million SEK on research development and establishment support for the university and continues to support by increasing financial resources.

Society speaks back

How can the situation of academic work in co-evolution processes with society be comprehended? If our aims are to produce knowledge encountering the need of society and being robust enough for sustainable purposes, then we have to be serious about how we understand our knowledge producing systems. Socially robust knowledge can only be produced in a mixed environment. The knowledge will then be exposed to more intensive testing in various contexts. It will not be pre-determined but open to re-negotiations (Nowotny et al., 2001). In addition the site of problem identification moves from the academy to the agora[7], where science meets society and contextualisation occurs. We are facing processes of non-linear character. This is far from our traditional perceptions of sequential processes in first knowledge making in basic research followed by applied research or dissemination to exploitation of the knowledge in products for a private or public market. Nowotny et al. (2003, p. 191) articulated this issue clearly in

> "reliable knowledge, the traditional goal of scientific inquiry, is no longer (self?) sufficient in the more open knowledge environments that are now emerging; knowledge also needs to be 'socially robust', because its validity is no longer determined solely, or predominantly, by narrowly circumscribed scientific communities, but by much wider communities of engagement comprising knowledge producers, disseminators, traders and users." Strathern (2003, p.275) adds "Accountability is, of course, at the heart of the argument about socially-robust science, and its converse, scientifically robust accountability."

---

[6] A local organisation / system / within which several active partners cooperate for creating innovations, economic and societal growth.
[7] The agora is central places for public life. The concept agora embrace the political arena and the market place – and goes beyond both (Nowotny et al 2003, p. 192).

What is highlighted in our practice and reference literature is that science and society are subject to the same driving forces in

- pervasiveness of a new economic rationality
- transformation of time and space (not the least as effects of ICT)
- demands for self-organising capacity
- generation of uncertainties and risks[8].

These processes can be described as science and society becoming transgressive fostering society to talk back to science. Jasanoff (2003, p.225) addresses the driving force for society to speak back in stating that uncertainties and risks are

"part of the modern human condition, woven into the very fabric of progress. The problem we urgently face is how to live democratically and at peace with the knowledge that our societies are inevitably 'at risk' ".

An important dimension of how science and society now speaks back and forth is the issue of input of resources and output of results. In the linear way of thinking science and society we are used to focus on the input of resources whether it comes from the government, public or private funding agencies etc.. Gulbrandsen (2004, p.109) argues that

"One of the most pressing interrogations for science policymakers the last 20-30 years has centred on output; how to secure an output from research that complies with economic, social, cultural and ethical concerns. Or reformulated to suit our more immediate concern: How can universities assure that choices made by scientists and engineers on campus contribute to responsible innovation? This challenge has by no means been satisfactory answered."

It gets increasingly evident that 'society speaks back' in forms of requiring to take part not only in the input phase but in the whole process (which more likely is non linear) up to the output of results. We have experienced in the NetPort context and on a municipality level how society represented by the local government explicitly manifest the *need* and *engagement* in being involved in the whole input - operation - output process. "Input is not enough"[9].

The *need* comes from the budget process in the local government to have local tax resources approved for the input to NetPort including research and infrastructure requests of the university. The local government directors need good arguments of the relevance of this 'investment' in order to convince the

---

[8] Beck 1992.
[9] statement by the local government commissioner in Karlshamn.

local parliament to vote in favour of the 'investment'.

The *engagement* comes from the mutual 'project' of fostering sustainable development of the local and regional society. The prerequisite for this 'project' is a triple helix-like process (Etzkowitz, Leydesdorff, 1997), which in our case is nurtured by a constant, almost daily dialogue. In this dialogue, which is a kind of agora, mutual understandings starts to find its expressions and that in very concrete ways and a co-evolution process takes place. For us, who have been involved, we talk about an

> "establishment of the institution of a 'kitchen cabinet'. A generous, open, inviting, allowing arena had to be created for the construction of new questions and dreams .... We need a lot of 'kitchen cabinets' on campus to cater for the polycentric, interactive and multipartite processes of knowledge-making we may dream of. A vision that entails transformative processes, changing research cultures and "teaching smart people how to learn".[10] (Gulbrandsen, 2004, p.120).

In summary with the situated knowledges that I have experienced within a distributed knowledge production system, I hope to make sense, when it comes to my claim on epistemological pluralism for the transformation needed at technical faculties. Below I will elaborate on why and how feminist technoscience can be a resource for developing epistemological pluralism and thus innovation systems.

3. Feminist technoscience as a resource

The gender research conducted within engineering sciences at technical faculties has come to focus on the fundamental knowledge issues of the areas and on their development of theories and methodologies. Engineering sciences are characterised by classifications, standardisations and formalisations about which there is general consensus. Gender research within technoscience is very much engaged in studying this basis and developing new ways of approaching the core of knowledge production, in order to strengthen science's ability to bring about change and development. This research has made an impact by showing which understandings of knowledge, science and technology dominate and have consequences in terms of creating realities. Internationally, gender research within technoscience provides an epistemological foundation for a variety of choices and decisions in society, which is increasingly dependent on research and technology. This research is thus no longer simply about drawing attention to the perspectives, experiences and needs of women.

As stated above international gender research is strongly linked to dominant

---

[10] See Argyris (1991) and Nowotny *et al* (2001).

technical fields of our time, where information and communication technology is one. The pertinent questions of boundaries and the transgression of the boundaries between science, technology, politics and society insist on terminology like technoscience. One of the scientists in the forefront of developing complex understanding and practice of this terminology is Donna Haraway. When focusing boundaries we have to keep in mind that boundaries "do not sit still" (Barad, 2003, p. 817) underscoring our complex realities.

A joint feature of gender research within technoscience is its research transforming ambitions. In many ways this is an obvious basis. In an international perspective we are dealing with an increasingly radical project of transformation (Trojer, 2000).

In the research transforming activities within feminist technoscience, there are some fundamental points of departure. For instance it is not good enough for a researcher to discover and map a waiting reality "out there" (context of discovery). Research must focus on the *context of production as well as context of implication* (Nowotny et al., 2001, 2003). As Gulbrandsen states (Trojer, Gulbrandsen, 1996)

"Time is ripe for us as partakers in the modern research complexes, to develop a readiness to think and feel ourselves as part of the problem, and learn how to use this, our implicatedness, as resources for transformatory projects."

Or as Donna Haraway notices (1997a)

"Technology is not neutral. We're inside what we make, and it's inside us. We're living in a world of connections – and it matters which one get made and unmade."

Gulbrandsen (2004) emphasizes the character of research as reality producing / world producing.

The emphasis on *transformation*, out of identified needs, as a prime goal for gender research, is essential. From the very beginning it was perceived inadequacies and imbalances in established research that motivated a growing feminist critique of science. This science critique developed from issues about women to realise and focus on problems concerning how science is constructed and practiced. Sandra Harding formulated this in her groundbreaking book "The Science Question in Feminism" (Harding, 1986). Harding argued for a shift of focus, from "the woman question in science", by which she meant, "What is to be done about the situation of women in science?" (Harding, 1986, p. 9) and towards what is often called "the science question in feminism", where she argued for and pointed to a reflexive turn, where transformation work of feminists also includes ourselves, as part of the problem and part of the solution.

The notion of *situated knowledge* is emphasized in the technoscientific reflections. Haraway (1991, p.196) stresses the following; what we can reasonably bring about in our knowledge production can never be more than partial translations. Translations are always interpretative, critical and partial. These constitute the very condition to be heard, when we are claiming rational knowledge, in the sense of relevance. Rational knowledge is founded within a process of ongoing critical interpretations among a number of interpreters. Rational knowledge includes power sensitive conversations. Haraway states that the world and its phenomenon, neither speaks itself or disappears in favour of one particular chosen interpreter or master decoder. The codes of the world do not find themselves silently waiting to be read.

We can ask ourselves why the research activity like the one at the division of Technoscience Studies is deeply involved in the development of NetPort and is one of several driving forces in these development processes. Some answers are found in identified potentials within this research (Rydhagen, Trojer 2003, Björkman, Elovaara, Trojer, 2005), namely to;

- expand the knowledge frames and practices for technology development in increasingly complex realities
- open up preferential rights of interpretation in selections of standards, which always are reality producing activities
- develop epistemological infrastructures relevant to a society heavily dependent on research and technology
- establish new arenas for developing understandings of relations between research, political sector and industry

create driving forces for inter- and transdisciplinary constellations.

4. Building epistemological infrastructures

As a conclusion I recognize the necessity for co-evolution processes in core activities of the technical university, where I am working. Relevance and situated knowledges compose keystones in our attempts to open up for the needed epistemological pluralism. We notice the transformation of the situated knowledge production in our context to move *from* contract negotiation / input focus *towards* co-evolution / the whole chain (input-operation-output) focus. Higher demand is obvious on the university and other stakeholders to argue for their relevance in order to become an accepted partner in the present ICT knowledge development. On the contrary, from a university perspective this demand does not make academic knowledge production less motivating, less quality strong and less desirable occupation.

What are the challenges we as academics and feminist technoscientists at technical faculty and as co-workers in NetPort is facing in the near future? The foremost challenge is the added value the core activities have to develop on a local, national and international level. The requirement is an intensified cooperation between the main triple helix actors – university, local government and private or public sector. We have to go further in the process of trilateral arrangements and sometimes even assuming the role of the other when needed and join in the efforts for the added, unique value. What is helping us is our engagement in generating epistemological pluralism relevant and appropriate enough for our located needs. This implies to continuously develop our understanding and practice of transformation, reality production (worldmaking), relevance and situated knowledges.

Karen Barad moves in linked epistemology fields and nurture the development of epistemological pluralism. She argues (2003) that

> "We" are not outside observers of the world. Nor are we simply located at particular places in the world; rather, we are part of the world in its ongoing intra-activity. This is a point Niels Bohr tried to get at in his insistence that our epistemology must take account of the fact that we are a part of that nature we seek to understand....We are part of the world in its differential becoming".

I want to highlight the concept of intra-activity. What Barad means is that the notion of intra-activity constitutes a reworking of the traditional notion of causality. She is looking for alternatives to representationalism[11] and shifts the focus from *"questions of correspondence between descriptions and reality (e.g., do they mirror nature or culture?) to matters of practices / doings / actions"* and bring to the forefront the issues of ontology, materiality and agency. Barad states that the discursive practices and material phenomena are mutually implicated in the dynamics of intra-activity and are not ontologically or epistemologically prior (neither can be explained in terms of the other),. *Intra-activity is neither a matter of strict determinism nor constrained freedom. The future is radically open at every turn*

References

Argyris, C. 1991. "Teaching Smart People How to Learn" *Harvard Business Review*, May-June.
Barad, K. 2003. "Posthumanist Performativity: Toward an Understanding of How Matter Comes to Matter, Signs." *Journal of Women in Culture and Society*, vol. 28, no. 3.

---

[11] Compare the contexts of production and implication (Nowotny et al., 2001)

Beck, U. 1992. *Risk Society: Towards a New Modernity*. Sage, London..
Björkman, Ch, Elovaara, P, Trojer, L, 2005, "Feminist Technoscience Rearranging in the Black Box of Information Technology", to appear ,in Susanne Maaß, Heidi Schelhowe, Carola Schirmer, Isabel Zorn eds, *Information Technology from a Gender Perspective– Epistemology, Construction and Empowerment*. VS-Verlag,, 2005
Etzkowitz H., Leydesdorff L. eds, 1997. *Universities and the Global Knowledge Economy: A Triple Helix of University-Industry-Government Relations*. Pinter, London.
Gibbons M., Limoge C., Nowotny H., Schwartzman S., Scott P., Trow M. 1994. *The new production of knowledge*. SAGE Publications, London, Thousand Oaks & New Dehli.
Gulbrandsen E. 2004. "How can universities become more active partners in innovation systems? Lessons from the Nordic countries?" in Gulbrandsen E., Nsengiyumva A., Rydhagen B., Trojer L. 2004. *ICT, innovation systems and the role of universities in societal development - a (post)colonial strain?* National University of Rwanda Press.
Haraway, D. 1991. *Simians, Cyborgs, and Women. Reinvention of Nature*. Routledge, New York.
—. 1997a. *Wired* 5.02 Feb.
—. 1997b. *Modest_Witness@Second_Mil-lenium. Female Man_Meets_OncoMouse. Feminism and Technoscience*, Routledge, New York and London.
—. 2003. *Companion Species Manifesto. Dogs, People and Significant Otherness*. Chicago, Prickly Paradigm Press.
—. 2003. "Cyborgs to Companion Species: Reconfiguring Kinship" in *Technoscience. Chasing Technoscience. Matrix for Materiality*. D. Idhe and E. Selinger ed, Bloomington, Indiana University Press: 58-82.
Harding, S. 1986. *The Science Question in Feminism*. Cornell University Press, Ithaca and London.
Henningsson, S., Trojer, L. 2005. "Why Triple Helix?", Bulletin of the KPZK, (Polish abbreviation of 'Polish National Committee for Space Economy and Regional Planning'), Polska Akademia, Studia Regionalia, nr 217
Jasanoff S. 2003. "Technologies of Humility." *Minerva* 41, Kluwer Academic Publishers.
Nowotny, H., Scott, P and Gibbons M. 2001. *Re-Thinking Science. Knowledge and the Public in an Age of Uncertainty*. Polity Press, Cambridge UK.
Nowotny, H., Scott, P. and Gibbons M. 2003. *Introduction. 'Mode 2' Revisited: The New Production of Knowledge*. Minerva 41, Kluwer Academic Publishers.
Rydhagen, B. and Trojer, L. 2003. "ICT and the Role of Universities - a

Technopolitical and Postcolonial Challenge." web proceedings, the International conference Information Technology, Transnational Democracy and Gender – RELOADED, Luleå University of Technology, Sweden, 14th to 16th November 2003.

Strathern M. 2003. "Re-Describing Society", *Minerva* 41, Kluwer Academic Publishers.

Trojer, L, Gulbrandsen, E, "Authority in Transformation." *The European Journal of Women's Studies*, vol. 3, issue 2, 1996.

—. Genusforskningens Relevans, Slutrapport från integreringsarbete i åtta svenska forskningsråd (The Relevance of Gender Research. Final Report from Work of Integration within Eight Swedish Research Councils), 2000. Rapport från forskningsrådens expertgrupp för genusforskningens integrering (Report from the Expert Group of the Research Councils for Integration of Gender Research), (www.bth.se/tks/teknovet.nsf under document)

Wagner, I. 1994. "Connecting Communities of Practice, Feminism, Science and Technology" in *Women's Studies Int. Forum* vol.17. no. 2/3, Elsevier Science

CHAPTER TWENTY FIVE

COMPUTER ETHICS IN (HIGHER) EDUCATION

PHILIP BREY

1. Introduction

Computer ethics is a major new field of study that addresses ethical issues in the use, development and management of information technology, as well as in the formulation of general societal policies regarding the regulation of information technology in society (Johnson, 2000; Tavani, 2003; Spinello, 2000; Baird et al., 2000; Forester and Morrison, 1994; Baase, 1997). Increasingly, computer ethics is a subject that is taught in universities, high schools, and other educational settings. This paper addresses the role of computer ethics in the education system, focusing specifically on university education and university policy. It will also, more briefly, address its role in high school education and high school policies. As my main thesis, I will be arguing that universities have a vital role in generating awareness of ethical issues in the use, development and management of information technology. As such I will be arguing, universities should be addressing these ethical issues in two ways: in computer ethics policies: given the importance of information technology in the practices of today's universities, and given the possibilities of unethical use of this technology by students and staff, universities should ensure that they have policies regarding the use and management of information technology by students and staff. in computer ethics education: given the importance of information technology in virtually every contemporary profession, universities should ensure that their curricula pay attention to ethical issues in the use, management or development of information technology. Such education should be part of more general education on the societal aspects of information technology. Sections 2 and 3 cover the first of these two points: computer ethics policies in the university. In section 2, I will discuss a variety of ethical issues regarding the use and management of information technology by students and staff. In section 3, I will focus on one specific issue: academic freedom and free speech, and the importance of good policies on this issue in the use and management of information technology on campus.   Sections 4 through 7 consider the second point, that of computer ethics education, which will be related to the broader issue of education on societal aspects of information technology. In section 4, I will outline a field of study which I call social and humanistic studies of computing (SHC) and contrast this with applied studies of societal aspects of computing (ASC). In section 5, I will argue for the importance of both SHC and ASC in university curricula and relate their roles to academic and professional functions of university education. In section 6, I will describe how courses in SHC and ASC may be taught in practice, illustrating this with a description of the minor ICT and Society which I have helped to develop at my university, and with a description of a course in Computers and Society. In section 7, I will assess the relation of computer ethics to SHC and ASC, and its role in the university curriculum. I will outline educational goals for computer ethics education and provide a brief description of a course in computer ethics that meets these goals.   In the concluding section I will briefly summarize my points and consider how my analysis of computer ethics in university education and policy would translate to a different area: that of secondary or high school education.

2. Information technology and ethical student and staff behaviour

In this section, I will address the question of how the use of computers in education changes the settings in which moral values function, for students and staff members. My focus will be on the new moral challenges and new possibilities for immoral behaviour for students and staff that may arise with the use of information technology in higher education. These moral challenges arise in part because electronic environments afford new types of actions that may require new moral codes, such as copying software and hacking. Yet, they also arise in part because certain types of immoral actions, such as plagiarism and invasions of privacy, are easier to perform in electronic settings, as well as harder to detect or control. What follows are six types of morally questionable behaviour that depend on the use of computers and computer networks in (higher) education. Digital plagiarism

Plagiarism has always existed in education, including higher education, where it is one of the major forms of academic dishonesty. Assignments handed in by students may turn out to be copied from fellow students or to be taken over, in part or in whole, from existing published works. In a way, computers and the Internet only add to the means that students have at their disposal to commit plagiarism. However, they make it much easier to do and much harder to detect. As Austin and Brown have argued, plagiarism has become easier for students in two ways: "word processing programs allow students to easily "cut and paste" information from the Internet or other electronic media to develop a paper that appears to be original work" and "students' use of Internet information that may be unavailable in traditional sources makes documenting academic dishonesty more difficult to faculty." (1999, p. 21; see also Hinman, 2002). Particularly worrisome, as they point out, is the existence of "term paper mills," which offer pre-written term papers to students on a range of topics, and many of which also offer to write papers specifically for students for a fee.

Breaking copyright and software theft

It is well known that the illegal copying of copyrighted media (texts, music works, movies and software programmes) is widespread throughout society. Moreover, many people who engage in such activity do not consider themselves to be doing something that is patently immoral. This is certainly true for college students. Cohen and Cornwell (1989) and Glass and Wood (1996), for example, found that a large majority of college students do not perceive the illegal copying of software as unethical.

This attitude of college students seems to match developments in the current information age, in which the Internet increasingly functions as the most important information medium that people use. Hinman (2002) has argued that the very structure of the Internet undermines the notion of private intellectual property on the web: "The inner dynamic of the Web moves us increasingly toward a much more communal notion of property". As he explains, the Web stimulates copying because the very nature of browser technology necessitates making copies, because perfect copies can be made at virtually no cost, and because making digital copies does not involve physical theft from the person who owns the original (34). It may be added to this that many information sources on the Web are not obviously copyrighted, and many even lack an identifiable author (Kolko, 2002). Lipinski and Britz (1999) argue, moreover, that digital copying can often be morally, if not legally, defended because of the fact that access to information is a critical need in an age of information that may in some cases override proprietary rights.

Hence, the traditional legal paradigm of intellectual property is increasingly challenged by a new paradigm that emphasises unrestrained access to, and use of, information. It is difficult to find an adequate moral compass to navigate the new landscape, not only for students, but for staff as well. Moral and legal confusion may moreover also result from the vagueness of "fair use" provisions in copyright law, that do not clearly state when copying for personal use or display in classroom settings is permitted, and from the existence of corporate licences at universities, or departments therein, that may permit students to freely use or copy media that they do not own themselves.

Hacking

Hacking is breaking into computer systems for unauthorized purposes, which may be either malicious or nonmalicious. Hacking may involve, for example, snooping around on someone's personal computer through remote access, intentionally modifying or destroying files to which one has not been granted access, releasing computer viruses, stealing passwords or files, exposing personal information, and stealing electronic money (see Forester and Morrison, 1994, ch. 5 and Baase, 1997, ch. 7). Students and staff members at both virtual and conventional universities may engage in hacking for a variety of reasons. They may simply be unaware that they are breaking into a computer system, they may just be curious, they may be out to harm someone, they may want to benefit themselves, or they may have entirely different reasons. Malicious hacking is clearly morally problematic, but nonmalicious hacking has been defended by hackers as morally acceptable and socially harmless or even beneficial (cf. Baase, p. 242). Clearly, universities need clear policies and guidelines on hacking (including policies that define what kinds of computer systems access are unauthorized for whom) and probably need to distinguish malicious from nonmalicious hacking.

Improper use of computer resources

Hacking is the use of computer resources to which one is not supposed to have access. However, students and staff may also have authorized access to computer resources, but then go on to use these resources improperly. They may have a university Internet account, or they may use a computer system or computer network or computer software that is owned by the university, or they may use computerized services offered by the university, and do so in a way that does not meet the university's standards for proper use of that particular resource. For example, students may use their student account to run their own Internet business, contrary to the university's policies. Or students may open up a popular website or service that generates loads of traffic that incapacitates the university's server, e.g., peer to peer downloads of MP3 files. Or staff members may use the university's server or computer systems to download or view or store content that is either illegal or against the university's policies (e.g., racist or fascist materials or pornography). Or members of the academic community may spread computer viruses or worms. Clearly, universities need policies regarding the proper use of computer resources in an academic context by students and staff.

(Anonymous) harassment and hate speech

In universities there may be various electronic means of communicating messages to other members of the academic community, as well as to persons outside the university: e-mail, electronic bulletin boards, IRC (the exchange of short one-on-one messages without a significant time lag), collaborative virtual environments and web pages constitute some of the most important ones. As in face-to-face communication, these computer-mediated forms of communication can be used to send threatening, obscene, inflammatory or harassing messages. These may include discriminatory messages, used to disparage individuals or groups based on gender, race, sexual orientation, religion, age, or disability. Such messages are generally not considered to be acceptable in an academic setting, as educators strive to ensure that the classroom, if not the campus at large, functions as a safe, nonthreatening environment for students as well as for staff. In this, the same principles apply for virtual classrooms and campuses as for their physical counterparts (cf. Ferganchick-Neufang, 1998).

Moreover, in curbing harassing and obscene messages, educators will simultaneously have to make sure that they are not unduly limiting free speech (see also Section 3). As Baase has pointed out (p. 212), speech on computer systems is often treated differently from other forms of speech, and there is a tendency for less tolerance for offensive talk that takes place online. If this is true, then extra care must be taken to ensure that student discussion in the virtual classroom can take place as freely as student discussion in the physical classroom. It would be a loss if students would be more hesitant to voice their opinions because they are using an electronic medium. A feature of computer-mediated communication that deserves special mention is the ease by which anonymous or pseudonymous messages can be sent, for example through anonymous remailer services. Baase (1997, 214-5) points out that anonymous messages posted over the Internet can have good and bad uses. She claims that anonymity provides protection for victims of violence and abuse and users of illegal drugs who seek counseling and advice and for whistleblowers who wish to report on unethical or illegal activity in their organisation without fear of retribution. However, anonymity can also be used for criminal and antisocial purposes: to perpetuate fraud, to harass people, to threaten or libel people with impunity, and ruin their reputation by spreading rumors (Baase, p. 214-5; see also Kling et al., 2000). Universities may hence want to consider having policies for anonymous electronic communication.

Breaches of informational privacy and confidentiality

Privacy is generally considered to be an individual right in Western countries, and many nations have privacy laws (or data protection laws, as they are sometimes called in Europe). It is nowadays generally recognized that new technologies, and particularly information and communication technologies, raise new privacy issues, for example concerning electronic databases and online privacy (e.g., Cate, 1997; Agre and Rotenberg, 1998). Many of these new privacy issues can be expected to apply to the use of universities that make a lot of use of online instruction and communication. In such universities, many important activities of members of the university can in principle be monitored or recorded electronically. This includes not only student administration but also classroom discussion, student-to-student and student-to-faculty e-mail contact, and the online behaviour of students in general. The walls of classrooms and offices at such a university are much more permeable than those of classical universities, making eavesdropping much easier, and it happens much more frequently that the things that are said and done in them are recorded so as to be available for later scrutiny, or can be copied for distribution.

At many (conventional) universities, privacy policies remain limited to student privacy policies that protect student records from being accessed by third parties without authorization. Since many student records are nowadays stored in electronic format, these policies must be supplemented with good system security. Electronic records should be adequately protected so as to avoid unauthorized access to them. Many universities nowadays also have policies that address the electronic posting of grades, which are considered to be privacy-sensitive.

Many more privacy issues can be raised at a university that has much of its communication and instruction online, however. Consider, first, the confidentiality of classroom or group discussion or one-to-one and one-to-many. Can students be sure that these discussions are not logged or monitored by administrators, that they are not made accessible on public networks, and that access to them cannot be easily hacked? In a study of privacy in online learning environments, Tu (2002) argues that class discussions over a connection that is not secure may either inhibit discussion or force students to take risks in disclosing more personal information. He argues in favor of more private interaction environments, which he claims to be "key to increasing interactivity" (315). As he claims: "A sound learning environment will allow learners to adjust to the ideal levels of privacy and give students more secure and more comfortable environments to increase their social presence to enhance social interaction" (315). Other relevant online privacy issues that may occur include:

Personal information on public computers. When students or staff use publicly accessible computers, they may unknowingly leave personal information behind, such as cached web pages (accessed web pages that are left in temporary storage on the disk drive and may remain there even after a browser is closed) and cookies (small files that are put on a hard disk by a web site to identify users and their preferences), that are then available for inspection by others. File sharing. Student or faculty computers may contain software that makes files on them accessible to other users on the campus network and outside without knowledge of the owner, or may allow files to be stored on a central server that are then accessible to others without their permission. This could allow strangers to read these files that may contain personal information. Publicly accessible databases. Many universities have databases that have public access, for example databases that contain directories for students and staff. These databases may contain privacy-sensitive information for which students and staff have given no permission. University web pages and bulletin boards. Web pages maintained by the university, by faculty or by students may contain personal information that invades the privacy of others. Likewise, postings and repostings (forwarded messages) on bulletin boards or in other electronic forums may contain personal information of third parties for which no authorization has been given. Search engines. Search engines can be used to collect personal information about students or staff. Specifically, a university's own search engine may be used to collect personal information that is found on the university's intranet or campus network. If such a search engine has access to many sites, it may give a detailed profile of people. It may tell about a student, for example, what courses (s)he is enrolled in, what student groups (s)he is a member of, and what campus events (s)he has participated in. Third party market research. Students constitute an interesting population for some marketers and market researchers, and they may try to enlist educators to help them acquire information on students, or solicit directly to students. The data collected by these parties is likely to be privacy-sensitive.

Clearly, then, universities will need privacy policies to protect the privacy rights of students and staff and to create secure learning environments in which members of the community interact with each other on a basis of trust.

Based on the previous discussion, I suggest that universities should consider developing policies regarding the use of information technology that include some or all of the following: Policies concerning digital plagiarism and academic dishonesty in online assessment. Policies concerning copyright and software theft. Policies concerning hacking. These should be supplemented by clear access guidelines to different systems and should probably distinguish malicious from nonmalicious hacking. Policies concerning the proper use of university computer resources. Policies concerning online anonymity and pseudo-anonymity, online harassment and hate speech, which should at the same time, not impose unacceptable limits on free speech. Privacy policies for personal information stored in databases and for online privacy.

3. Academic freedom and information technology

Intellectual freedom is the freedom to use one's intellect in a way of one's own choosing, and to both hold, receive and disseminate ideas without restraint. The American Library Association defines it as "the right of every individual to both seek and receive information from all points of view without restriction" and holds that intellectual freedom "provides for free access to all expressions of ideas through which any and all sides of a question, cause or movement may be explored." Intellectual freedom has often been defended as a core Western value, as a necessary prerequisite for democracy and cultural progress (cf. Morse, 2001).

Academic freedom is intellectual freedom as it exists within the academy: it is the free pursuit of knowledge by scholars and students. Clark, in an important study of the higher education system, claims that academic freedom involves freedom of research, freedom of teaching, and freedom of learning (1983, p. 248). As he points out, the liberties of academic freedom are sought at various levels: students seek freedom to learn what they want, scholars seek freedoms in teaching and research within their department, departmental groups seek self-determination within the university, and the university seeks autonomy from the state and from outside groups (p. 248). Basic to this push for liberties is, according to Clark, "the desire for individual self-expression". Teachers want to teach to be able to say what they please without restraint or fear of retribution. Those who learn want to learn in a way that helps realize their life plan: they want be able to choose what they learn, how they learn it, and at what pace they learn it. In discussing academic freedom and information technology, some authors have argued that information technology enhances academic freedom for students by offering them more choice, for instance by making a university education available through e-learning for students (e.g. employed persons or disabled persons) who are unable to physically attend classes. More generally, also, authors have been emphasizing the greater informational freedom that results from the Internet as an education medium, as it enhances opportunities for academic communication, information retrieval and teaching. However, many authors also identify challenges to academic freedom that may arise from the use of computers and the Internet in education. A major challenge that has been discussed is the challenge of content selection with resulting limitations on free speech. Academic freedom means, amongst others, free access to information and freedom of speech for both students and faculty. When speech or information is carried by a digital medium, however, limitations may be imposed quite easily: an administrator, system operator or list moderator may block certain types of messages, delete certain web pages or block certain e-mail addresses in a matter of seconds. Thus, both students and faculty are in a dependent position concerning their ability to acquire information and voice opinions via computer networks.

Regarding free access to information, universities sometimes place filters on their Internet traffic that effectively block access to certain web sites or to bulletin boards or messages that contain certain types of content (Rosenberg, 2001). Filtering or blocking may be done for efficiency reasons, for instance because it is found that certain sites, such as adult sites, generate a large amount of web traffic that causes net congestion. However, it may also be done as a form of censorship, to prevent users from having access to certain types of information that are considered immoral or illegal or otherwise undesirable. For instance, access may be blocked to sites with adult content, with racist or fascist content, or with illegal software available for download. Though such efforts are understandable, it may be questioned if such content control can be reconciled with the demands of academic freedom. Moreover, the use of filtering software has a reported disadvantage, which is that it invariably filters too much. Filters usually block access to messages based on the occurrence in them of certain key words. This ignores context, however, and so often leads to 'suitable' content being blocked. For instance, sites or messages may be blocked that study pornography rather than containing it, or challenge racism instead of promoting it. Regarding free speech, universities may try to exercise control over the types of speech that are exercised by students and staff over the university network. They may, for example, have policies against certain types of speech that are considered undesirable, may remove or block messages that do not adhere to such policies. For example, the University of California, San Diego imposed a speech code in 1995 that stated: "The use of University resources such as electronic mail to disparage individuals or groups on the basis of gender, race, sex, sexual orientation, age, disability, or religion, is strictly prohibited and violates University policy." (quoted in Baase, 1997, p. 212). Universities may also monitor speech by eavesdropping on on-line communications and accessing student and faculty files on university servers.

While many forms of content control at universities probably result from efforts to protect individuals and groups from harassment and libel and foster a secure academic environment, there is nevertheless a serious risk that academic freedom and free speech are limited in the process. The ability to voice unpleasant and dissenting opinions has always been central to academic freedom and to freedom of speech, and a necessary prerequisite for social and intellectual criticism. When student and faculty fear that their electronically communicated views and opinions may be reprimanded or blocked, or worry that their communication may be (anonymously) monitored by parties who are in a position of power relative to them, free speech may be stifled and academic freedom may be adversely affected as a result. A serious and continuous effort is needed, therefore, to balance any the need to protect individuals and groups from harassment against the need to promote free speech and academic freedom.

In conclusion, the following policy recommendations may be made to universities regarding the use of information technology in a way that respects academic freedom and free speech: Universities, whether conventional or electronic/virtual, should be committed to protecting academic freedom, which includes freedom of research, freedom of learning and freedom of teaching, as well as overall freedom of speech. Their policies and procedures should reflect this commitment.

Universities should be very cautious about filtering, blocking or removing electronic information or messages, monitoring computer systems and electronic communications of students and staff, and proposing speech codes for electronic communications. If any such actions are to be taken at all, they should respect as well as possible academic and intellectual freedom as well as personal privacy.

4. Computer ethics and social and humanistic studies of computing

I will now turn to the issue of computer ethics education in the university. Computer ethics as a field of study is (arguably) part of a wider field of study which may be called social and humanistic studies of computing (SHC). SHC are studies by scholars in the humanities and social sciences of computers and their roles in society. I define SHC as theoretical or nonapplied studies of the way in which various forms of information technology shape, and are themselves shaped by, aspects of their social context. By the social context of computer systems, I mean any aspect of individuals, collectives or social systems that constitutes part of the environment within which one or more computer systems are used. Hence, a study of the psychological effects of regular Internet use is a study in SHC. So is a study of the influence of computer networks on the structure of large organisations, a study of cultural practices of users of mobile computing devices, a study of cultural images of computers throughout history, of or a study of the role of information technology in globalization. Studies in SHC hence consider any sort of way in which information and communication technologies (ICTs) relate to their larger context of use. Studies in SHC are theoretical, as opposed to applied. Their primary aim is not to change practices or develop policies. It is only to understand.

Over the past twenty or so years, the amount of research within the scope of SHC, as defined here, has increased dramatically. Still, SHC is not often seen as a coherent field of study. There has been some effort by social scientists, however, to turn social studies of computing into a field, for example by the late Rob Kling, former editor of the journal The Information Society, who has been promoting the label 'social informatics' to designate social studies of computing. But on most counts, the coherence within the field of SHC is limited. Nevertheless, there are nowadays specialized journals that help give it coherence, such as The Information Society, Computers and Society, New Media and Society, Information Technology & People and Information, Communication and Society, as well as specialized societies and conference series.

Next to the emergence of SHC, there has been an emergence of various kinds of applied research on societal aspects of computing. Here, there is even less coherence between the various approaches that exist. Therefore, when I speak of applied studies of societal aspects of computing (ASC), I do not refer to a field but just an existing set of studies and approaches that are often unrelated to each other. Research in ASC has in common that it is not primarily concerned with a theoretical understanding of the social context of computer systems, although such theoretical knowledge usually plays a useful role in applied research. Instead, research in ASC is concerned with developing effective tools for professionals in various fields for coping with various societal aspects of computer systems. Such studies include applied studies in computer law, computer-assisted education, management and computing, and e-commerce, amongst others. SHC and ASC are hence complementary in the way they approach societal or nontechnical aspects of ICTs: the first is concerned with gaining a theoretical understanding, the second with developing practical know-how.

5. SHC and ASC in the university curriculum

Let me now turn to the question of the role that both SHC and ASC should have in the university curriculum. I take university education to have both an academic and a professional function. In some study programmes, the academic function is emphasised. These are programmes that lead to an academic degree. They are aimed at equipping students with theoretical knowledge within a field and with research skills for developing more theoretical knowledge in that field. Other university study programmes lead to a professional degree. In such programmes, the educational emphasis is on professional knowledge and skills, and the research skills that are taught relate to research aimed at developing applied forms of knowledge, or on applying knowledge in specific contexts.

Now, it is certainly not the case that the academic and professional functions of university education are mutually exclusive. Academic study programmes always also have a professional role, in that they train students to become members of a certain profession. This is the profession of an academic scientist, equipped with research skills for furthering a specialized field. Conversely, professional degree programmes at university level tend to have an academic component, in that they emphasise academic, theoretical knowledge and skills. Theoretical knowledge acquired in a professional university programme is considered important as a theoretical background for more applied tasks. For instance, a mechanical engineer should have a basic training in Newtonian mechanics because this theoretical knowledge is relevant to the applied knowledge and skills that are the primary focus of a mechanical engineering programme.

However, theoretical knowledge is not just important as a preliminary to mastering applied knowledge and skills. It is frequently also considered important for the more general academic outlook that is the landmark of university education. This general academic outlook is realized through courses in general education, some of which emphasise cultural literacy and societal knowledge, others of which emphasise general cognitive and professional skills. Someone with a university degree, whether academic or professional, is not just expected to excel in his or her field, but also to adhere to certain minimum standards of cultural literacy, and to have good general cognitive skills. That is, he or she is supposed to have an above average understanding of society, culture and history, and to have above average cognitive skills in analysis and synthesis.

To summarize, some university programmes focus on academic education, emphasizing theoretical knowledge and research skills, whereas others emphasise nonacademic professional knowledge and skills. Yet, every university programme promotes a general academic outlook by offering courses in general education that are outside one's specialty. Given this characterization of university education, there are at least two reasons why is advisable to make education in SHC and ASC a required part of today's university curriculum.

First of all, there are good reasons to suppose that the general education component in a university programme should pay attention to issues in SHC. This is because, I claim, such a programme would give a shallow and outdated picture of society if it left out an analysis of the great changes that information technology is effecting in virtually every sector of society. The economy, government, education, health care, religion, scientific research, the media, entertainment, the arts, organisations, the workplace, interpersonal relations, and many other core institutions of society are being transformed through information and communication technologies. If one were living at the time that the industrial revolution took place, one would not want a general education programme to focus on preindustrial society. Instead, one would want it to pay attention to industrialization processes and the changes these are affecting. Likewise, one would expect a contemporary general education programme to pay attention to the current information revolution, including the roles and effects of information technologies.

Education in SHC might not just be desirable within an education programme because it is an important part of a general education component. It might also provide part of the background or context within which a good professional is able to situate his or her work. This role of SHC education can perhaps be illustrated best by looking at computer science curricula. Computer science curricula focus on knowledge and skills by which computer professionals may design, operate or manage certain types of technologically complex systems. Much of the knowledge this requires is technological: it pertains to the rules according to which these systems operate. However, computer systems also have to make a good fit with their social context. Users have to be able to use them well, organisations have to benefit from them, and sometimes society as a whole is supposed to benefit as well. A good fit between a computer system and its social context is not the mere result of it executing certain input-output functions without error. The technology also has to work in harmony with its social context. Therefore, a broader understanding of how computer systems impact and fit in with various aspects of their social context is, if not necessary, then at least highly advisable if one is to be a good computer scientist. And this means that education in SHC is defensible as a required component in computer science curricula. Second, within the professional component of a university programme, there is a clear need for specialized courses dealing with the role of information technology within someone's specific profession. That is, there is a special need for courses in ASC. Nowadays, there are few professions left in which information technology does not play an important role. Obviously, nearly every professional will be using information technologies as an end-user. But it is not the role of information technology in their profession I am referring to. It is not clear that special courses in ASC are required to be a better end-user of information technology. Instead, what are required are just courses that teach one how to use the technology, and these are not courses in ASC because they do not normally focus on contextual aspects of information technology. However, next to end-users, many professionals are also decision-makers regarding information technology. That is, in the course of their professional duties, they may be deciding that certain computer systems will be used, purchased or implemented, they may be deciding by whom and for what they will be used, and they may shape or influence various policies regarding the development, acquisition and use of information technologies. Because, increasingly, professionals have to make such IT-related choices, and because of the great impact such choices may have because of the revolutionary transformative power of information technology, it is increasingly important to include relevant education components on ASC in professional curricula. For example, in a policy programme, it would nowadays be advisable to have a course on policy and information technology, because of the likelihood that professionals in this field will be making policy choices in which information technologies play key roles. Likewise, in an education studies programme, it would be advisable to have education on computers, because of the profound impact that computers are having on education. I conclude that because of the general education requirement in university curricula, and in some cases also because of the professional function of curricula (as in the case of computer science), education in SHC is highly advisable. Specifically, it would be advisable to have a required course on "Computers and Society" across the university curriculum. Moreover, an equally good case can be made that professional programmes should contain at least one relevant course in ASC. This course should focus on the role of information technology within that specific professional field and should convey professional knowledge and skills that enable intelligent professional choices regarding the role of information technology within that field. For some programmes, one course in SHC and one course in ASC may not be enough. It certainly would not be enough for programmes that train one to be a computer professional. Specifically, I would propose that a computer science programme would devote at least 10% of its professional component on SHC and ASC. This means that not more than 90% of the professional component should be devoted to the technical aspects of computer systems, and at least 10% should consider the fit between computer systems and their social context.

6. Teaching SHC and ASC

In this section, I will take SHC teaching at my own university, The University of Twente in the Netherlands, as an example. The University of Twente, grants academic degrees in engineering and applied social science. There are bachelor and master programmes in various engineering fields, such as electrical engineering, computer science, and design engineering, and bachelor and master programmes in various applied social science fields, such as education, policy and business administration. Students follow a three-year bachelor programme which includes a half-year minor programme in a field different from their area of specialization, after which they follow a one-year or two-year master programme. Students are free to choose a minor programme to their liking and they also have some amount of choice regarding the master programmes they may follow immediately after completing a specific bachelor programme.

At my university, I have taken the initiative to start a new interdisciplinary minor programme called ICT and Society. This minor is the equivalent of half-a-year of university education, or 820 study hours, and is stretched over the course of an entire academic year. In the academic year in which they take the minor, students hence have 50% time to work on the minor and 50% time to take courses in their own field. The minor ICT and Society is not currently a required minor for any degree programme at my university, but it is a recommended minor for several programmes. The aim of the minor ICT and Society is twofold. The primary aim is to acquaint students with basic issues in SHC. A secondary aim is to teach general professional skills for decision-making in relation to computer systems. This is a general ASC component of the major. Students have a degree of freedom to tailor the ASC component to their own professional area. In this way, the minor ICT and Society equips students with the basic understanding and skills to provide them with general education in this vital area and to deal with the social context of computing in their prospective careers. To further these two aims, the ICT and Society minor is set up to have the following structure. In the first trimester of the academic year, students take three introductory courses. The first is a basic course on the technical aspects of computer systems. This course aims to familiarize students with basic properties of computer systems and the ways they are used in society. Computer science students participating in the minor do not have to take this course, and have the option of taking another course relevant to their professional interests, such as a course in computer law (which is not a required course in their own professional curriculum). The second course, taught by me, is a basic course on computers and society. It treats social aspects of computing as one would expect in a course dealing with basic SHC issues. The third course is a course on the role of computer systems in organisations (both governmental and commercial). This topic was considered by us to be an important SHC topic for the students at our university, because most will be assuming important roles in commercial or governmental organisations. This is why we decided to devote a special course to it. In the second trimester, students take applied courses that can be characterized as courses in ASC. One course provides students with tools to do technology assessment of information technologies. This course aims to enable students to do general assessments of the societal or organisational impacts of new computer systems. A second course focuses on two specific topics: e-commerce and e-government. It studies models and theories within these two areas and teaches about applications and application methodologies in both areas. A third course focuses on virtual communities, and looks at methods for investigating such communities, as well as at assessing the conditions under which such communities function well. In the third trimester, finally, students take up a small research project within one or more of the aforementioned areas. They may do so individually or (preferably) in small groups in which people from different disciplines work together. For many students, however, a half-year programme on ICT and Society may be too much of a good thing. I would not advise it to become a required minor for any programme, with a possible exception of the computer science curriculum. In the previous section, though, I argued for a required course Computers and Society across the university curriculum. I will now consider what such a course may look like. The aim of a course in computers and society would be to acquaint students with basic issues in SHC, that is, it would teach about the role of information technology in various sectors of society and regarding various aspects of their social context. A course on Computers and Society would leave students with a basic understanding of how ICT is transforming social institutions and practices. I now present a possible list of topics for a course in Computers and Society. Most courses would make a selection from this list:

1. ICT in contemporary society. A qualitative and quantitative assessment of the role of ICT in current society. A quick survey of the role of ICT and in various sectors of society (e.g., regarding work, the business world, medicine, education, government, the media, and everyday life), and related issues and problems. Key statistics on the users and uses of ICT.

2. The Information Revolution and the Information Society. A broad macro-perspective on the way in which ICT has changed the economy and social institutions in recent history. With a brief introduction to some theoretical perspectives, e.g., Beniger's theory of the Control Revolution (Beniger, 1986) or Castells' trilogy on the information age (e.g., Castells, 2000).

3. Social history of ICT and its role in society. A historical survey of the birth and spread of the digital computer, and social and cultural changes resulting from it. Attention is paid to changing functions of the computer in the workplace, in the economy, and in organisations, to past social struggle, and to images of and discourses on ICT.

4. ICT and the economy. An assessment of the role of ICT in the economy and of the difference between Fordist and post-Fordist economies. A consideration of the role of producers and consumers in this process.

5. ICT and politics. An assessment of the way in which ICT is transforming politics, both regarding the relation of citizens to the state, the relation of corporations to the state and its citizens, and the hierarchical structure of organisations. A treatment of specific political issues like privacy, freedom, democracy, and social justice.

6. ICT and law. An assessment of the way in which ICT is transforming law. Problems and issues like informational freedom, privacy, and intellectual property.

7. ICT and social structure. An assessment of the way in which social structures, roles, relationships and behaviours are changing because of ICT. Topics may include the 'digital divide' between 'information-haves and have-nots,' changing roles of various social groups (e.g., women, the elderly), the changing structure of social relationships, and changes in communication.

8. ICT and culture. An assessment of the way in which cultural beliefs, practices and experiences are changing because of ICT. This may include an assessment of the changing role of media, of the changing role of communication and information, changes in lifestyles, and the emergence of new cultural forms.

9. ICT and human psychology. An assessment of psychological changes correlated with the use of ICT. Mental processing of information with new media; changes in personality and social psychology; changes in conceptions of reality, time and space.

10. ICT and the future. Current expectations and scenarios for future technologies and trends in the information society.

There are nowadays various good textbooks that could be used in such a course. A very good textbook is Richard S. Rosenberg, The Social Impact of Computers. Also excellent is The Network Society, written by my University of Twente colleague Jan van Dijk. Other books are the reader Computers in Society edite by Kathryn Schellenberg, Rob Kling's Computerization and Controversy: Value Conflicts and Social Choices, and Paul Winter's Computers and Society. I currently teach two rather broad courses on computers and society. The course that I offer in the context of the minor ICT and Society is called Humans and Information Technology. It is not currently a required course for any degree programme. The other course is called The Information Society and it is a required course for first-year computer science students. In both these courses I teach many of the topics that can be found in the above list. In this way, I hope to acquaint students with what I see as the main topics in Social and Humanistic studies of Computing.

7. Teaching Computer ethics

For computer science students, or for other students specializing to become a computer professional of some sort (e.g., students specializing in library science or computer-assisted education) it would be highly advisable to have, in addition to a required Computers and Society course, a required course in computer ethics. Computers and Society courses for non-IT professionals should preferably include an ethics component, which considers ethical aspects of the use of information technology, and ethical aspects of social and policy choices that are made in society regarding information technology. To understand the role of computer ethics in the university curriculum, an understanding is needed of the kind of knowledge and skills that are the hallmark of it. I will try to arrive at such an understanding by analyzing the goals of computer ethics education and its relation to the goals of education in SHC and ASC. To start with the second issue, is computer ethics a form of social and humanistic studies of computing, aimed at a theoretical understanding of ethical aspects of computing, or is it rather a form of applied research on societal aspects of computing, aimed at developing practical professional tools? If one would take as one's point of departure Jim Moor's influential conception of computer ethics, one would have to conclude it is both. Moor claims: "On my view, computer ethics is the analysis of the nature and social impact of computer technology and the corresponding formulation and justification of policies for the ethical use of such technology." (1985, p. 266). Quite clearly, the analysis Moor refers to in the first part of his statement is a central concern of SHC, whereas the formulation and justification of policies referred to in the second part clearly belongs to ASC. Thus we have more fundamental studies in computer ethics that belong to SHC and that are aimed at an understanding of ethical issues relating to computers and their uses, and we have more applied studies in computer ethics, that belong to ASC and that are aimed at arriving at specific policies. In teaching a course on computer ethics, one may of course emphasise either the more fundamental or the more applied dimension of computer ethics. In a professional programme for computer science students, one may want to opt for a course in computer ethics that is mostly applied, and that focuses on professional roles of computer scientists. In a programme in policy studies, or in law, or in science, technology and society, one would likely emphasise more fundamental issues in computer ethics. Normally, however, a course in computer ethics would integrate both dimensions. Regarding privacy, for example, it would both teach general moral theory on privacy, specific moral analyses of informational privacy, the various ways in which privacy considerations come up in contemporary computer systems and their uses, existing privacy law and policies, and professional responsibilities for protecting privacy. An ideal course in computer ethics, then, should have both the goal of promoting an understanding of major ethical issues in computing, as well as providing aspiring professionals with tools for giving content to their own professional responsibility in dealing with computer systems. In constructing such a course, one should begin with a selection of moral issues regarding computers that can be considered to be the most pressing in contemporary society. These will include many well-known issues in the computer ethics literature. My own selection would certainly include issues of privacy, autonomy, justice (with special emphasis on the problem of the so-called 'digital divide'), democracy, (informational) freedom and quality of life. Second, one should opt for a 'rich' presentation of these issues, in which one treats both (i) their moral worth and significance; (ii) the way they come up in current computing controversies (include here a consideration of one or more exemplary cases); (iii) past policies and laws that have been devised to deal with them; and (iv) professional responsibilities regarding the issue and ways in which professionals may deal with them. The way in which the professional component of a computer ethics course is set up will depend strongly on the nature of the professional programme within which the course is situated. Obviously, in a law programme, a course in computer ethics would focus on ethical issues in computer law, and how to deal with them professionally. In a programme in education studies, a course in computer ethics would focus on ethical issues in designing education programmes involving computers and in using computers in the classroom. In a programme in computer science, there should be special emphasis on ethical issues in the design of computer systems and software (cf. Friedman and Nissenbaum, 1997; Brey, 1998, 2000), as well as in their maintenance and their operation. In all cases, the emphasis should not just be on the ethical issues that come up in these professions, but also on the professional responsibility to deal with them, and the practical procedures one may follow in dealing with them.

8. Conclusion and implications for high school education

In this essay, I have argued for the importance of computer ethics policies and computer ethics education in higher education. I have argued that universities should have policies that address the ethical use and management of information technology on campus by students and staff. Relevant ethical issues include digital plagiarism and academic dishonesty in online assessment, copyright and software theft, the proper use of university computer resources, hacking, informational and online privacy, online anonymity and pseudonymity, online harassment and hate speech, and academic freedom and free speech online. I have also argued for the importance of computer ethics education in higher education, which I have situated as part of a broader effort to help students understand societal aspects of information technology. I have argued in favor of a required course in university curricula on Computers and Society, that acquaints students with basic issues regarding the role of ICT in contemporary society, and a required course in ASC in professional programmes, that focuses on the role of information technology within the relevant professional field and that conveys professional knowledge and skills that enable intelligent choices regarding the role of information technology within that field. I have also argued for computer ethics as a required course in professional programmes that prepare students to become computer professionals. These courses should both acquaint students with major ethical issues in computing, and provide them with practical tools for giving content to their own professional responsibility in relation to computer systems. Let me close by focusing on computer ethics policies and education on social and ethical aspects of IT in education prior to university, specifically in secondary or high school education. Regarding computer ethics policies, it will be clear that most of the policy issues for the use and management of information technology that apply to higher education also apply to secondary education: hacking, informational privacy, digital plagiarism, and so forth, are issues that may arise in high school just as much as they may arise at universities. One major difference may be the issue of academic freedom and freedom of speech. Because high school students have not yet reached adulthood, high schools arguably have an obligation to protect students from certain online content or ideas, unlike universities. Also they may arguably go futher than universities in limiting free speech in order to protect students from harassment and to provide a safe learning environment. However, opinions on how far high schools may go on these points are bound to differ.

Let me turn, finally, education on social and ethical aspects of IT in secondary education. One difference between higher and secondary education is that in secondary education, there is less of an expectation that students will have a serious decision-making responsibility regarding information technology in their future profession. Hence, education in SHC and ASC at the secondary school level may not be justified by reference to the future profession of secondary education students. However, the previously presented argument for attention to SHC in general education certainly applies to secondary education as well. Therefore, acquainting students with the role of ICT in society should be considered a legitimate and important topic in secondary education. Next to this, I think there are also good reasons why an attention to ethical issues regarding ICT has a place in secondary education. Secondary education is the learning phase at which ethics can first be taught. Moral issues like abortion, the death penalty, and genetic engineering are great issues to explore in secondary school, not through an emphasis on moral theory, but though an emphasis on cases, and moral learning through a joint discussion of such cases. Their own morality in their everyday life should certainly also be a topic. In relation to this, it would be very useful to discuss with students the ethical issues that come up for users of information technology, for example in using the

Internet, and to discuss also their own moral stance on these issues, as (potential) users of the technology. Such a discussion is particularly important because information technology is not yet a technology that has reached "closure" (Pinch & Bijker, 1987). That is, the interpretations, rules, policies and patterns of behaviour surrounding information technology are not yet as fixed as they are around many other technologies. The world of cyberspace is not yet an orderly society. It is still a bit like the Wild West, and as this vast new space is being colonized, and made into an orderly society, everyone should be asking the question of what kind of society we want it to be. We, as adults, should not just ask this question of ourselves and to each other, but also to the new generation that will inhabit it.

References

Agre, P. & Rotenberg, M. 1998. *Technology and Privacy: The New Landscape.* Cambridge and London: MIT Press.

Austin, M.J. & Brown, L.D. 1999. "Internet plagiarism: Developing strategies to curb student academic dishonesty." *The Internet and higher education* 2:21-33.

Baase, S. 1997. *A gift of fire: Social, Legal and ethical issues in computing.* Upper Sadle River: Prentice Hall.

Baird, R. M. and Ramsower, R. & Rosenbaum, S.E. eds, 2000. *Cyberethics.* New York: Prometheus Books.

Beniger, J. 1986. *The Control Revolution: Technological and Economic Origins of the Information Sociey.* Cambridge, MA: Harvard University Press.

Brey, P. 1998. "The Politics of Computer Systems and the Ethics of Design." in *Computer Ethics: Philosophical Enquiry* (ed, J. van den Hoven), Rotterdam University Press, Rotterdam.

—. 2000. "Disclosive Computer Ethics" *Computers and Society* 30: 4, 10-16.

—. 2003. "Ethical Issues for the Virtual University." Report for the cEVU Project (EuroPACE/European Commission). To appear online on www.cevu.org.

Castells, M. 2000. *The Rise of The Network Society*, 2nd ed. Blackwell.

Cate, F. 1997. *Privacy in the Information Age. Washington.* D.C. Brookings Institutions Press.

Chester, A. and Gwynne, G. 1998. "Online Teaching: Encouraging Collaboration through Anonymity." *Journal of Computer Mediated Communication* 4 (2).

Clark, B.R. 1983. *The higher education system: Academic organization in cross-national perspective.* Berkeley: University of California press.

Cohen, E. and Cornwell, L. 1989. "A question of ethics: developing information

system ethics." *Journal of Business Ethics* 8: 431-437.
Dijk, J. van 1999. *The Network Society*. Sage.
Forester, T. and Morrison, P. 1994. *Computer Ethics: Cautionary Tales and Ethical Dilemmas in Computing*. 2nd ed. Cambridge and London: MIT Press.
Friedman, B. and Nissenbaum, H. 1997. *Bias in Computer Systems, in Human Values and the Design of Computer Technology.* (ed. B. Friedman), Cambridge University Press, Cambridge.
Glass, R. and Wood., W. 1996. "Situational Determinants of Software Piracy: An Equity Theory Perspective." *Journal of Business Ethics* 15: 1189-1198.
Hinman, L.M. 2002. "The impact of the internet on our moral lives in academia." *Ethics and information technology* 4: 31-35.
Johnson, D. 2000. *Computer Ethics*, 3rd ed. Upper Sadle River: Prentice Hall.
Kling R, Lee Y, Teich A, and Frankel M.S. 2000. "Anonymous communication policies for the internet: Results and recommendations of the AAAS conference and assessing anonymous communication on the internet: Policy deliberations." In: Baird, R. M. & Ramsower, R. & Rosenbaum, S.E. eds, *Cyberethics*. New York: Prometheus Books.
Kling R., ed., *Computerization and Controversy: Value Conflicts and Social Choices*. 2nd ed. Academic Press.
Kolko, B. 2000. "Intellectual property in synchronous and collaborative virtual space." In: In: Baird, R., Ramsower, R. & Rosenbaum, S. (eds.) *Cyberethics*. New York: Prometheus Books. Lipinski, T.A. and Britz, J.J. 1999. "Deconstructing (the concept of) Intellectual Property: Designing and Incorporating Alternative Models of Property Ownership in the New Millennium and the Protection of Indigenous Knowledge." Proceedings of Ethicomp 99. Luiss University, Rome, 5-8 October 1999. CD-ROM (1-13).
Moor, J. 1985. "What is Computer Ethics?" *Metaphilosophy*, 16, 266-275.
Morse, J.F. 2001. "Intellectual freedom and economic sufficiency as educational entitlements." *Studies in philosophy and education* 20:201-211.
Olt, M.R. 2002. "Ethics and distance education: strategies for minimizing academic dishonesty in online assessment." *Online journal of distance learning administration*, vol. 5 (3). Unpaginated. See: http://www.westga.edu/~distance/ojdla/fall53/olt53.html
Pinch, T., and Bijker, W. 1987. "The Social Construction of Facts and Artifacts: Or How the Sociology of Science and the Sociology of Technology Might Benefit Each Other." in Bijker, W., Pinch, T., and Hughes, T., eds., *The Social Construction of Technological Systems: New Directions in the Sociology and History of Technology. Cambridge*. MA: MIT Press, 1987.
Rosenberg, R. 1997. *The Social Impact of Computers*. 2nd ed. Academic Press.
—. 2001. "Controlling access to the internet: the role of filtering." *Ethics and*

Information Technology 3:35-54.
Schellenberg, K. ed, 1999. *Computers in Society.* 8th ed. McGraw-Hill Higher Education.
Spinello, R. 2000. *Cyberethics. Morality and Law in Cyberspace.* Sudbury, MA: Jones and Bartlett Publishers.
Tavani, H. 2003. "Ethics and Technology: Ethical Issues in an Age of information and Communication Technology."
Wiley. Tu, Chih-Hsiung 2002. "The relationship between social presence and online privacy." *The internet and higher education* 5:293-318.
Winters, P. 1997. *Computers and Society.* Greenhaven Press.

These two sections are based on a study that discusses ethical aspects of the use and management of information technology in higher education, called Ethical Issues for the Virtual University (Brey, 2003). The report was written for the cEVU project coordinated by EuroPACE and supported by the European Committee, for a publication for the European Committee. An online version is due to appear on http://www.cevu.org.

These four sections, and the corresponding part in the conclusion, are based on the paper "The role of social and ethical studies of IT in the university curriculum" presented at FINE (Foundations of Information Ethics), Hiroshima, Japan, February 27-28, 2001.

See, amongst others, the Stanford Privacy Project at:
http://www.stanford.edu/group/privacyproject/ and Spinello, 2000, ch. 5.
See Olt (2002) for a discussion of strategies for minimizing academic dishonesty in online assessment. See, e.g., the 1999 statement on copyright of the American Association of University Professors at:
http://www.aaup.org/statements/Redbook/Spccopyr.htm
Intellectual Freedom and Censorship Q and A of the American Library Association at :
http://www.ala.org/Content/NavigationMenu/Our_Association/Offices/Intellectual_Freedom3/Basics/Intellectual_Freedom_and_Censorship_QandA.htm

CONTRIBUTORS

Gregory Chaitin, IBM Watson Research Center in New York His paper was a given as *Alan Turing Lecture on Computing and Philosophy* at E-CAP 2005 (European Computing And Philosophy Conference).

Luciano Floridi is Associate Professor of Logic and Epistemology, Dipartimento di Scienze Filosofiche, Università degli Studi di Bari and Fellow of St Cross College and member of the Faculty of Philosophy and of the OUCL (Computer Science Department), University of Oxford.

Patrick Allo is Research Assistant of the Fund for Scientific Research at Vrije Universiteit Brussel.

Ahti-Veikko Pietarinen is Adjunct Professor and Post-Doctoral Fellow of the Academy of Finland, University of Helsinki

Lars-Göran Johansson is Associate Professor in Theoretic Philosophy at Uppsala Universitet

Gang Liu is Deputy Director, Faculty of Philosophy of Science and Technology Institute of Philosophy Research Center for Science Technology and Society (STS), Chinese Academy of Social Sciences (CASS), China

Werner Ceusters is Professor at NYS Center of Excellence in Bioinformatics & Life Sciences, Ontology Research Group and Executive Director, European Center for Ontological Research, Saarland University, Germany.

Barry Smith is Professor at University at Buffalo and Director, National Center for Ontological Research Saarland University. His paper was a given as a *Carl Linnaeus Lecture on Ontology* at E-CAP 2005.

Katherine Munn, Institute for Formal Ontology and Medical Information Science, Saarland University, Germany.

Ruth Hagengruber is Professor at Paderborn University, Germany.

Uwe V. Riss is Senior Researcher, SAP Research, CEC Karlsruhe, Germany.

Raymond Turner is Professor at Department of Computer Science, University of Essex.

Amnon H. Eden is Lecturer with the University of Essex, and a research fellow with the Center For Inquiry, University of Essex.

Pedro C. Marijuán, Fundación CIRCE CPS, University of Zaragoza, Spain.

Raquel del Moral, Universidad de Zaragoza, Spain

Søren Brier is Associated Professor at the Department of Management, Politics and Philosophy Copenhagen Business School, Copenhagen, Denmark.

Arturo Carsetti is Professor of Philosophy of Science at the University of Rome "Tor Vergata", Rome, Italy.

Peter Århem is Professor at Nobelinstitute for Neurophysiology, Karolinska Institutet, Stockholm, Sweden.

Paavo Pylkkänen is Associate Professor in Theoretical Philosophy at the University of Skövde, Sweden.

Pauli Brattico is a Post-doc Fellow of the Academy of Finald, University of Helsinki, Finland.

Marcin Milkowski is Assistant Professor at the Institute of Philosophy and Sociology, Polish Academy of Sciences, Poland.

Otto Lappi, University of Helsinki, Finland.

Pius ten Hacken, University of Wales Swansea, United Kingdom.

Graeme Hirst is Professor at the Department of Computer Science, University of Toronto.

Tarja Knuuttila is Ph.D. Research Fellow (Academy of Finland), University of Helsinki, Finland.

Alexander Riegler is Professor at Vrije Universiteit, Brussel, Belgium.

Terrell Bynum is Professor of Philosophy at Southern Connecticut State University, Director of the Research Center on Computing and Society here, and Visiting Professor at De Montfort University in Leicester, England. His paper was a given as a *Georg Henrik von Wright Lecture on Ethics* at E-CAP 2005.

Lena Trojer is Professor at School of Technoculture, Humanities and. Planning, Blekinge Institute of Technology, Blekinge, Sweden.

Philip Brey is Associate Professor of philosophy and vice chair of the department of philosophy, University of Twente, the Netherlands.